Contents

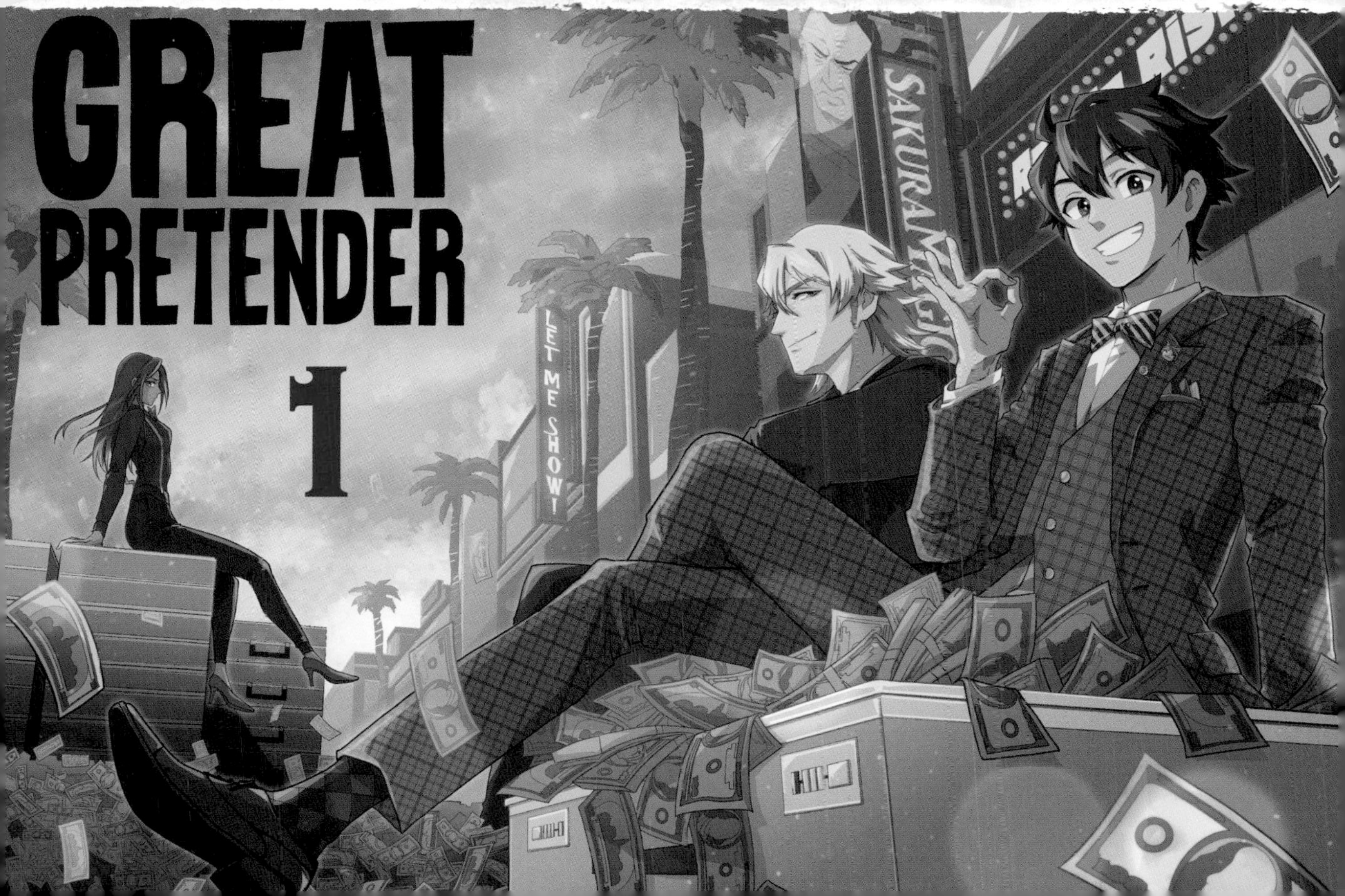
GREAT
PRETENDER
1
LET ME SHOW!
SAKURA

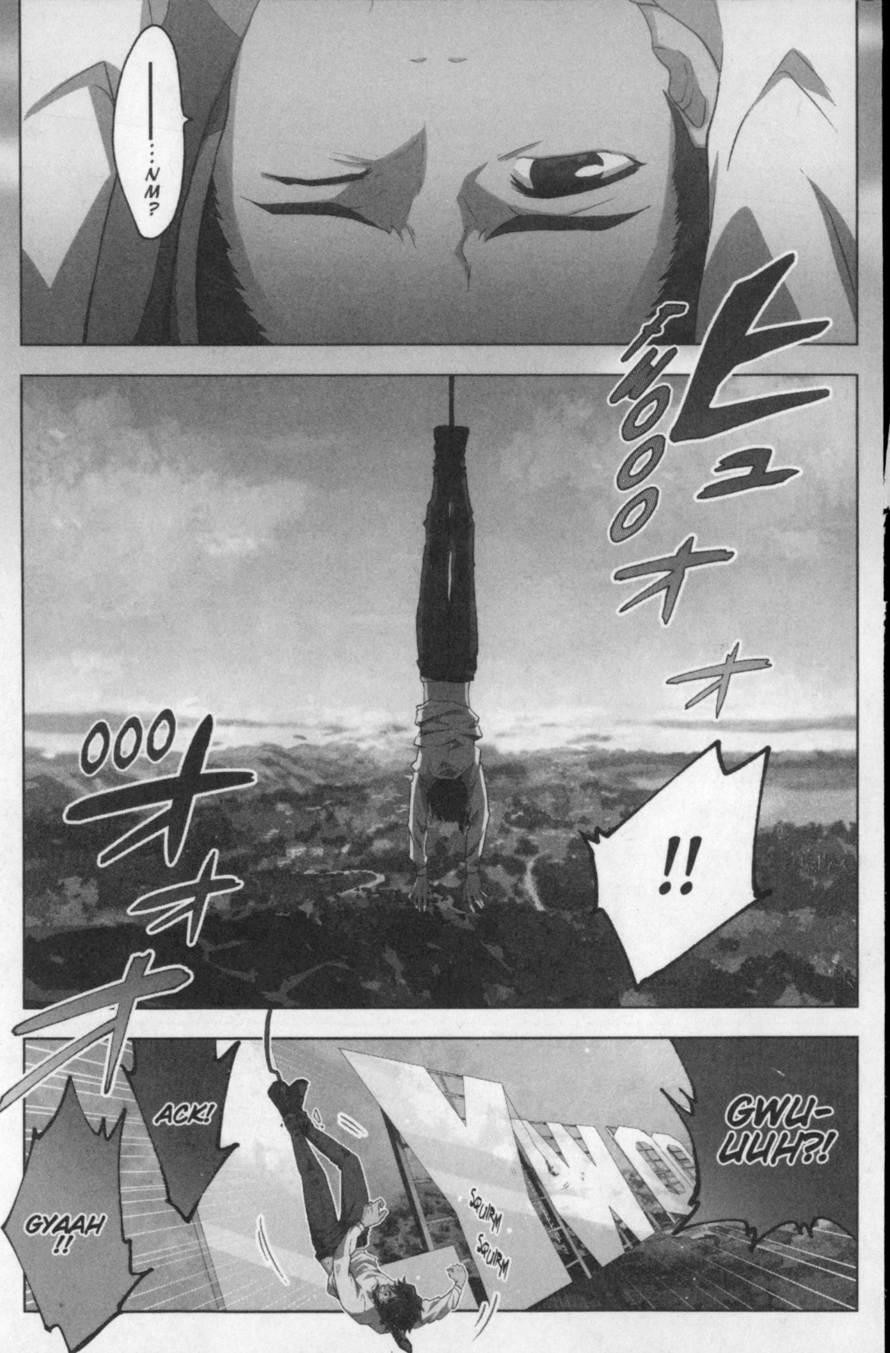
—...NM?
ヒュ
ooo
オォ
!!
OOO
オォォ
GWU-UUH?!
SQUIRM
SQUIRM
ACK!
GYAAH!!

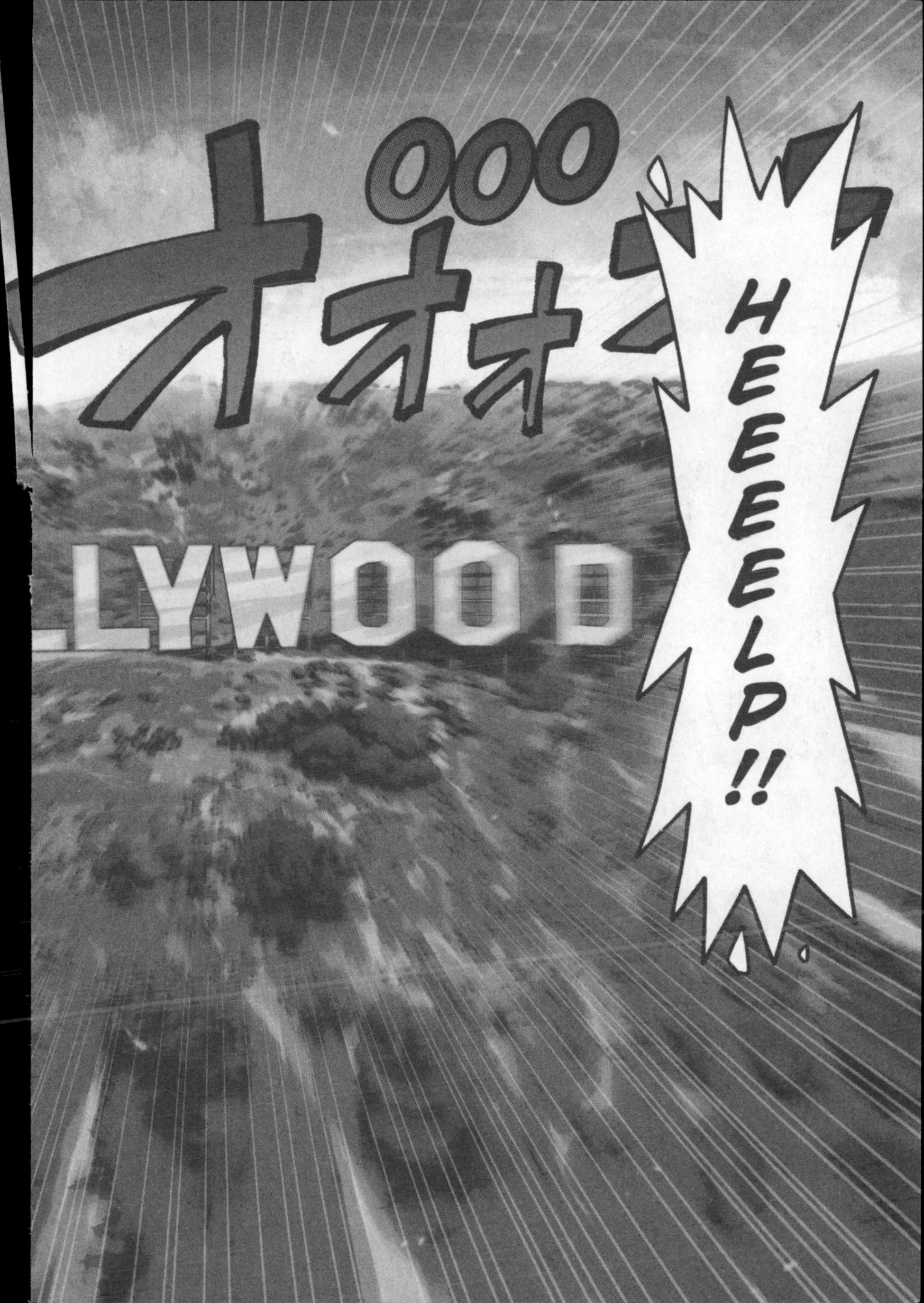
オォォォ
HEEEEELP!!
LYWOOD

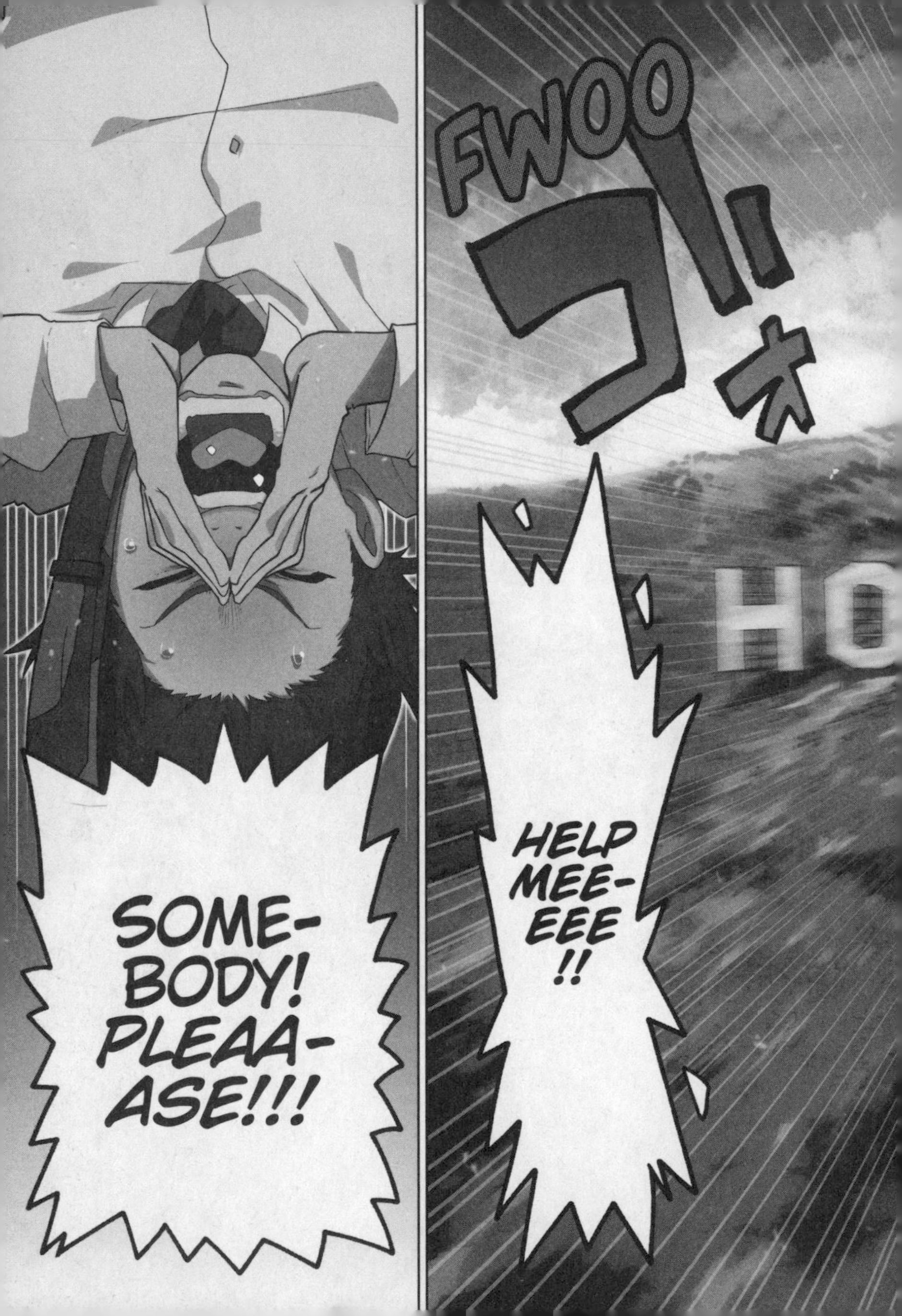
FWOO
ゴォ
HO
HELP MEEE-EEE!!
SOME-BODY! PLEAA-ASE!!!

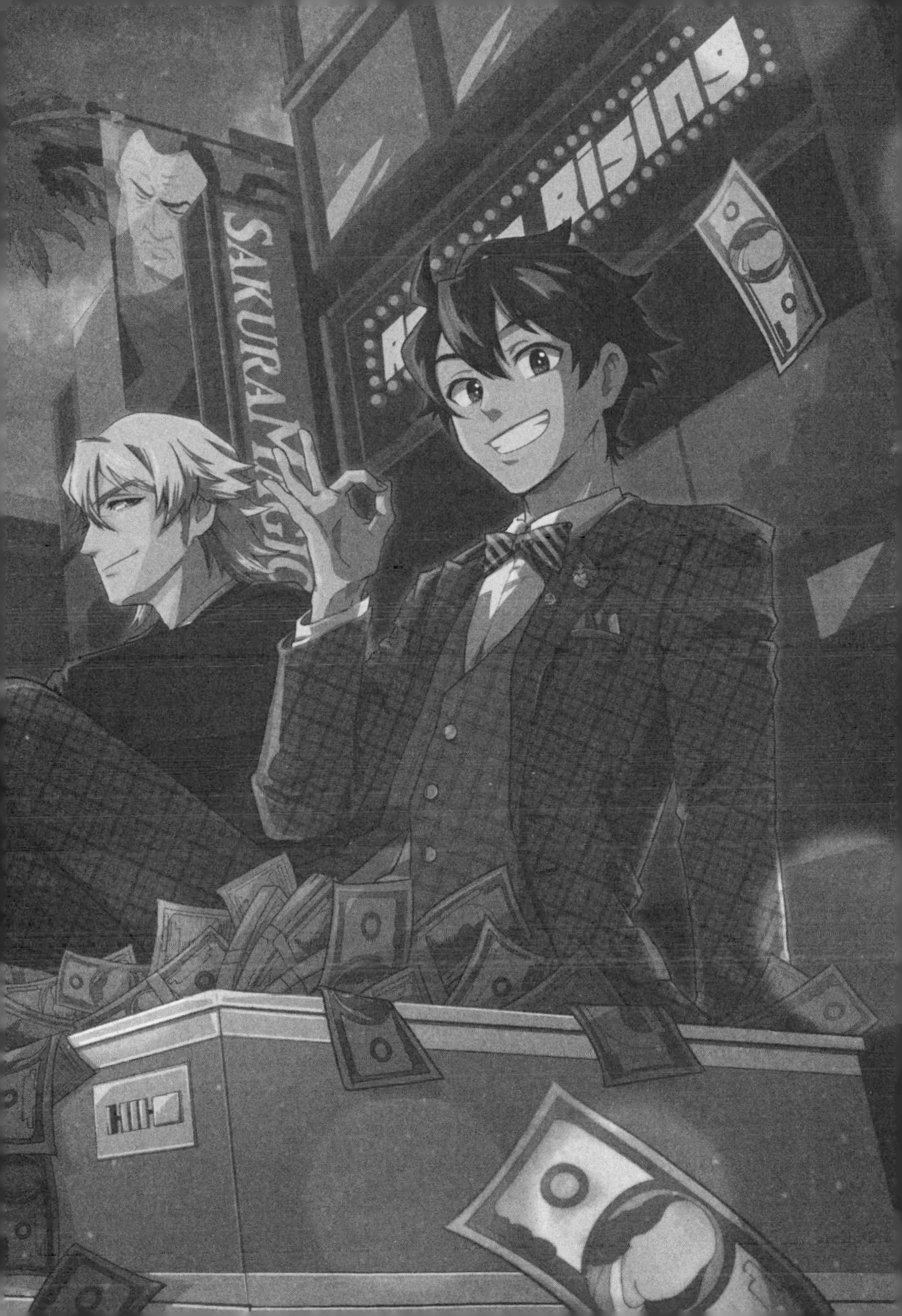
RISING

#01
Los Angeles Connection ①

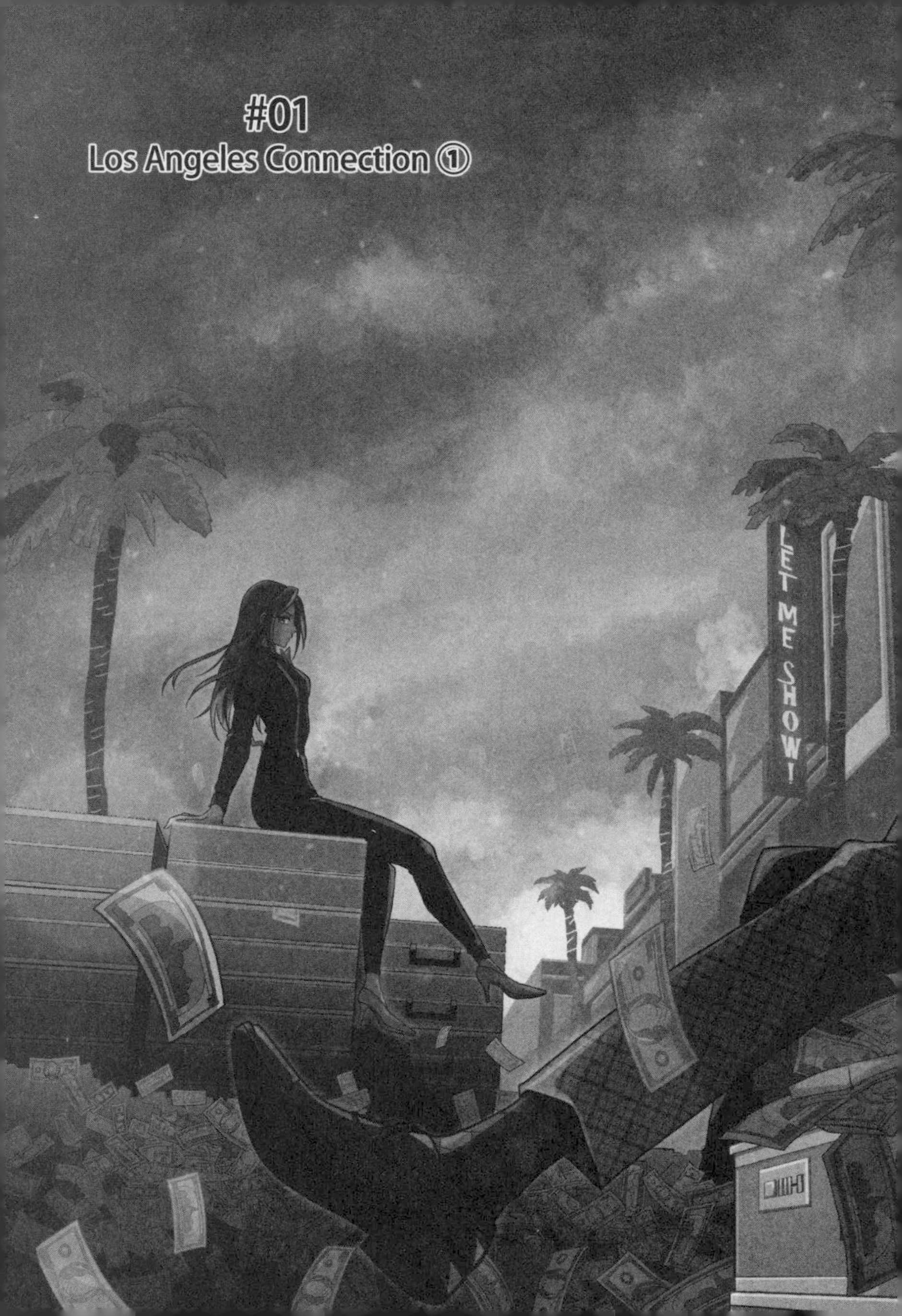
LET ME SHOW!

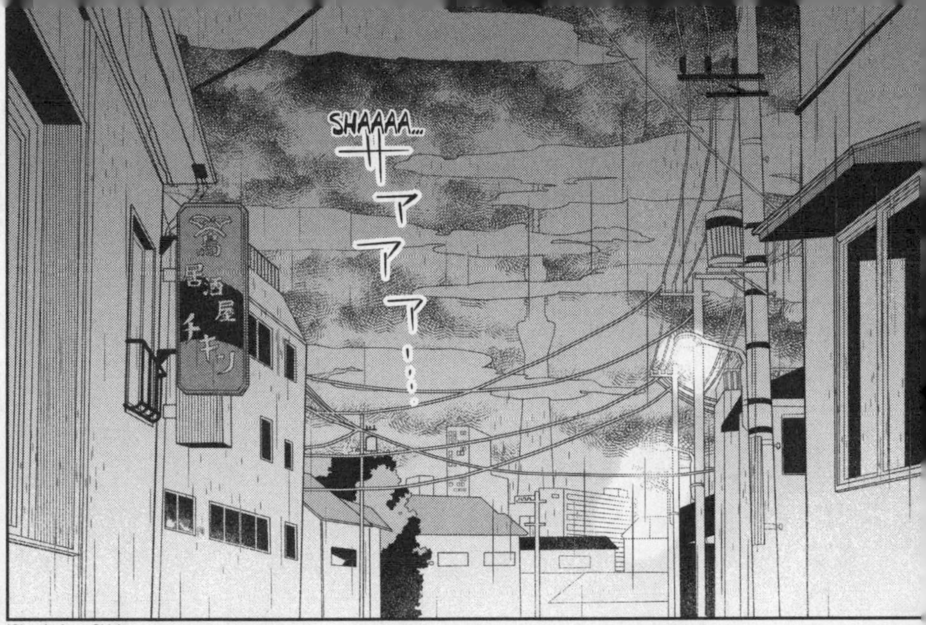
SHAAAA...
サアアア・・・
居酒屋
チキン

*Sign: Izakaya Chicken

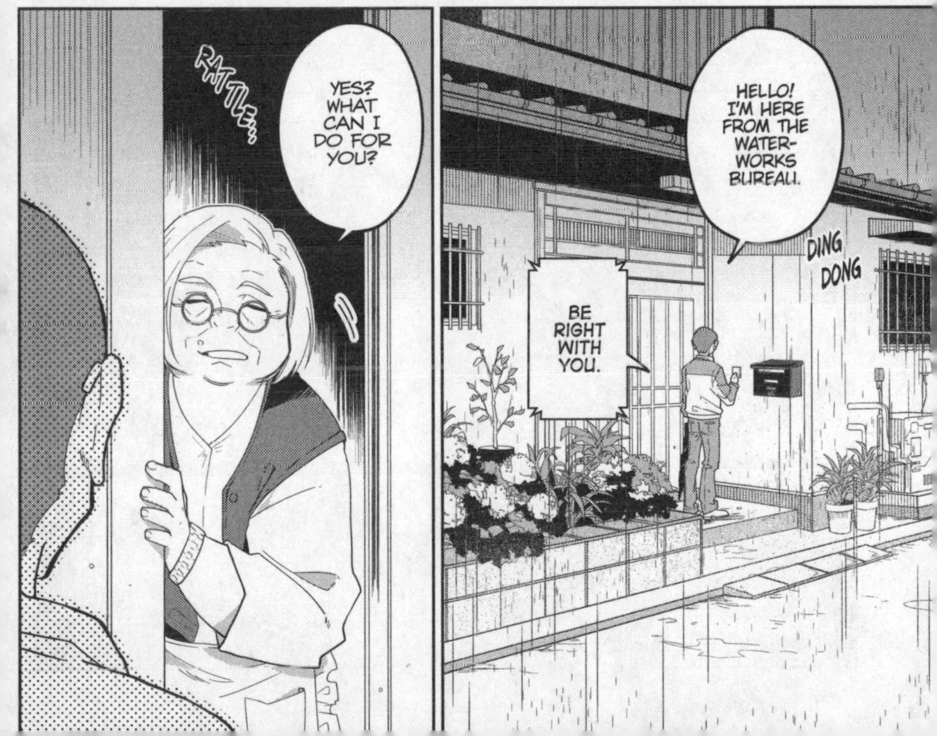
HELLO! I'M HERE FROM THE WATER-WORKS BUREAU.
DING DONG
BE RIGHT WITH YOU.
RATTLE...
YES? WHAT CAN I DO FOR YOU?

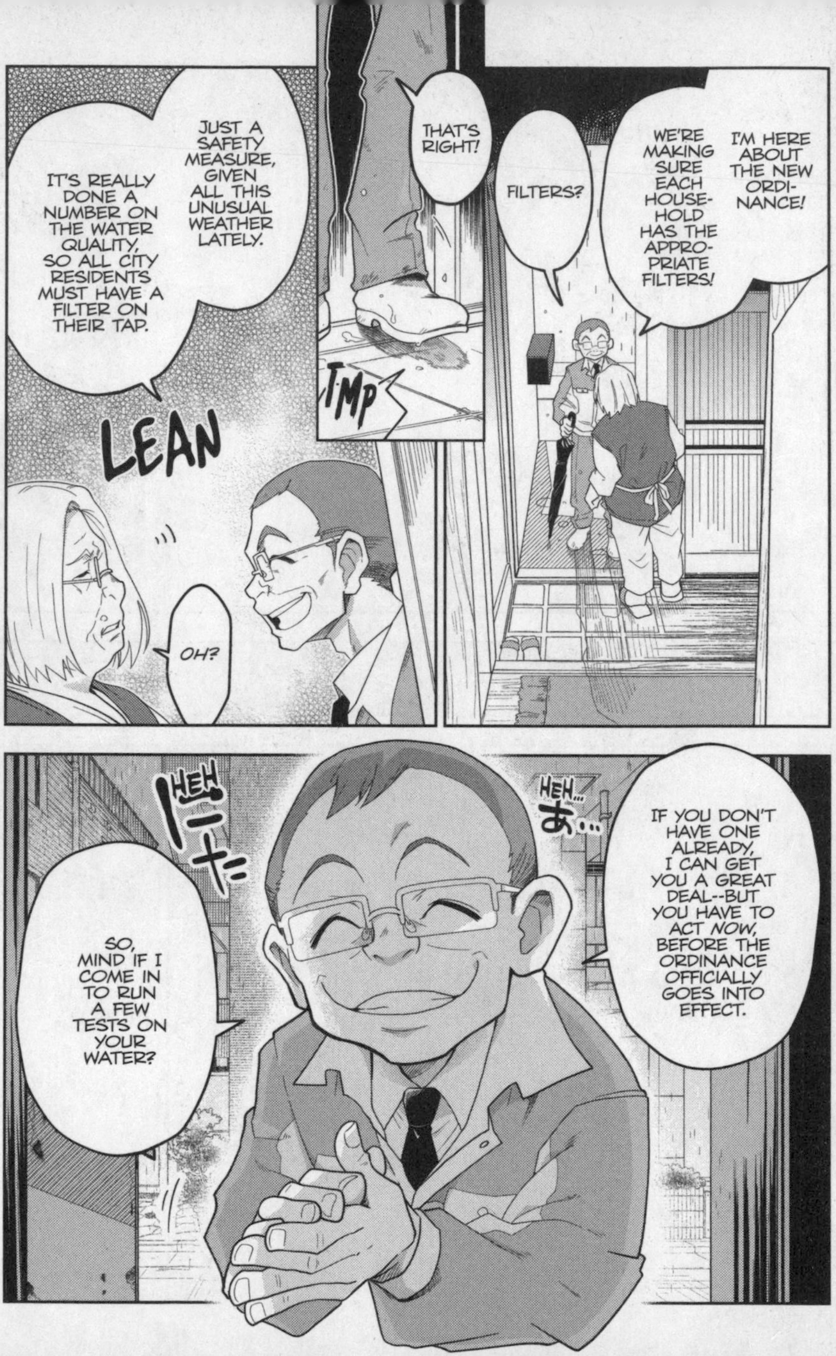
I'M HERE ABOUT THE NEW ORDINANCE!
WE'RE MAKING SURE EACH HOUSEHOLD HAS THE APPROPRIATE FILTERS!
FILTERS?
THAT'S RIGHT!
TMP
JUST A SAFETY MEASURE, GIVEN ALL THIS UNUSUAL WEATHER LATELY.
IT'S REALLY DONE A NUMBER ON THE WATER QUALITY, SO ALL CITY RESIDENTS MUST HAVE A FILTER ON THEIR TAP.
LEAN
OH?
IF YOU DON'T HAVE ONE ALREADY, I CAN GET YOU A GREAT DEAL--BUT YOU HAVE TO ACT *NOW*, BEFORE THE ORDINANCE OFFICIALLY GOES INTO EFFECT.
HEH... あ...
HEH
SO, MIND IF I COME IN TO RUN A FEW TESTS ON YOUR WATER?

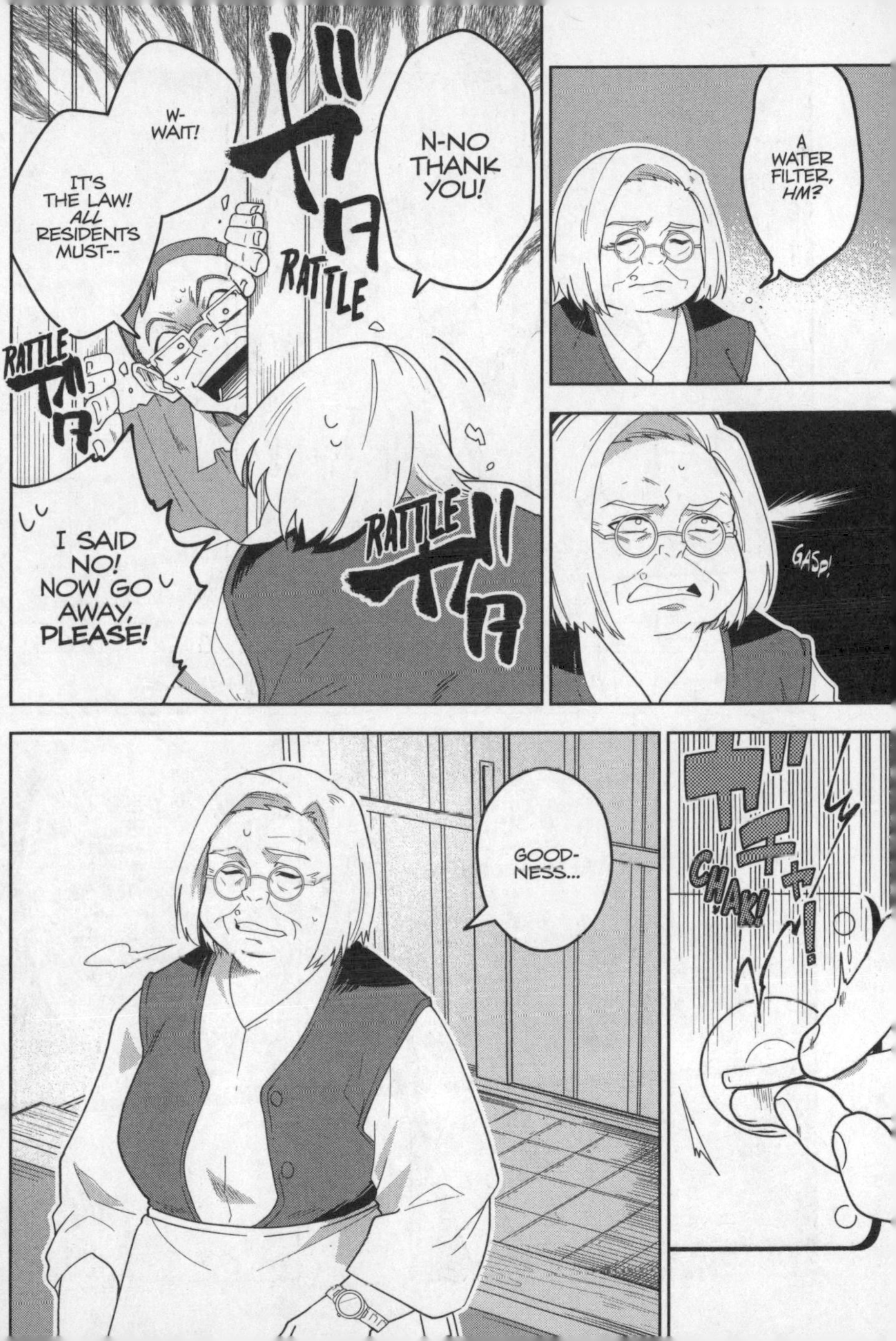
A WATER FILTER, HM?
GASP!
N-NO THANK YOU!
RATTLE
W-WAIT! IT'S THE LAW! ALL RESIDENTS MUST--
RATTLE
RATTLE
I SAID NO! NOW GO AWAY, PLEASE!
CHAK!
GOODNESS...

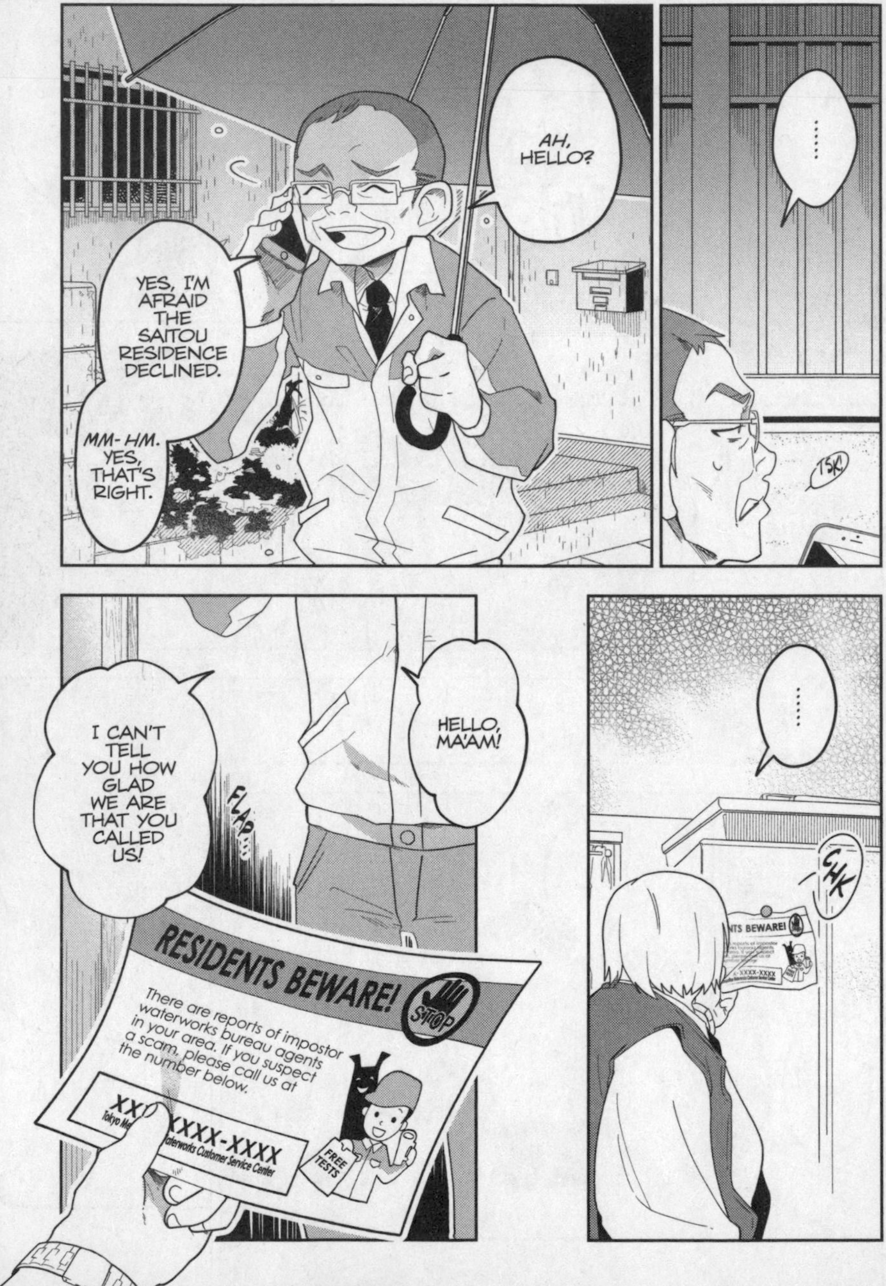
......
TSK
AH, HELLO?
YES, I'M AFRAID THE SAITOU RESIDENCE DECLINED.
MM-HM. YES, THAT'S RIGHT.
......
CHK
HELLO, MA'AM!
I CAN'T TELL YOU HOW GLAD WE ARE THAT YOU CALLED US!
FLAP
RESIDENTS BEWARE!
STOP
There are reports of impostor waterworks bureau agents in your area. If you suspect a scam, please call us at the number below.
XXXX-XXXX
Waterworks Customer Service Center
FREE TESTS

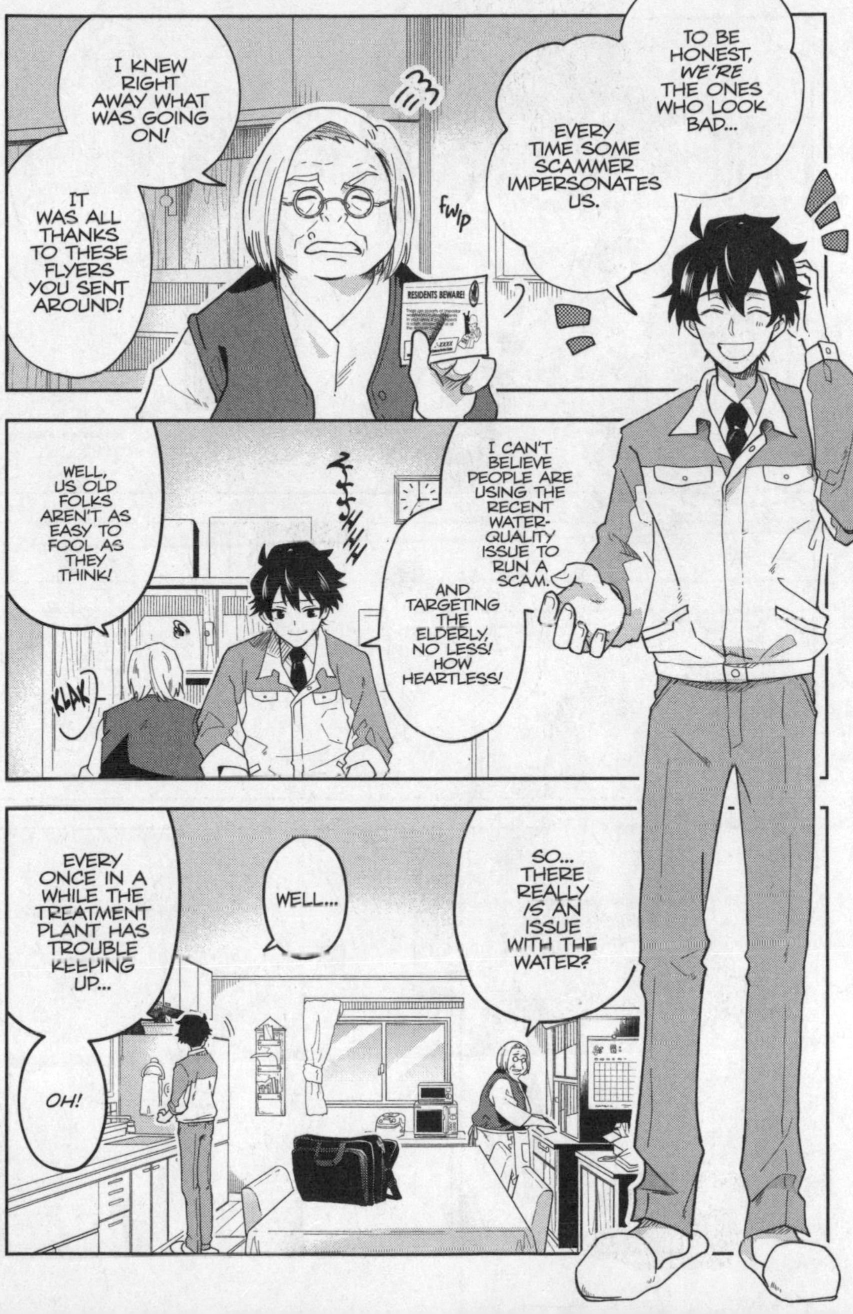
TO BE HONEST, *WE'RE* THE ONES WHO LOOK BAD...
EVERY TIME SOME SCAMMER IMPERSONATES US.
I KNEW RIGHT AWAY WHAT WAS GOING ON!
FWIP
RESIDENTS BEWARE!
IT WAS ALL THANKS TO THESE FLYERS YOU SENT AROUND!
I CAN'T BELIEVE PEOPLE ARE USING THE RECENT WATER-QUALITY ISSUE TO RUN A SCAM.
AND TARGETING THE ELDERLY, NO LESS! HOW HEARTLESS!
WELL, US OLD FOLKS AREN'T AS EASY TO FOOL AS THEY THINK!
KLAK
SO... THERE REALLY *IS* AN ISSUE WITH THE WATER?
WELL...
EVERY ONCE IN A WHILE THE TREATMENT PLANT HAS TROUBLE KEEPING UP...
OH!

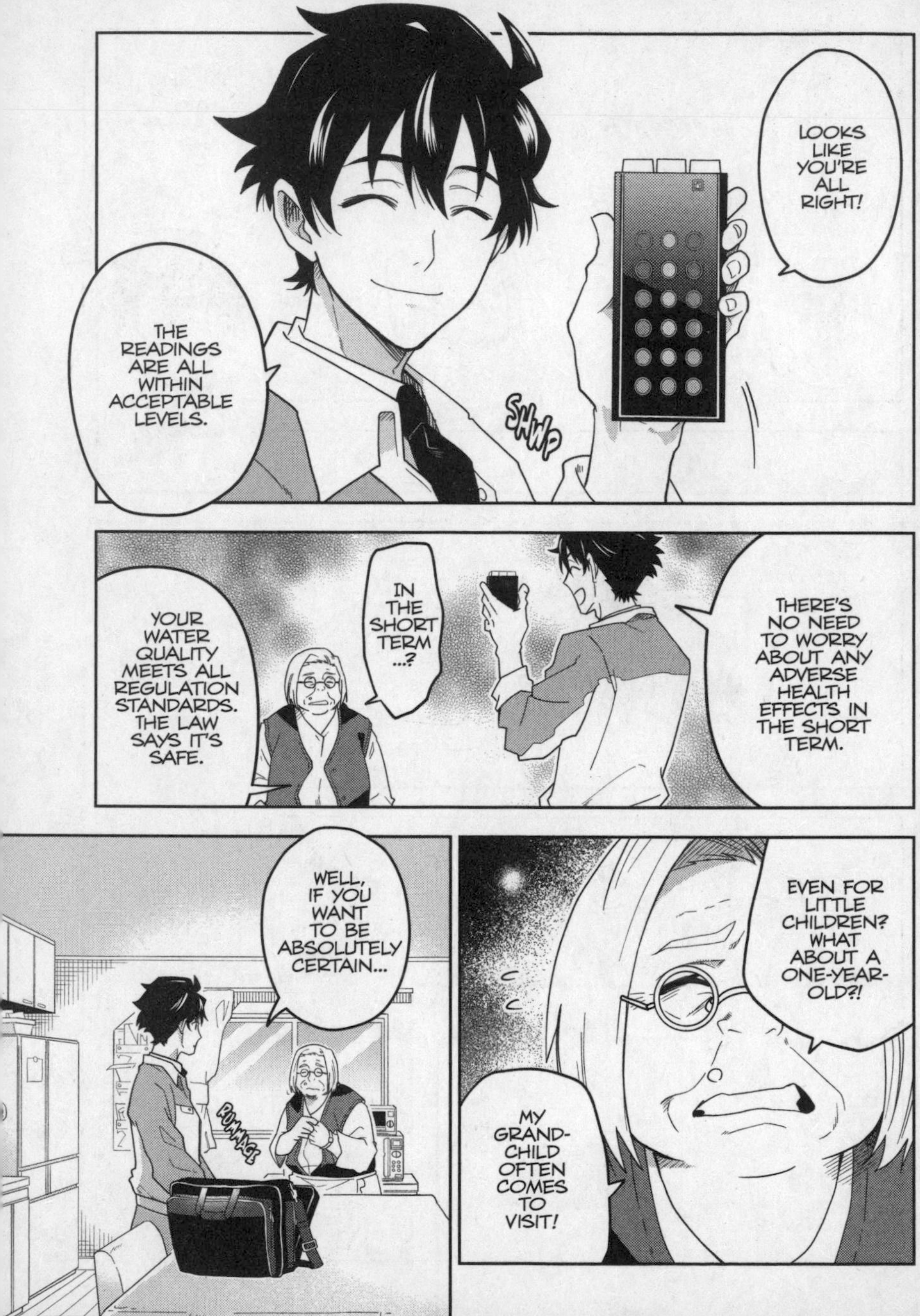
LOOKS LIKE YOU'RE ALL RIGHT!
THE READINGS ARE ALL WITHIN ACCEPTABLE LEVELS.
SHWP
THERE'S NO NEED TO WORRY ABOUT ANY ADVERSE HEALTH EFFECTS IN THE SHORT TERM.
IN THE SHORT TERM ...?
YOUR WATER QUALITY MEETS ALL REGULATION STANDARDS. THE LAW SAYS IT'S SAFE.
EVEN FOR LITTLE CHILDREN? WHAT ABOUT A ONE-YEAR-OLD?!
MY GRAND-CHILD OFTEN COMES TO VISIT!
WELL, IF YOU WANT TO BE ABSOLUTELY CERTAIN...
RUMMAGE

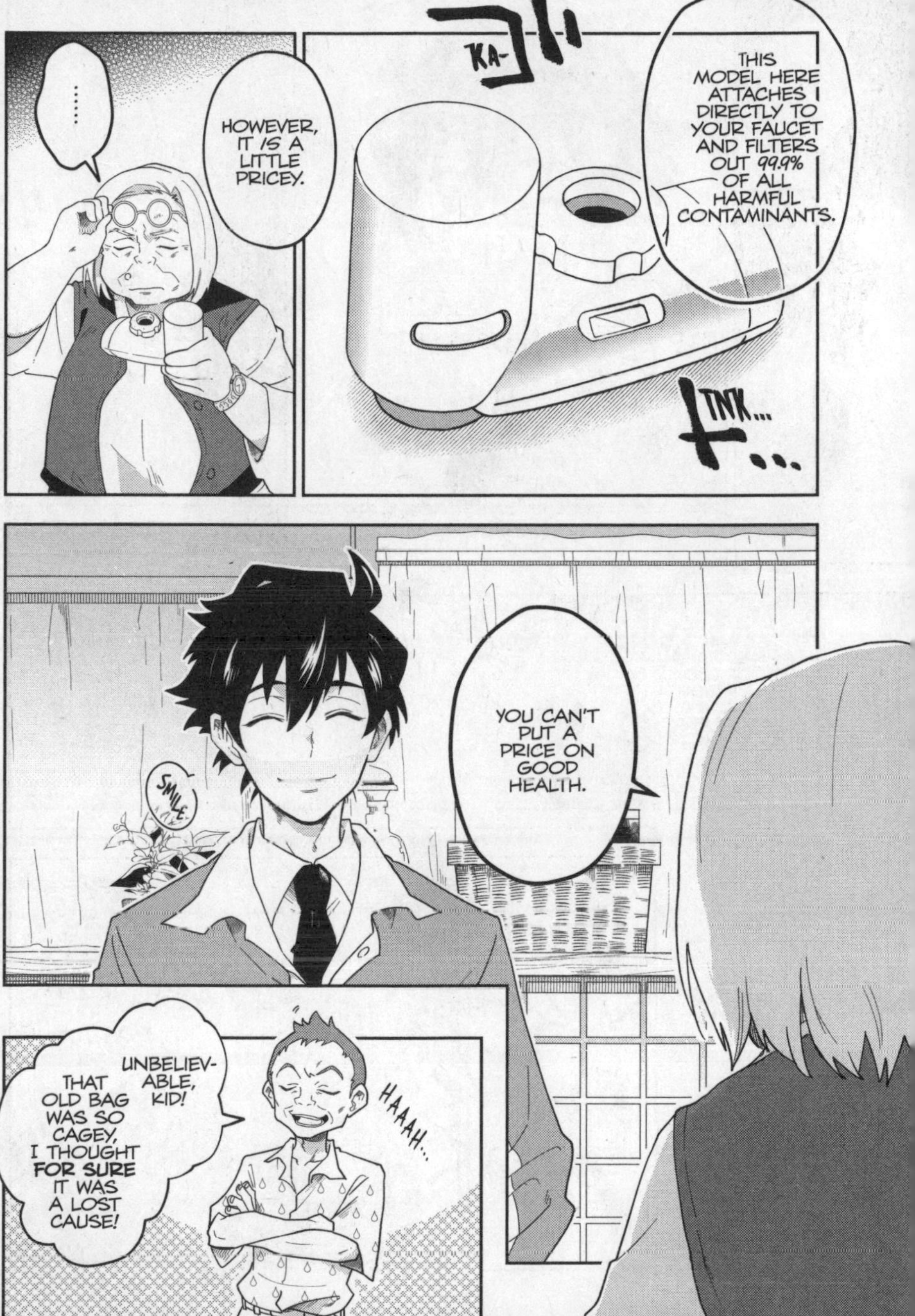
KA-
THIS MODEL HERE ATTACHES DIRECTLY TO YOUR FAUCET AND FILTERS OUT 99.9% OF ALL HARMFUL CONTAMINANTS.
TNK...
HOWEVER, IT IS A LITTLE PRICEY.
......
YOU CAN'T PUT A PRICE ON GOOD HEALTH.
SMILE
HAAAH...
UNBELIEV-ABLE, KID! THAT OLD BAG WAS SO CAGEY, I THOUGHT **FOR SURE** IT WAS A LOST CAUSE!

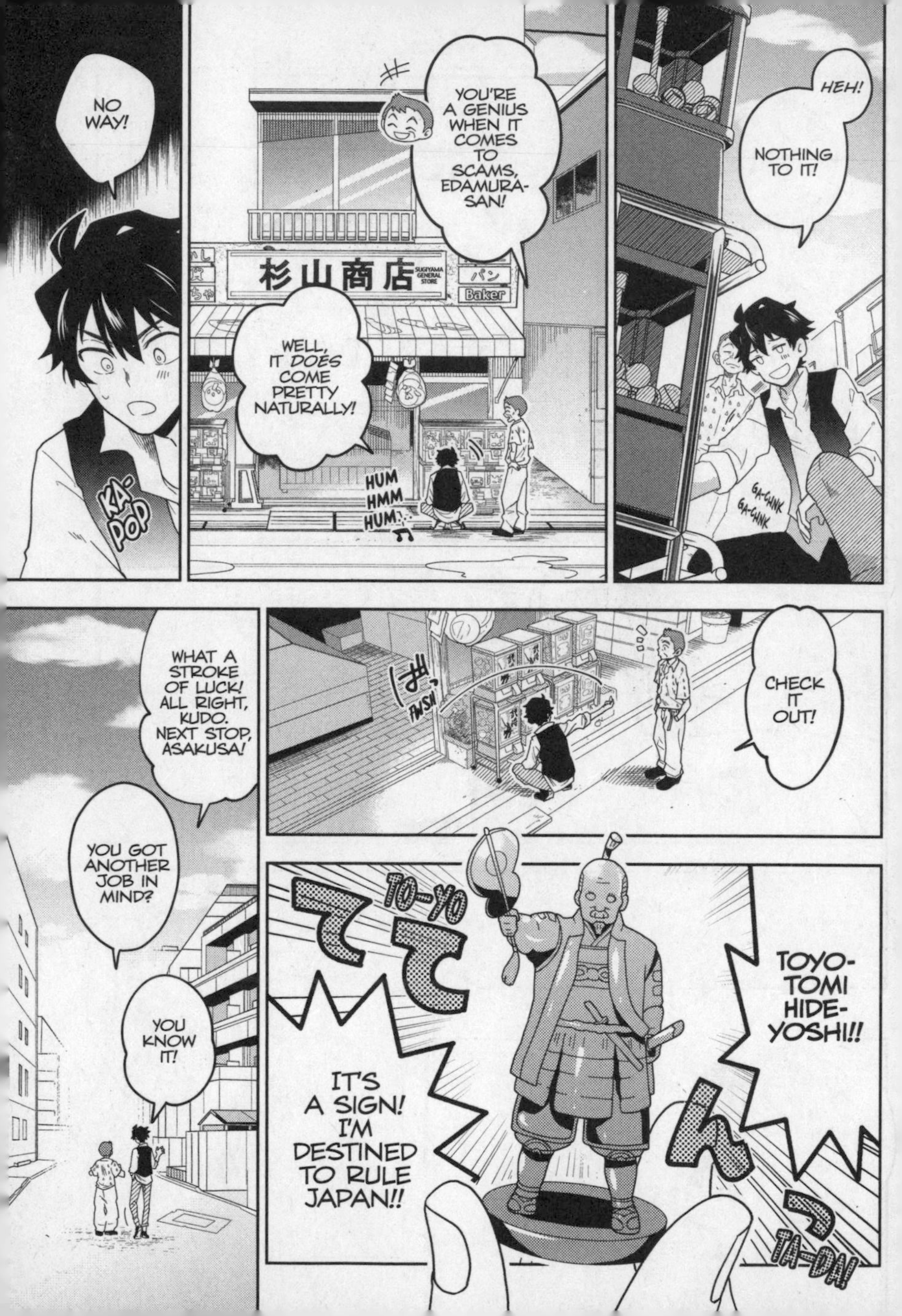
HEH!
NOTHING TO IT!
GA-CHNK GA-CHNK
YOU'RE A GENIUS WHEN IT COMES TO SCAMS, EDAMURA-SAN!
杉山商店
SUGIYAMA GENERAL STORE
パン
Baker
WELL, IT *DOES* COME PRETTY NATURALLY!
HUM HMM HUM
NO WAY!
KA-POP
CHECK IT OUT!
FWSH
TOYO-TOMI HIDE-YOSHI!!
TO-YO
IT'S A SIGN! I'M DESTINED TO RULE JAPAN!!
TA-DA
WHAT A STROKE OF LUCK! ALL RIGHT, KUDO. NEXT STOP, ASAKUSA!
YOU GOT ANOTHER JOB IN MIND?
YOU KNOW IT!

<EXCUSE ME.>

ASAKUSA.

BUSTLE
BUSTLE
BUSTLE
BUSTLE

<I'M SORRY?>

<DID YOU DROP THIS?>

<YOU'D BETTER CHECK INSIDE.>

<ISN'T IT YOURS?>

......

<WOW...>

BULGE

HEY ?!

<SORRY! THAT'S MINE!>

FWIP

HIC!

ぱっ SNIPE

OH! THANKS, PAL!

?!

I-I THINK I'D BETTER TAKE IT TO THE POLICE!

SNIFF

WHAT THE HELL?! HAND IT OVER!

....

HOW DO I KNOW YOU'RE TELLING THE TRUTH?!

BICKER BICKER

THERE'S A TON OF CASH IN HERE-- 300,000 YEN!

OH, C'MON! I'M TELLIN' YA, IT'S MINE!

BURP?!

I'LL GIVE YA 2,000 YEN!

THAT MATH DOESN'T ADD UP!!

SHWFF

TSK!

TMP

YOU WANT A REWARD FOR FINDING IT. HOW 'BOUT 10%?

OH, I GET IT.

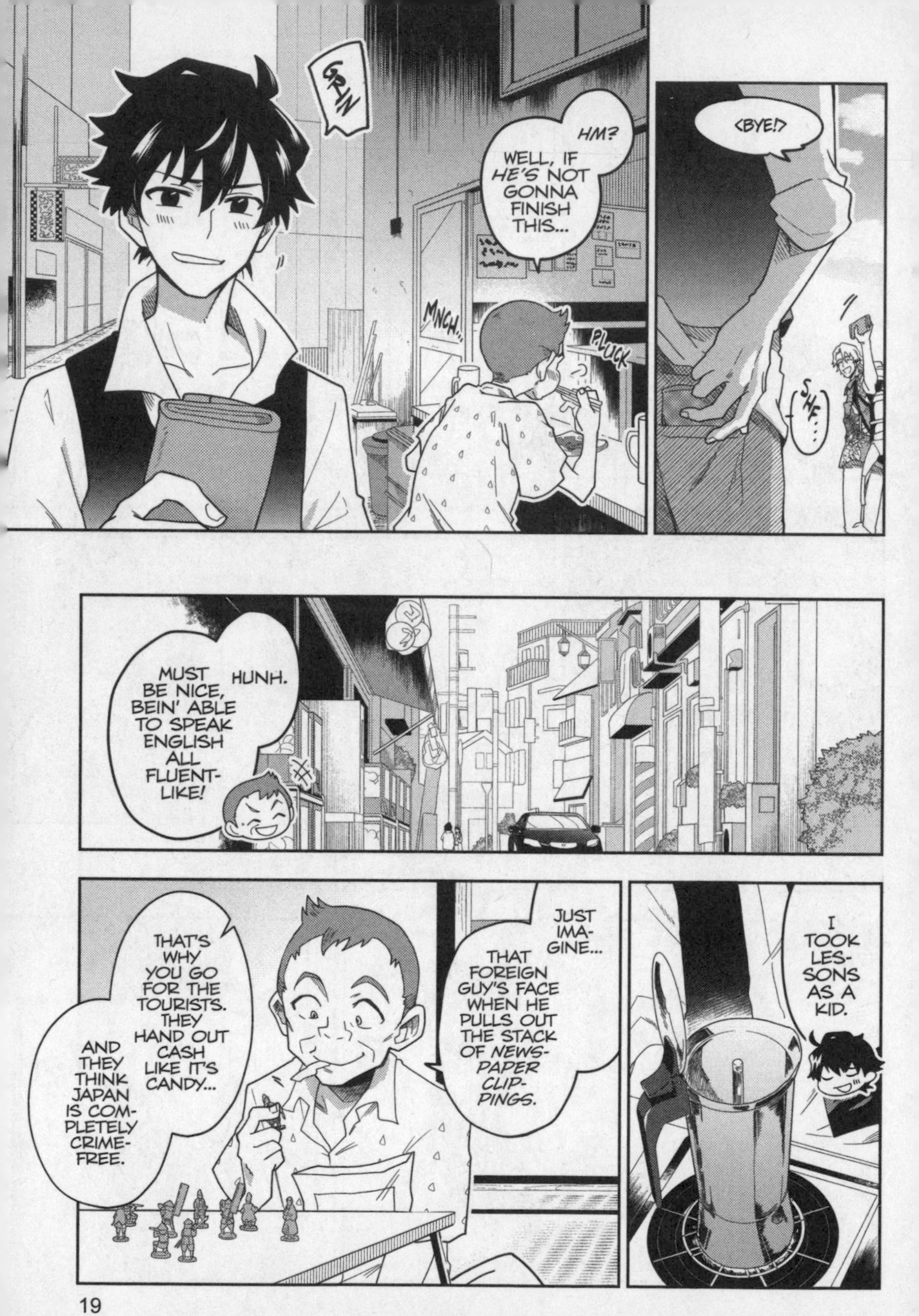
<BYE!>
SHF...
HM?
WELL, IF HE'S NOT GONNA FINISH THIS...
GRIN
MNCH...
PLUCK
HUNH.
MUST BE NICE, BEIN' ABLE TO SPEAK ENGLISH ALL FLUENT-LIKE!
I TOOK LES-SONS AS A KID.
JUST IMA-GINE...
THAT FOREIGN GUY'S FACE WHEN HE PULLS OUT THE STACK OF NEWS-PAPER CLIP-PINGS.
THAT'S WHY YOU GO FOR THE TOURISTS. THEY HAND OUT CASH LIKE IT'S CANDY...
AND THEY THINK JAPAN IS COM-PLETELY CRIME-FREE.

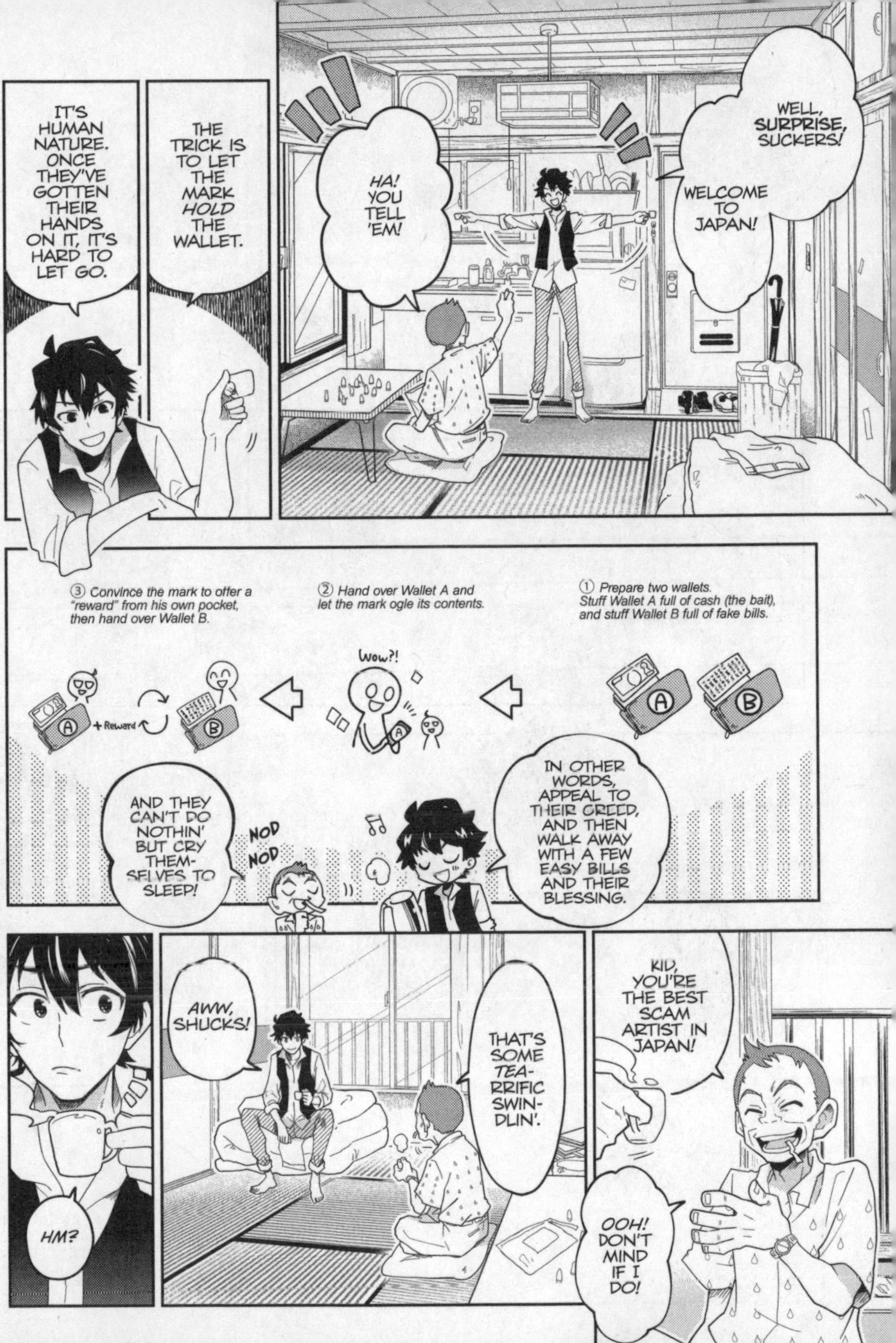
WELL, SURPRISE, SUCKERS!
WELCOME TO JAPAN!
HA! YOU TELL 'EM!
THE TRICK IS TO LET THE MARK HOLD THE WALLET.
IT'S HUMAN NATURE. ONCE THEY'VE GOTTEN THEIR HANDS ON IT, IT'S HARD TO LET GO.
① Prepare two wallets. Stuff Wallet A full of cash (the bait), and stuff Wallet B full of fake bills.
A
B
② Hand over Wallet A and let the mark ogle its contents.
Wow?!
A
③ Convince the mark to offer a "reward" from his own pocket, then hand over Wallet B.
B
A
+ Reward
IN OTHER WORDS, APPEAL TO THEIR GREED, AND THEN WALK AWAY WITH A FEW EASY BILLS AND THEIR BLESSING.
NOD NOD
AND THEY CAN'T DO NOTHIN' BUT CRY THEM-SELVES TO SLEEP!
KID, YOU'RE THE BEST SCAM ARTIST IN JAPAN!
OOH! DON'T MIND IF I DO!
THAT'S SOME TEA-RRIFIC SWIN-DLIN'.
AWW, SHUCKS!
HM?

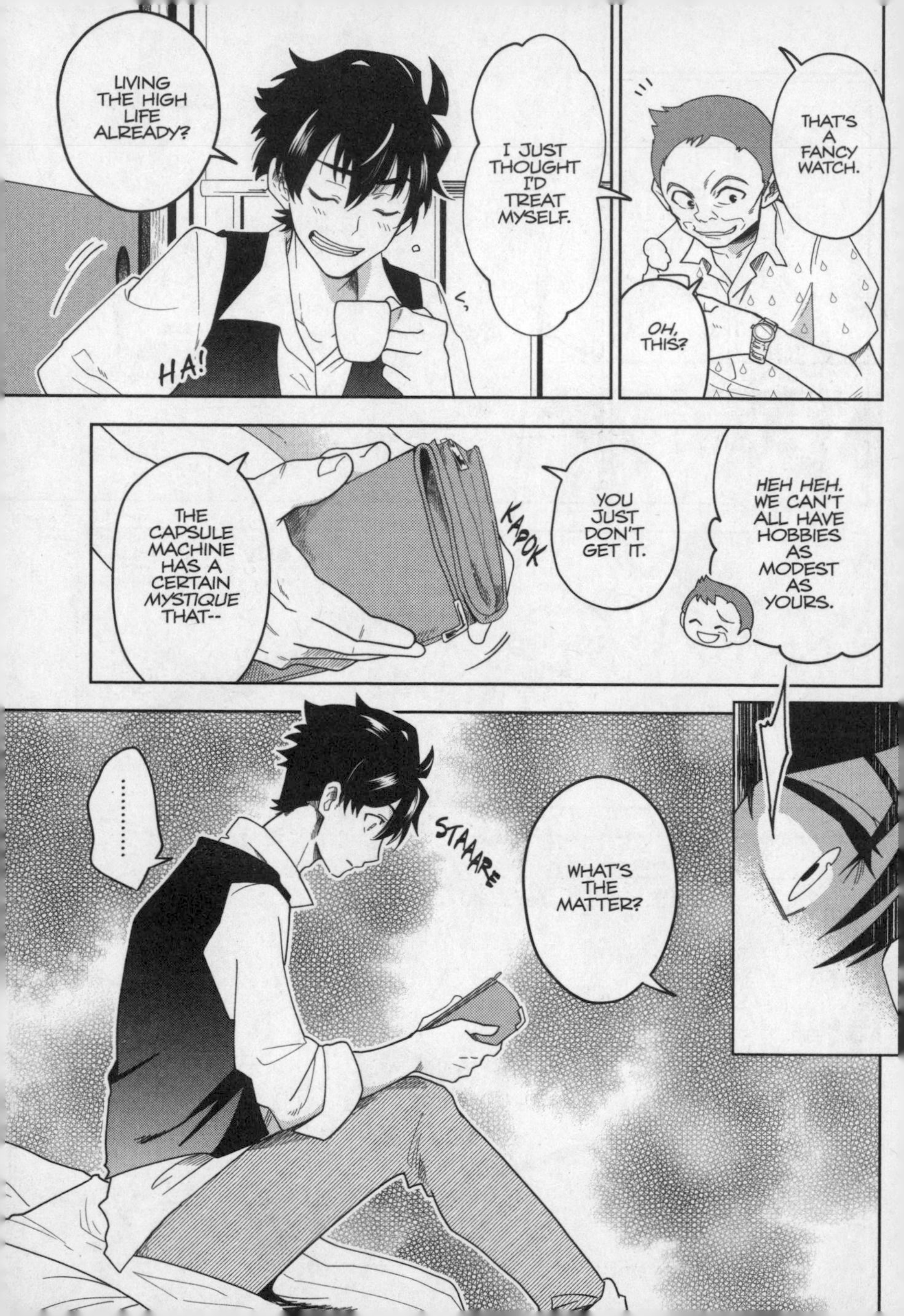
THAT'S A FANCY WATCH.
OH, THIS?
I JUST THOUGHT I'D TREAT MYSELF.
LIVING THE HIGH LIFE ALREADY?
HA!
HEH HEH. WE CAN'T ALL HAVE HOBBIES AS MODEST AS YOURS.
YOU JUST DON'T GET IT.
KAPOK
THE CAPSULE MACHINE HAS A CERTAIN MYSTIQUE THAT--
WHAT'S THE MATTER?
STAAARE
......

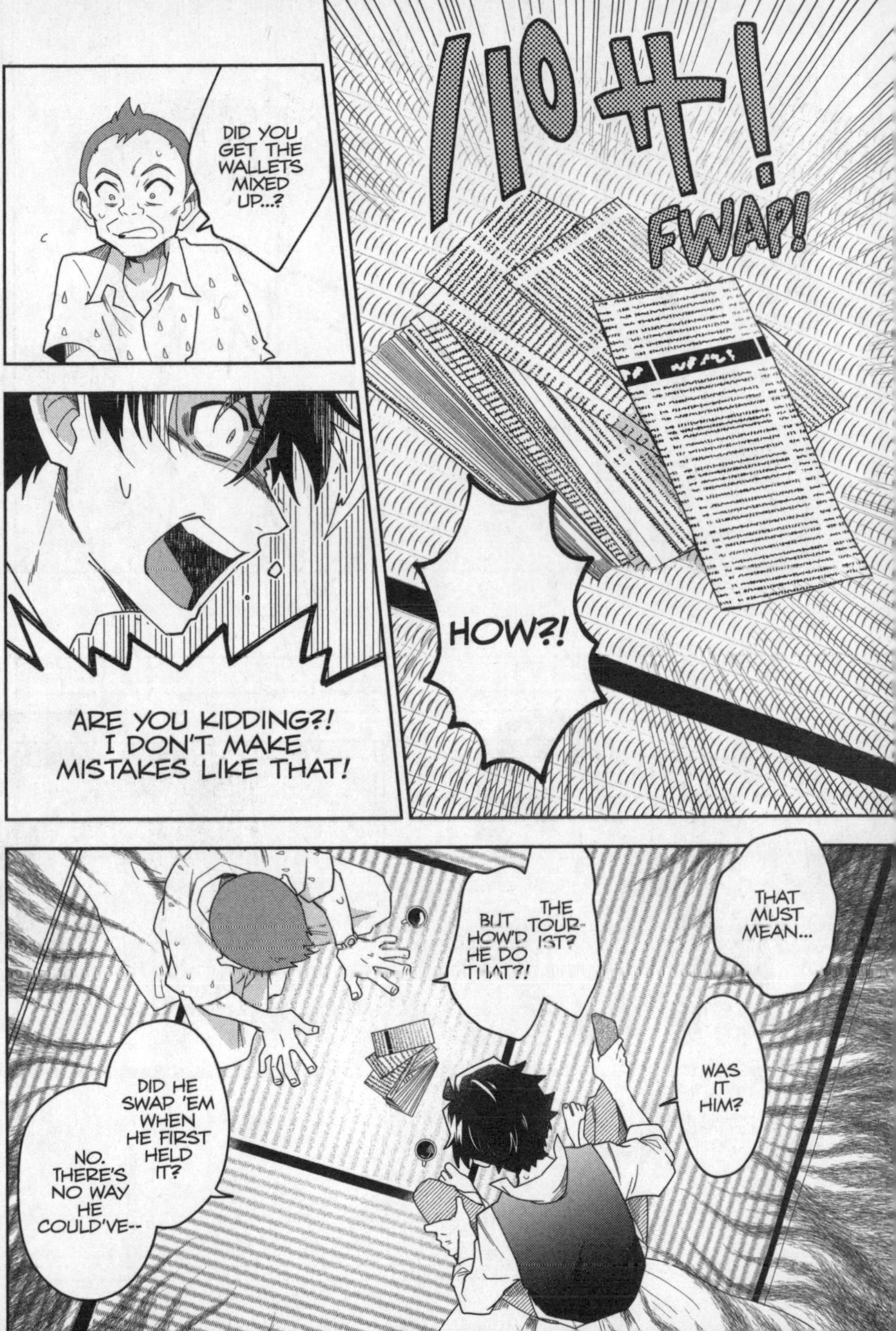
FWAP!
HOW?!
DID YOU GET THE WALLETS MIXED UP...?
ARE YOU KIDDING?! I DON'T MAKE MISTAKES LIKE THAT!
THAT MUST MEAN...
THE TOURIST?
BUT HOW'D HE DO THAT?!
WAS IT HIM?
DID HE SWAP 'EM WHEN HE FIRST HELD IT?
NO. THERE'S NO WAY HE COULD'VE--

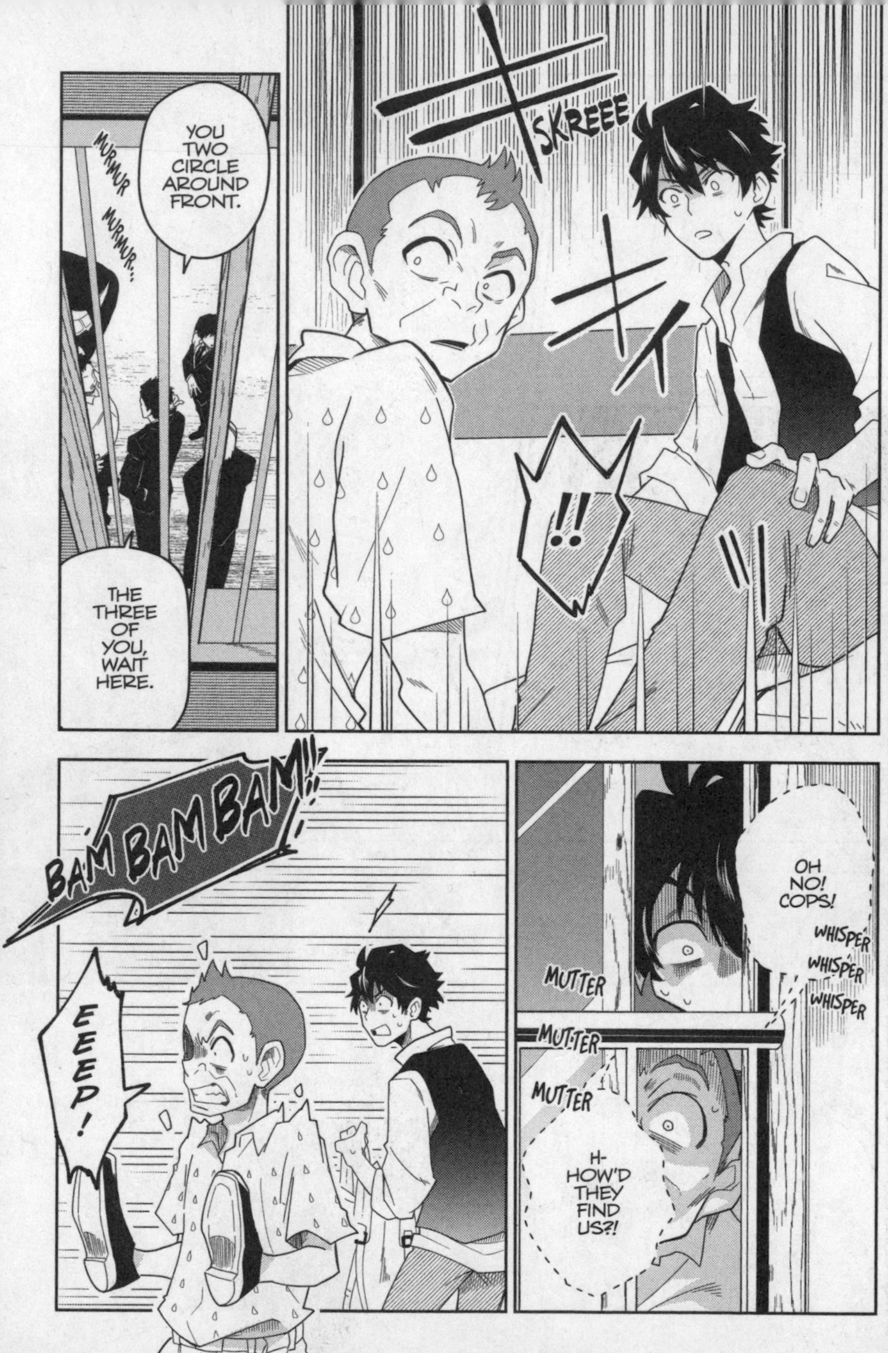
SKREEE
キイ
!!
MURMUR
MURMUR...
YOU TWO CIRCLE AROUND FRONT.
THE THREE OF YOU, WAIT HERE.
OH NO! COPS!
WHISPER
WHISPER
WHISPER
MUTTER
MUTTER
MUTTER
H-HOW'D THEY FIND US?!
BAM BAM BAM!!
EEEP!

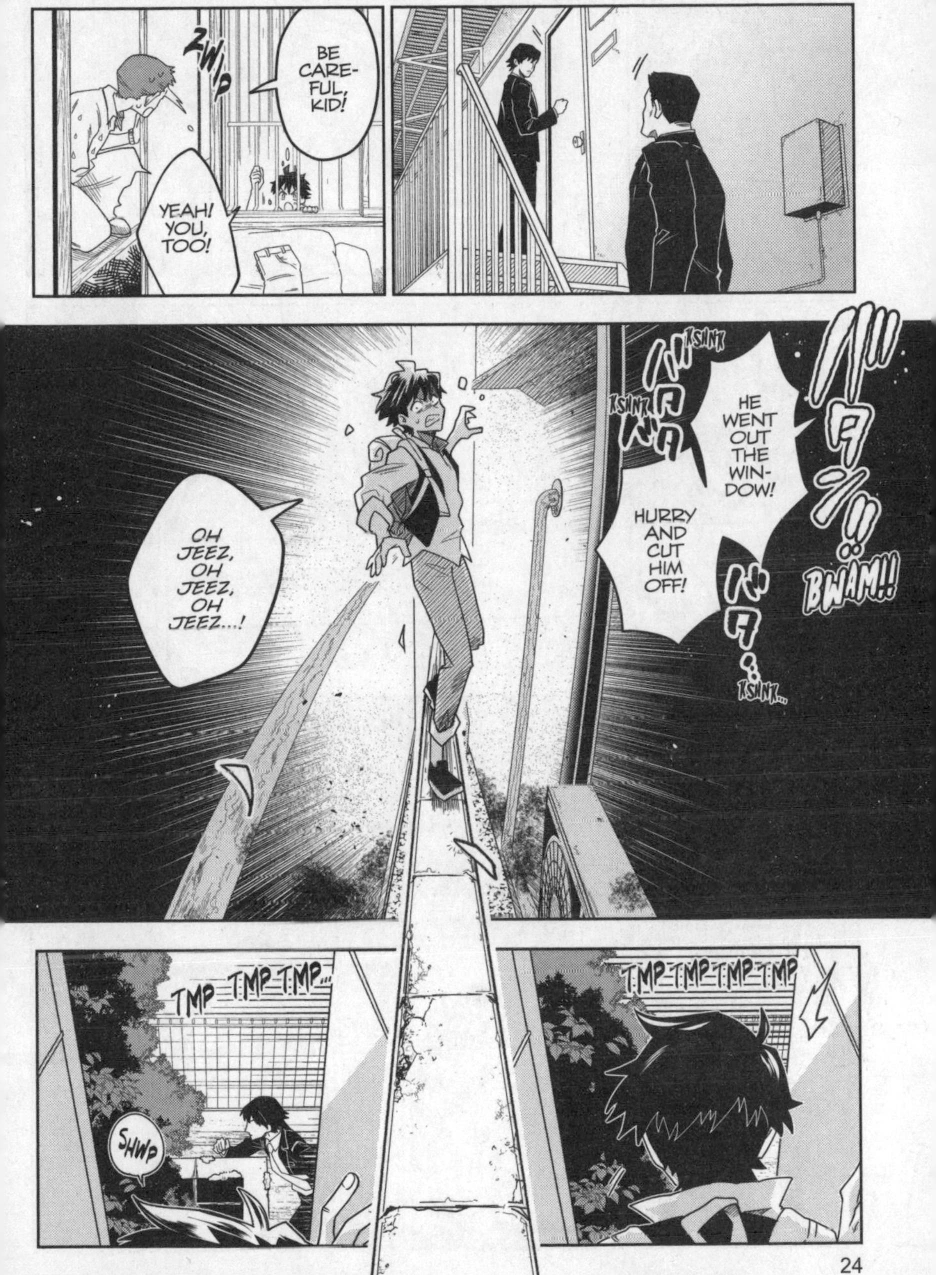

ZWIP
BE CAREFUL, KID!
YEAH! YOU, TOO!
KSHNK
KSHNK
HE WENT OUT THE WINDOW!
HURRY AND CUT HIM OFF!
BWAM!!
KSHNK...
OH JEEZ, OH JEEZ, OH JEEZ...!
TMP TMP TMP TMP
TMP TMP TMP...
SHWP

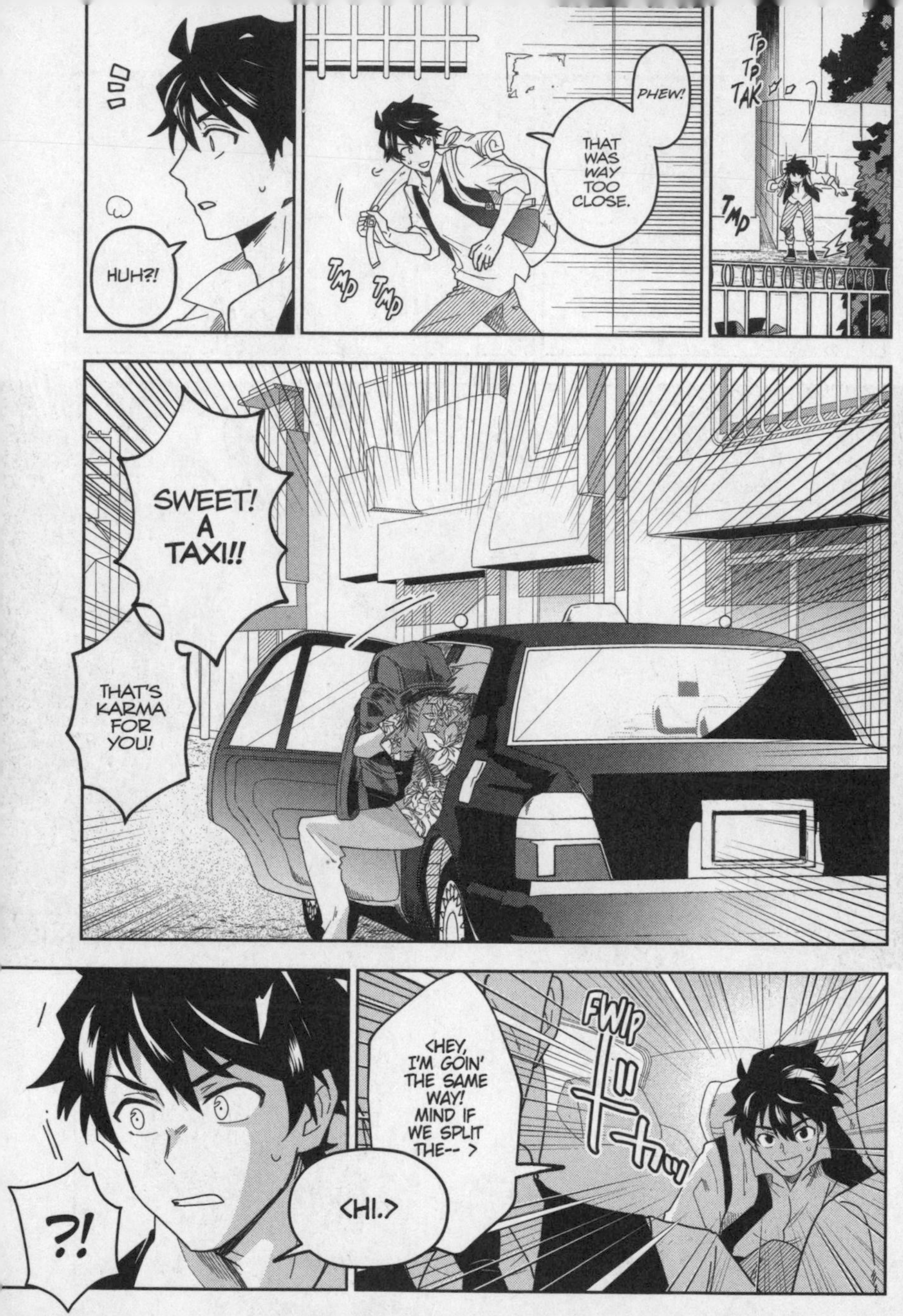
TP TP TAK
TMP
PHEW!
THAT WAS WAY TOO CLOSE.
TMP TMP
HUH?!
SWEET! A TAXI!!
THAT'S KARMA FOR YOU!
FWIP
<HEY, I'M GOIN' THE SAME WAY! MIND IF WE SPLIT THE-- >
<HI.>
?!

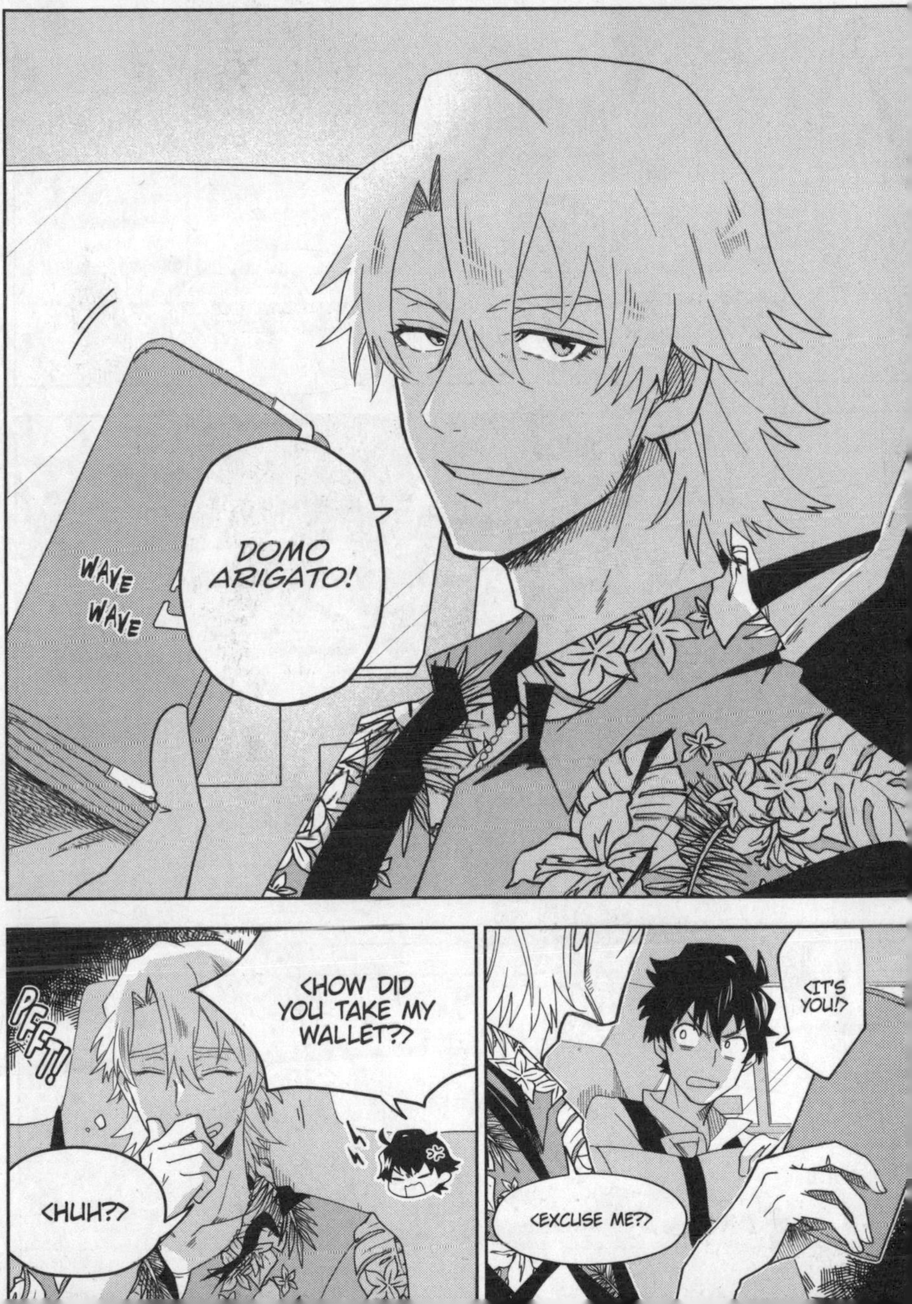
DOMO ARIGATO!
WAVE WAVE
<IT'S YOU!>
<EXCUSE ME?>
<HOW DID YOU TAKE MY WALLET?>
PFFT!
<HUH?>

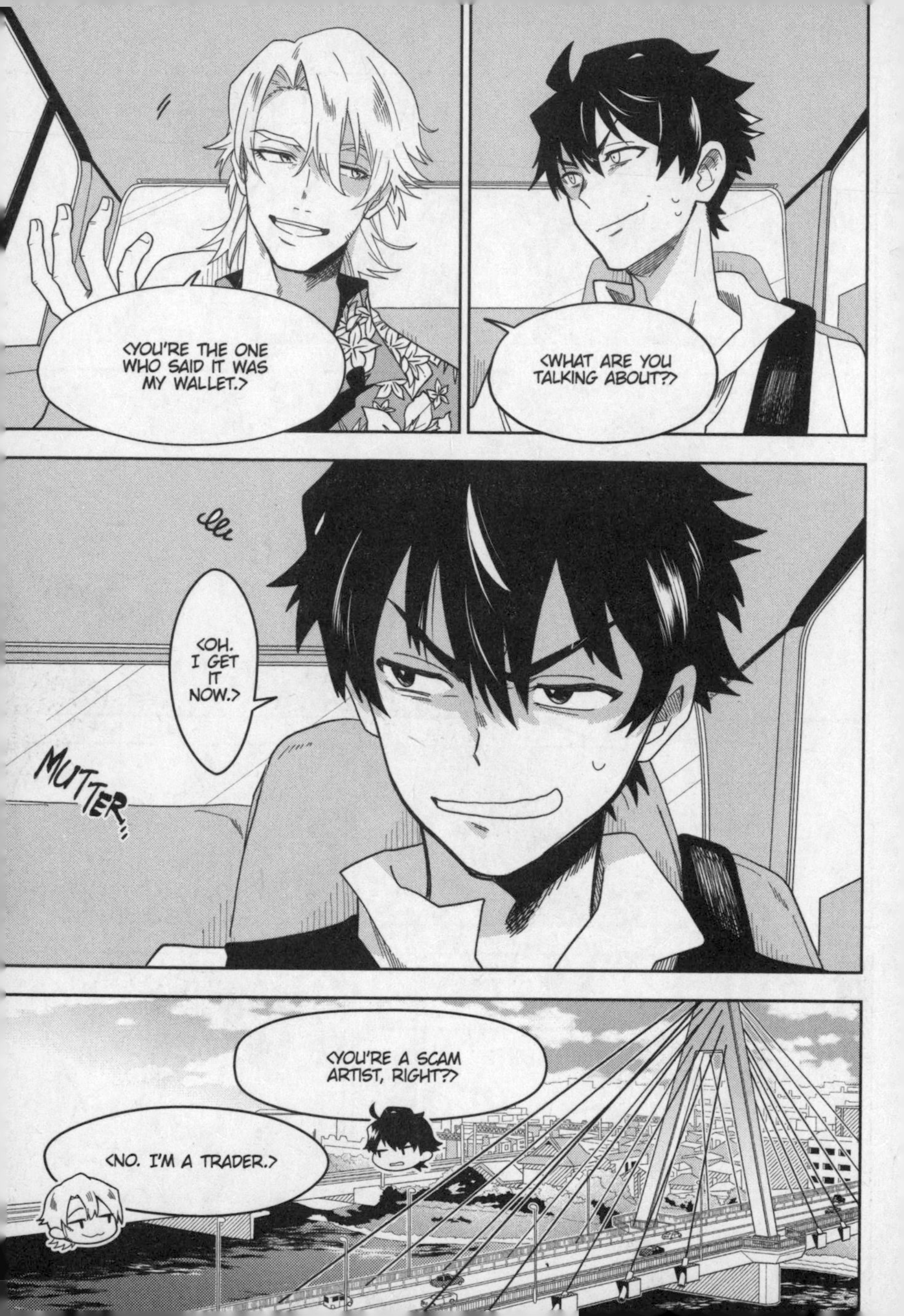
<WHAT ARE YOU TALKING ABOUT?>
<YOU'RE THE ONE WHO SAID IT WAS MY WALLET.>
<OH. I GET IT NOW.>
MUTTER...
<YOU'RE A SCAM ARTIST, RIGHT?>
<NO. I'M A TRADER.>

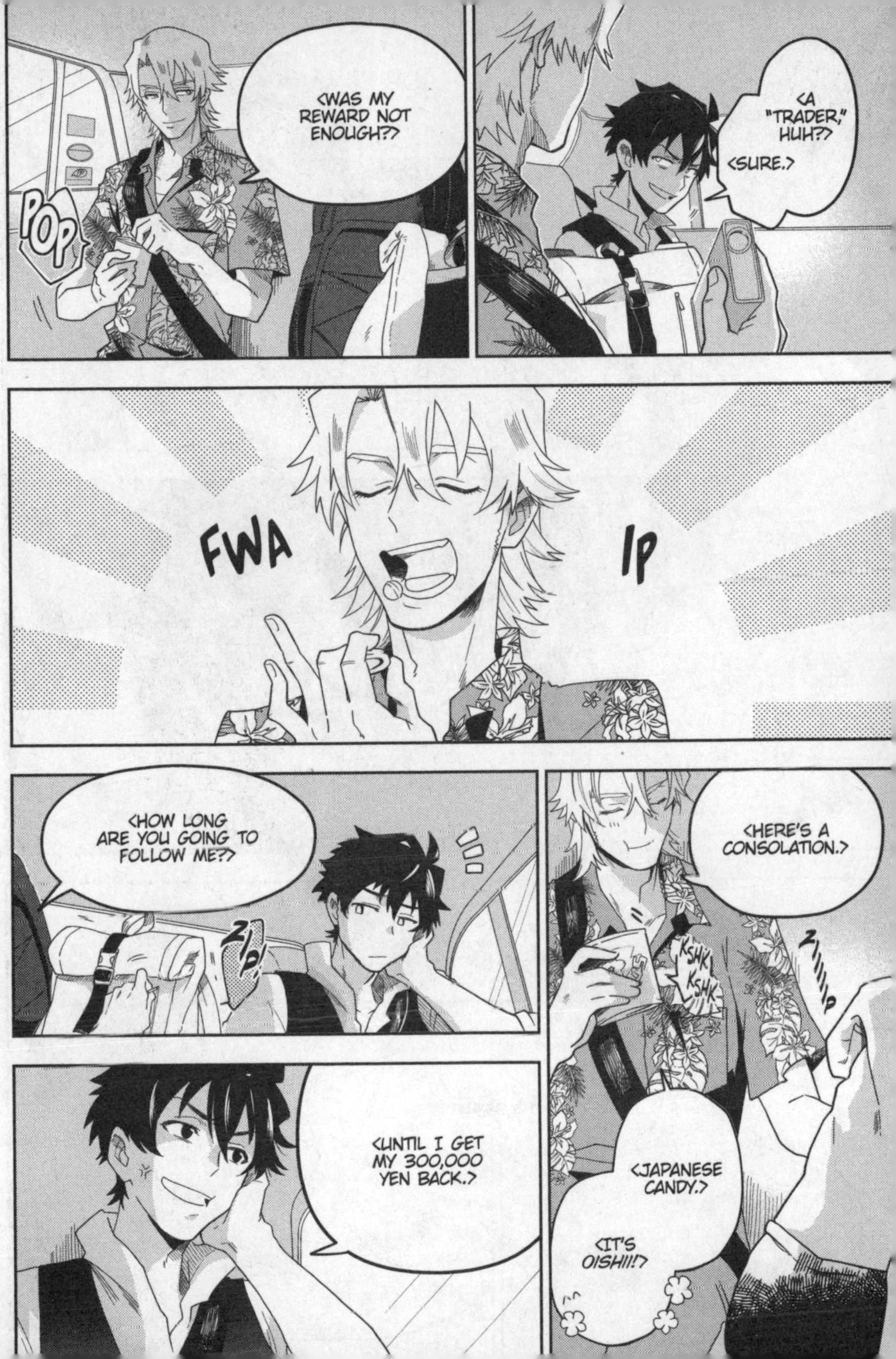
<A "TRADER," HUH?>
<SURE.>
<WAS MY REWARD NOT ENOUGH?>
POP
FWA IP
<HERE'S A CONSOLATION.>
KSHK KSHK
ZIIIIIP
<JAPANESE CANDY.>
<IT'S OISHII!>
<HOW LONG ARE YOU GOING TO FOLLOW ME?>
ZIP
<UNTIL I GET MY 300,000 YEN BACK.>

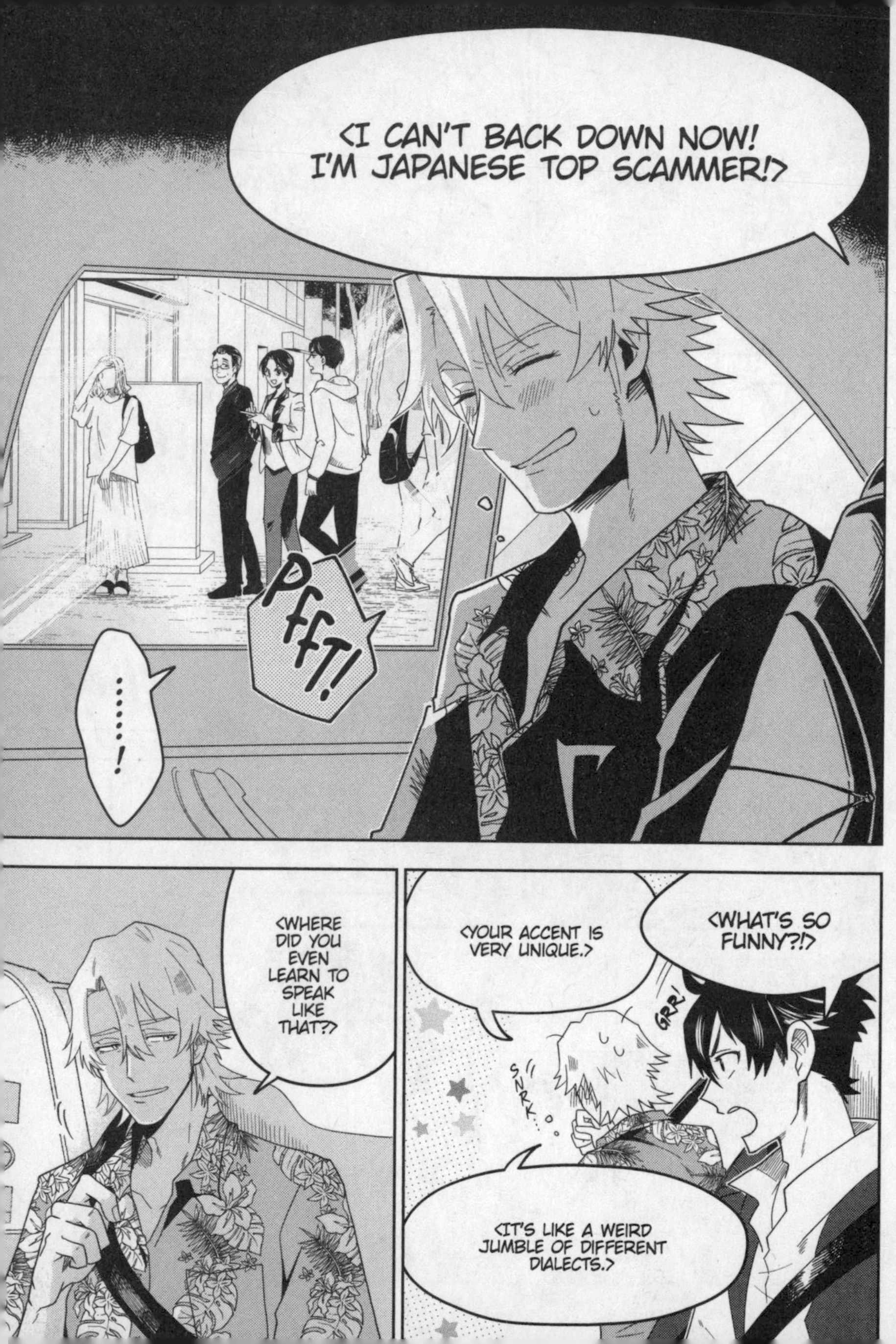
<I CAN'T BACK DOWN NOW! I'M JAPANESE TOP SCAMMER!>
PFFT!
......!
<WHAT'S SO FUNNY?!>
GRR!
<YOUR ACCENT IS VERY UNIQUE.>
SNRK...
<IT'S LIKE A WEIRD JUMBLE OF DIFFERENT DIALECTS.>
<WHERE DID YOU EVEN LEARN TO SPEAK LIKE THAT?>

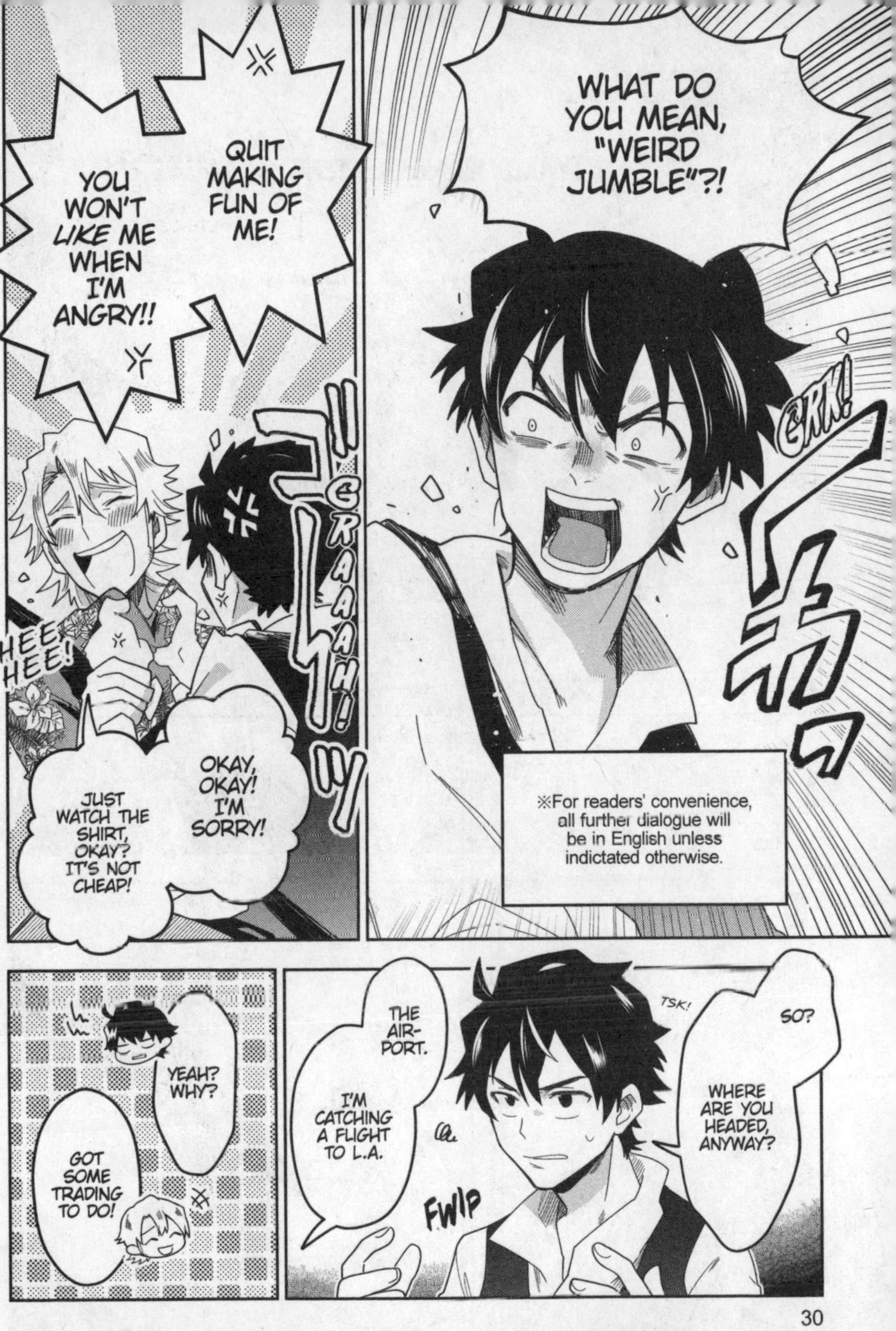
WHAT DO YOU MEAN, "WEIRD JUMBLE"?!
CRN!
※For readers' convenience, all further dialogue will be in English unless indictated otherwise.
QUIT MAKING FUN OF ME!
YOU WON'T LIKE ME WHEN I'M ANGRY!!
GRAAAAAH!!
HEE HEE!
OKAY, OKAY! I'M SORRY!
JUST WATCH THE SHIRT, OKAY? IT'S NOT CHEAP!
TSK!
SO?
WHERE ARE YOU HEADED, ANYWAY?
THE AIR-PORT.
I'M CATCHING A FLIGHT TO L.A.
FWIP
YEAH? WHY?
GOT SOME TRADING TO DO!

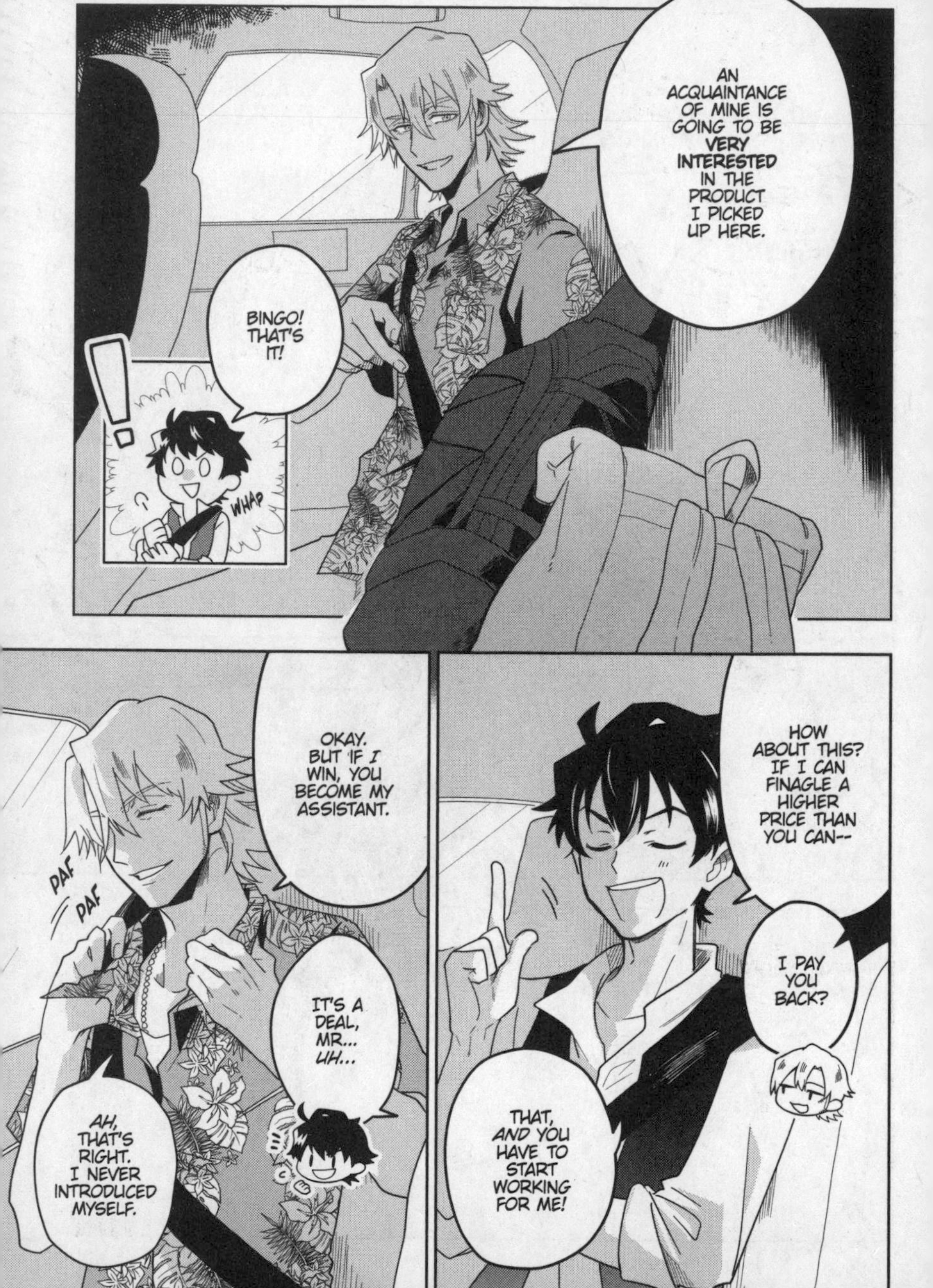
AN ACQUAINTANCE OF MINE IS GOING TO BE **VERY INTERESTED** IN THE PRODUCT I PICKED UP HERE.
BINGO! THAT'S IT!
WHAP
HOW ABOUT THIS? IF I CAN FINAGLE A HIGHER PRICE THAN YOU CAN--
I PAY YOU BACK?
THAT, *AND* YOU HAVE TO START WORKING FOR ME!
OKAY. BUT IF *I* WIN, YOU BECOME MY ASSISTANT.
PAF
PAF
IT'S A DEAL, MR... UH...
AH, THAT'S RIGHT. I NEVER INTRODUCED MYSELF.

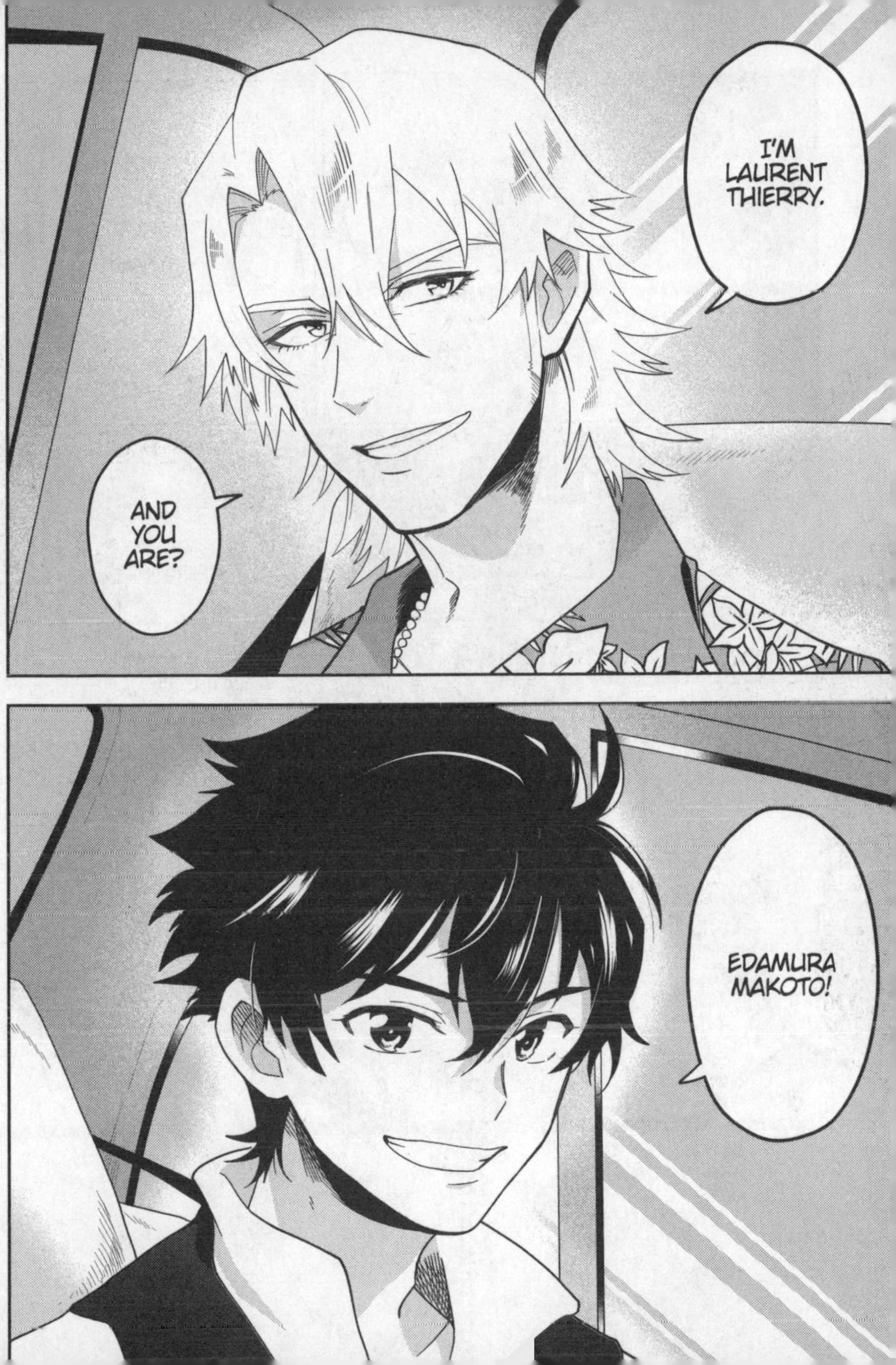
I'M LAURENT THIERRY.
AND YOU ARE?
EDAMURA MAKOTO!

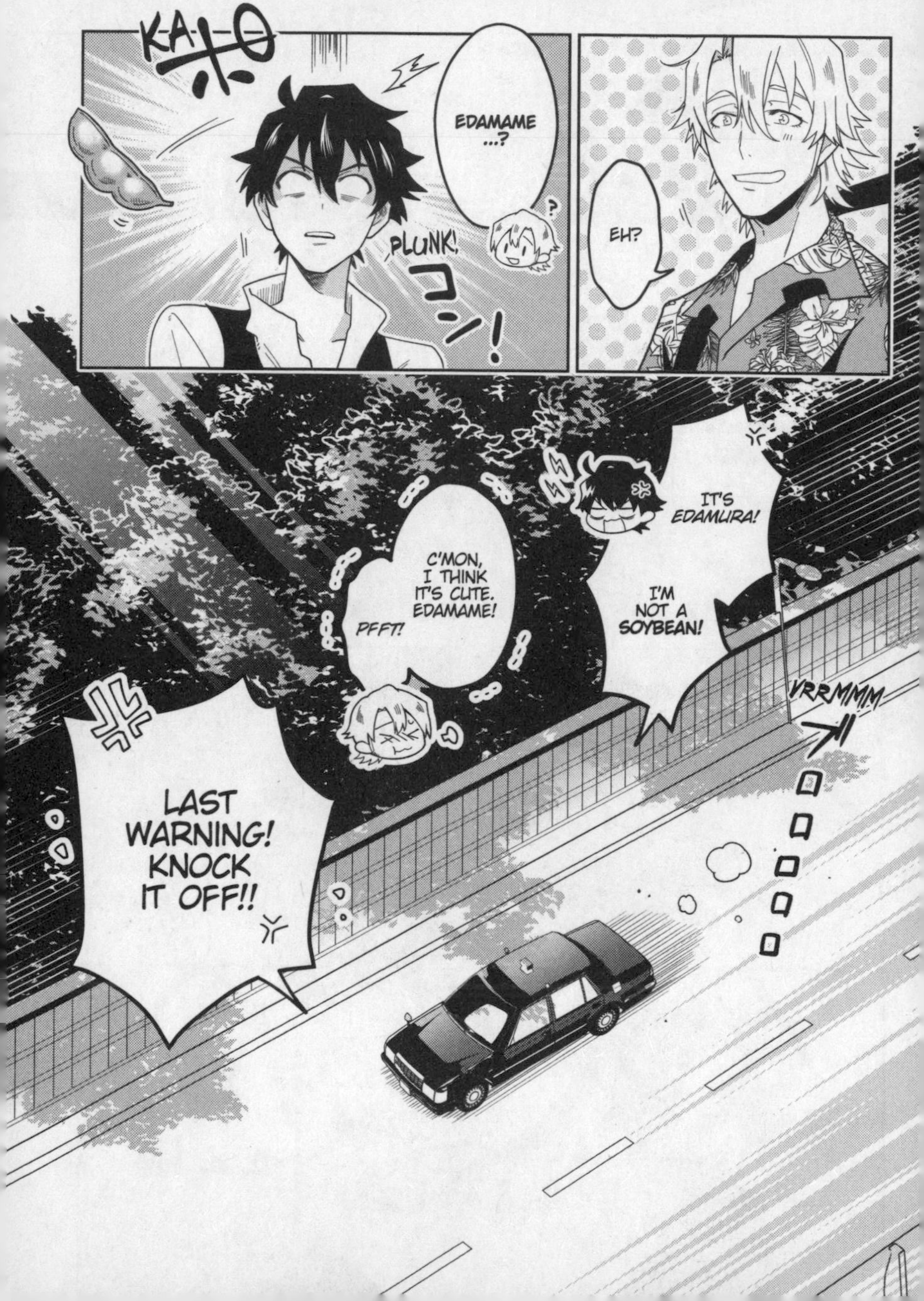
EH?
KA-O
EDAMAME ...?
?
PLUNK!
IT'S EDAMURA!
I'M NOT A SOYBEAN!
VRRMMM
C'MON, I THINK IT'S CUTE. EDAMAME!
PFFT!
LAST WARNING! KNOCK IT OFF!!

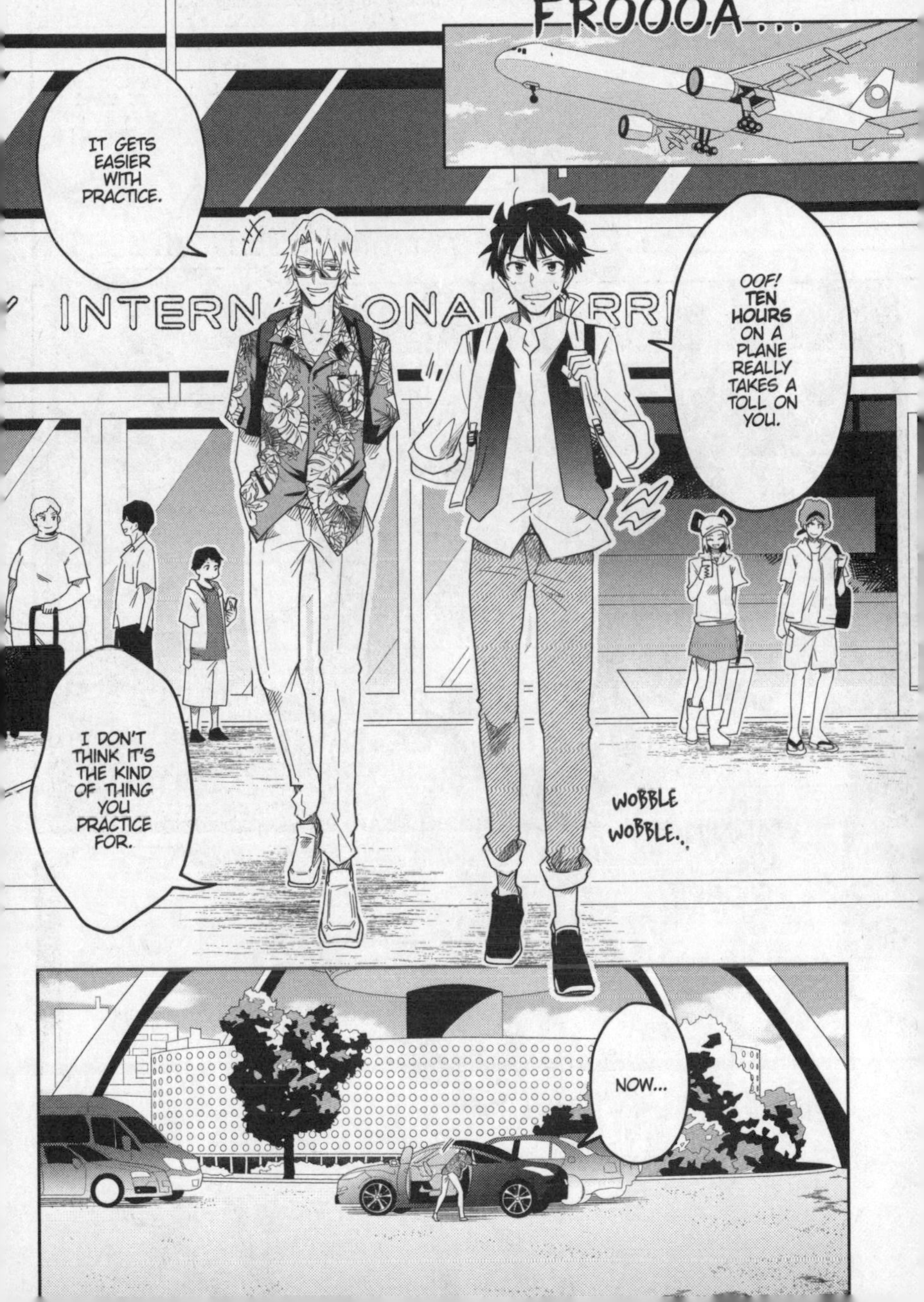
FROOOA...
OOF! TEN HOURS ON A PLANE REALLY TAKES A TOLL ON YOU.
IT GETS EASIER WITH PRACTICE.
I DON'T THINK IT'S THE KIND OF THING YOU PRACTICE FOR.
WOBBLE WOBBLE...
NOW...

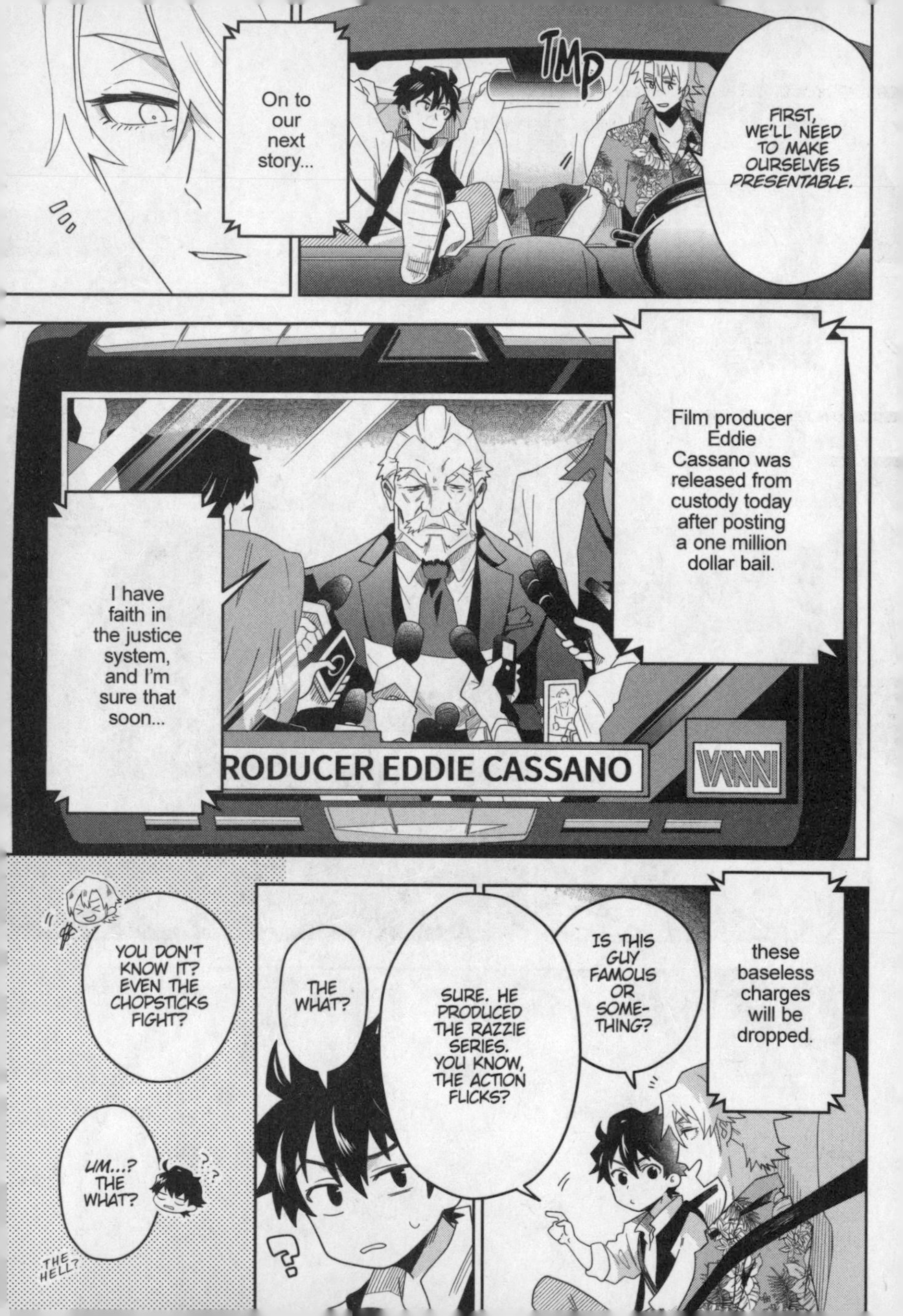
FIRST, WE'LL NEED TO MAKE OURSELVES PRESENTABLE.
TMP
On to our next story...
Film producer Eddie Cassano was released from custody today after posting a one million dollar bail.
I have faith in the justice system, and I'm sure that soon...
RODUCER EDDIE CASSANO
VANNI
these baseless charges will be dropped.
IS THIS GUY FAMOUS OR SOME-THING?
SURE. HE PRODUCED THE RAZZIE SERIES. YOU KNOW, THE ACTION FLICKS?
THE WHAT?
YOU DON'T KNOW IT? EVEN THE CHOPSTICKS FIGHT?
UM...? THE WHAT?
THE HELL?

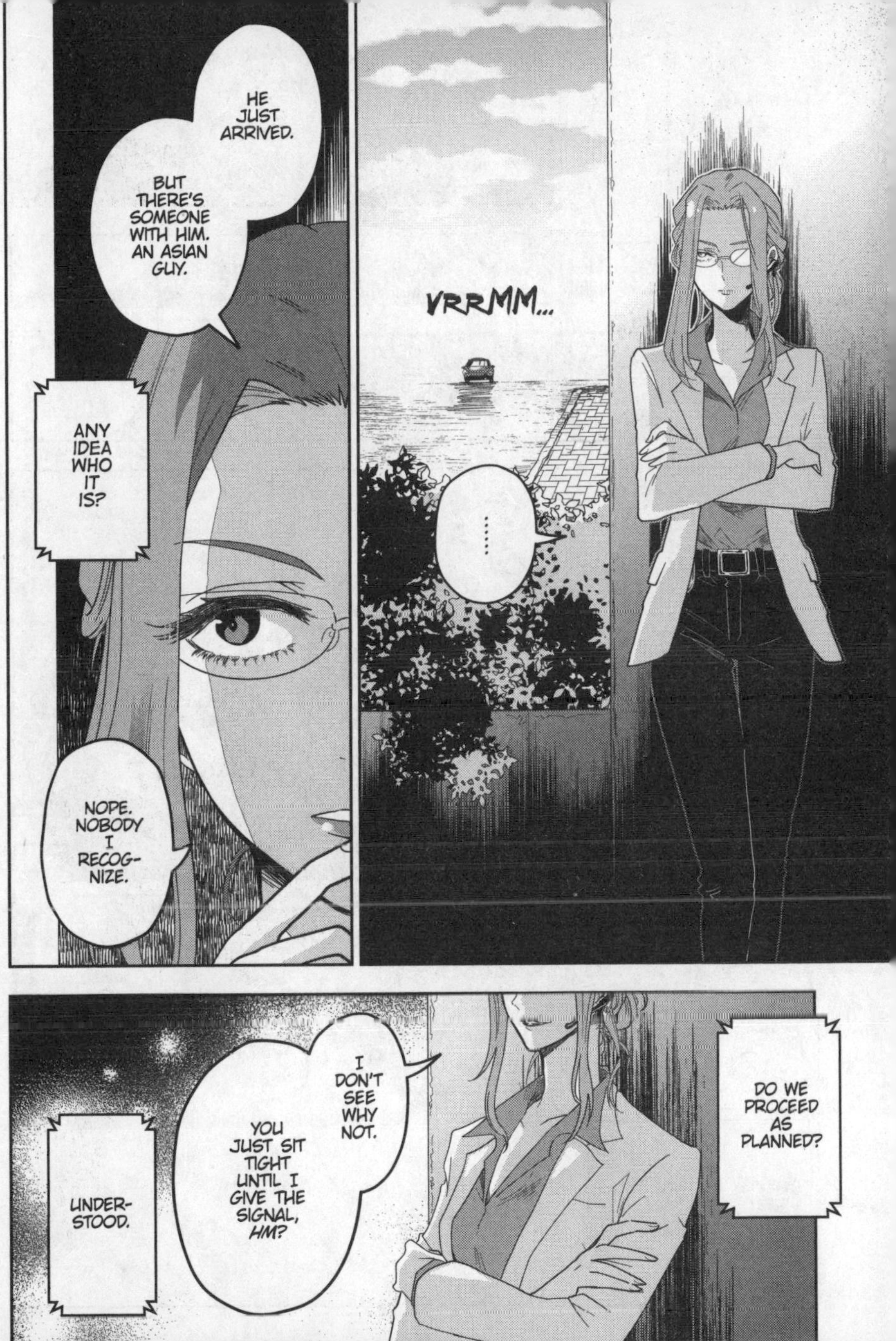
VRRMM...
......
HE JUST ARRIVED.
BUT THERE'S SOMEONE WITH HIM. AN ASIAN GUY.
ANY IDEA WHO IT IS?
NOPE. NOBODY I RECOG-NIZE.
DO WE PROCEED AS PLANNED?
I DON'T SEE WHY NOT.
YOU JUST SIT TIGHT UNTIL I GIVE THE SIGNAL, HM?
UNDER-STOOD.

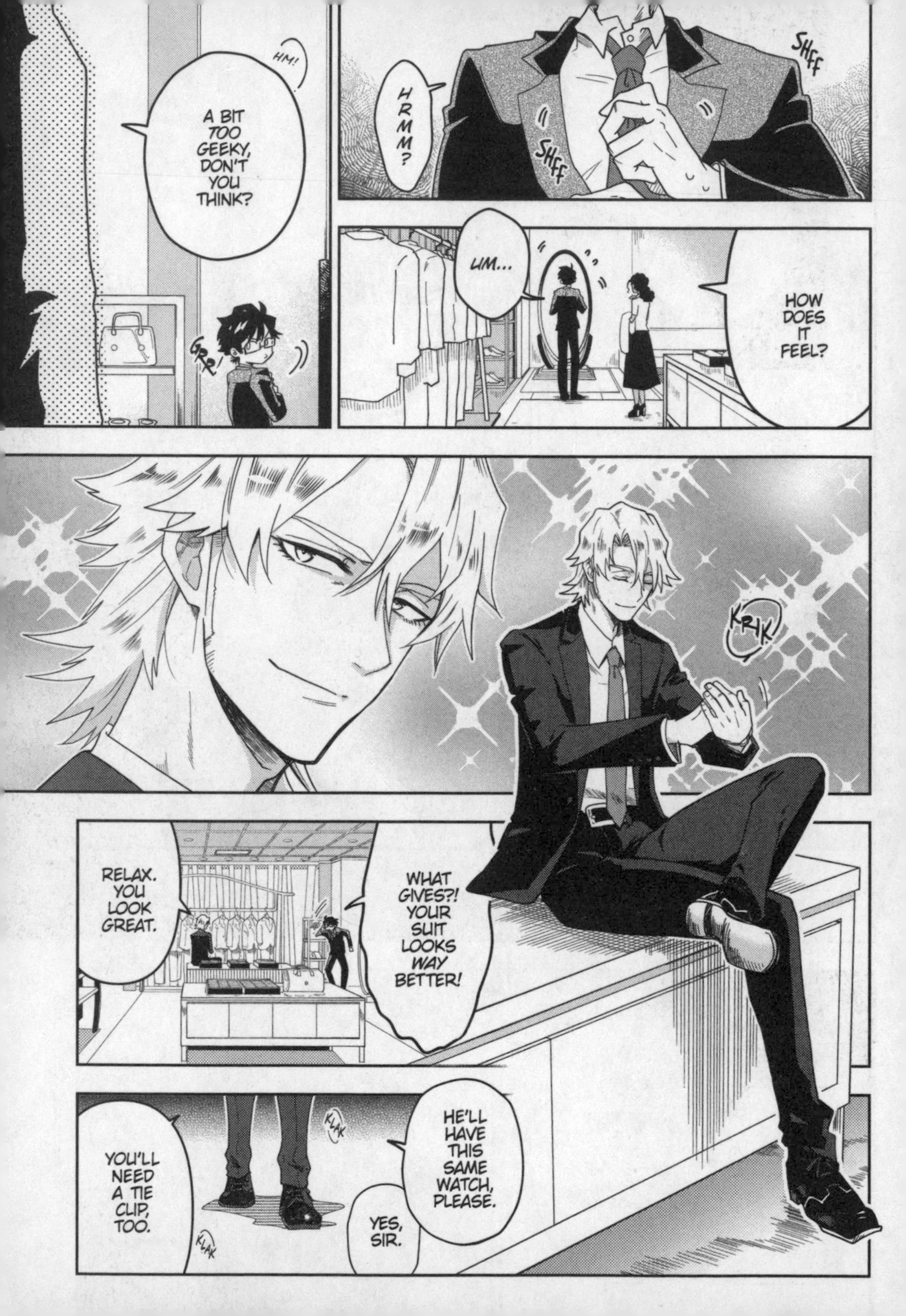
SHFF
HRMM?
SHFF
HOW DOES IT FEEL?
UM...
HM!
A BIT TOO GEEKY, DON'T YOU THINK?
GRR!
KRIK
WHAT GIVES?! YOUR SUIT LOOKS WAY BETTER!
RELAX. YOU LOOK GREAT.
HE'LL HAVE THIS SAME WATCH, PLEASE.
KLAK
YES, SIR.
YOU'LL NEED A TIE CLIP, TOO.
KLAK

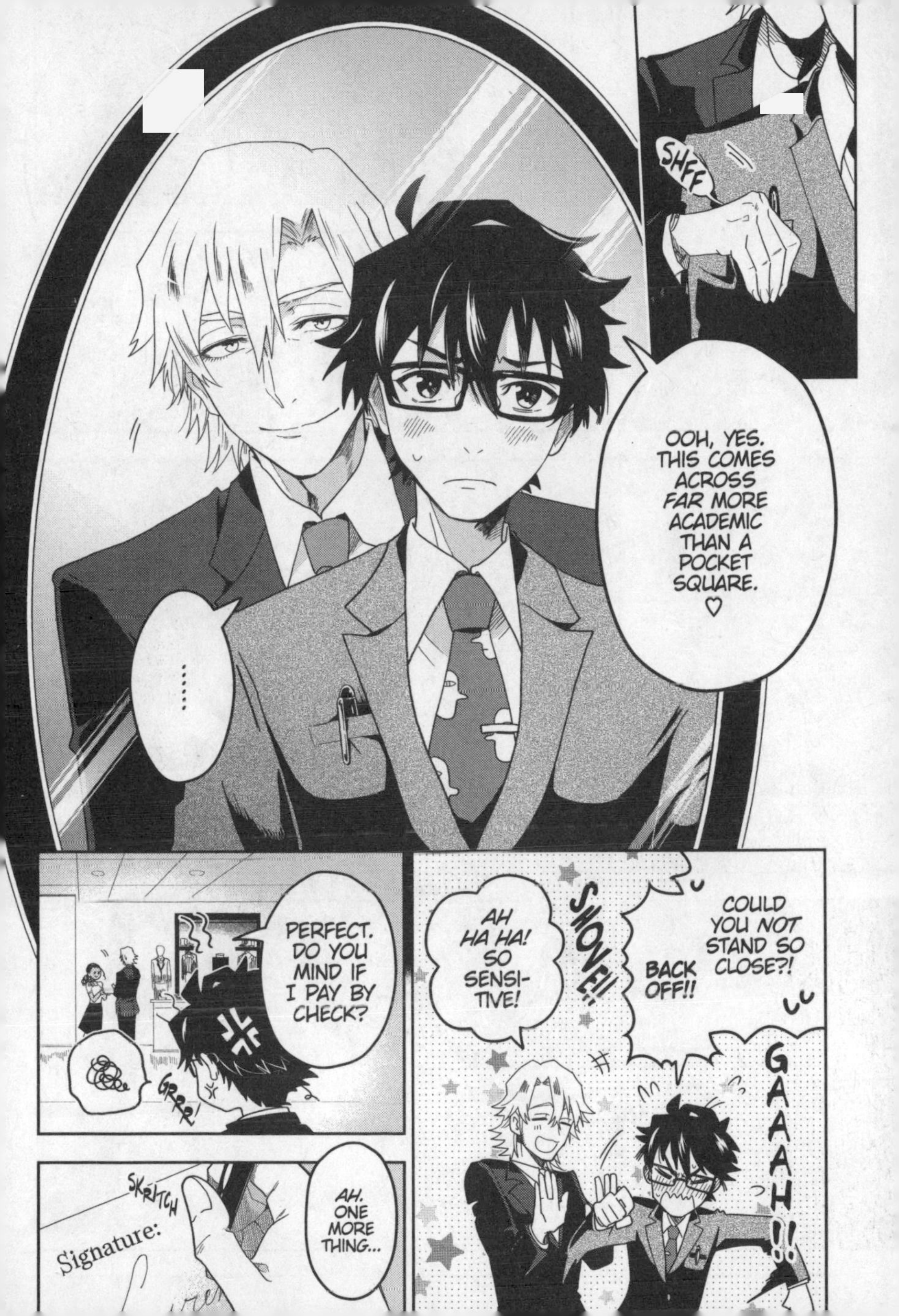
SHFF
OOH, YES. THIS COMES ACROSS FAR MORE ACADEMIC THAN A POCKET SQUARE. ♡
......
COULD YOU NOT STAND SO CLOSE?!
BACK OFF!!
SHOVE!!
AH HA HA! SO SENSI-TIVE!
GAAAH!!
PERFECT. DO YOU MIND IF I PAY BY CHECK?
GRRR!
SKRITCH
AH. ONE MORE THING...
Signature:

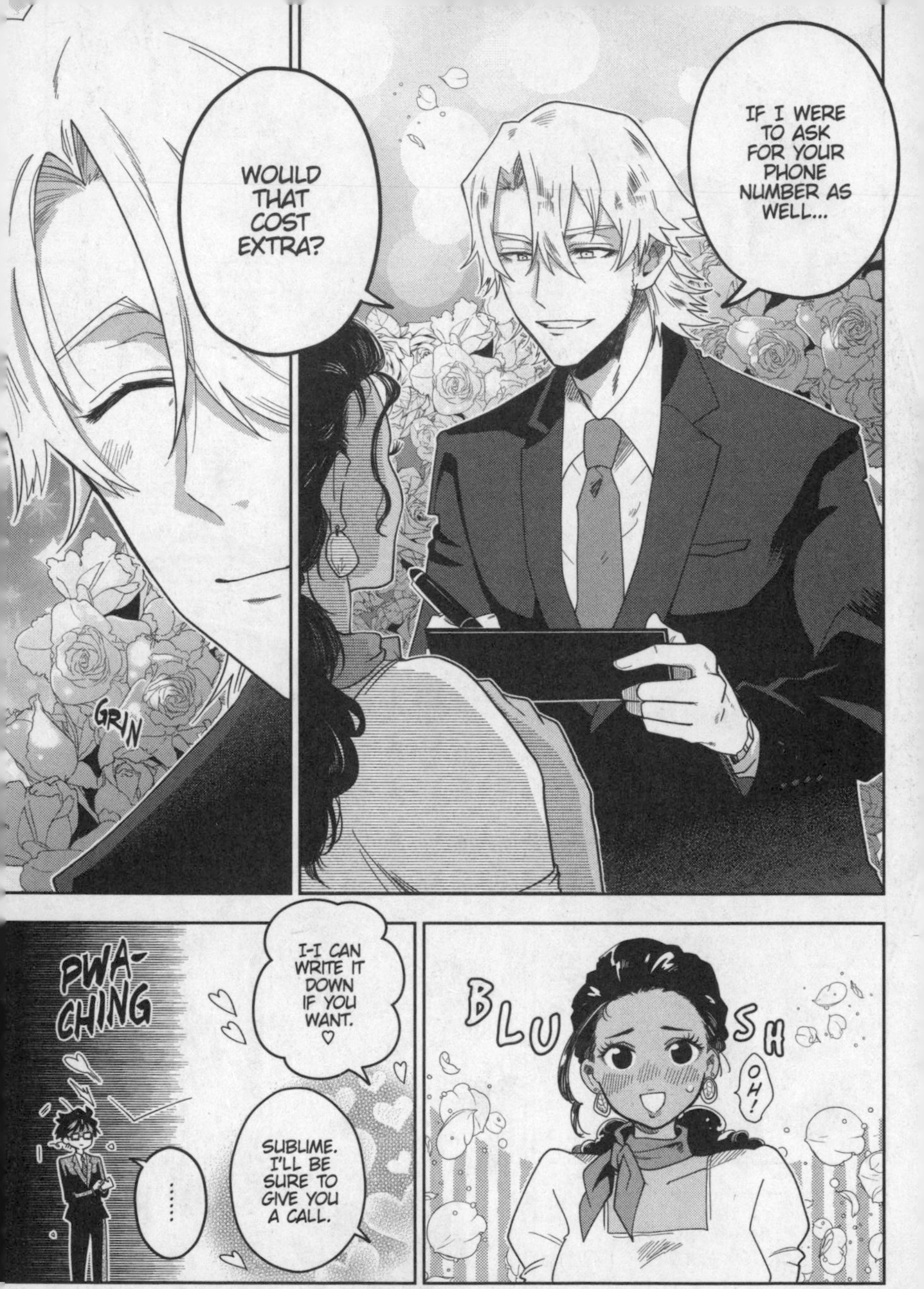
IF I WERE TO ASK FOR YOUR PHONE NUMBER AS WELL...
WOULD THAT COST EXTRA?
GRIN
BLUSH
OH!
I-I CAN WRITE IT DOWN IF YOU WANT. ♡
SUBLIME. I'LL BE SURE TO GIVE YOU A CALL.
......
PWA-CHING

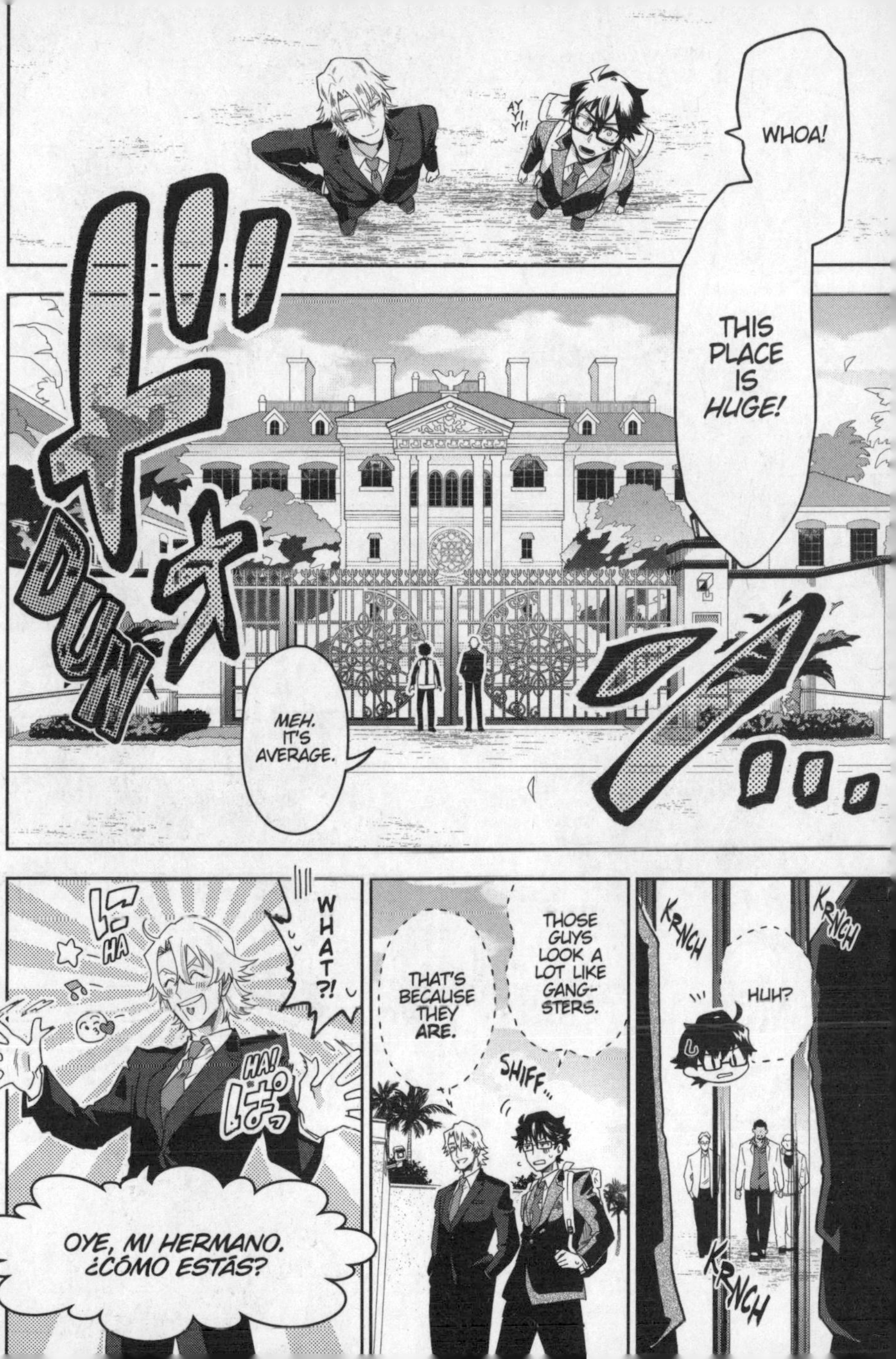
AY YI YI!
WHOA!
THIS PLACE IS HUGE!
DUN
MEH. IT'S AVERAGE.
KRNCH
KRNCH
HUH?
KRNCH
THOSE GUYS LOOK A LOT LIKE GANG-STERS.
THAT'S BECAUSE THEY ARE.
SHIFF...
WHAT?!
にこ
HA
HA!
ぱっ
OYE, MI HERMANO. ¿CÓMO ESTÁS?

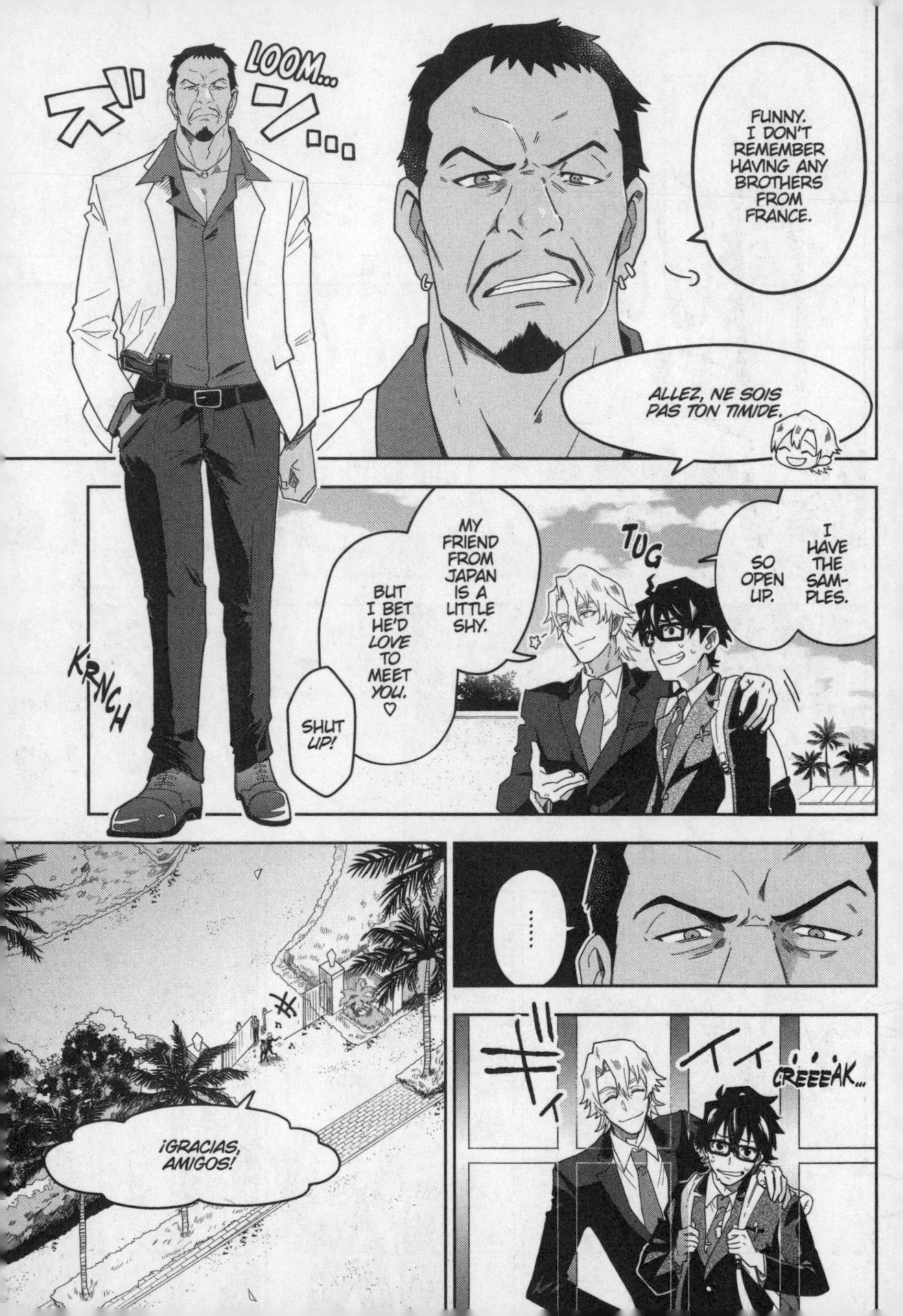
FUNNY. I DON'T REMEMBER HAVING ANY BROTHERS FROM FRANCE.
ALLEZ, NE SOIS PAS TON TIMIDE.
I HAVE THE SAMPLES.
SO OPEN UP.
TUG
MY FRIEND FROM JAPAN IS A LITTLE SHY.
BUT I BET HE'D LOVE TO MEET YOU. ♡
SHUT UP!
LOOM...
KRNCH
......
CREEEAK...
¡GRACIAS, AMIGOS!

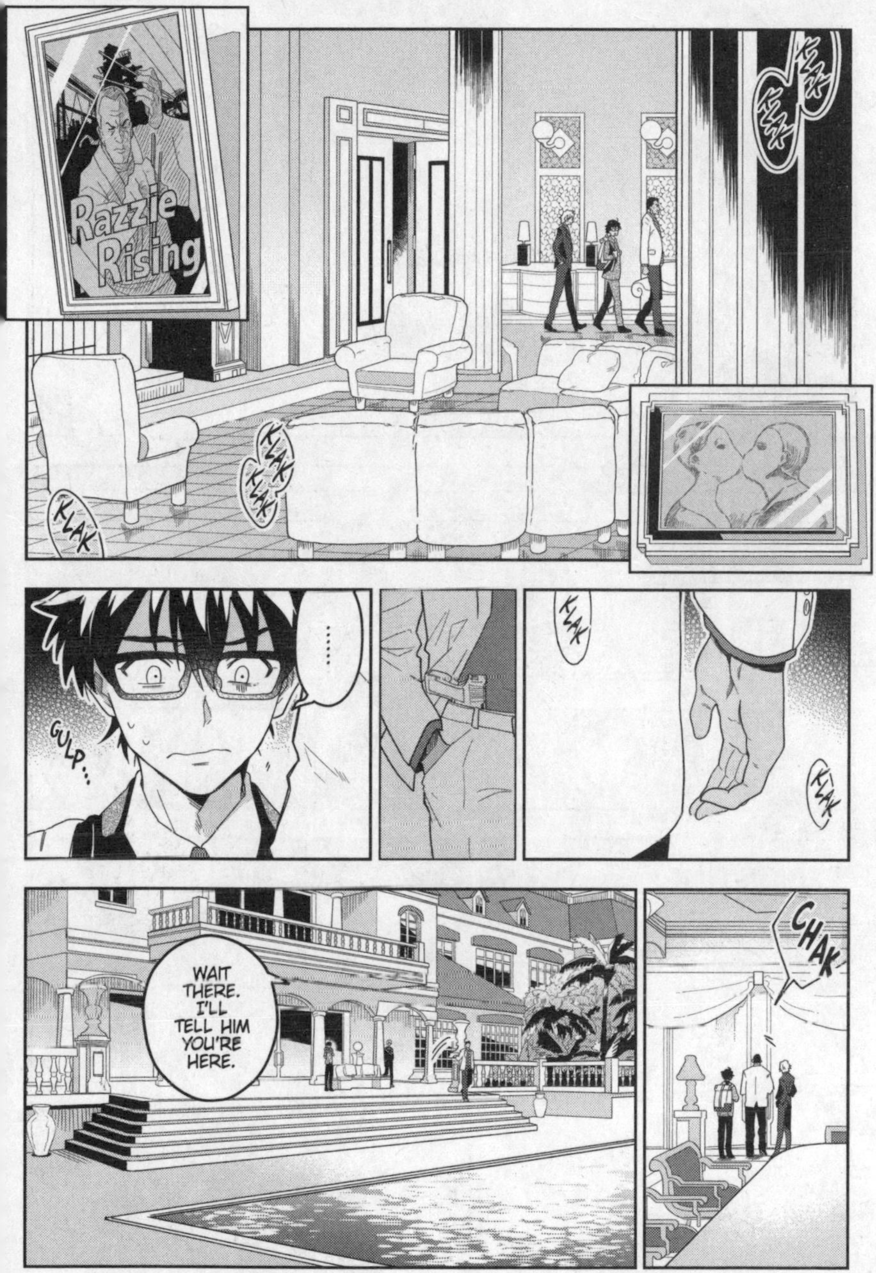
KLAK
KLAK
KLAK
KLAK
KLAK
Razzie Rising
KLAK
KLAK
......
GULP...
CHAK
WAIT THERE. I'LL TELL HIM YOU'RE HERE.

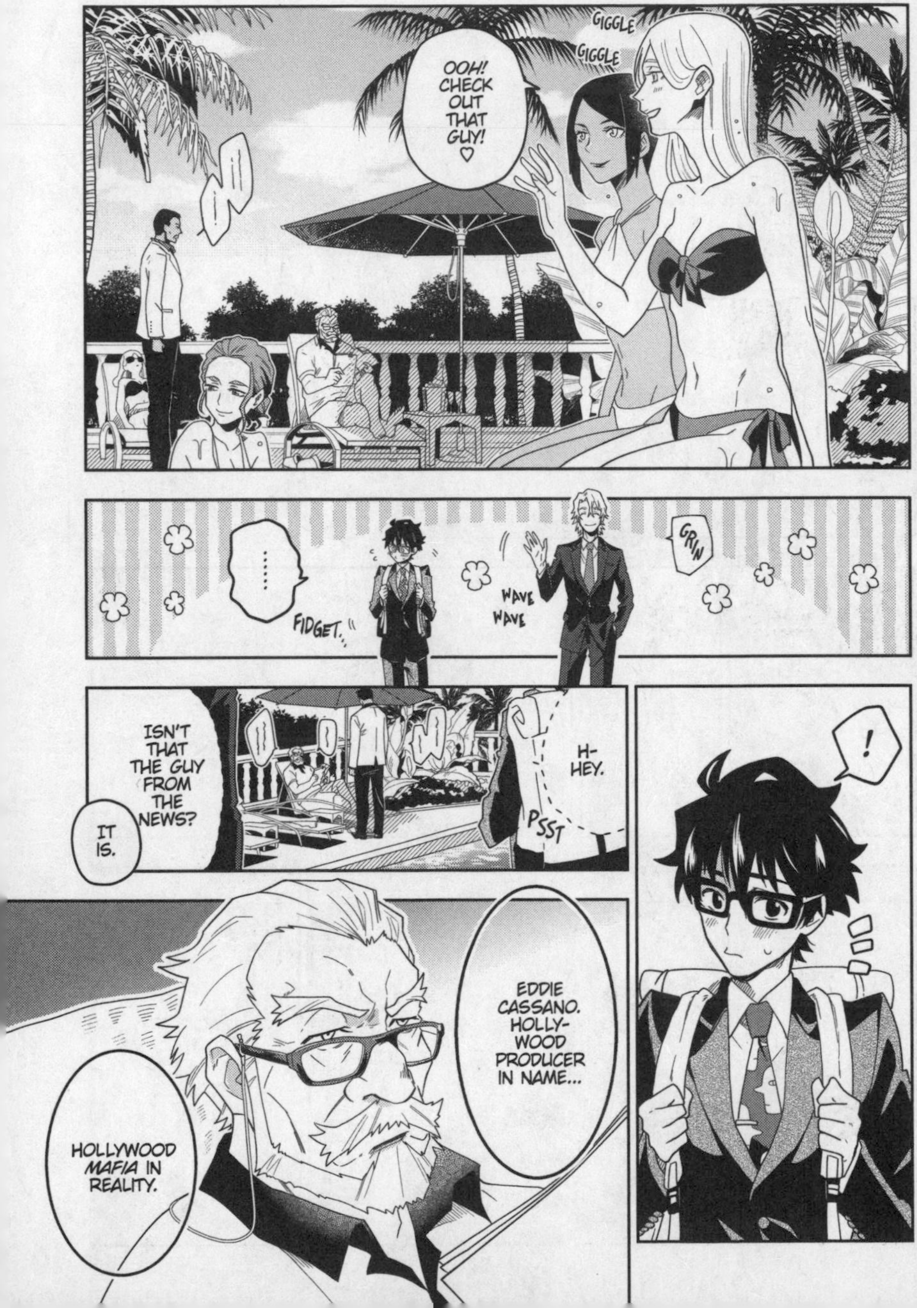
GIGGLE
GIGGLE
OOH! CHECK OUT THAT GUY! ♡
GRIN
WAVE WAVE
......
FIDGET
!
H-HEY.
PSST
ISN'T THAT THE GUY FROM THE NEWS?
IT IS.
EDDIE CASSANO. HOLLYWOOD PRODUCER IN NAME...
HOLLYWOOD *MAFIA* IN REALITY.

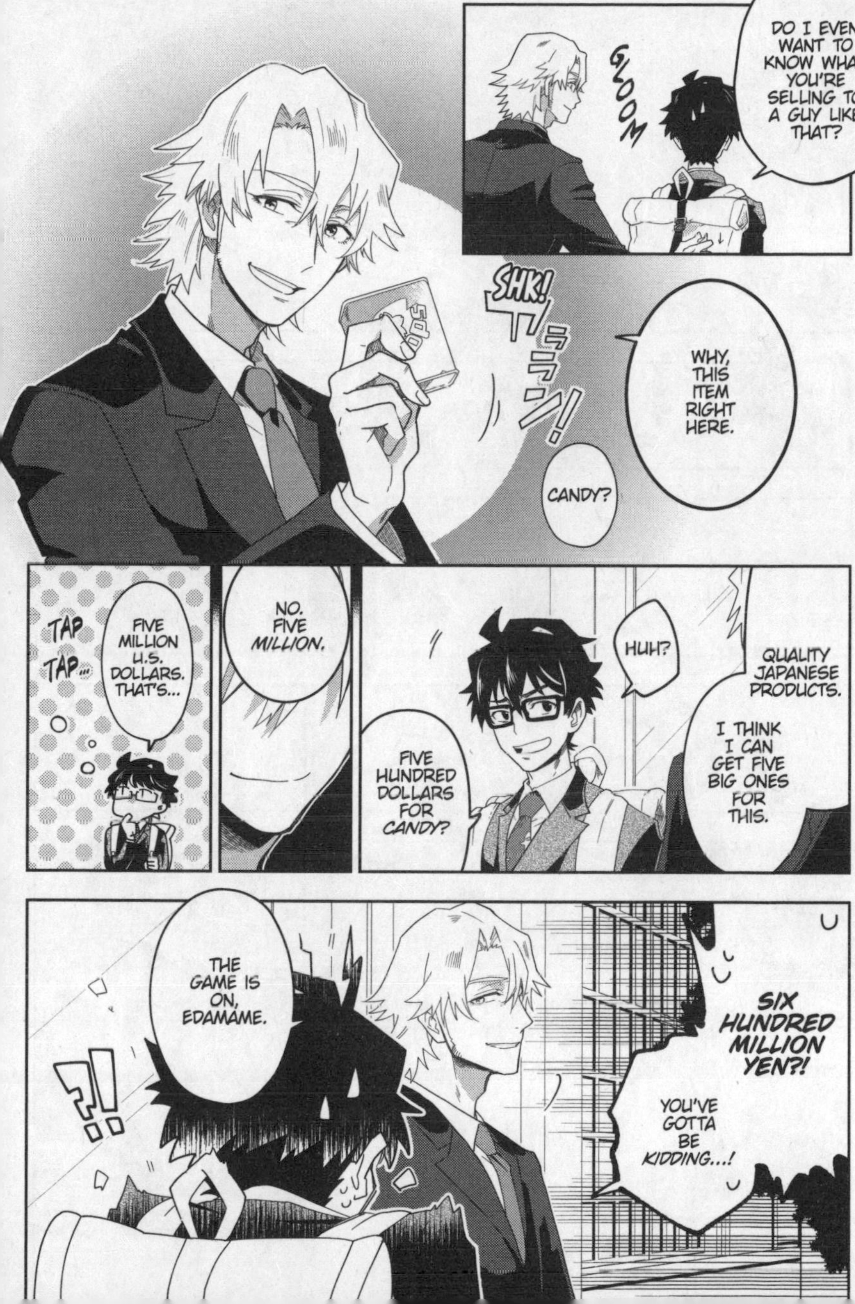
DO I EVEN WANT TO KNOW WHAT YOU'RE SELLING TO A GUY LIKE THAT?
GLOOM
SHK!
WHY, THIS ITEM RIGHT HERE.
CANDY?
QUALITY JAPANESE PRODUCTS.
I THINK I CAN GET FIVE BIG ONES FOR THIS.
HUH?
FIVE HUNDRED DOLLARS FOR CANDY?
NO. FIVE MILLION.
TAP TAP...
FIVE MILLION U.S. DOLLARS. THAT'S...
SIX HUNDRED MILLION YEN?!
YOU'VE GOTTA BE KIDDING...!
THE GAME IS ON, EDAMAME.

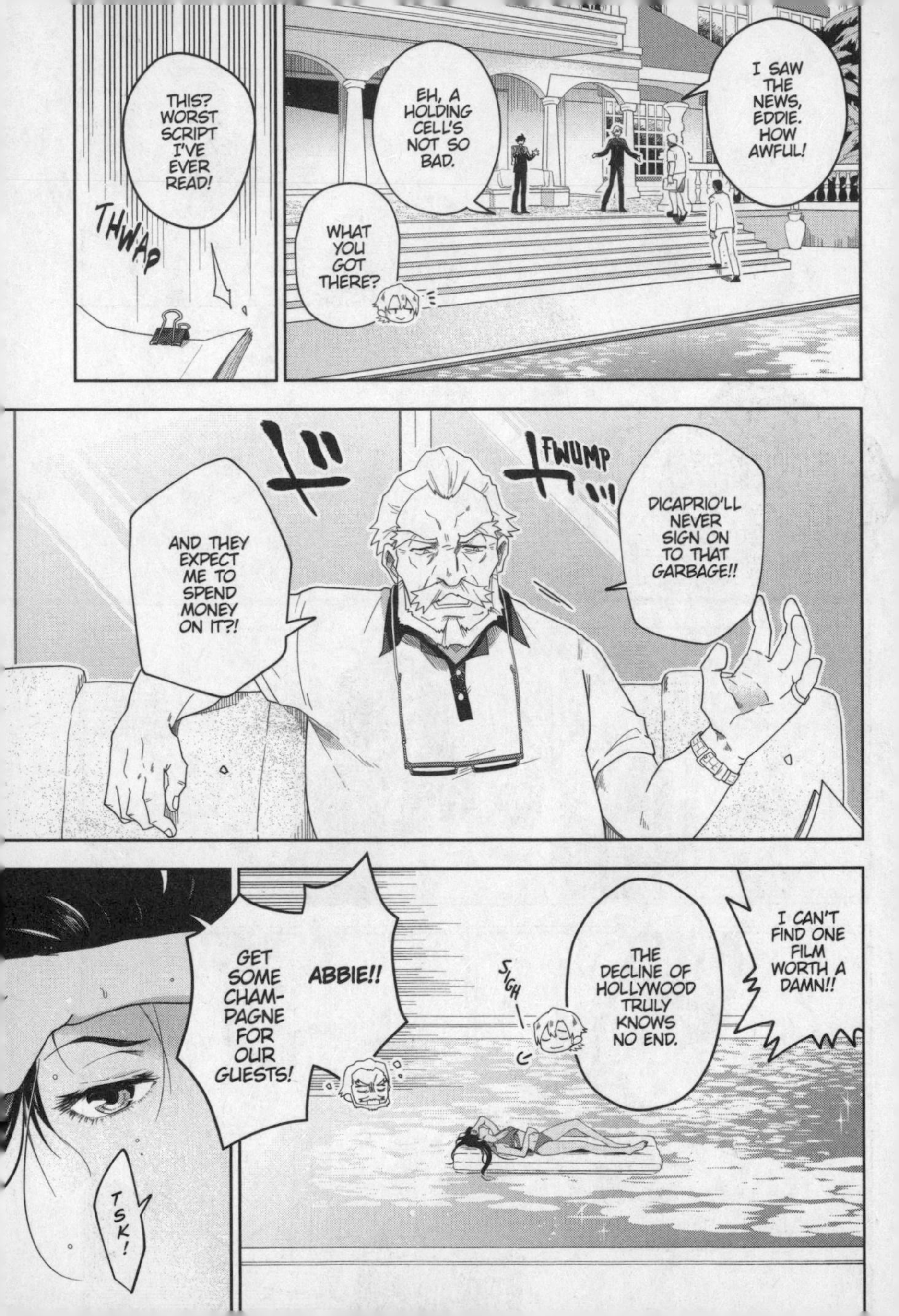
I SAW THE NEWS, EDDIE. HOW AWFUL!
EH, A HOLDING CELL'S NOT SO BAD.
WHAT YOU GOT THERE?
THIS? WORST SCRIPT I'VE EVER READ!
THWAP
FWUMP
DICAPRIO'LL NEVER SIGN ON TO THAT GARBAGE!!
AND THEY EXPECT ME TO SPEND MONEY ON IT?!
I CAN'T FIND ONE FILM WORTH A DAMN!!
THE DECLINE OF HOLLYWOOD TRULY KNOWS NO END.
SIGH
ABBIE!!
GET SOME CHAMPAGNE FOR OUR GUESTS!
TSK!

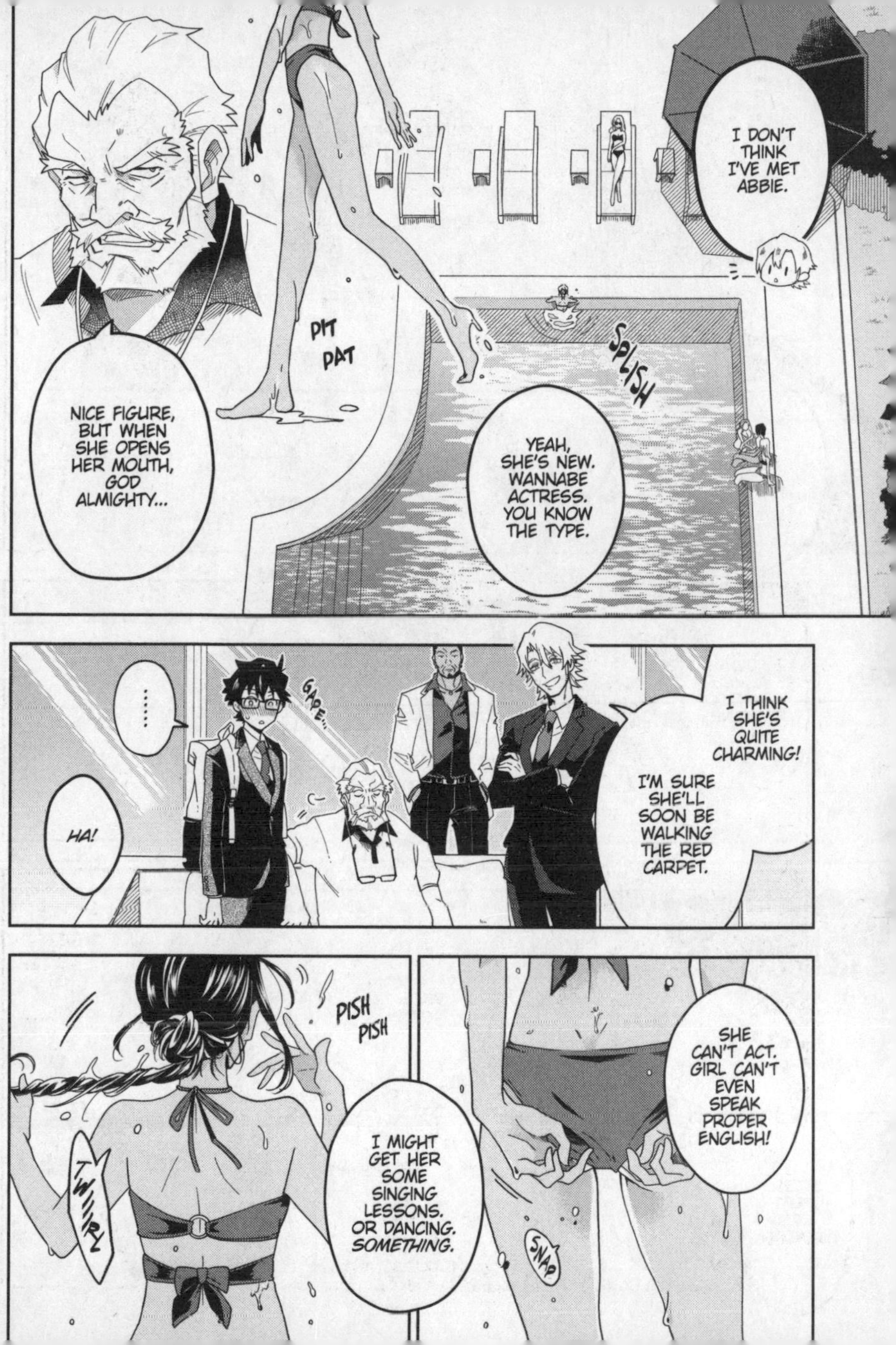
I DON'T THINK I'VE MET ABBIE.
SPLISH
YEAH, SHE'S NEW. WANNABE ACTRESS. YOU KNOW THE TYPE.
PIT PAT
NICE FIGURE, BUT WHEN SHE OPENS HER MOUTH, GOD ALMIGHTY...
I THINK SHE'S QUITE CHARMING!
I'M SURE SHE'LL SOON BE WALKING THE RED CARPET.
GAPE...
......
HA!
SHE CAN'T ACT. GIRL CAN'T EVEN SPEAK PROPER ENGLISH!
SNAP
PISH PISH
I MIGHT GET HER SOME SINGING LESSONS. OR DANCING. SOMETHING.
TWIIIRL

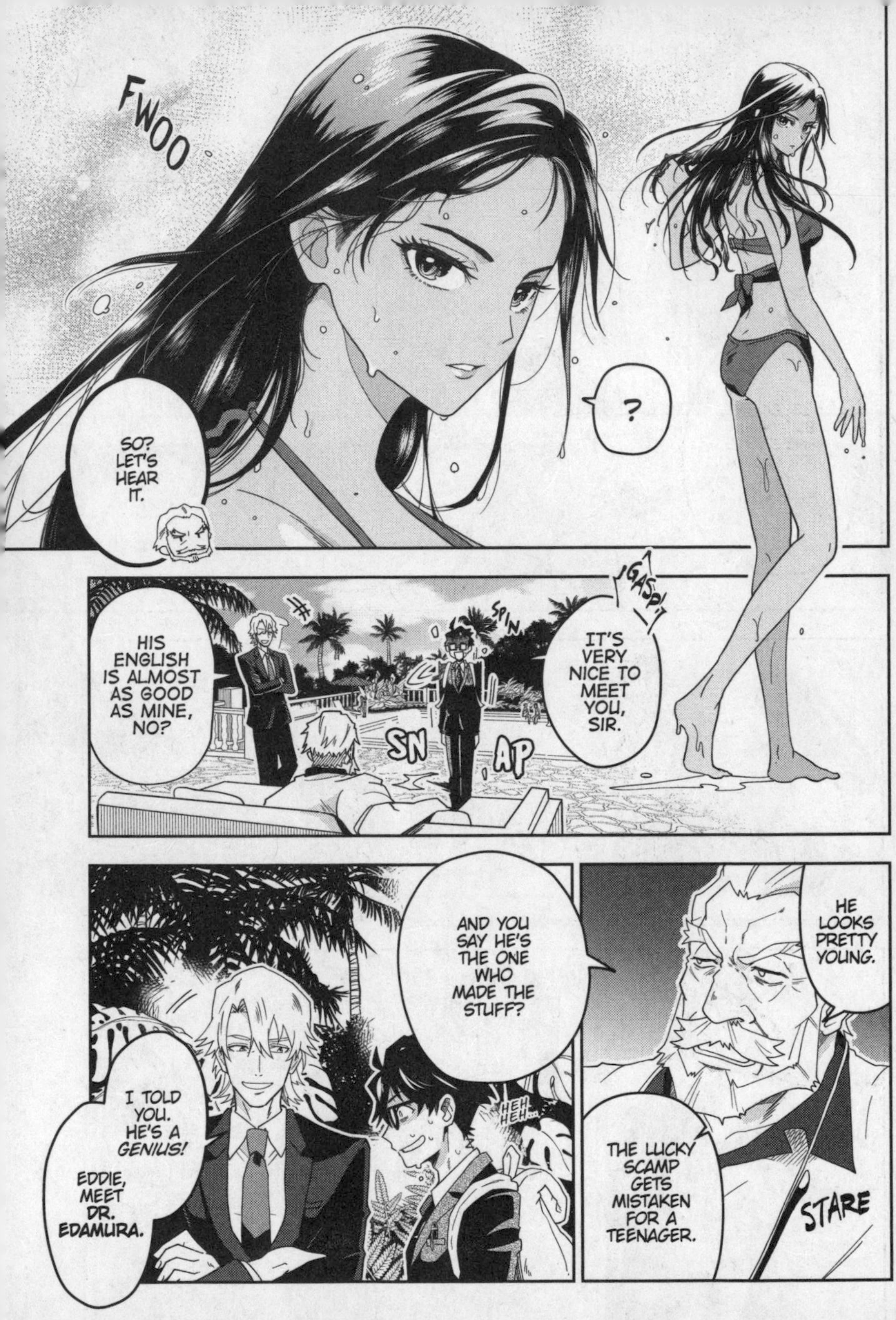
FWOO
?
SO? LET'S HEAR IT.
GASP!
IT'S VERY NICE TO MEET YOU, SIR.
SPIN
HIS ENGLISH IS ALMOST AS GOOD AS MINE, NO?
SNAP
HE LOOKS PRETTY YOUNG.
STARE
THE LUCKY SCAMP GETS MISTAKEN FOR A TEENAGER.
AND YOU SAY HE'S THE ONE WHO MADE THE STUFF?
HEH HEH...
I TOLD YOU. HE'S A GENIUS!
EDDIE, MEET DR. EDAMURA.

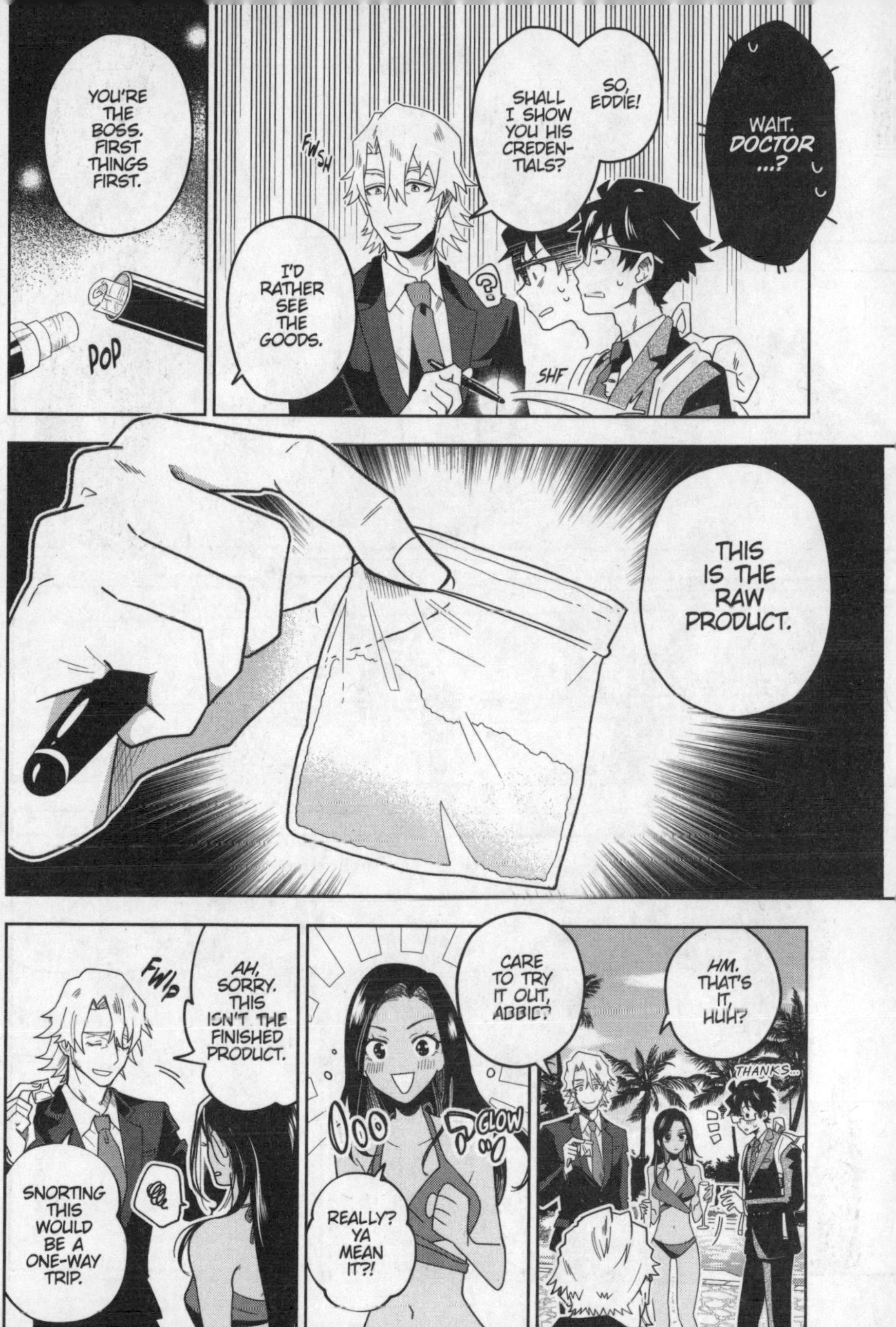
SO, EDDIE!
SHALL I SHOW YOU HIS CREDENTIALS?
WAIT. DOCTOR ...?
FWSH
I'D RATHER SEE THE GOODS.
SHF
YOU'RE THE BOSS. FIRST THINGS FIRST.
POP
THIS IS THE RAW PRODUCT.
HM. THAT'S IT, HUH?
THANKS...
CARE TO TRY IT OUT, ABBIE?
GLOW
REALLY? YA MEAN IT?!
FWIP
AH, SORRY. THIS ISN'T THE FINISHED PRODUCT.
SNORTING THIS WOULD BE A ONE-WAY TRIP.

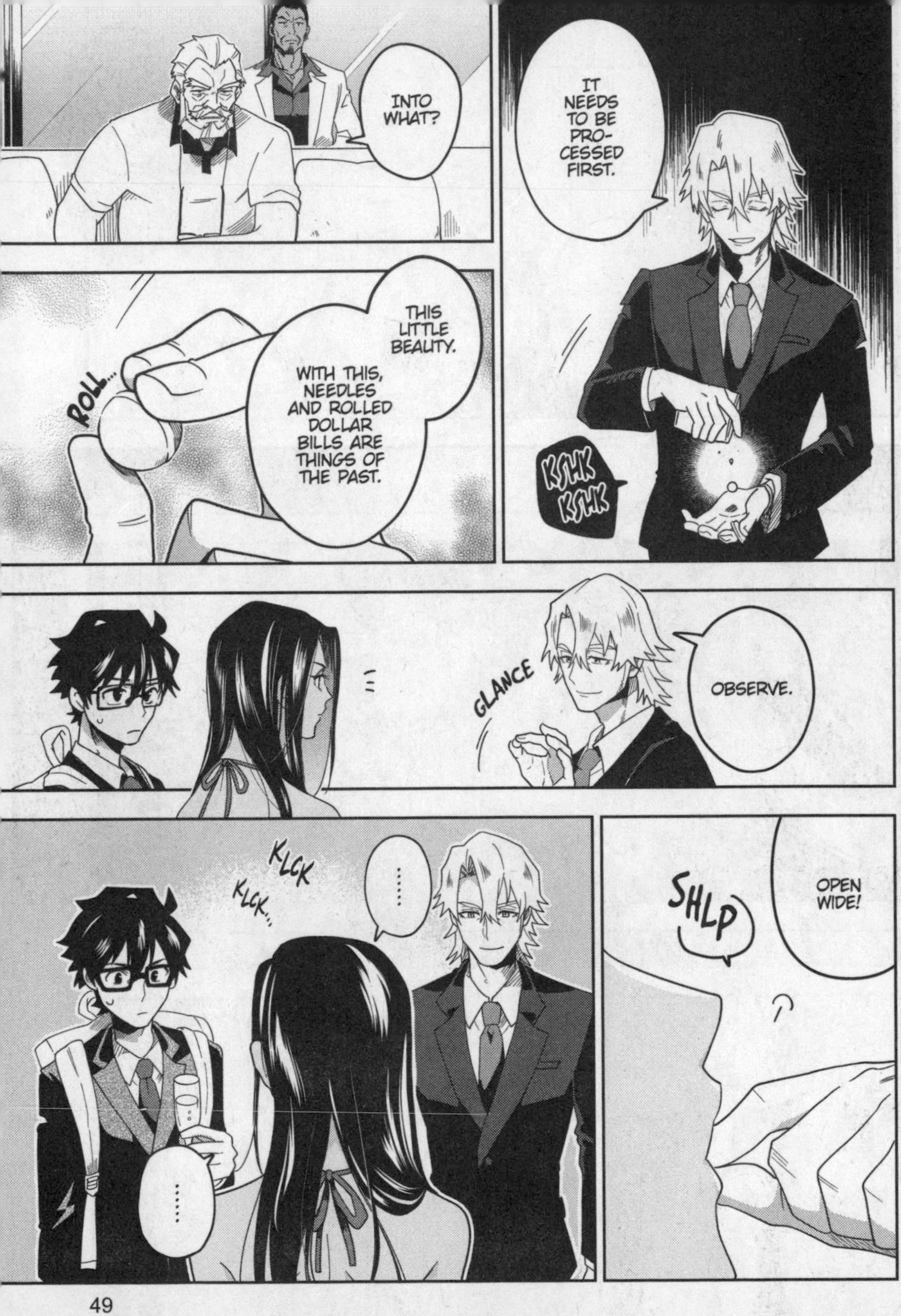
IT NEEDS TO BE PRO-CESSED FIRST.
KSHK KSHK
INTO WHAT?
THIS LITTLE BEAUTY.
WITH THIS, NEEDLES AND ROLLED DOLLAR BILLS ARE THINGS OF THE PAST.
ROLL...
OBSERVE.
GLANCE
OPEN WIDE!
SHLP
KLCK
KLCK...
......
......

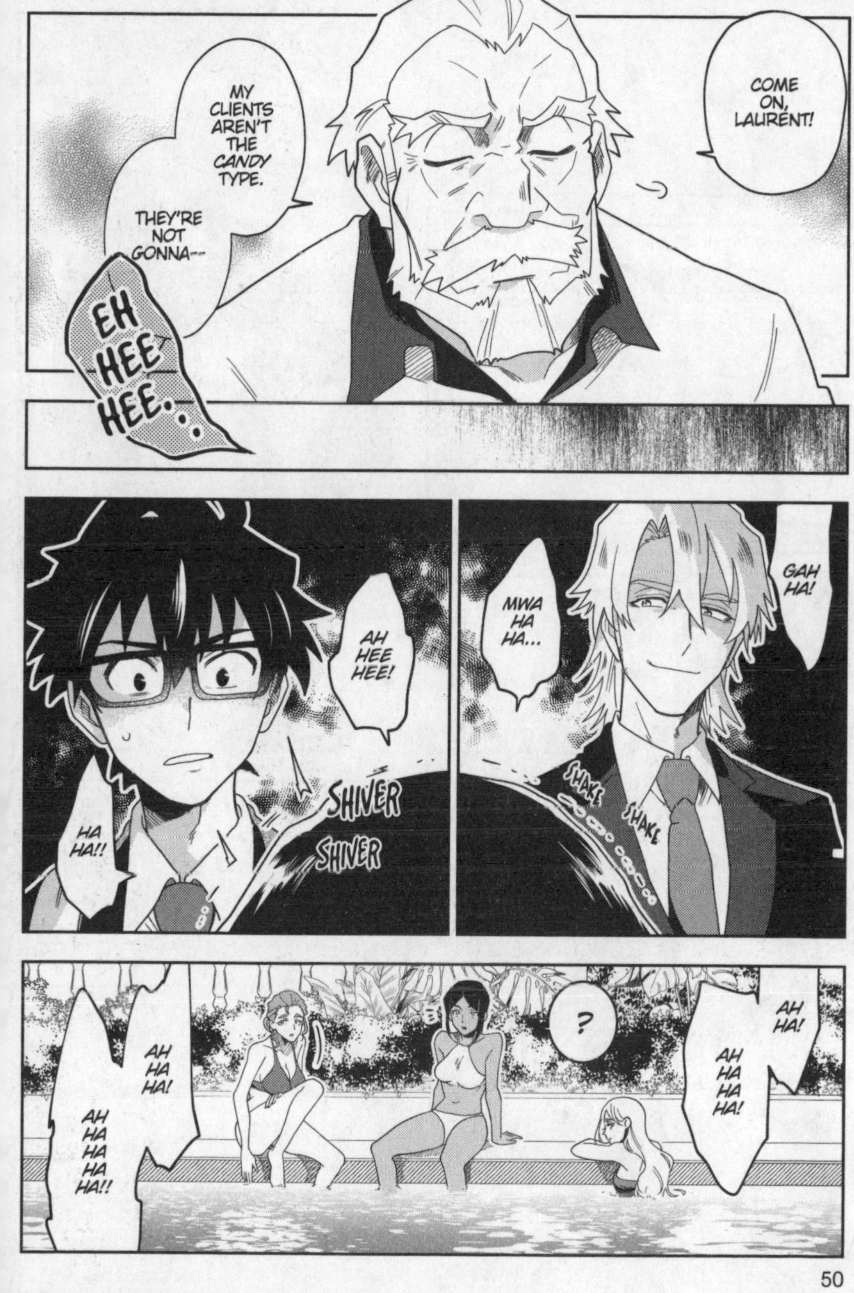
COME ON, LAURENT!
MY CLIENTS AREN'T THE CANDY TYPE.
THEY'RE NOT GONNA--
EH HEE HEE...
GAH HA!
MWA HA HA...
SHAKE
SHAKE
AH HEE HEE!
SHIVER
SHIVER
HA HA!!
AH HA!
AH HA HA HA!
?
AH HA HA!
AH HA HA HA HA!!

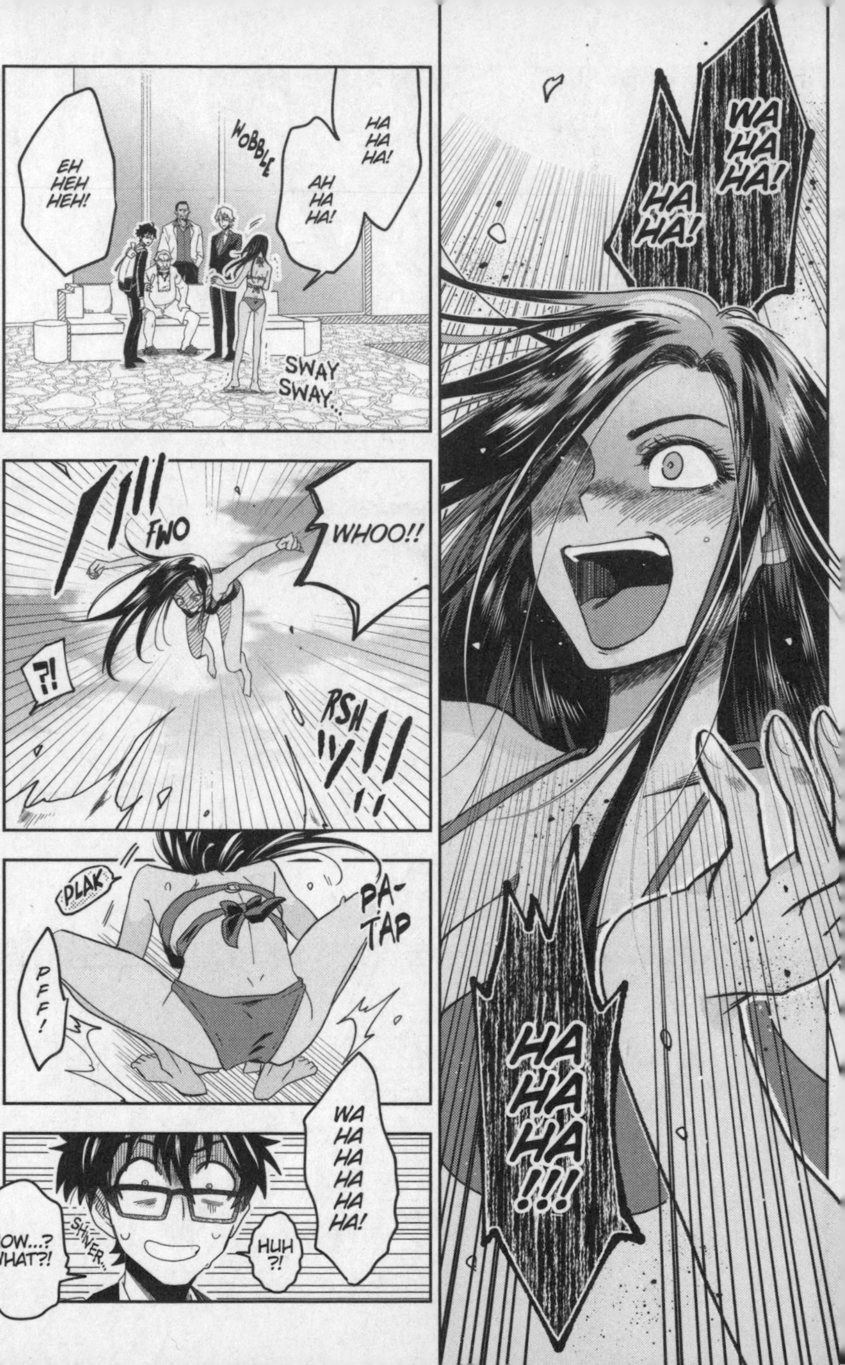
WA HA HA!
HA HA!
HA HA HA!!!
HA HA HA!
AH HA HA!
WOBBLE
EH HEH HEH!
SWAY SWAY...
WHOO!!
FWO
?!
RSH
PA-TAP
PLAK
PFF!
WA HA HA HA HA HA HA HA!
HUH ?!
SHIVER...
HOW...? WHAT?!

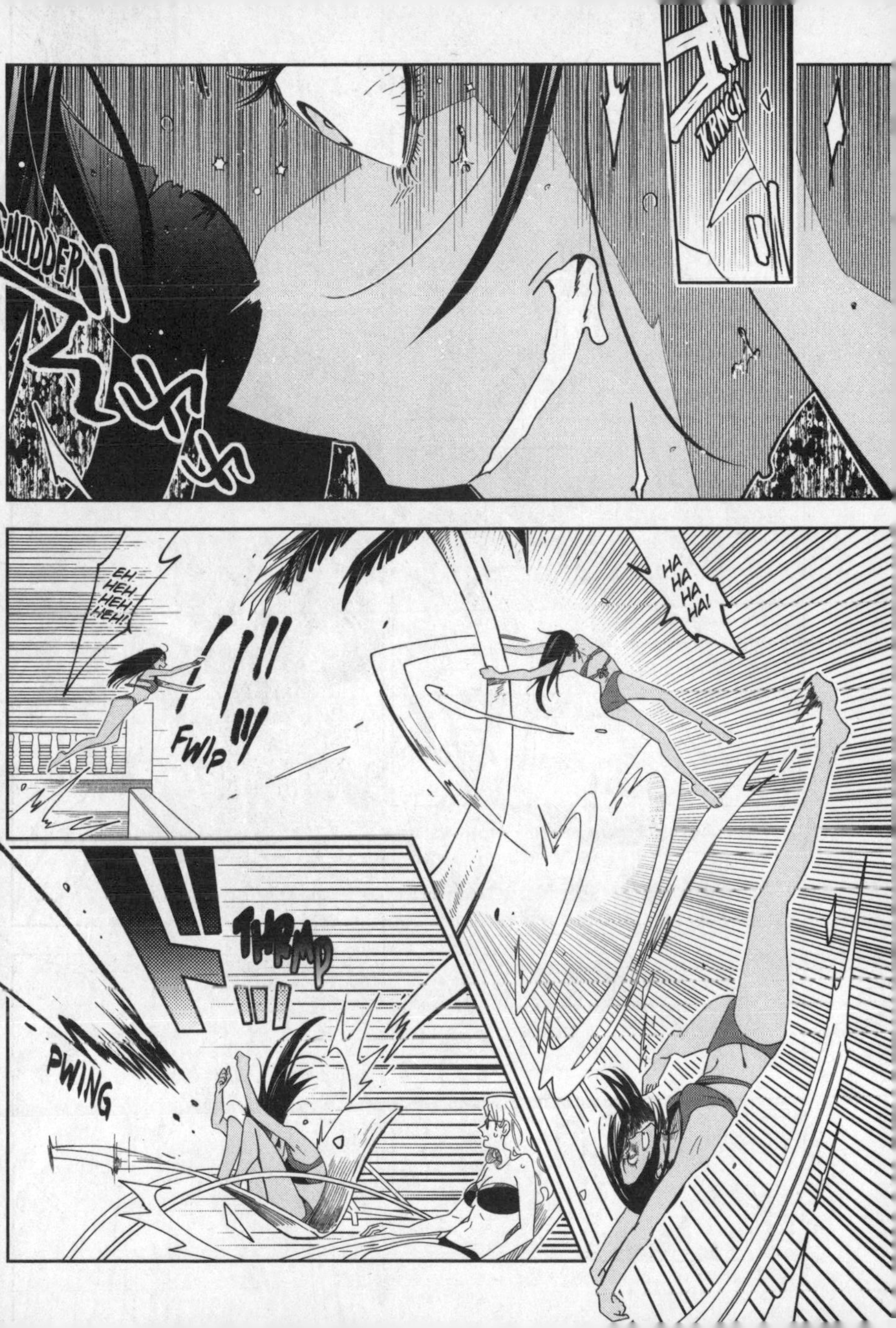
KRNCH
SHUDDER
HA HA HA HA HA!
EH HEH HEH HEH!
FWIP
THRMP
PWING

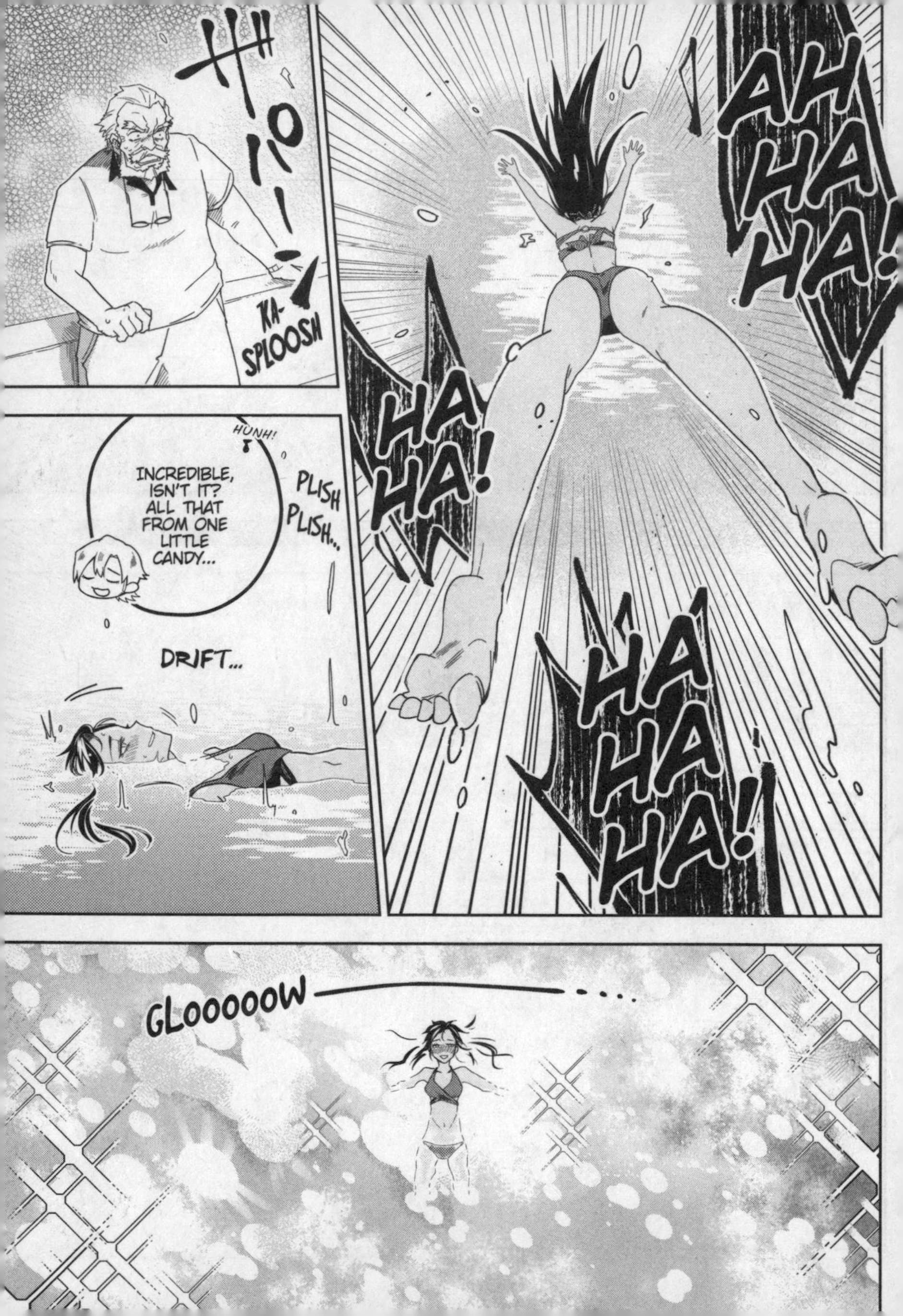

AH HA HA HA!
HA HA!
HA HA HA!
ザパーン
KA-SPLOOSH
HUNH!
INCREDIBLE, ISN'T IT? ALL THAT FROM ONE LITTLE CANDY...
PLISH PLISH...
DRIFT...
GLOOOOOW

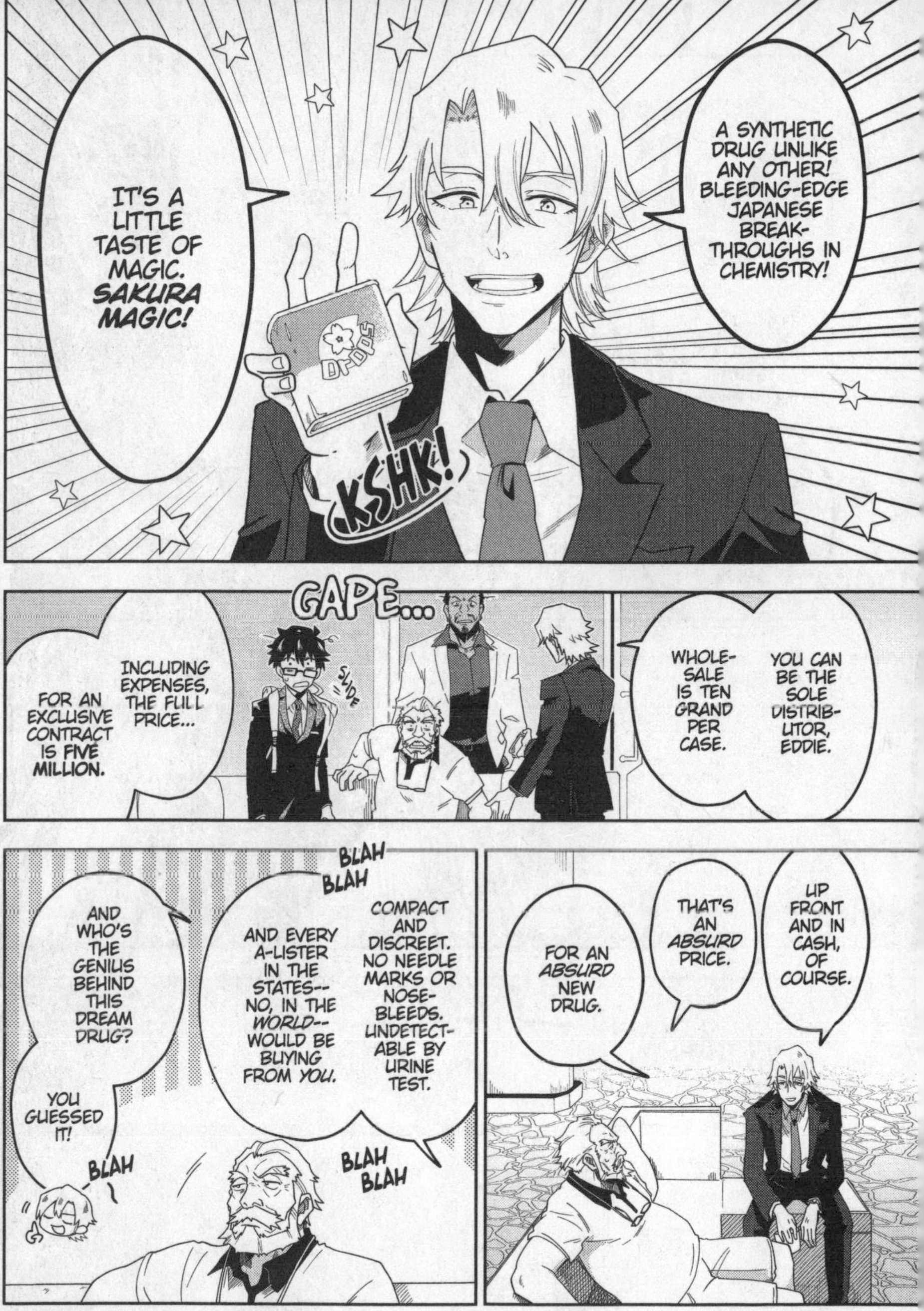
A SYNTHETIC DRUG UNLIKE ANY OTHER! BLEEDING-EDGE JAPANESE BREAK-THROUGHS IN CHEMISTRY!
IT'S A LITTLE TASTE OF MAGIC. **SAKURA MAGIC!**
Drops
KSHK!
GAPE...
YOU CAN BE THE SOLE DISTRIB-UTOR, EDDIE.
WHOLE-SALE IS TEN GRAND PER CASE.
INCLUDING EXPENSES, THE FULL PRICE...
FOR AN EXCLUSIVE CONTRACT IS FIVE MILLION.
SLIDE
UP FRONT AND IN CASH, OF COURSE.
THAT'S AN *ABSURD* PRICE.
FOR AN *ABSURD* NEW DRUG.
BLAH BLAH
COMPACT AND DISCREET. NO NEEDLE MARKS OR NOSE-BLEEDS. UNDETECT-ABLE BY URINE TEST.
AND EVERY A-LISTER IN THE STATES-- NO, IN THE *WORLD*-- WOULD BE BUYING FROM *YOU*.
AND WHO'S THE GENIUS BEHIND THIS DREAM DRUG?
YOU GUESSED IT!
BLAH
BLAH BLAH

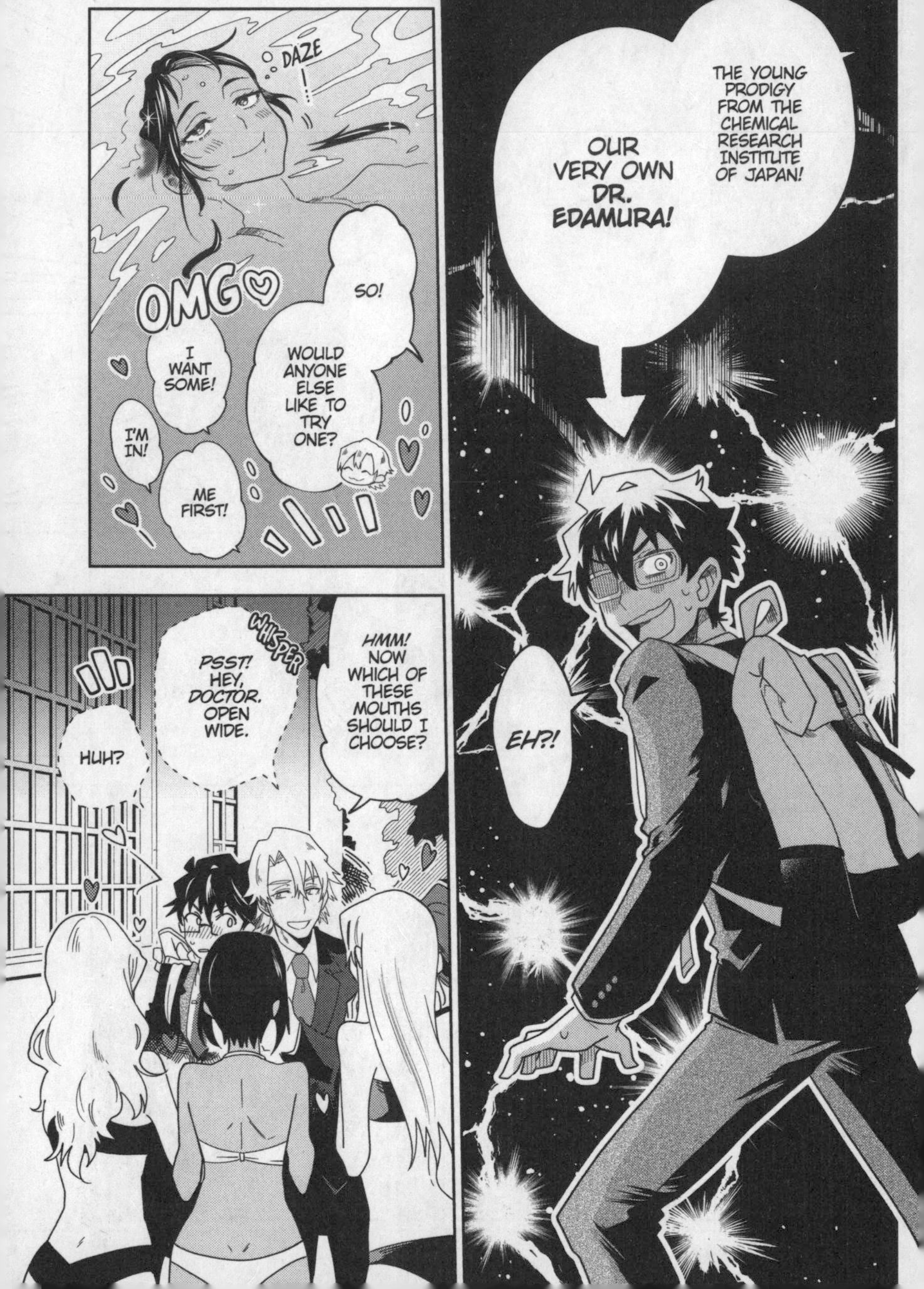
THE YOUNG PRODIGY FROM THE CHEMICAL RESEARCH INSTITUTE OF JAPAN!
OUR VERY OWN DR. EDAMURA!
EH?!
DAZE
SO!
WOULD ANYONE ELSE LIKE TO TRY ONE?
OMG
I WANT SOME!
I'M IN!
ME FIRST!
HMM! NOW WHICH OF THESE MOUTHS SHOULD I CHOOSE?
WHISPER
PSST! HEY, DOCTOR. OPEN WIDE.
HUH?

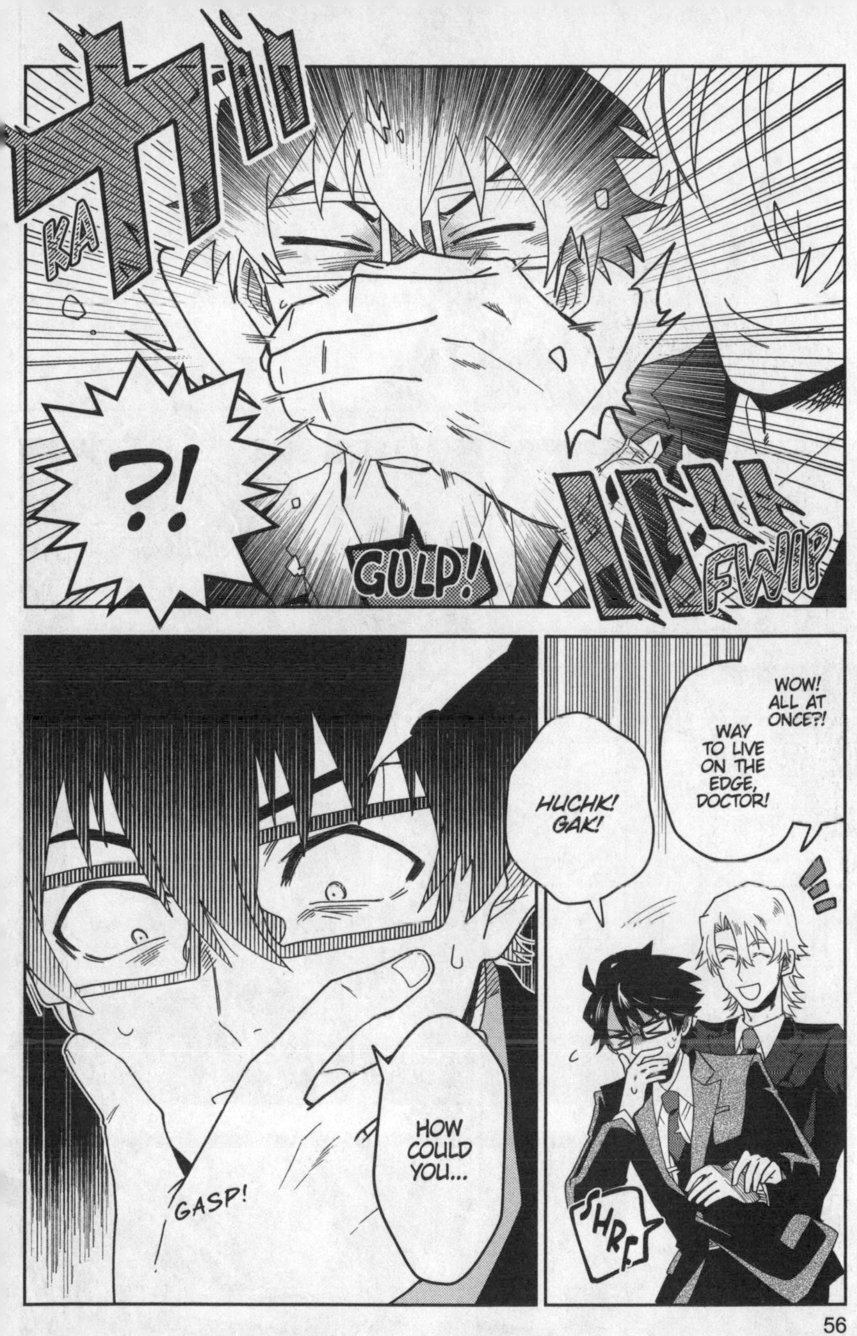
KA
FWIP
?!
GULP!
WOW! ALL AT ONCE?!
WAY TO LIVE ON THE EDGE, DOCTOR!
HUCHK! GAK!
SHRF
HOW COULD YOU...
GASP!

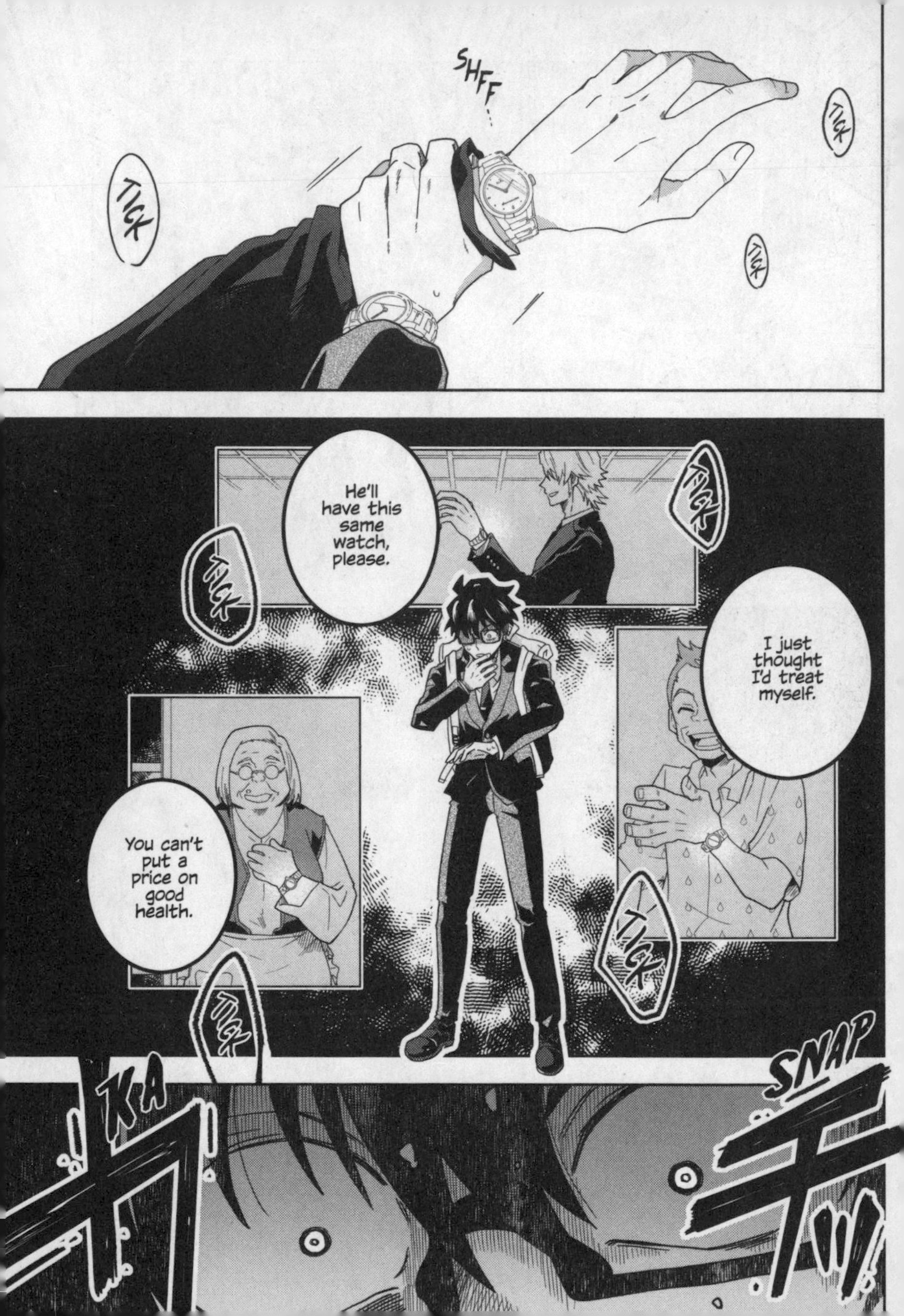
SHFF
TICK
TICK
TICK
TICK
He'll have this same watch, please.
TICK
I just thought I'd treat myself.
You can't put a price on good health.
TICK
TICK
SNAP
KA

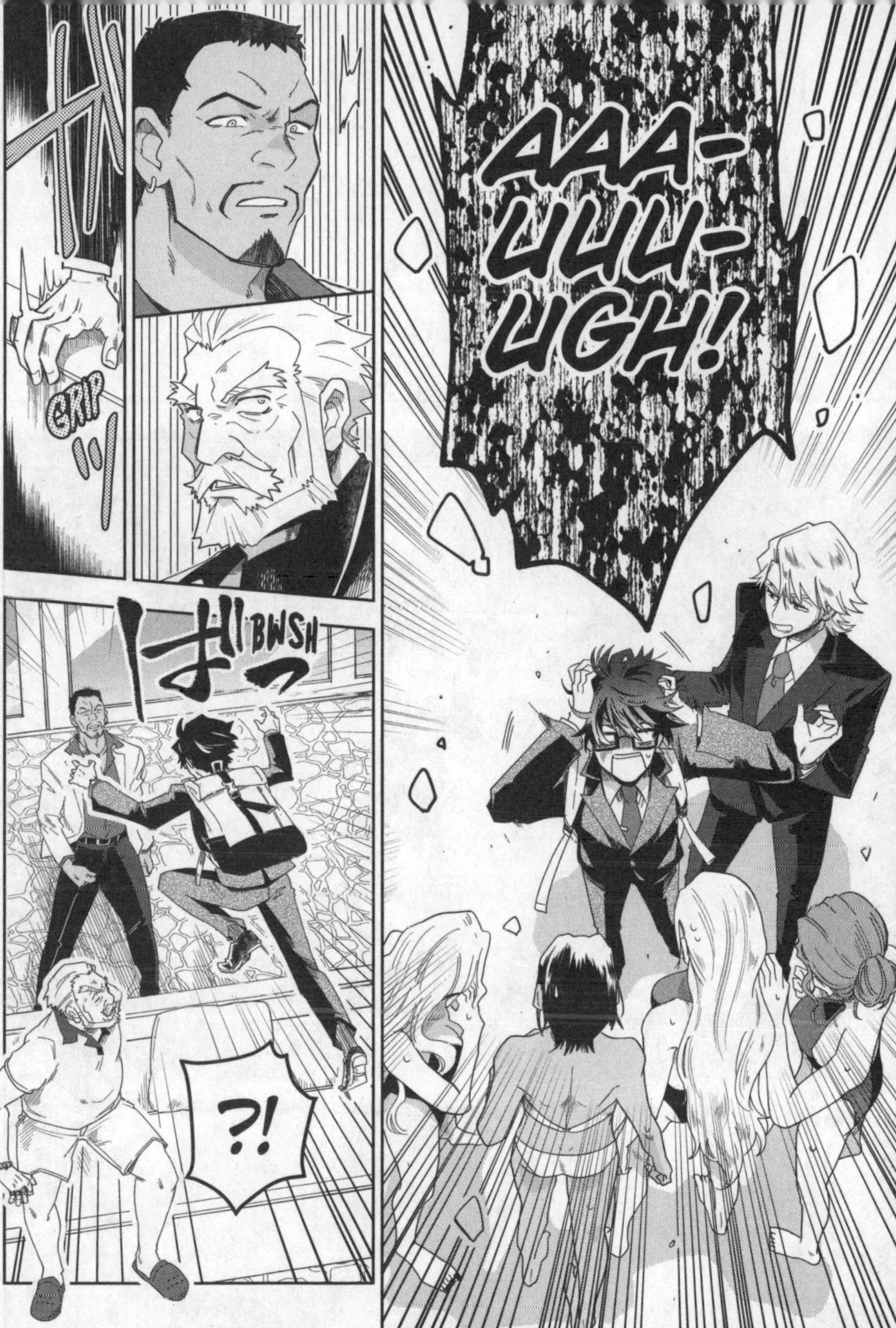
AAA-UUU-UGH!
GRIP
はっ BWSH
?!

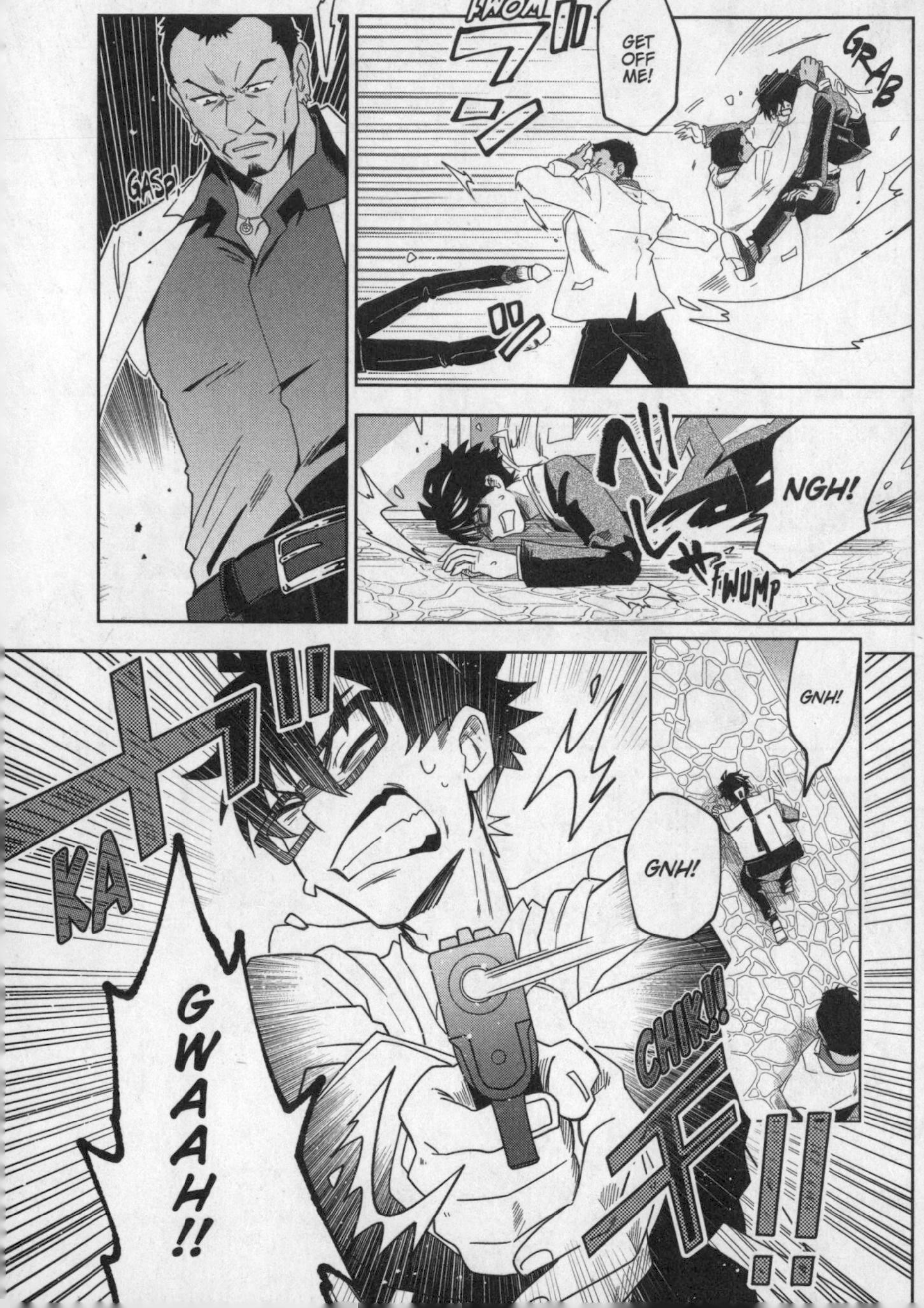
GRAB
GET OFF ME!
FWOM
NGH!
FWUMP
GASP!
GNH!
GNH!
CHIK!!
KA
GWAAH!!

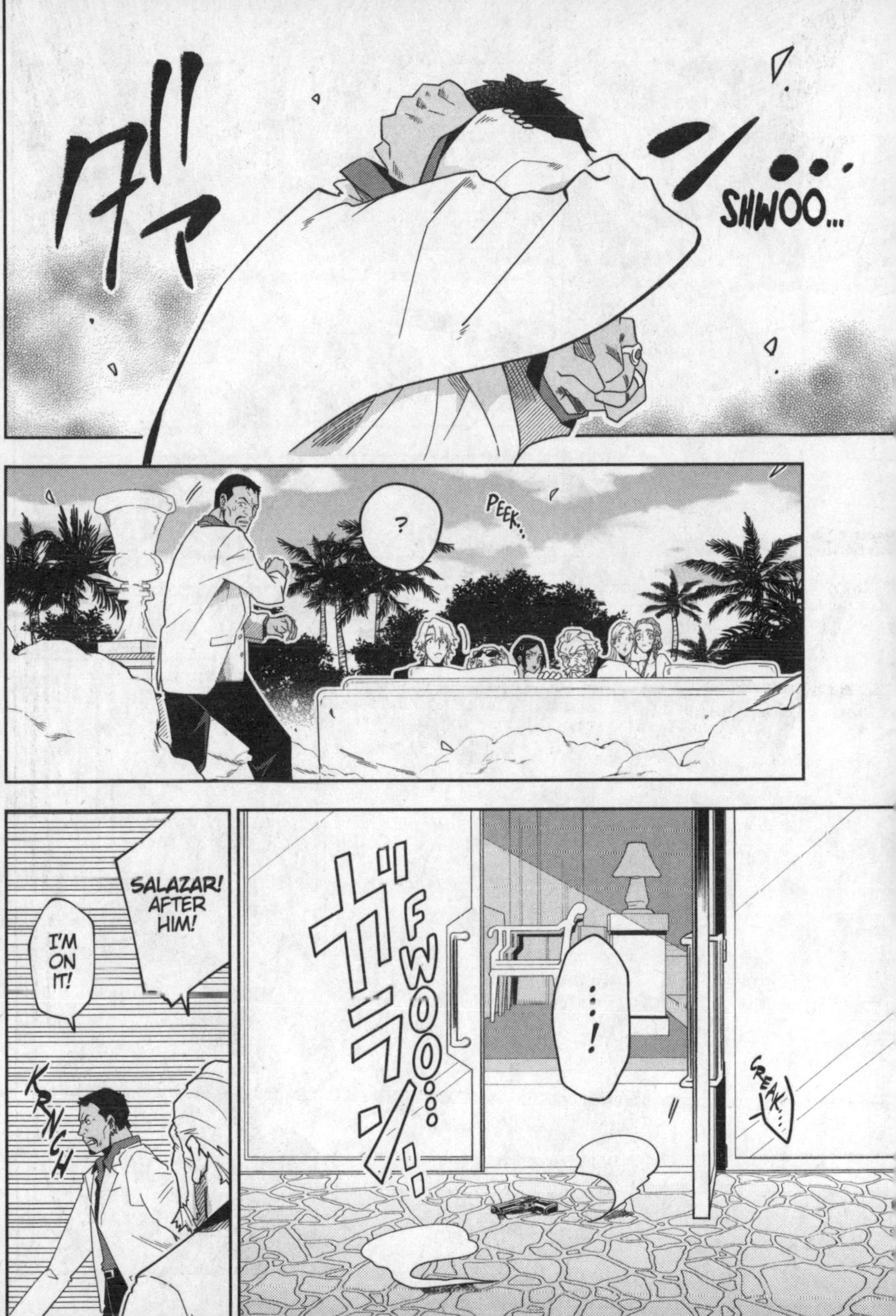

ダアン
SHWOO...
?
PEEK...
ガラッ
FWOO...
...!
CREAK...
SALAZAR! AFTER HIM!
I'M ON IT!
KRNCH

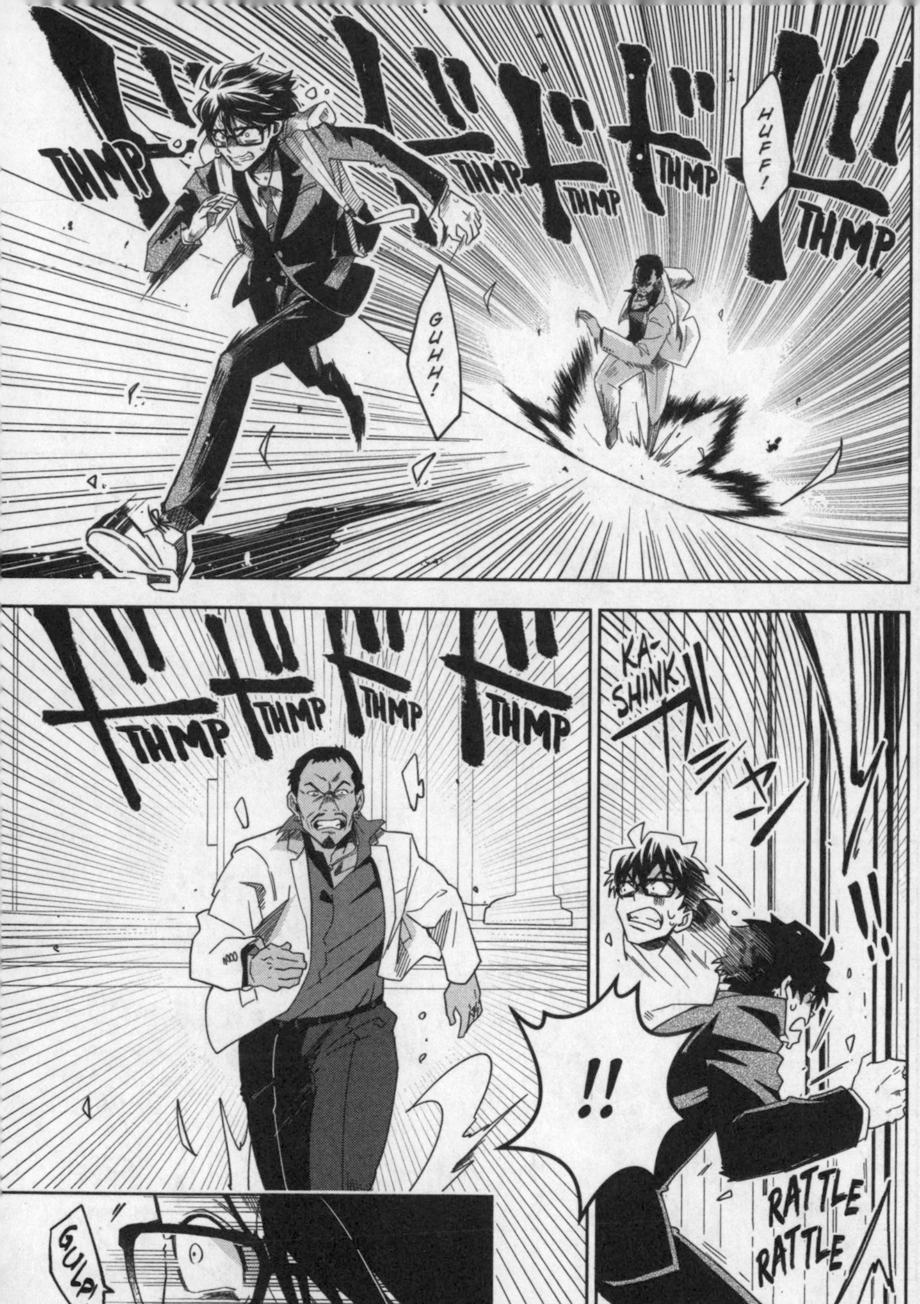

HUFF!
THMP
THMP
THMP
GUHH!
THMP
THMP
KA-SHINK
!!
RATTLE RATTLE
THMP
THMP
THMP
THMP
GULP!

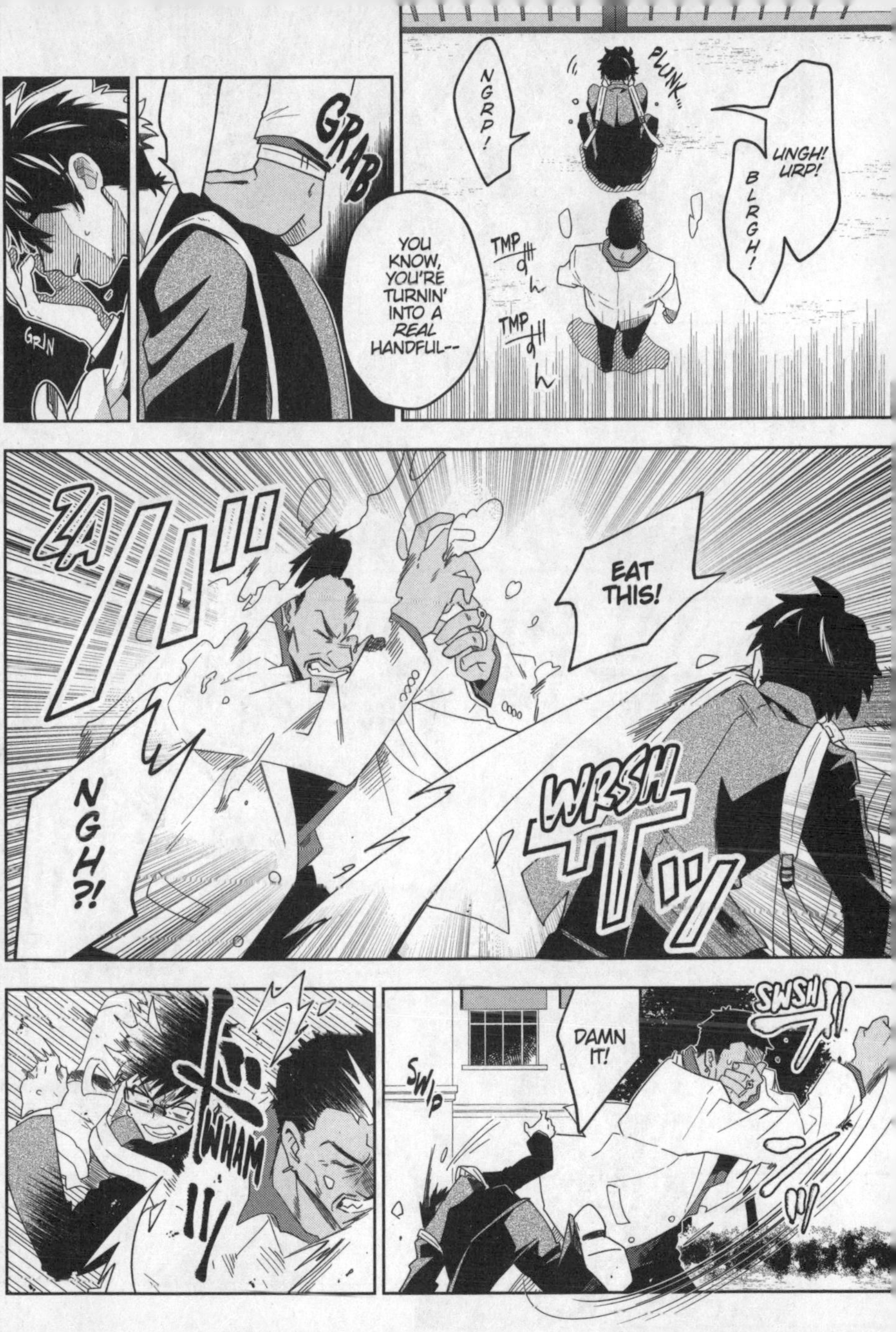
UNGH! URP!
BLRGH!
PLUNK...
NGRP!
TMP
TMP
GRAB
YOU KNOW, YOU'RE TURNIN' INTO A *REAL* HANDFUL--
GRIN
EAT THIS!
ZA
WRSH
NGH?!
SWSH
DAMN IT!
SWIP
WHAM

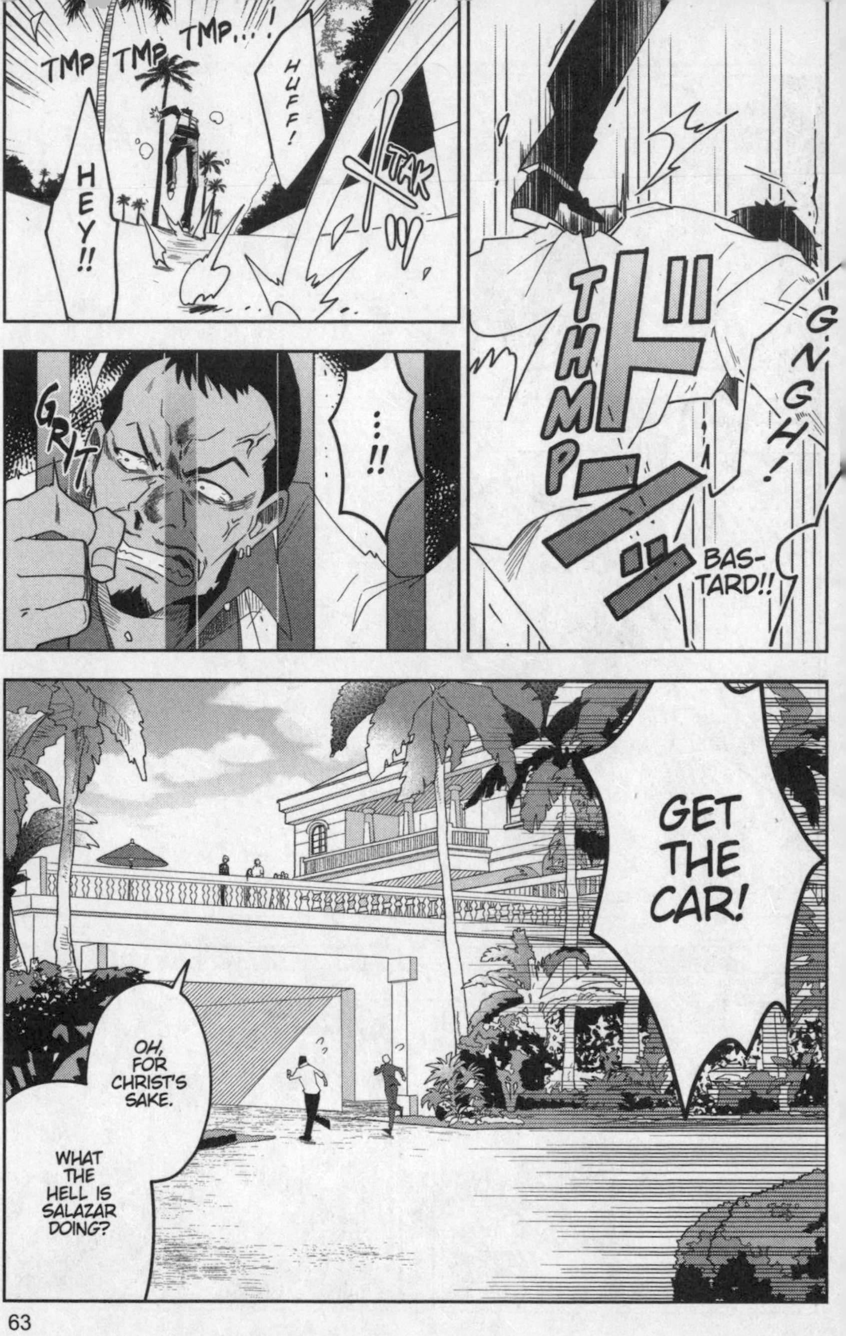
THMP
GNGH!
BAS-TARD!!
TMP TMP TMP...!
HUFF!
HEY!!
TAK
GRYT
...!!
GET THE CAR!
OH, FOR CHRIST'S SAKE.
WHAT THE HELL IS SALAZAR DOING?

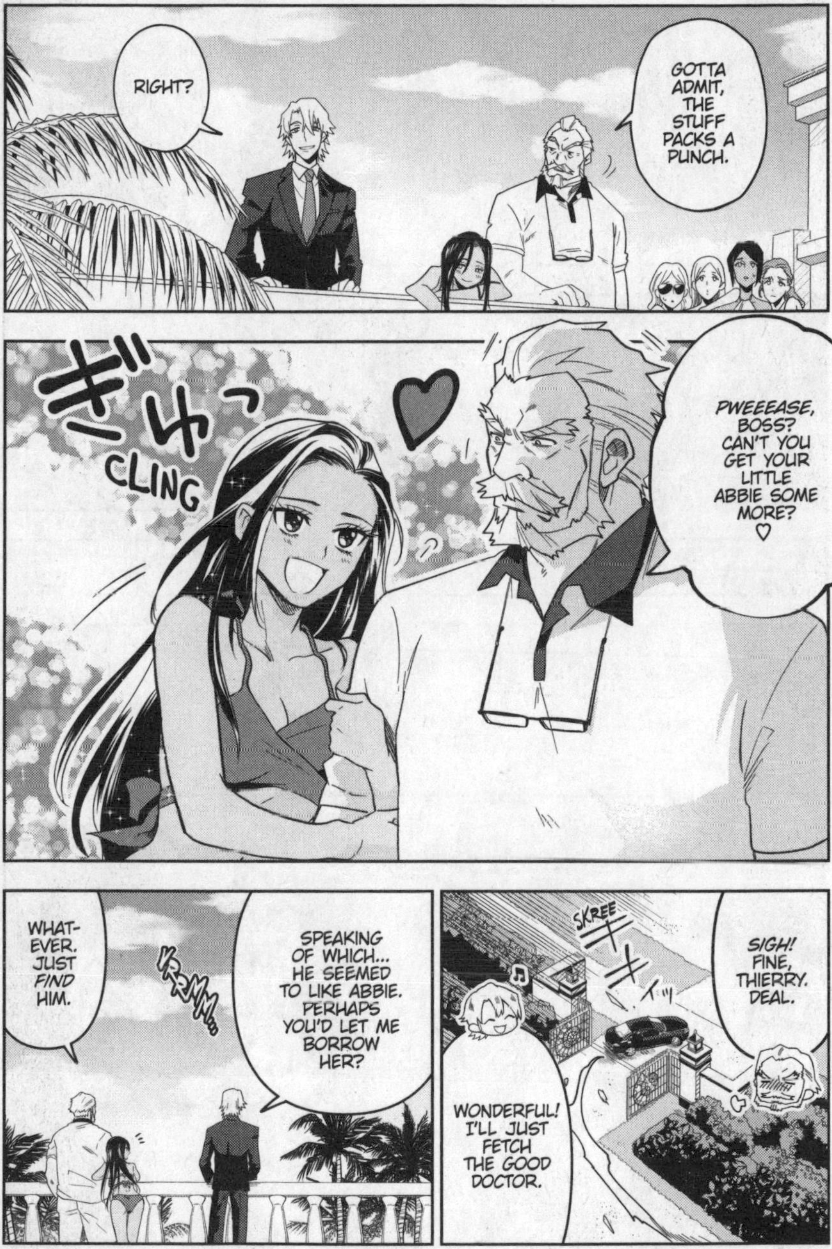
GOTTA ADMIT, THE STUFF PACKS A PUNCH.
RIGHT?
PWEEEASE, BOSS? CAN'T YOU GET YOUR LITTLE ABBIE SOME MORE? ♡
ギュッ
CLING
SIGH! FINE, THIERRY. DEAL.
SKREE
キイッ
WONDERFUL! I'LL JUST FETCH THE GOOD DOCTOR.
SPEAKING OF WHICH... HE SEEMED TO LIKE ABBIE. PERHAPS YOU'D LET ME BORROW HER?
WHAT-EVER. JUST FIND HIM.
VRRMM...

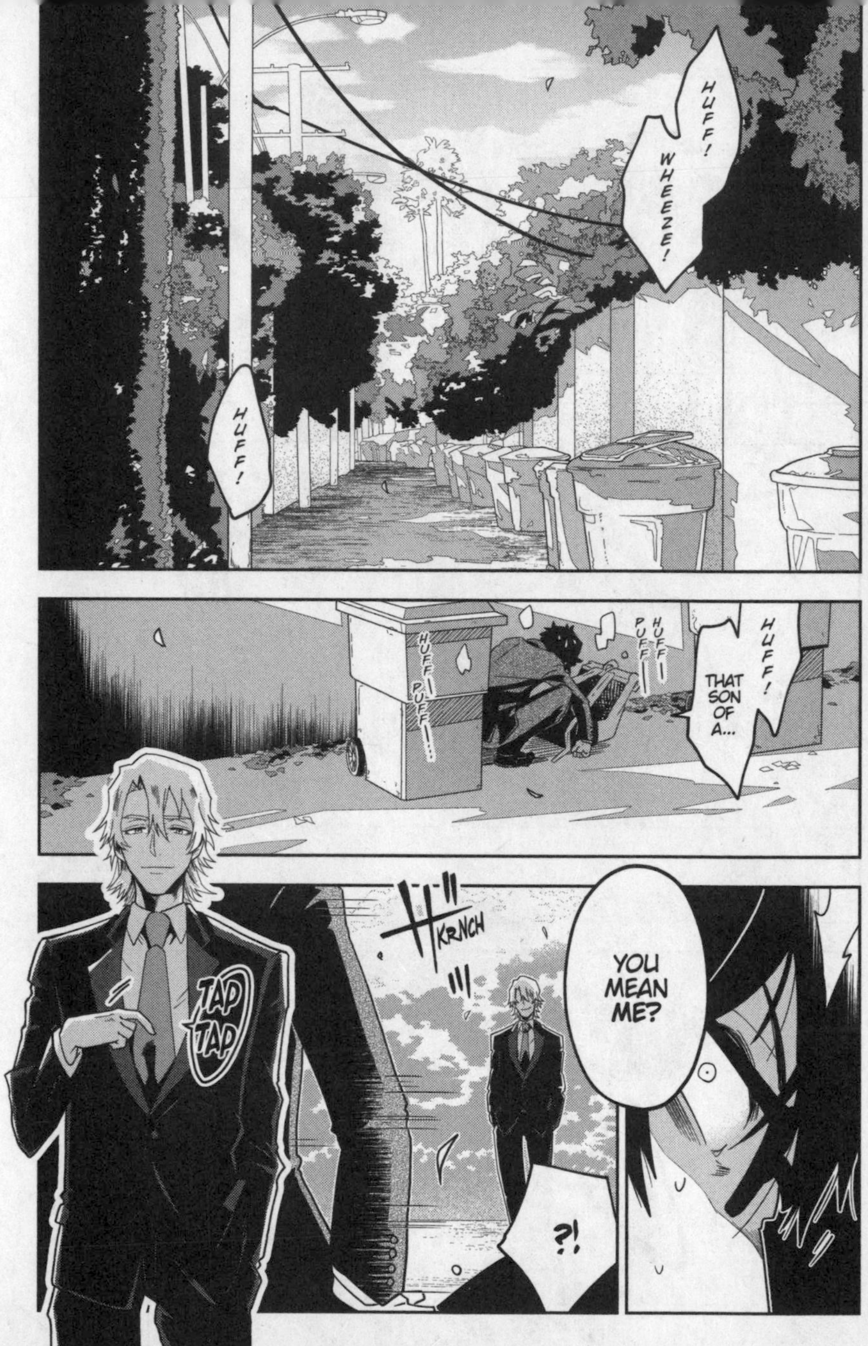
HUFF! WHEEZE!
HUFF!
HUFF! THAT SON OF A...
HUFF— PUFF—
HUFF— PUFF—...
YOU MEAN ME?
KRNCH
?!
TAP TAP

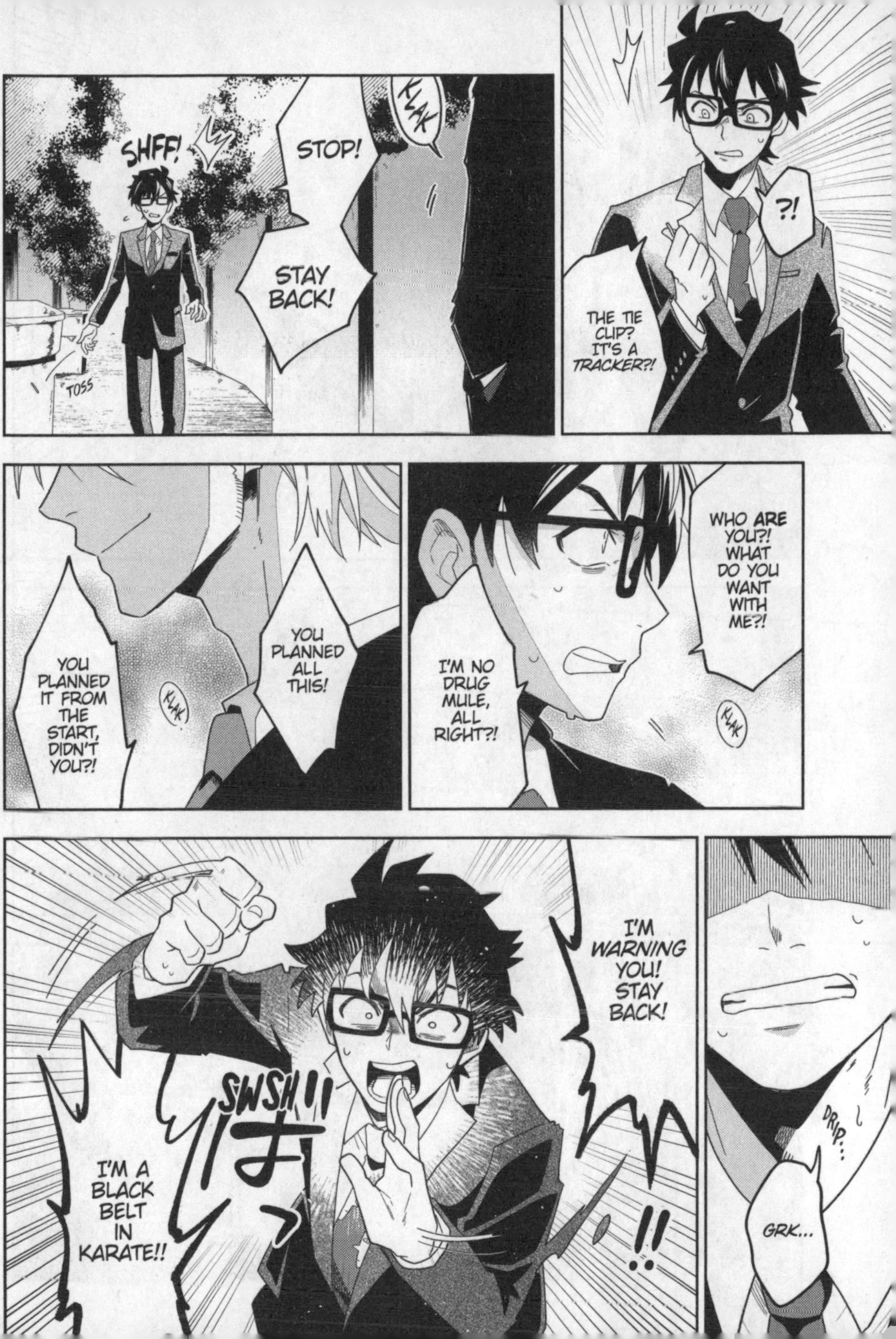
?!
THE TIE CLIP? IT'S A TRACKER?!
KLAK
STOP!
STAY BACK!
SHFF!
TOSS
WHO ARE YOU?! WHAT DO YOU WANT WITH ME?!
KLAK
I'M NO DRUG MULE, ALL RIGHT?!
YOU PLANNED ALL THIS!
KLAK
YOU PLANNED IT FROM THE START, DIDN'T YOU?!
DRIP...
GRK...
I'M WARNING YOU! STAY BACK!
!!
SWSH!!
は
I'M A BLACK BELT IN KARATE!!

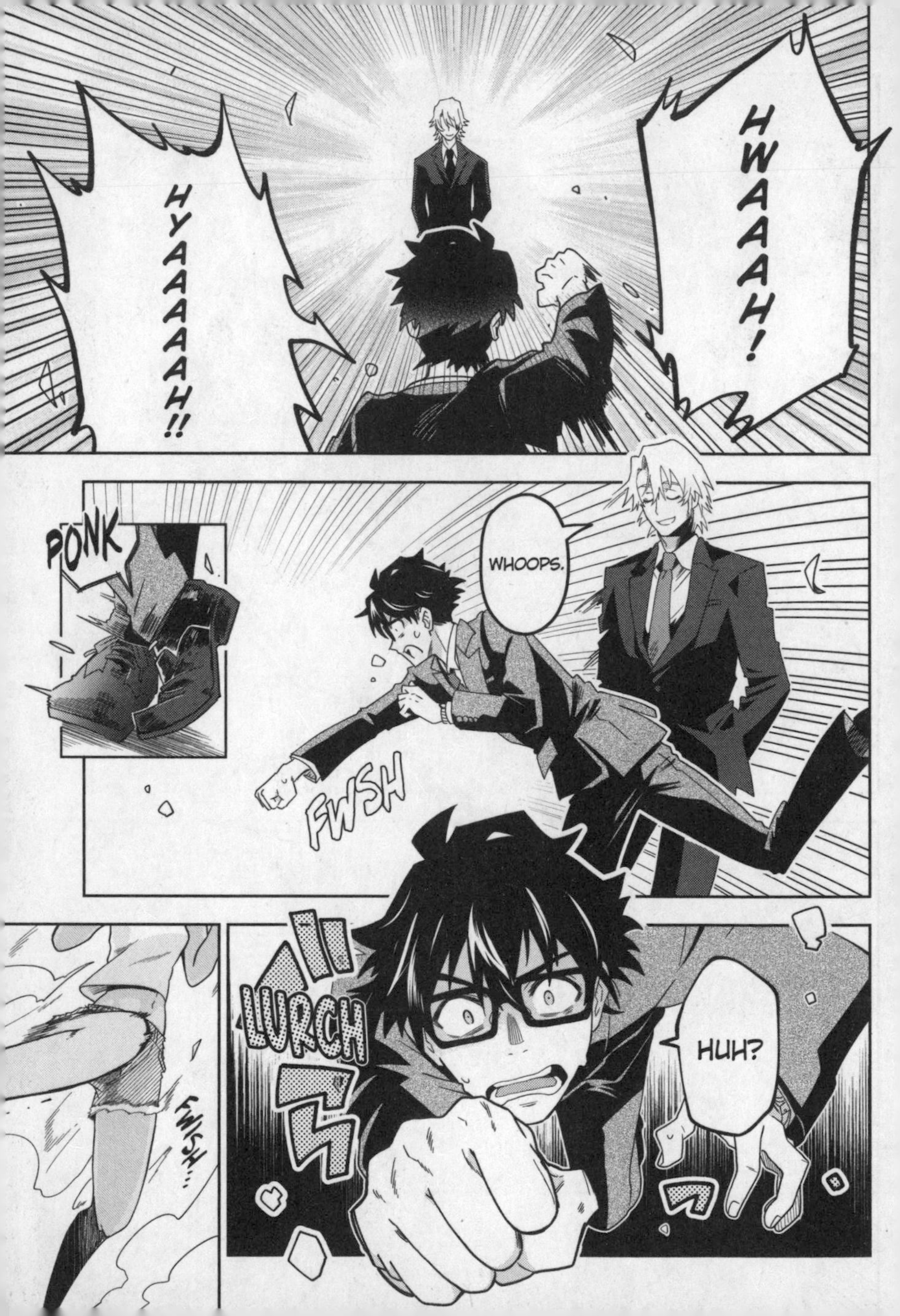

HWAAAAH!
HYAAAAAAH!!
WHOOPS.
FWSH
PONK
HUH?
LURCH
FWISH...

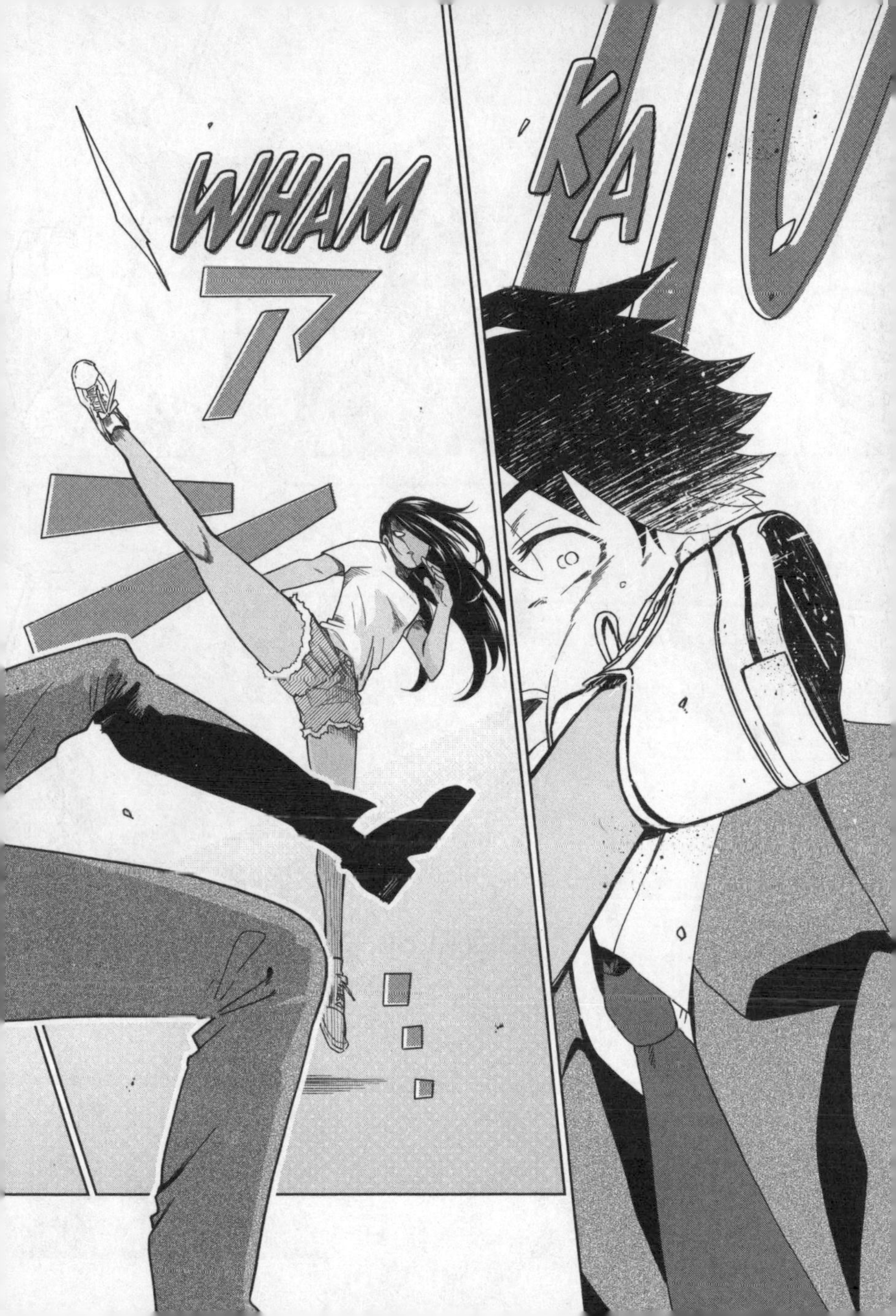
KA
WHAM

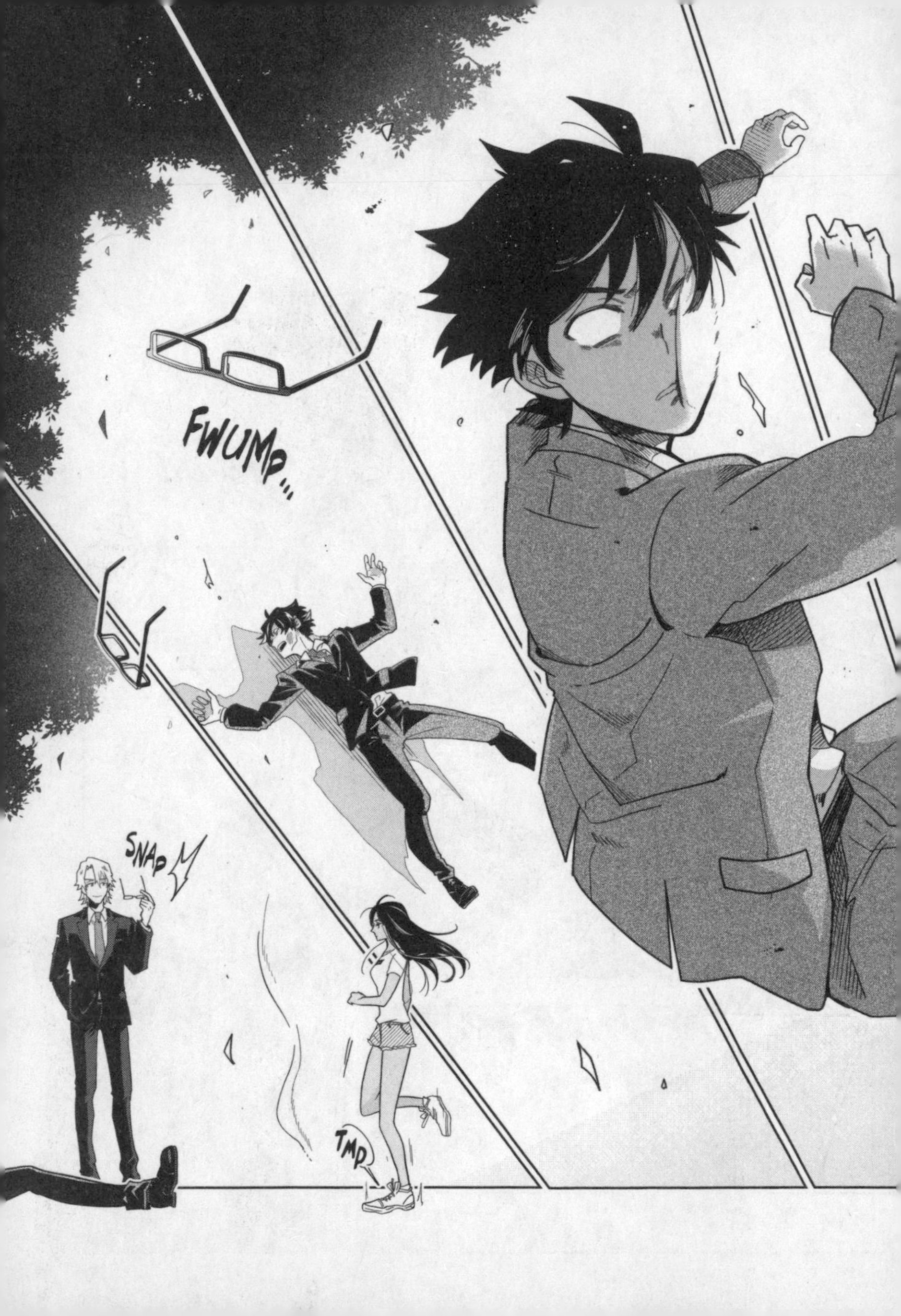
FWUMP...
TMP
SNAP

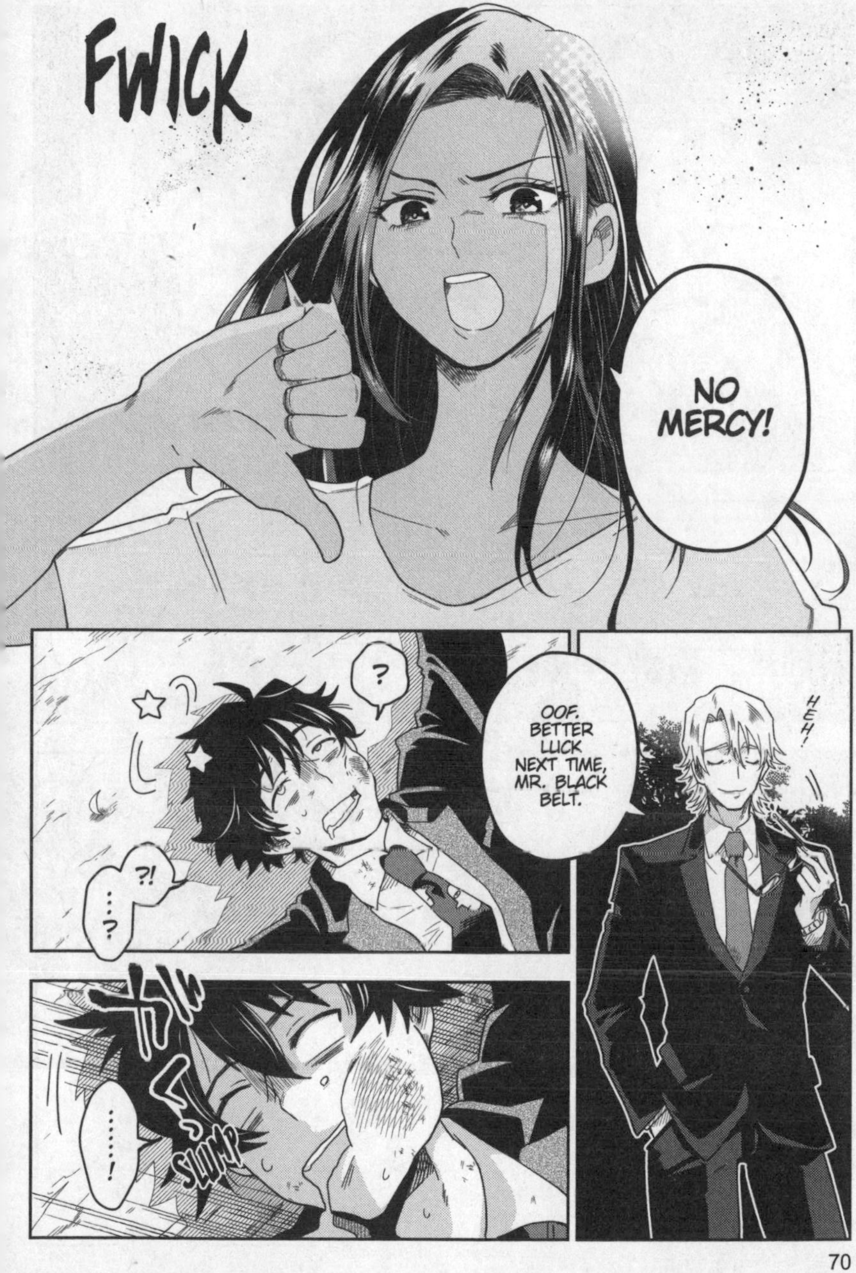
FWICK
NO MERCY!
OOF. BETTER LUCK NEXT TIME, MR. BLACK BELT.
HEH!
?
?!
...?
......!
SLUMP

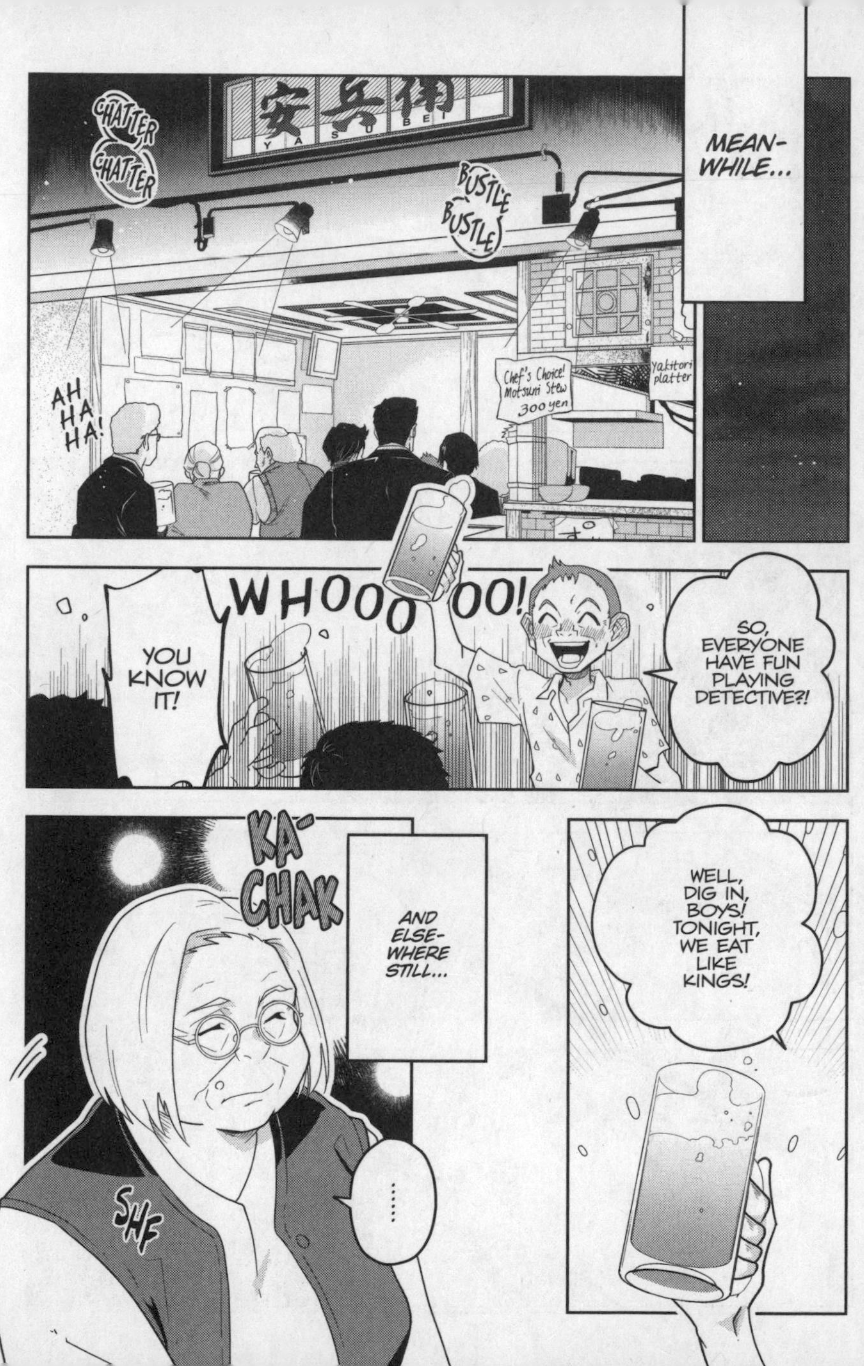
MEAN-WHILE...
安兵衛
YASUBEI
BUSTLE BUSTLE
CHATTER CHATTER
Yakitori platter
Chef's Choice! Motsuni Stew 300 yen
AH HA HA!
SO, EVERYONE HAVE FUN PLAYING DETECTIVE?!
WHOOOOO!
YOU KNOW IT!
WELL, DIG IN, BOYS! TONIGHT, WE EAT LIKE KINGS!
KA-CHAK
AND ELSE-WHERE STILL...
......
SHF

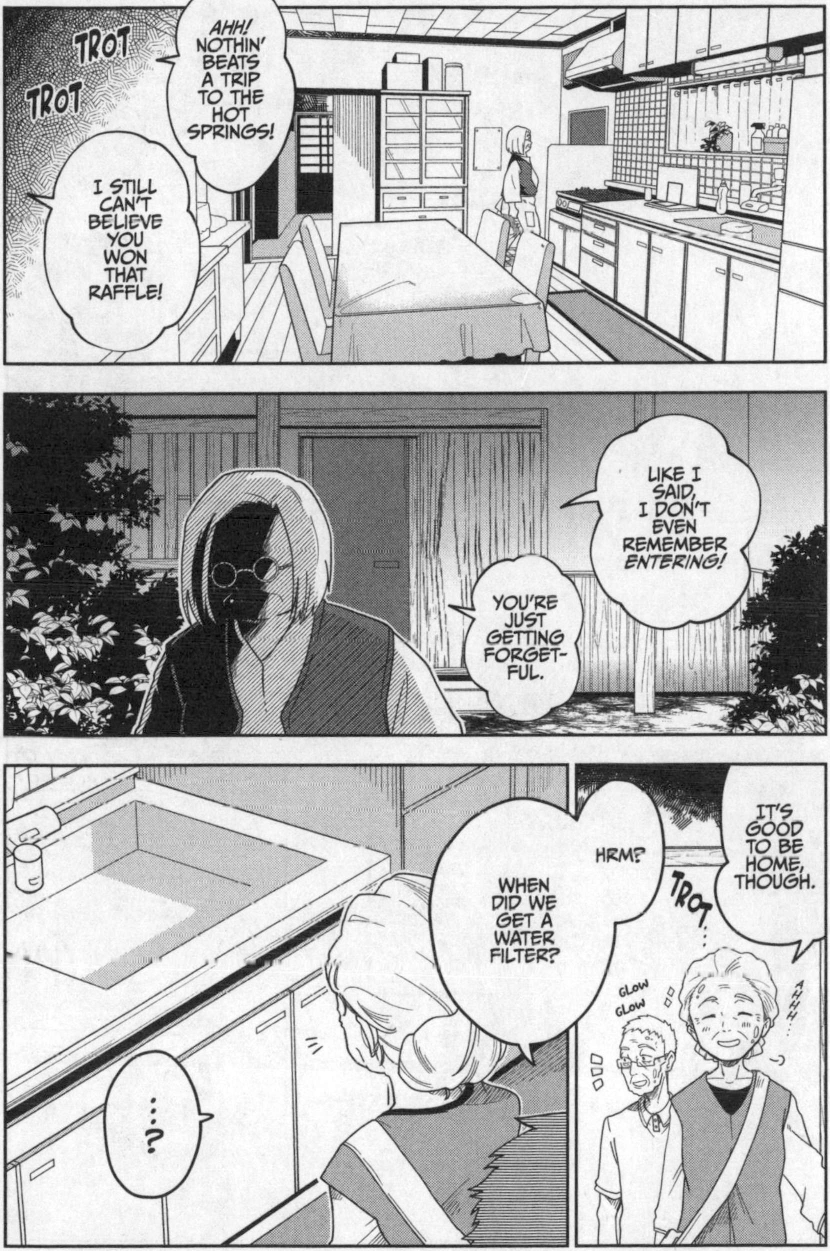
AHH! NOTHIN' BEATS A TRIP TO THE HOT SPRINGS!
TROT
TROT
I STILL CAN'T BELIEVE YOU WON THAT RAFFLE!
LIKE I SAID, I DON'T EVEN REMEMBER *ENTERING!*
YOU'RE JUST GETTING FORGET-FUL.
IT'S GOOD TO BE HOME, THOUGH.
TROT...
AHHH...
GLOW GLOW
HRM?
WHEN DID WE GET A WATER FILTER?
...?

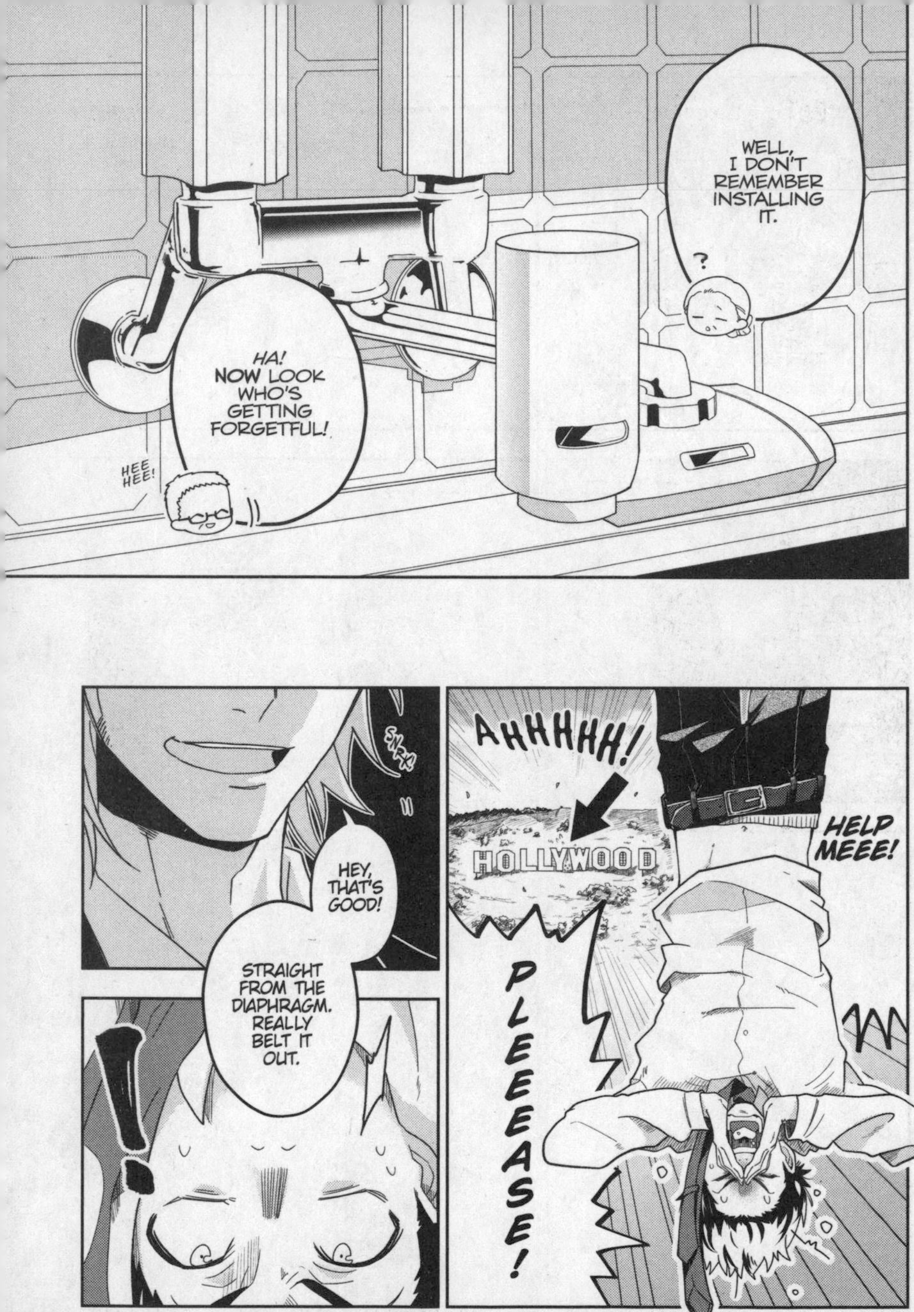
WELL, I DON'T REMEMBER INSTALLING IT.
HA! NOW LOOK WHO'S GETTING FORGETFUL!
HEE HEE!
AHHHHH!
HOLLYWOOD
HELP MEEE!
PLEEEASE!
HEY, THAT'S GOOD!
STRAIGHT FROM THE DIAPHRAGM. REALLY BELT IT OUT.
!

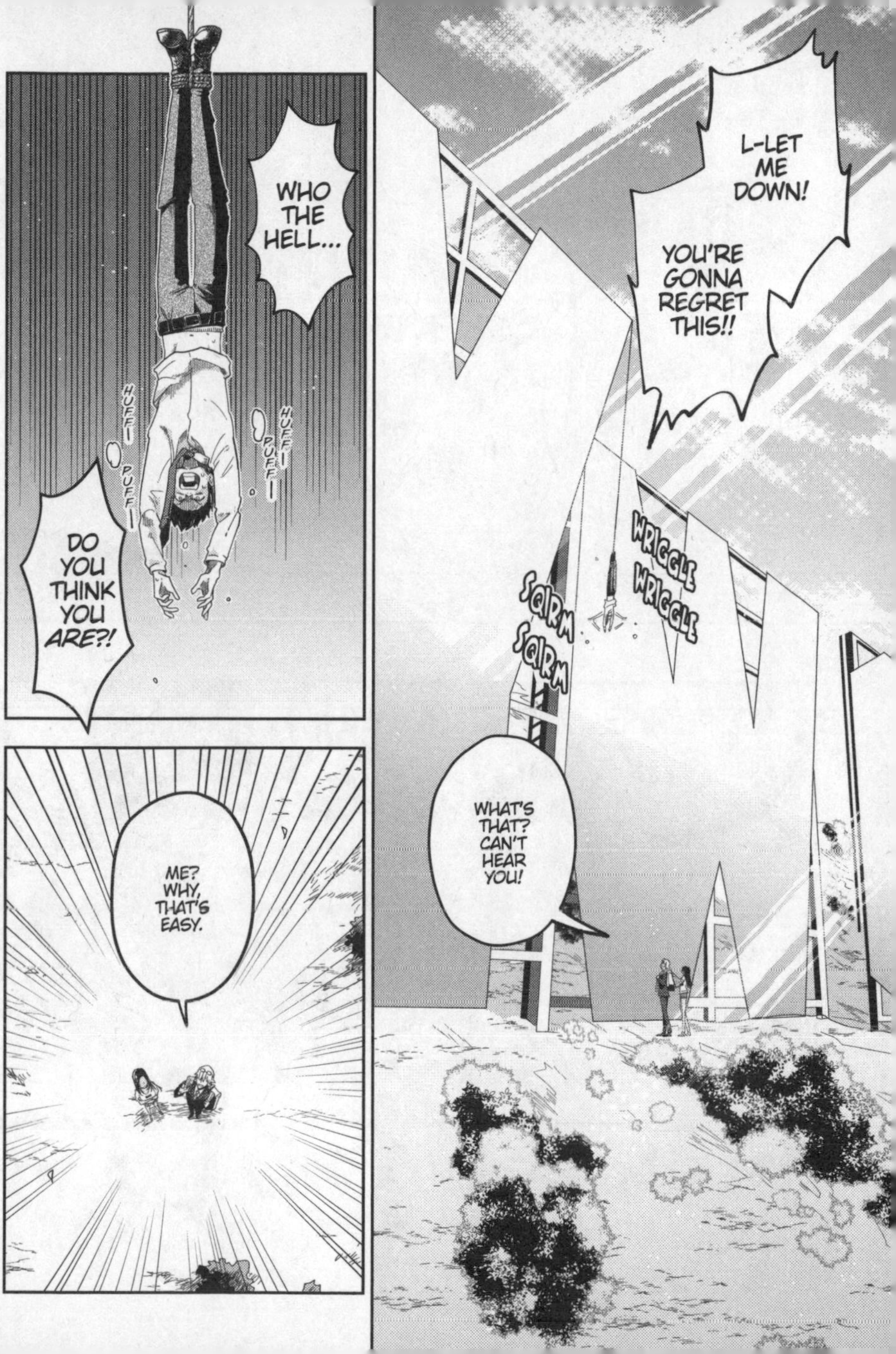
L-LET ME DOWN!
YOU'RE GONNA REGRET THIS!!
WRIGGLE WRIGGLE
SQIRM SQIRM
WHAT'S THAT? CAN'T HEAR YOU!
WHO THE HELL...
HUFF HUFF
PUFF PUFF
DO YOU THINK YOU ARE?!
ME? WHY, THAT'S EASY.

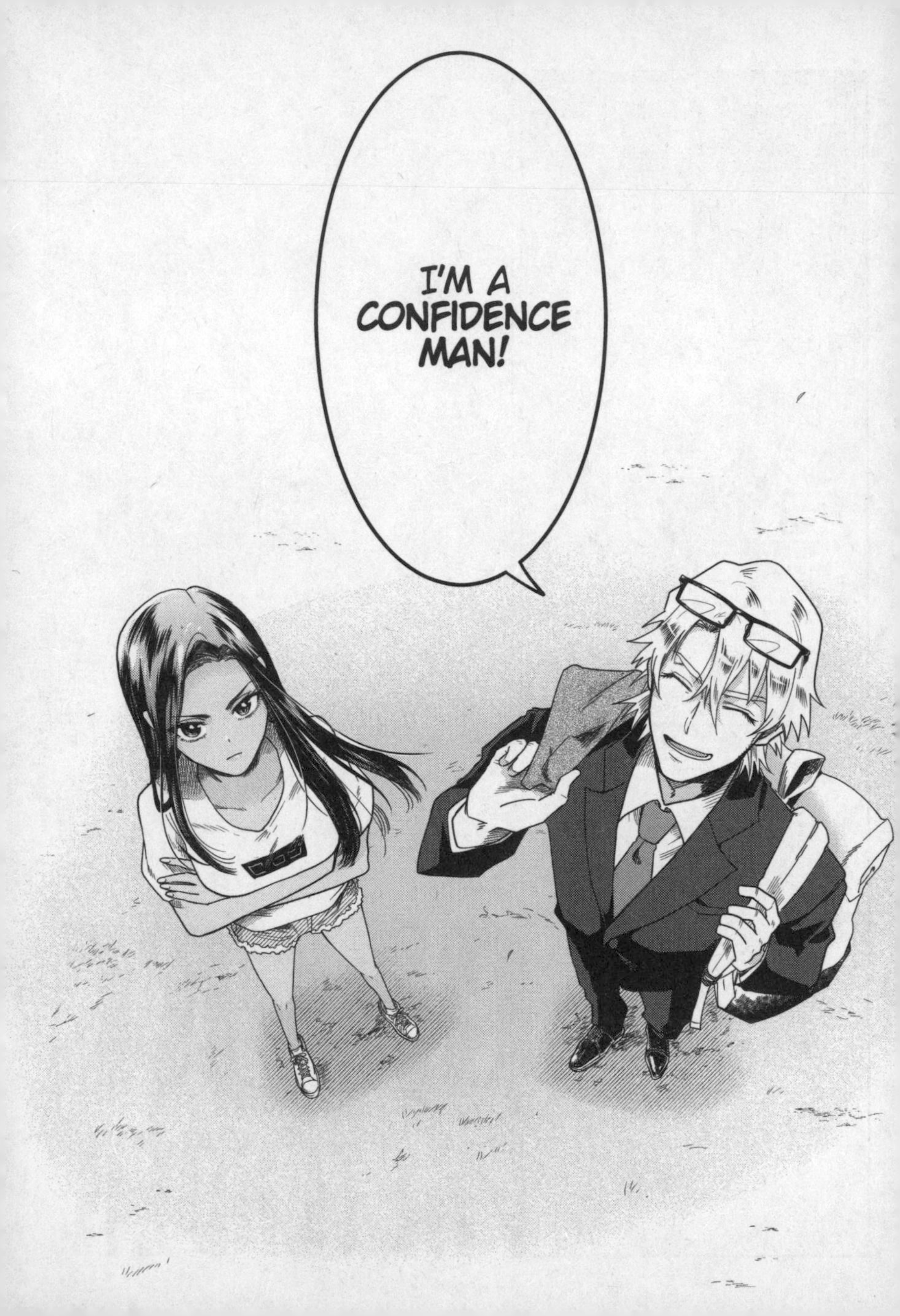
I'M A CONFIDENCE MAN!

GREAT
グレートプリテンダー
PRETENDER

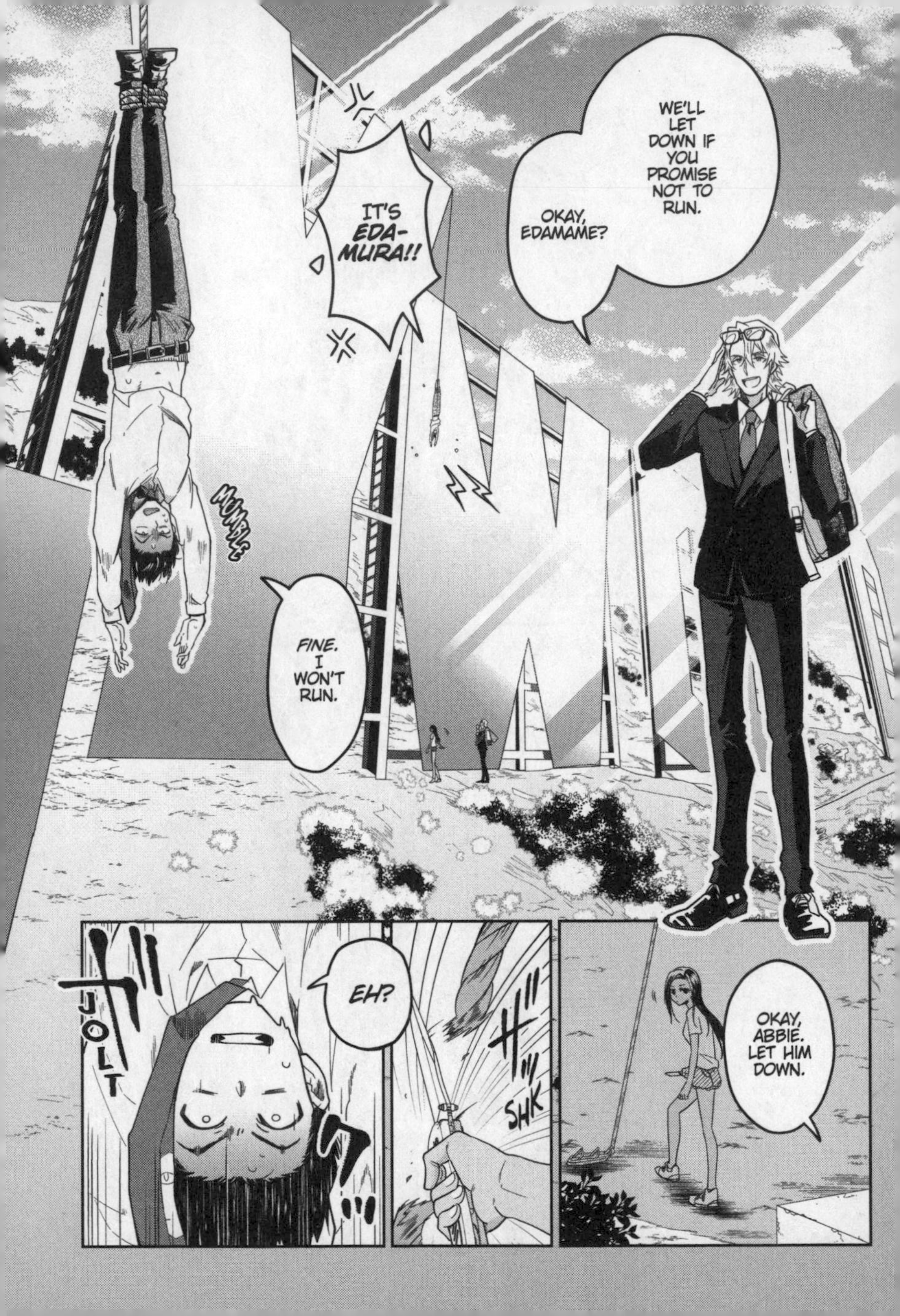
WE'LL LET DOWN IF YOU PROMISE NOT TO RUN.
OKAY, EDAMAME?
IT'S *EDAMURA!!*
MUMBLE
FINE. I WON'T RUN.
OKAY, ABBIE. LET HIM DOWN.
SHK
EH?
JOLT

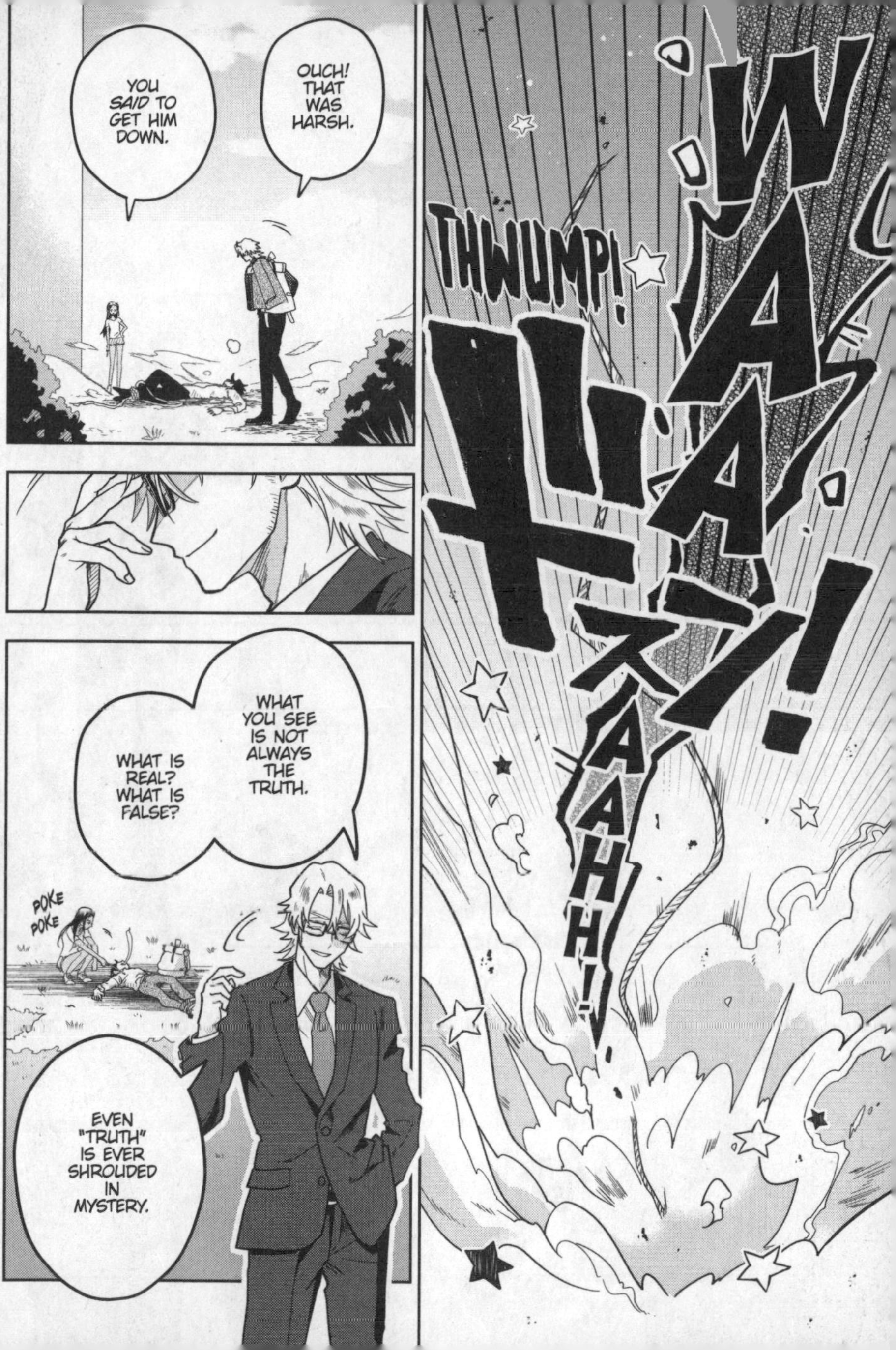
WAAAAHH!!
ドスン!
THWUMP!
OUCH! THAT WAS HARSH.
YOU SAID TO GET HIM DOWN.
WHAT YOU SEE IS NOT ALWAYS THE TRUTH.
WHAT IS REAL? WHAT IS FALSE?
POKE POKE
EVEN "TRUTH" IS EVER SHROUDED IN MYSTERY.

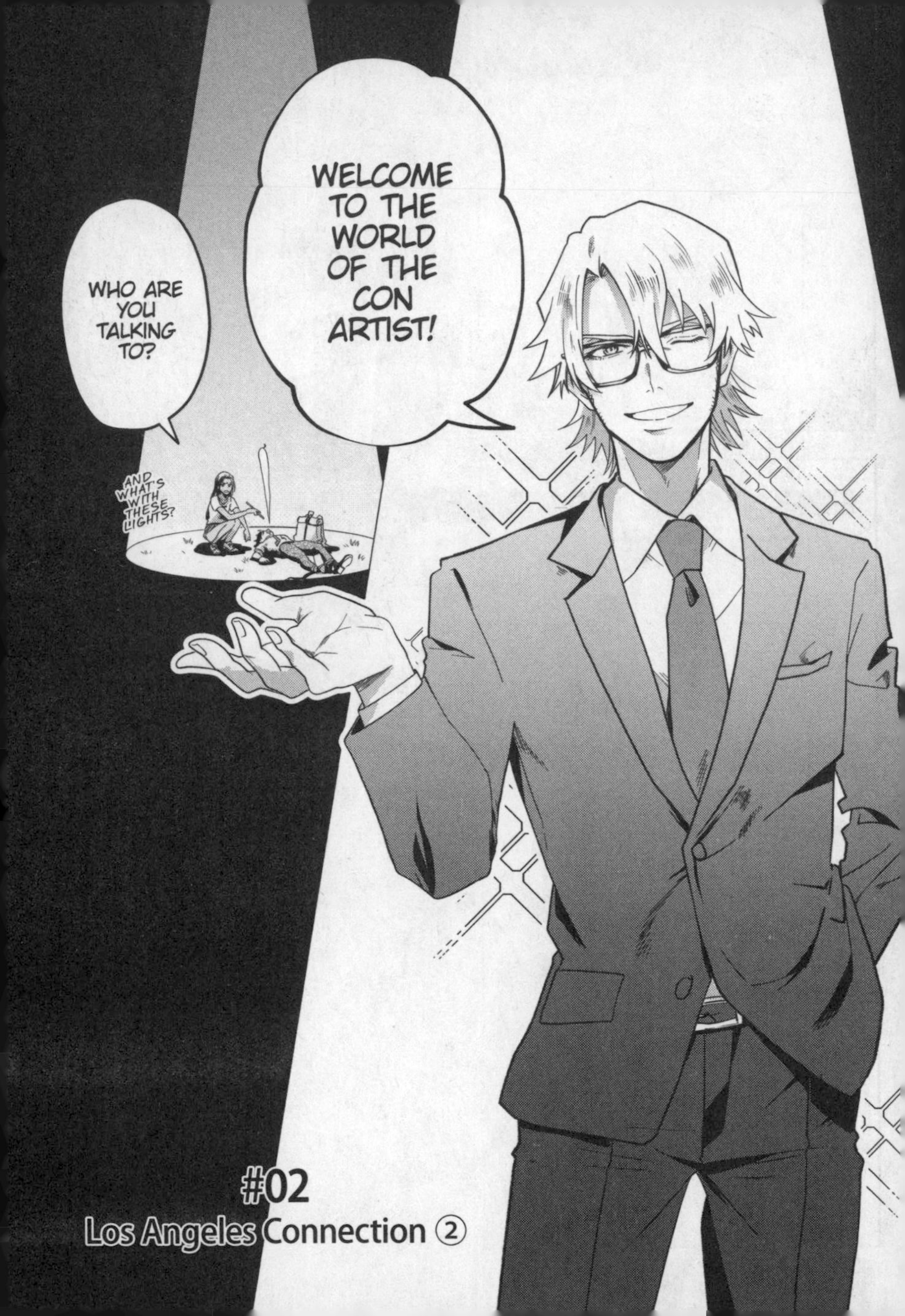
WELCOME TO THE WORLD OF THE CON ARTIST!
WHO ARE YOU TALKING TO?
AND WHAT'S WITH THESE LIGHTS?
#02
Los Angeles Connection ②

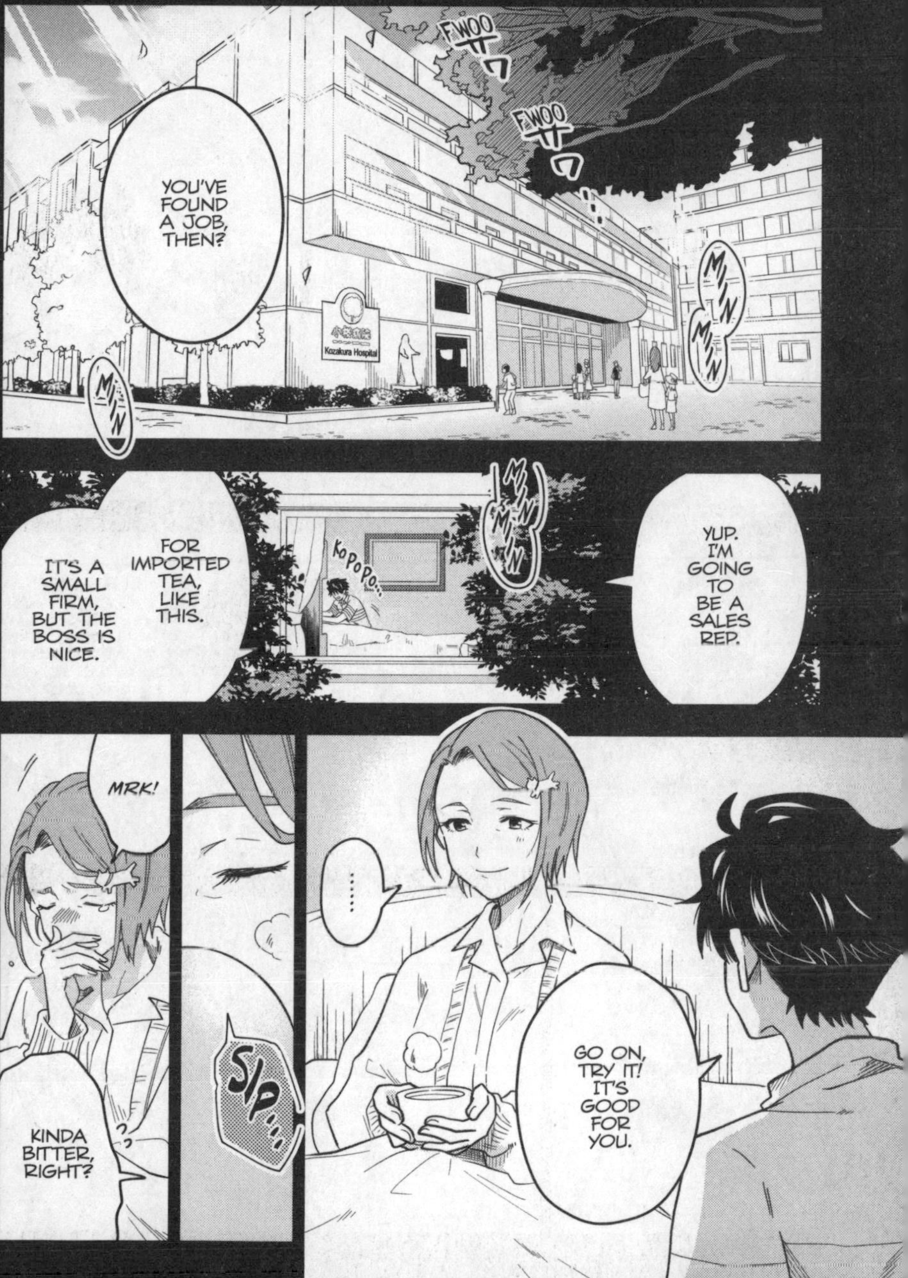
FWOO
FWOO
MIN MIN MIN
Kozakura Hospital
YOU'VE FOUND A JOB, THEN?
MIN
YUP. I'M GOING TO BE A SALES REP.
MIN MIN MIN
KOPOPO...
FOR IMPORTED TEA, LIKE THIS.
IT'S A SMALL FIRM, BUT THE BOSS IS NICE.
......
GO ON, TRY IT! IT'S GOOD FOR YOU.
SIP...
MRK!
KINDA BITTER, RIGHT?

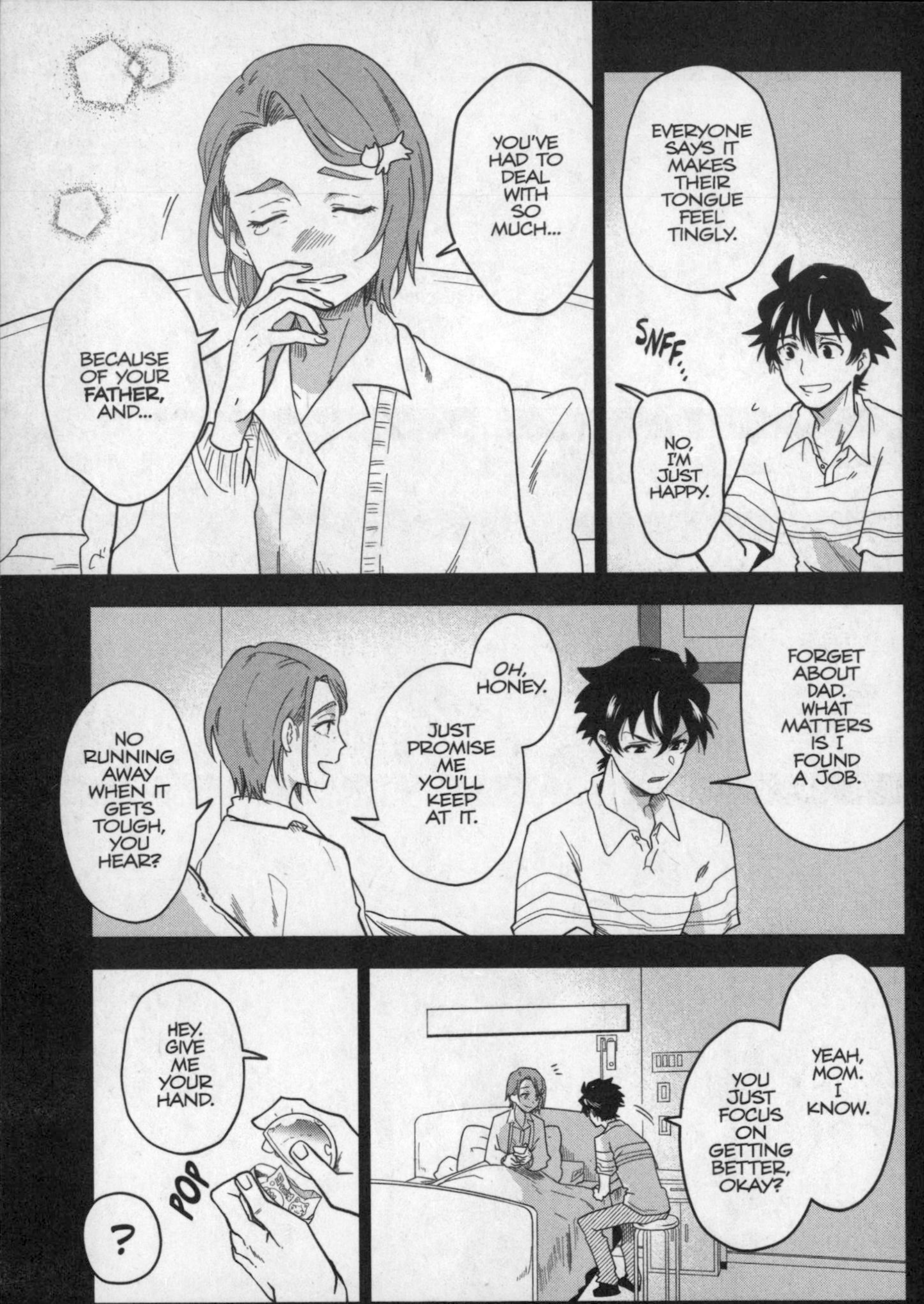
EVERYONE SAYS IT MAKES THEIR TONGUE FEEL TINGLY.
SNFF...
NO, I'M JUST HAPPY.
YOU'VE HAD TO DEAL WITH SO MUCH...
BECAUSE OF YOUR FATHER, AND...
FORGET ABOUT DAD. WHAT MATTERS IS I FOUND A JOB.
OH, HONEY.
JUST PROMISE ME YOU'LL KEEP AT IT.
NO RUNNING AWAY WHEN IT GETS TOUGH, YOU HEAR?
YEAH, MOM. I KNOW.
YOU JUST FOCUS ON GETTING BETTER, OKAY?
HEY. GIVE ME YOUR HAND.
POP
?

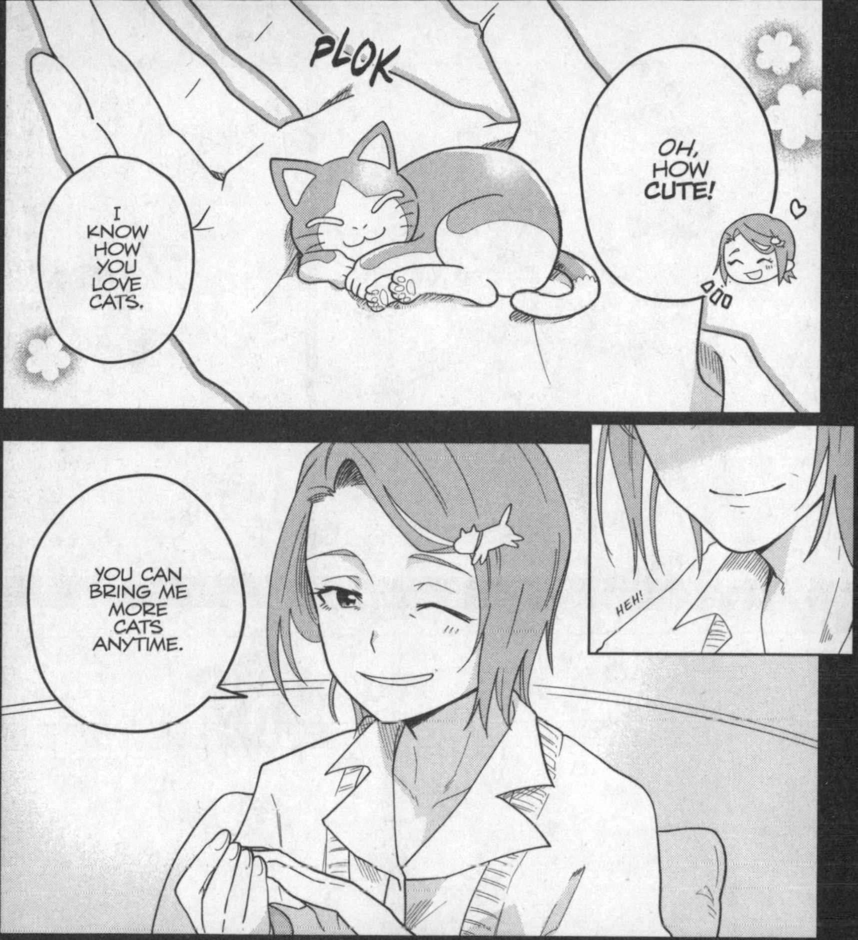
PLOK
OH, HOW CUTE!
I KNOW HOW YOU LOVE CATS.
HEH!
YOU CAN BRING ME MORE CATS ANYTIME.

Sign: Mankai Tea. The Original Mankai.

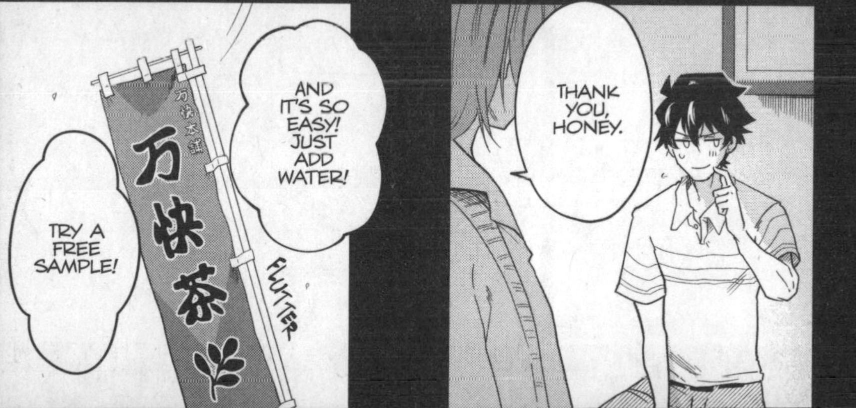
THANK YOU, HONEY.
AND IT'S SO EASY! JUST ADD WATER!
TRY A FREE SAMPLE!
万快茶
FLUTTER

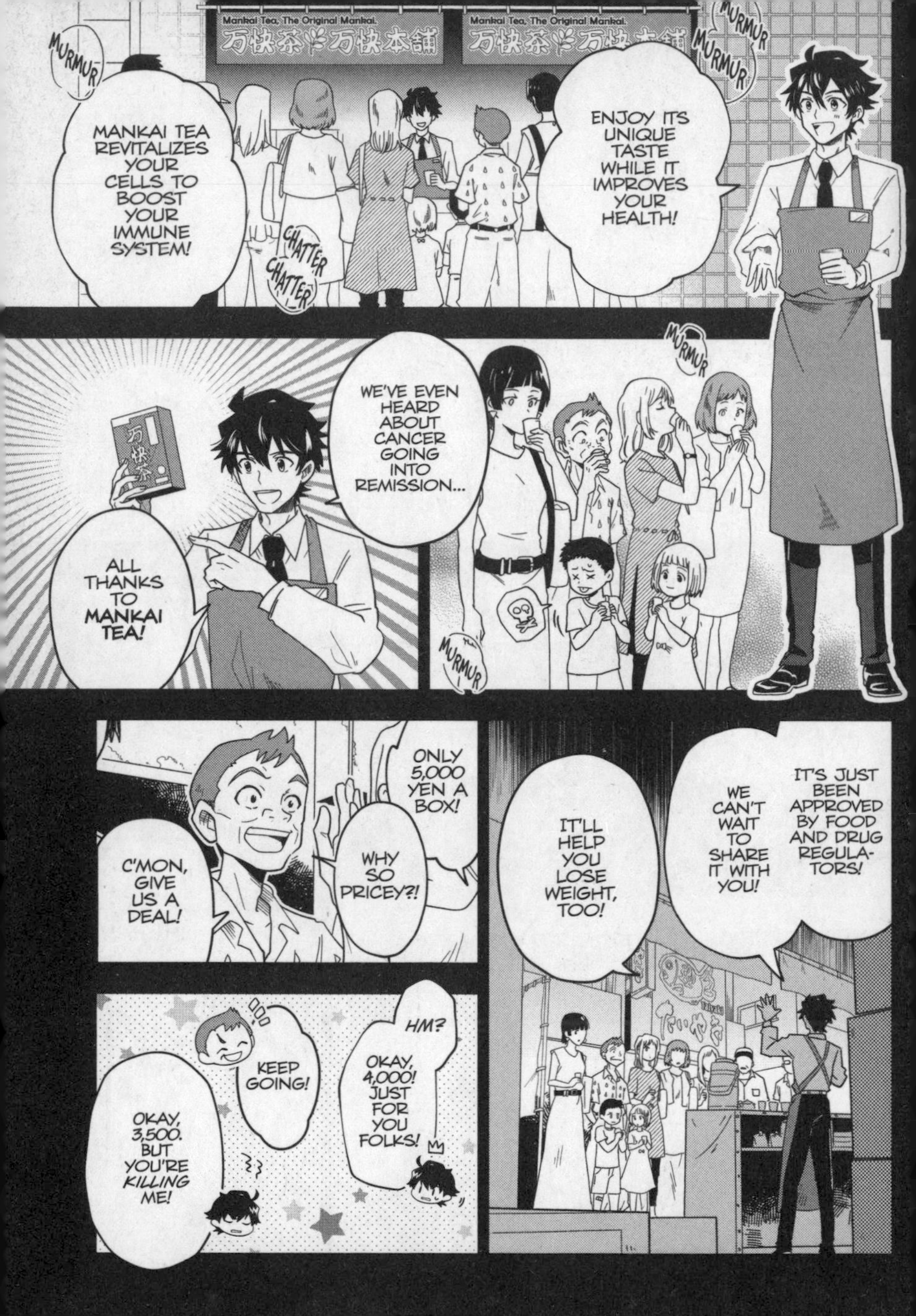
Mankai Tea, The Original Mankai.
万快茶🌿万快本舗
Mankai Tea, The Original Mankai.
万快茶🌿万快本舗
MURMUR MURMUR
ENJOY ITS UNIQUE TASTE WHILE IT IMPROVES YOUR HEALTH!
MURMUR
MANKAI TEA REVITALIZES YOUR CELLS TO BOOST YOUR IMMUNE SYSTEM!
CHATTER CHATTER
MURMUR
MURMUR
WE'VE EVEN HEARD ABOUT CANCER GOING INTO REMISSION...
万快茶
ALL THANKS TO MANKAI TEA!
IT'S JUST BEEN APPROVED BY FOOD AND DRUG REGULATORS!
WE CAN'T WAIT TO SHARE IT WITH YOU!
IT'LL HELP YOU LOSE WEIGHT, TOO!
ONLY 5,000 YEN A BOX!
WHY SO PRICEY?!
C'MON, GIVE US A DEAL!
HM?
OKAY, 4,000! JUST FOR YOU FOLKS!
KEEP GOING!
OKAY, 3,500. BUT YOU'RE KILLING ME!

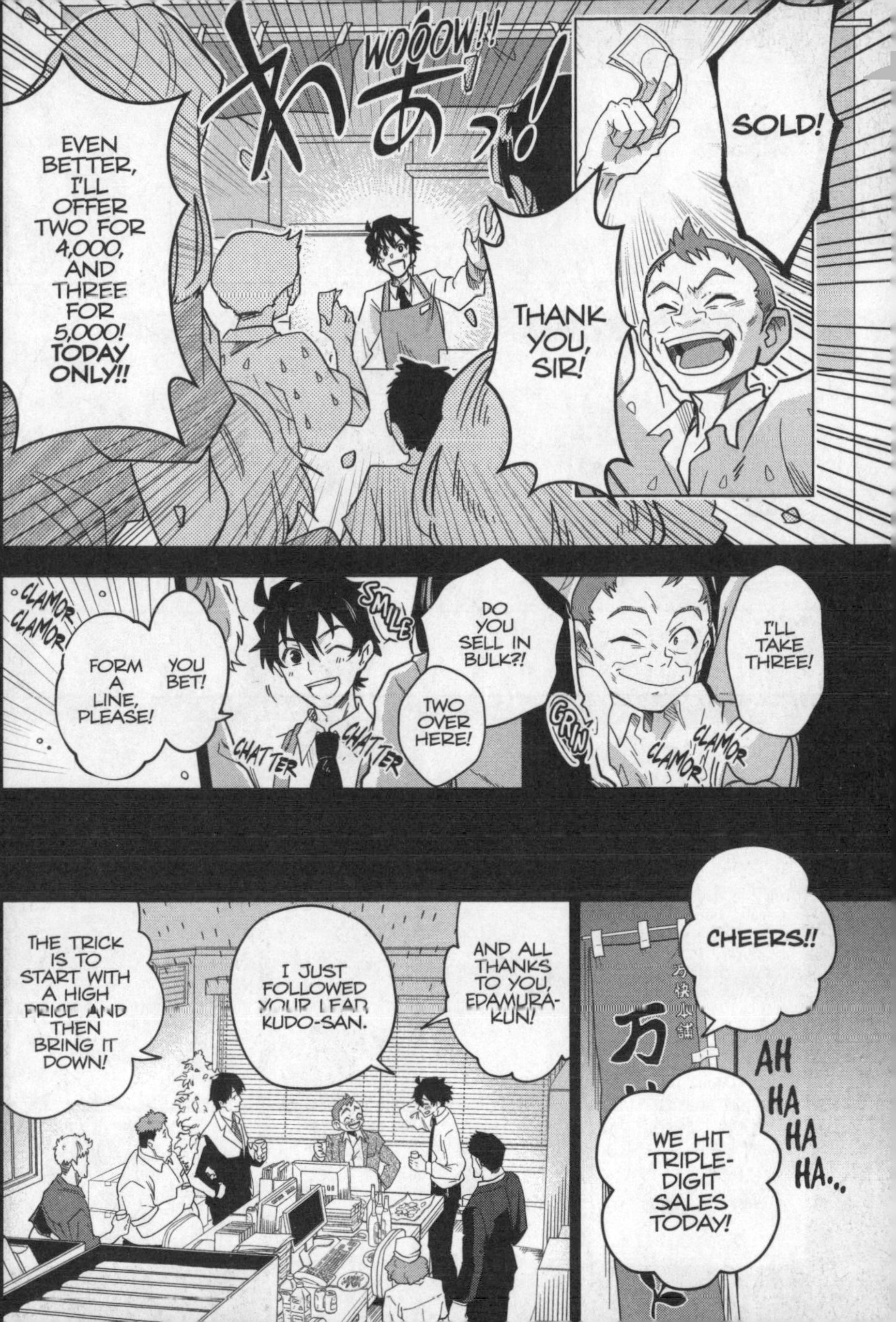
SOLD!
THANK YOU, SIR!
わあっ!!
WOOOW!!
EVEN BETTER, I'LL OFFER TWO FOR 4,000, AND THREE FOR 5,000! TODAY ONLY!!
I'LL TAKE THREE!
GRIN
CLAMOR CLAMOR
DO YOU SELL IN BULK?!
SMILE
YOU BET!
FORM A LINE, PLEASE!
TWO OVER HERE!
CHATTER CHATTER
CLAMOR CLAMOR
CHEERS!!
AH HA HA HA...
WE HIT TRIPLE-DIGIT SALES TODAY!
AND ALL THANKS TO YOU, EDAMURA-KUN!
I JUST FOLLOWED YOUR LEAD, KUDO-SAN.
THE TRICK IS TO START WITH A HIGH PRICE AND THEN BRING IT DOWN!

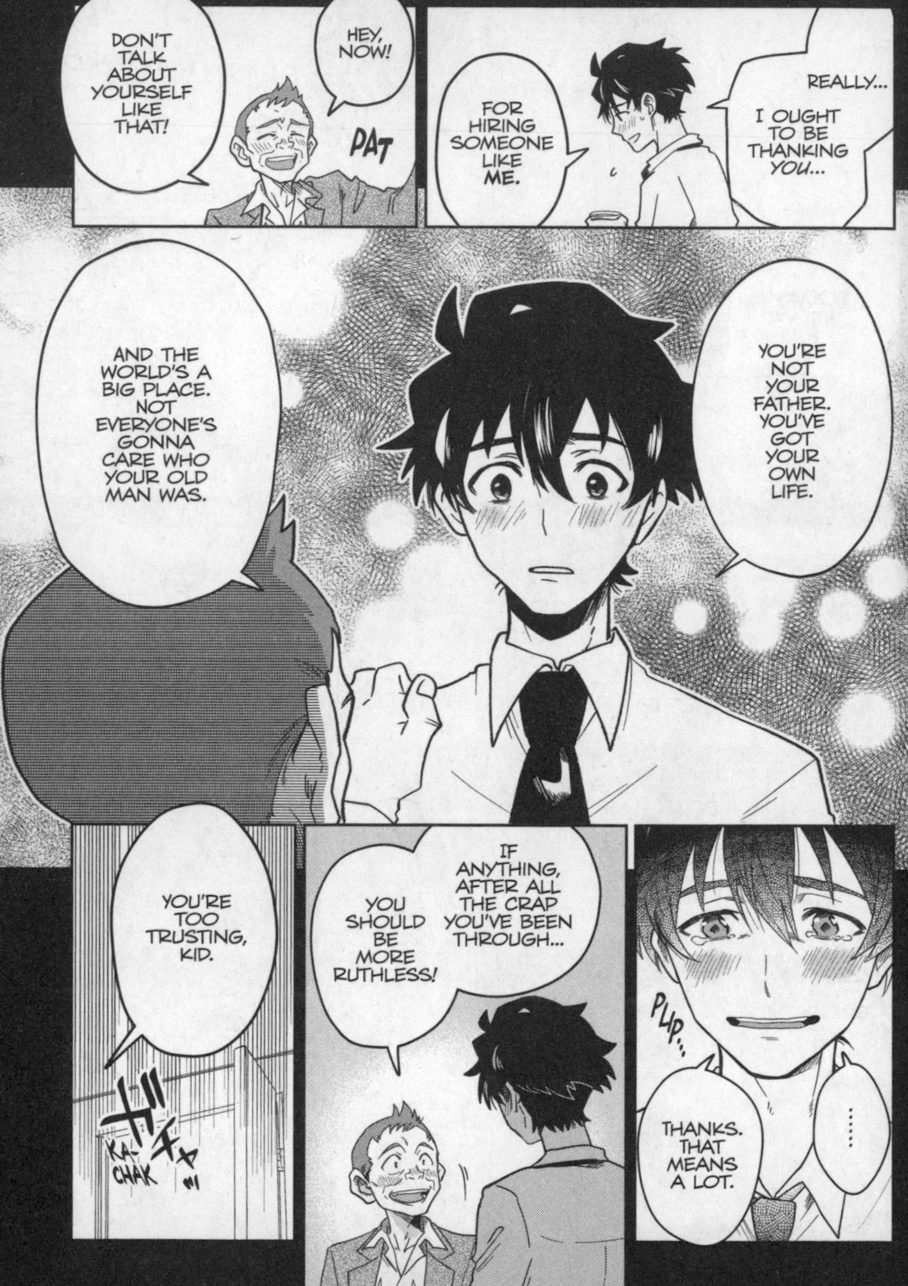
REALLY... I OUGHT TO BE THANKING *YOU*...
FOR HIRING SOMEONE LIKE ME.
HEY, NOW!
PAT
DON'T TALK ABOUT YOURSELF LIKE THAT!
YOU'RE NOT YOUR FATHER. YOU'VE GOT YOUR OWN LIFE.
AND THE WORLD'S A BIG PLACE. NOT EVERYONE'S GONNA CARE WHO YOUR OLD MAN WAS.
PLIP...
......
THANKS. THAT MEANS A LOT.
IF ANYTHING, AFTER ALL THE CRAP YOU'VE BEEN THROUGH...
YOU SHOULD BE MORE RUTHLESS!
YOU'RE TOO TRUSTING, KID.
KA-CHAK

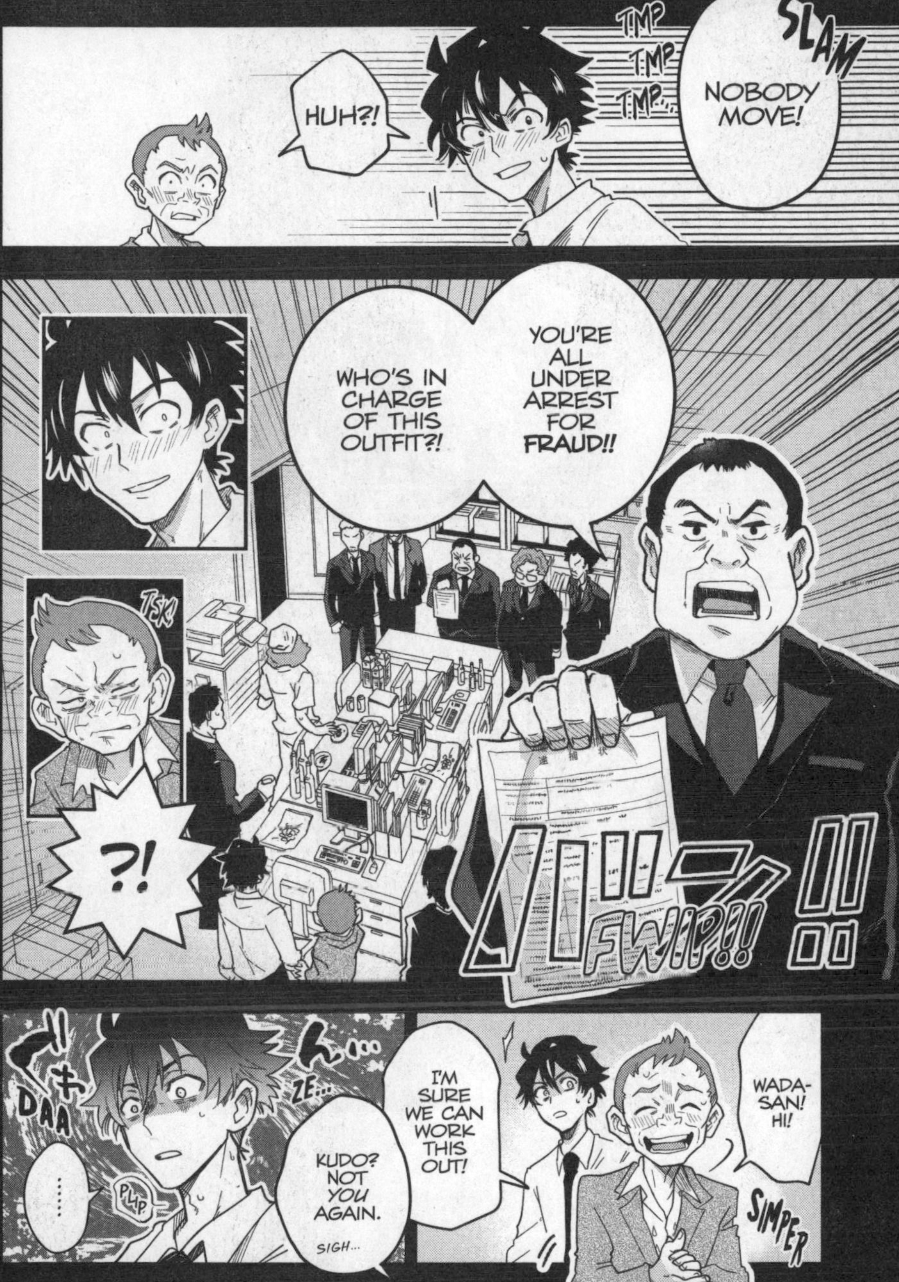
SLAM
NOBODY MOVE!
TMP TMP TMP...
HUH?!
YOU'RE ALL UNDER ARREST FOR FRAUD!!
WHO'S IN CHARGE OF THIS OUTFIT?!
FWIP!!
TSK!
?!
WADA-SAN! HI!
I'M SURE WE CAN WORK THIS OUT!
SIMPER
ZE...
KUDO? NOT YOU AGAIN.
SIGH...
PLIP
......
DAA

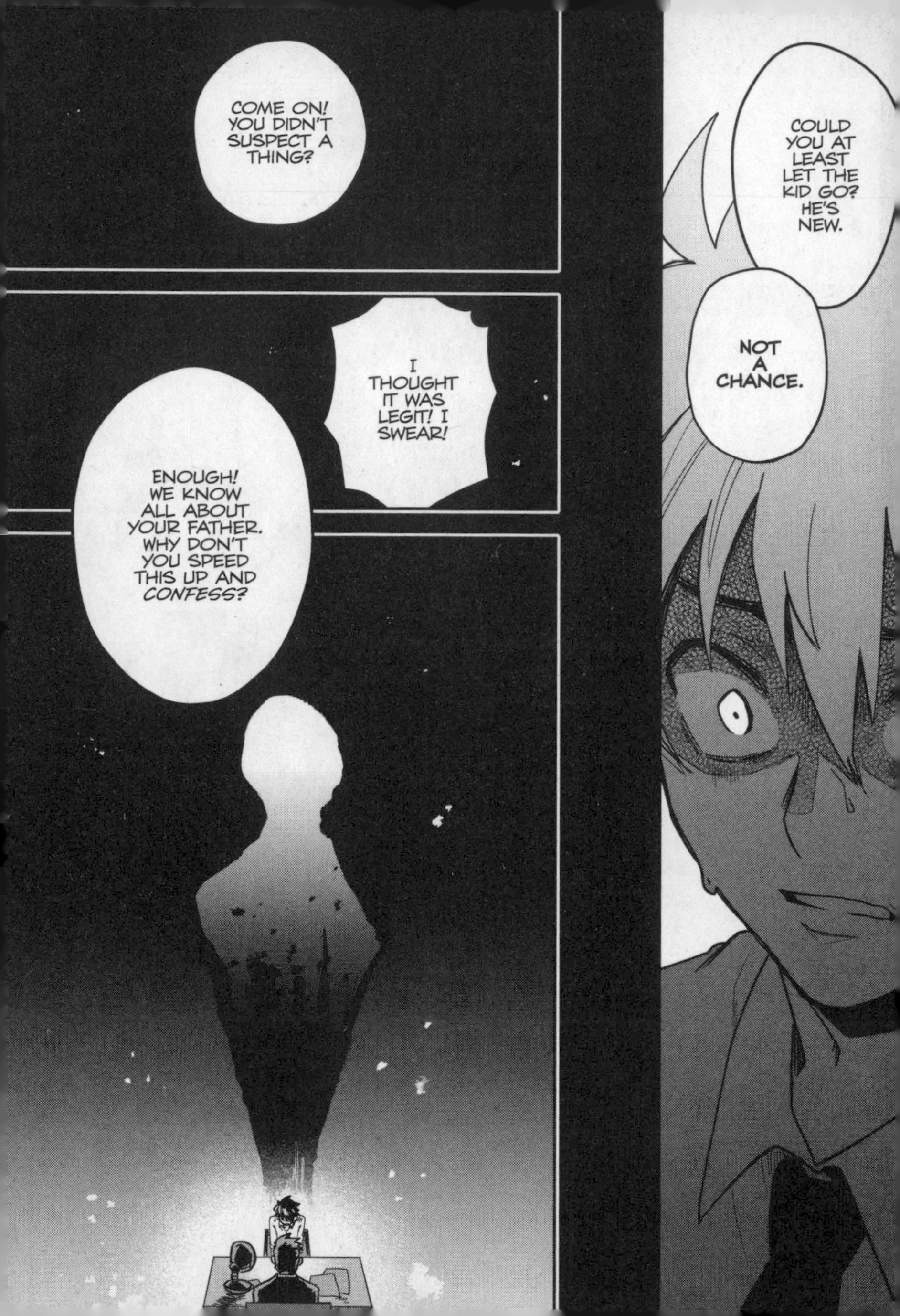
COULD YOU AT LEAST LET THE KID GO? HE'S NEW.
NOT A CHANCE.
COME ON! YOU DIDN'T SUSPECT A THING?
I THOUGHT IT WAS LEGIT! I SWEAR!
ENOUGH! WE KNOW ALL ABOUT YOUR FATHER. WHY DON'T YOU SPEED THIS UP AND *CONFESS?*

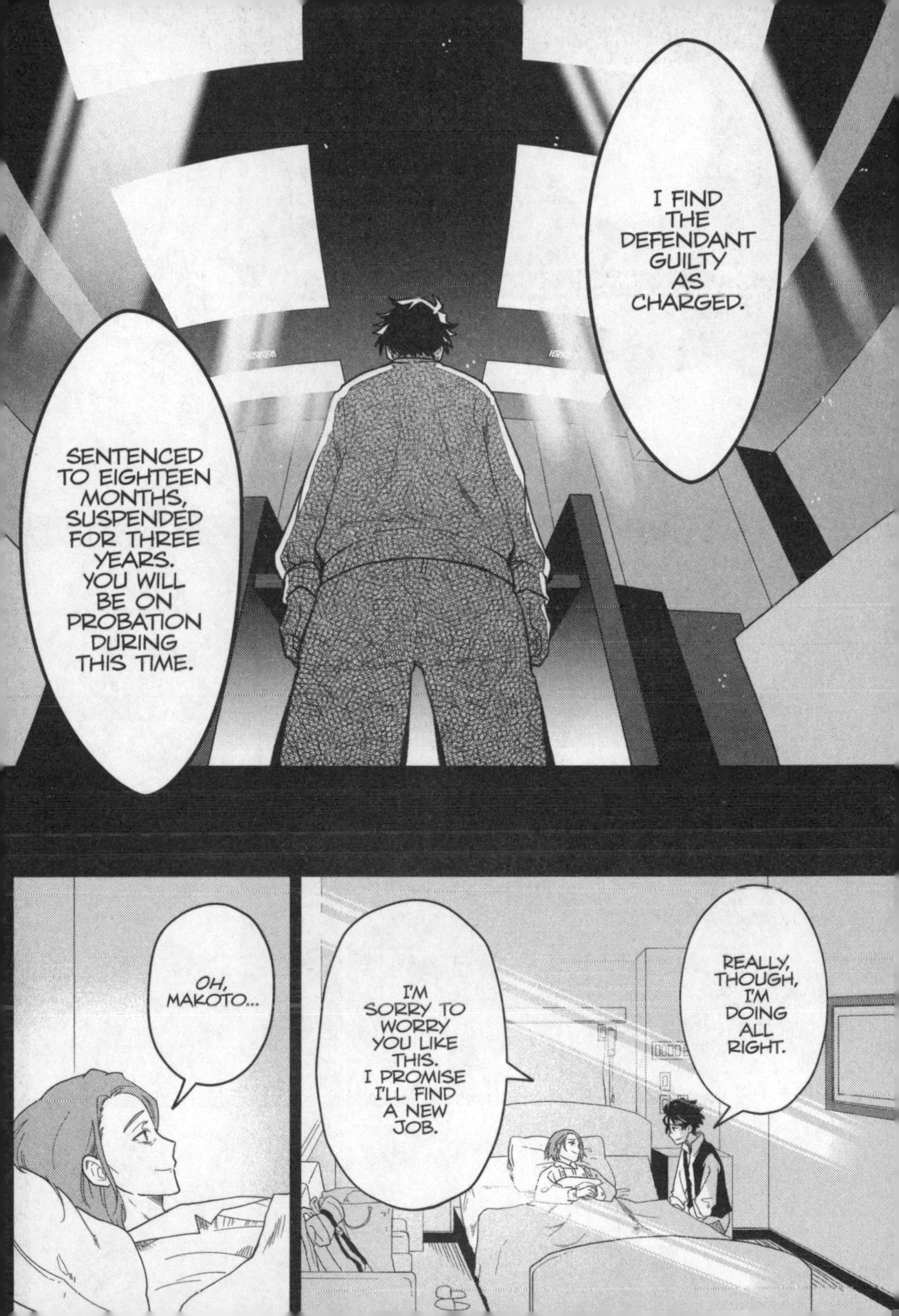
I FIND THE DEFENDANT GUILTY AS CHARGED.
SENTENCED TO EIGHTEEN MONTHS, SUSPENDED FOR THREE YEARS. YOU WILL BE ON PROBATION DURING THIS TIME.
REALLY, THOUGH, I'M DOING ALL RIGHT.
I'M SORRY TO WORRY YOU LIKE THIS. I PROMISE I'LL FIND A NEW JOB.
OH, MAKOTO...

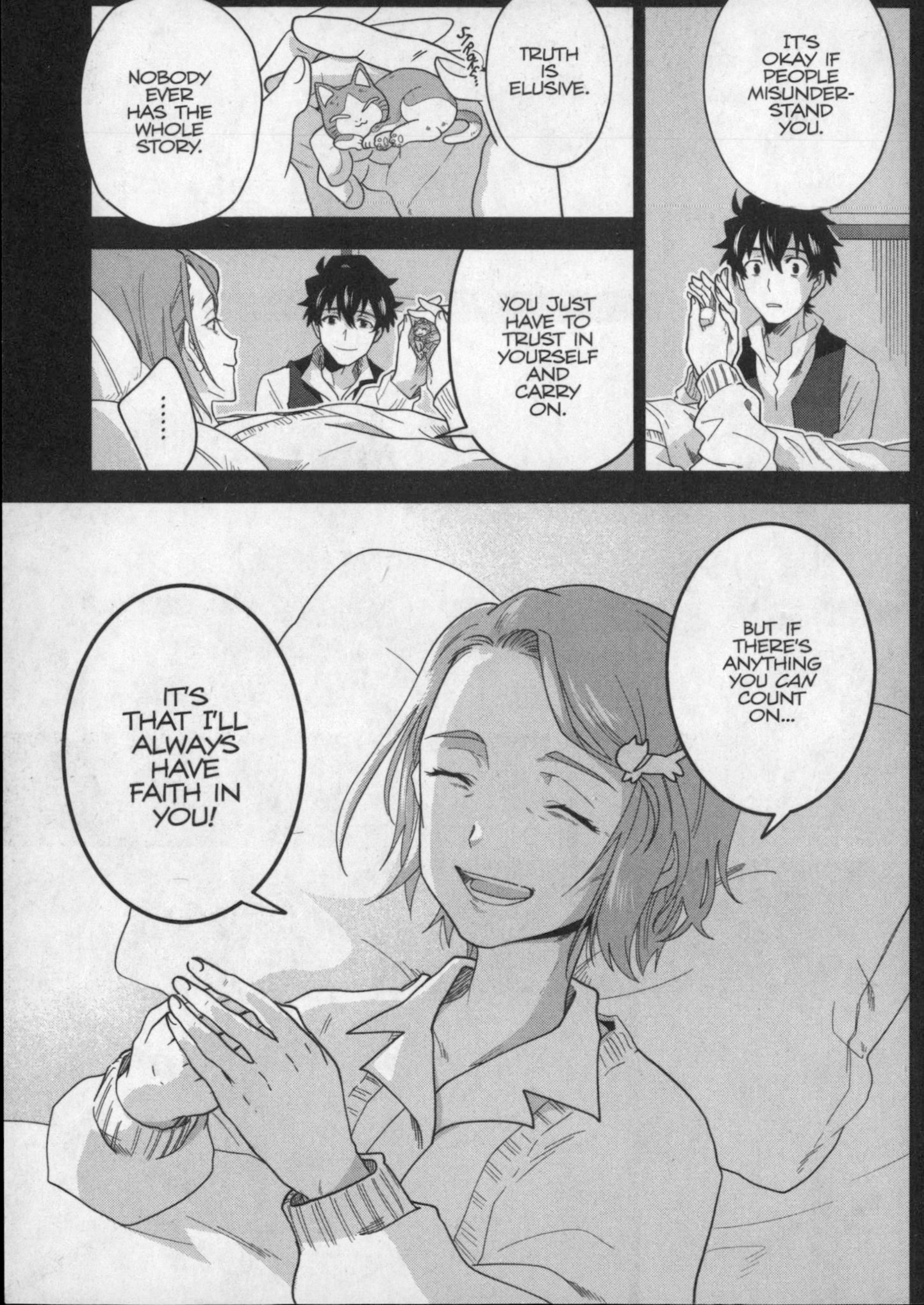
IT'S OKAY IF PEOPLE MISUNDER-STAND YOU.
STROKE...
TRUTH IS ELUSIVE.
NOBODY EVER HAS THE WHOLE STORY.
YOU JUST HAVE TO TRUST IN YOURSELF AND CARRY ON.
......
BUT IF THERE'S ANYTHING YOU *CAN* COUNT ON...
IT'S THAT I'LL ALWAYS HAVE FAITH IN YOU!

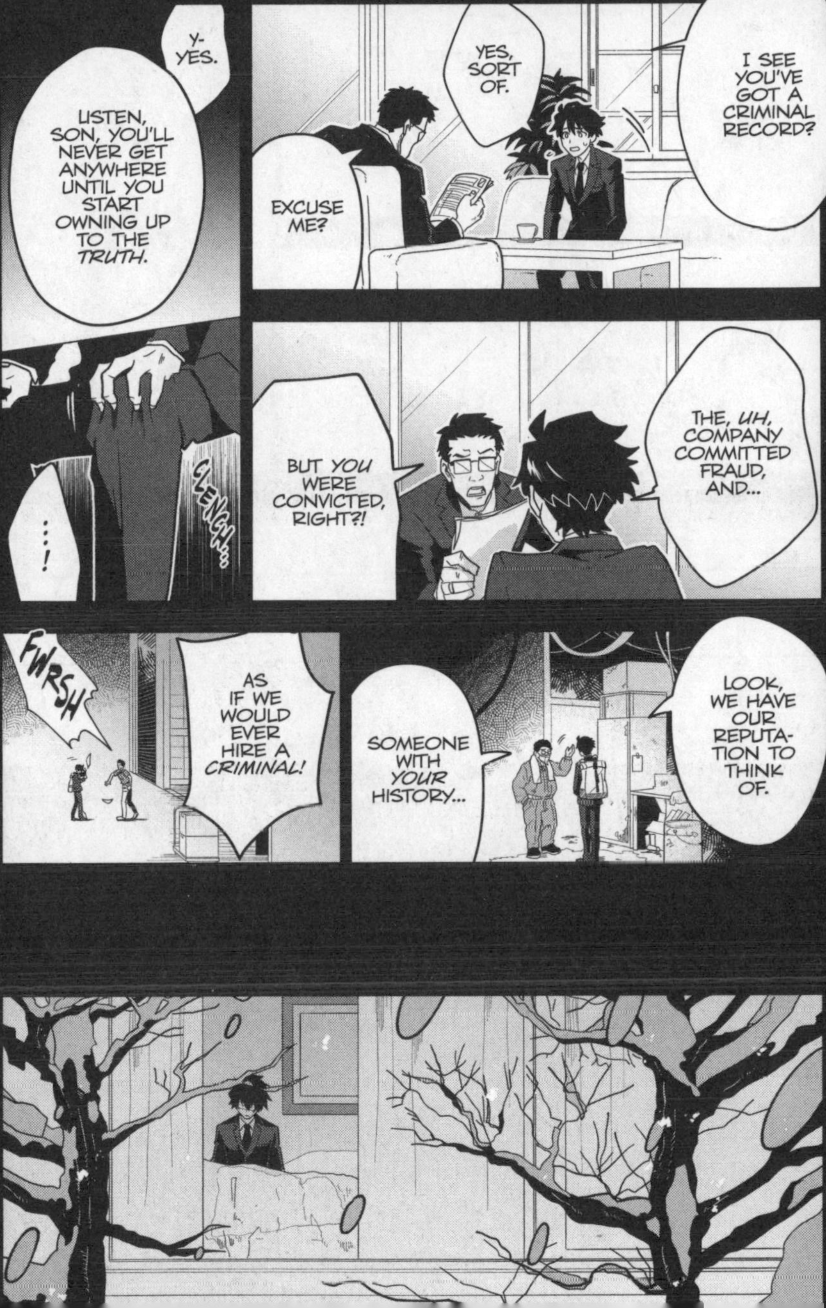
I SEE YOU'VE GOT A CRIMINAL RECORD?
YES, SORT OF.
EXCUSE ME?
THE, UH, COMPANY COMMITTED FRAUD, AND...
BUT YOU WERE CONVICTED, RIGHT?!
Y- YES.
LISTEN, SON, YOU'LL NEVER GET ANYWHERE UNTIL YOU START OWNING UP TO THE TRUTH.
CLENCH...
...!
LOOK, WE HAVE OUR REPUTATION TO THINK OF.
SOMEONE WITH YOUR HISTORY...
AS IF WE WOULD EVER HIRE A CRIMINAL!
FWRSH

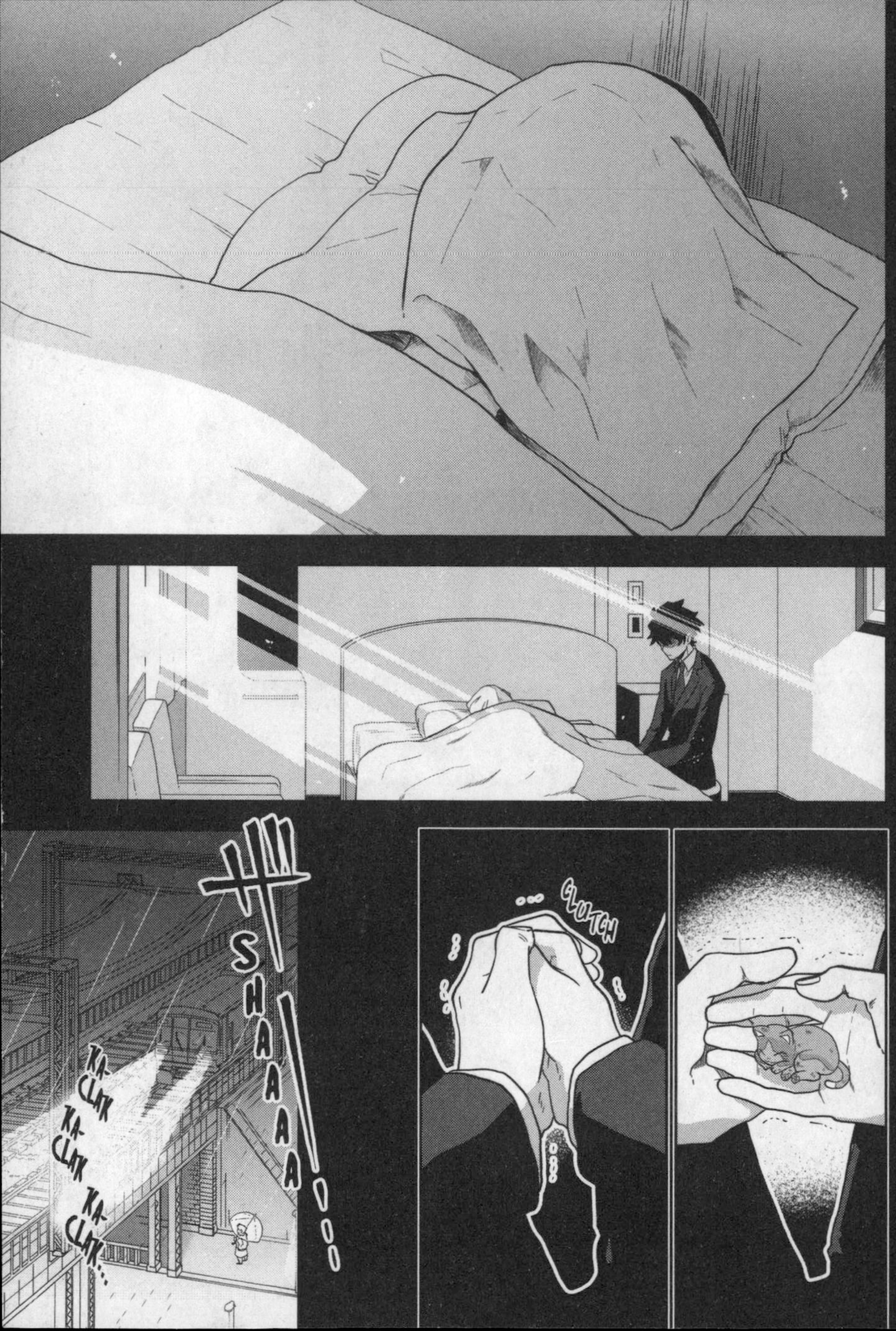
CLUTCH
SHAAAAA...!!
KA-CLAK KA-CLAK KA-CLAK...

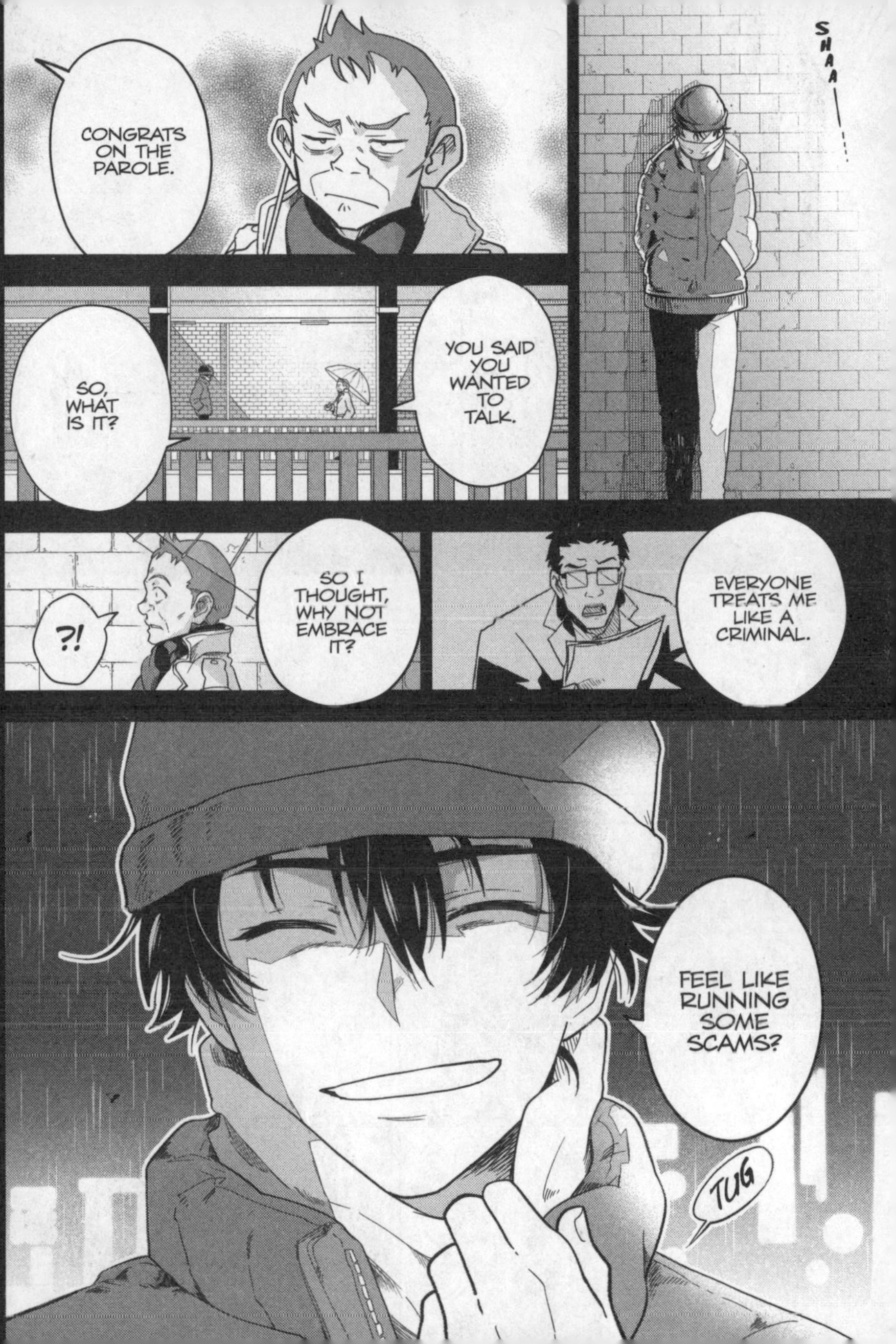
SHAA---
CONGRATS ON THE PAROLE.
YOU SAID YOU WANTED TO TALK.
SO, WHAT IS IT?
EVERYONE TREATS ME LIKE A CRIMINAL.
SO I THOUGHT, WHY NOT EMBRACE IT?
?!
FEEL LIKE RUNNING SOME SCAMS?
TUG

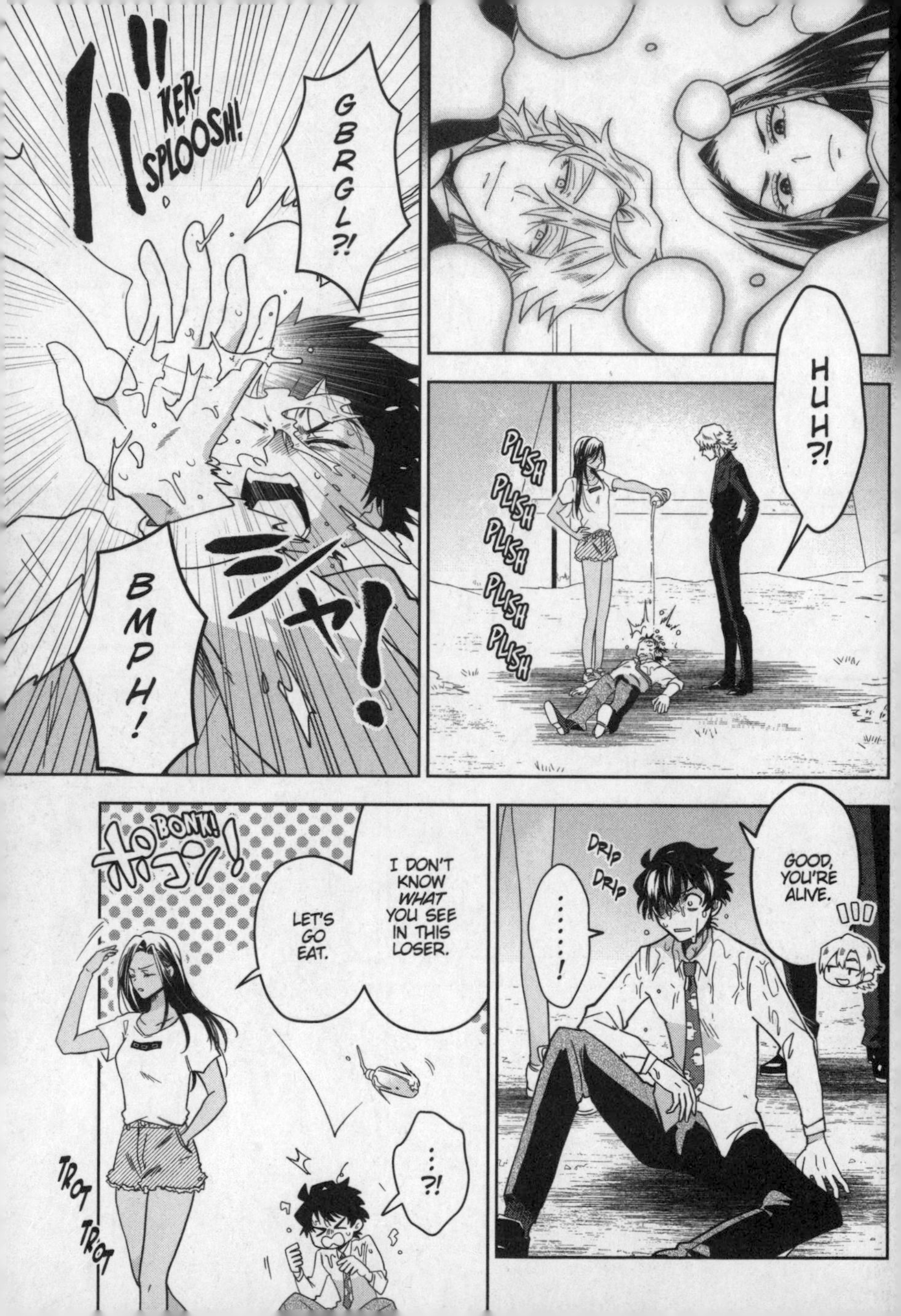
HUH?!
PLISH PLISH PLISH PLISH PLISH PLISH
KER-SPLOOSH!
GBRGL?!
BMPH!
GOOD, YOU'RE ALIVE.
......!
DRIP DRIP
BONK!
I DON'T KNOW WHAT YOU SEE IN THIS LOSER.
LET'S GO EAT.
...?!
TROT TROT

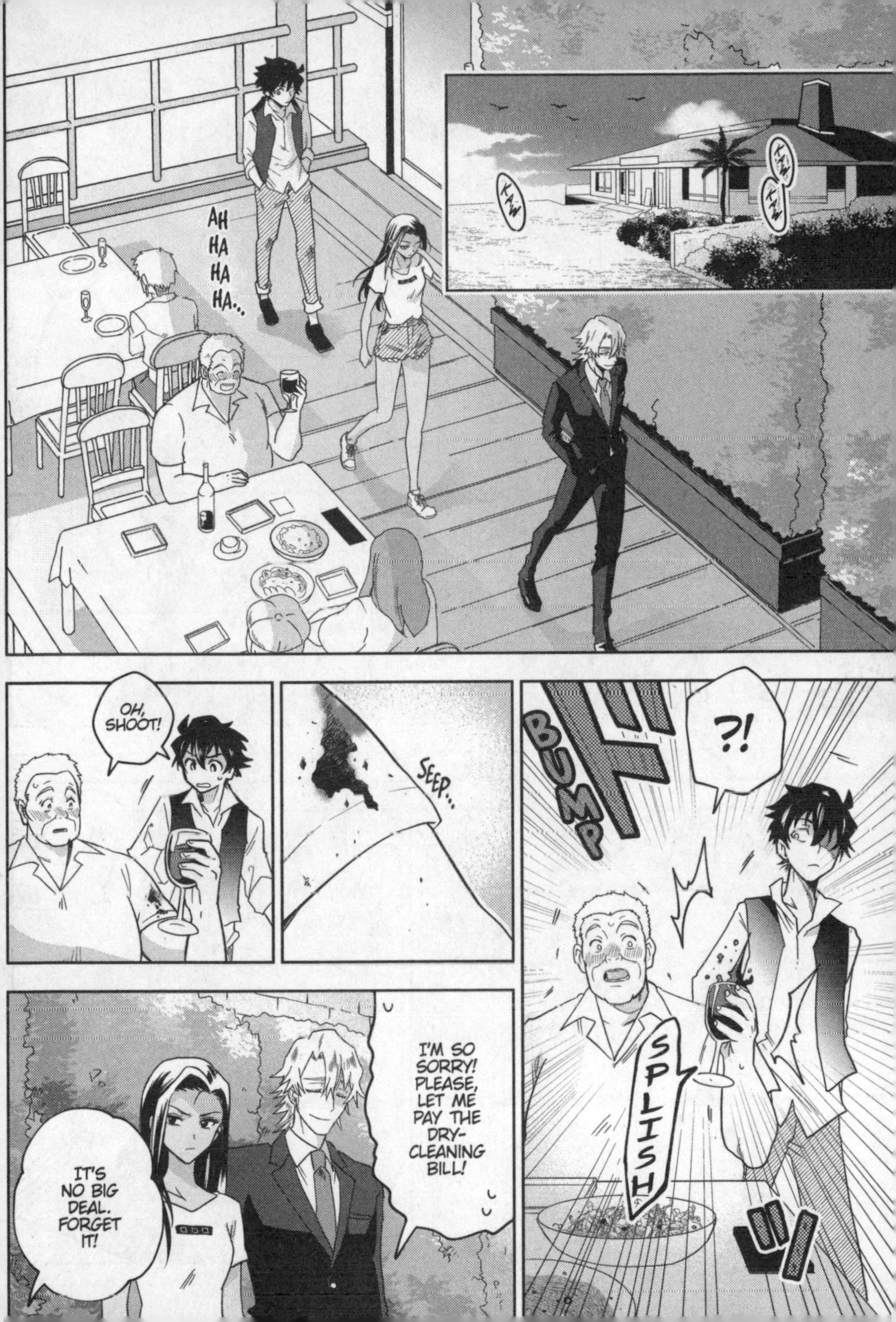
KAW
KAW
KAW
AH HA HA HA...
?!
BUMP
SPLISH
SEEP...
OH, SHOOT!
I'M SO SORRY! PLEASE, LET ME PAY THE DRY-CLEANING BILL!
IT'S NO BIG DEAL. FORGET IT!

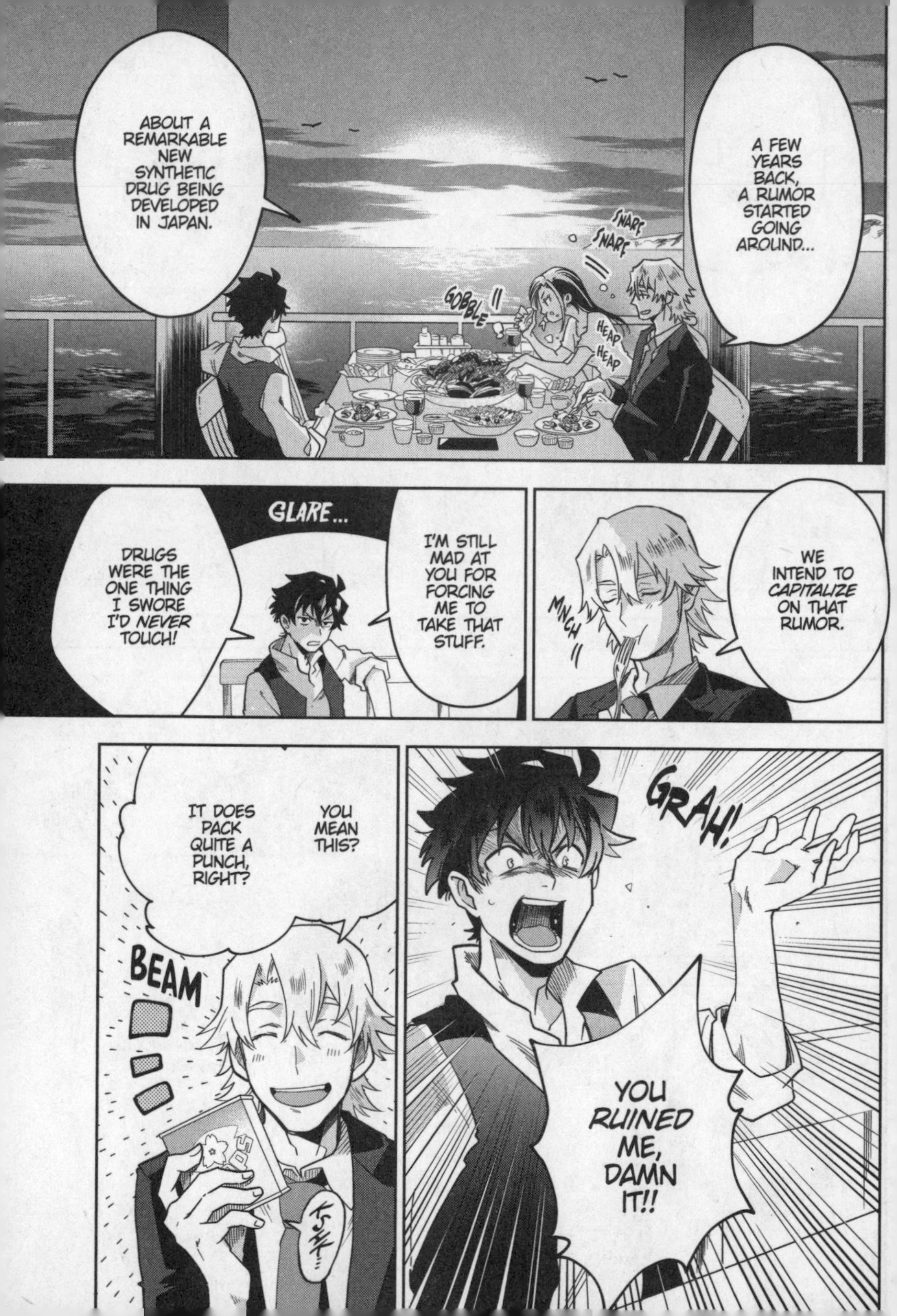
A FEW YEARS BACK, A RUMOR STARTED GOING AROUND...
ABOUT A REMARKABLE NEW SYNTHETIC DRUG BEING DEVELOPED IN JAPAN.
SNARF SNARF
GOBBLE
HEAP HEAP
WE INTEND TO *CAPITALIZE* ON THAT RUMOR.
MNCH
GLARE...
I'M STILL MAD AT YOU FOR FORCING ME TO TAKE THAT STUFF.
DRUGS WERE THE ONE THING I SWORE I'D *NEVER* TOUCH!
GRAH!
YOU RUINED ME, DAMN IT!!
YOU MEAN THIS?
IT DOES PACK QUITE A PUNCH, RIGHT?
BEAM

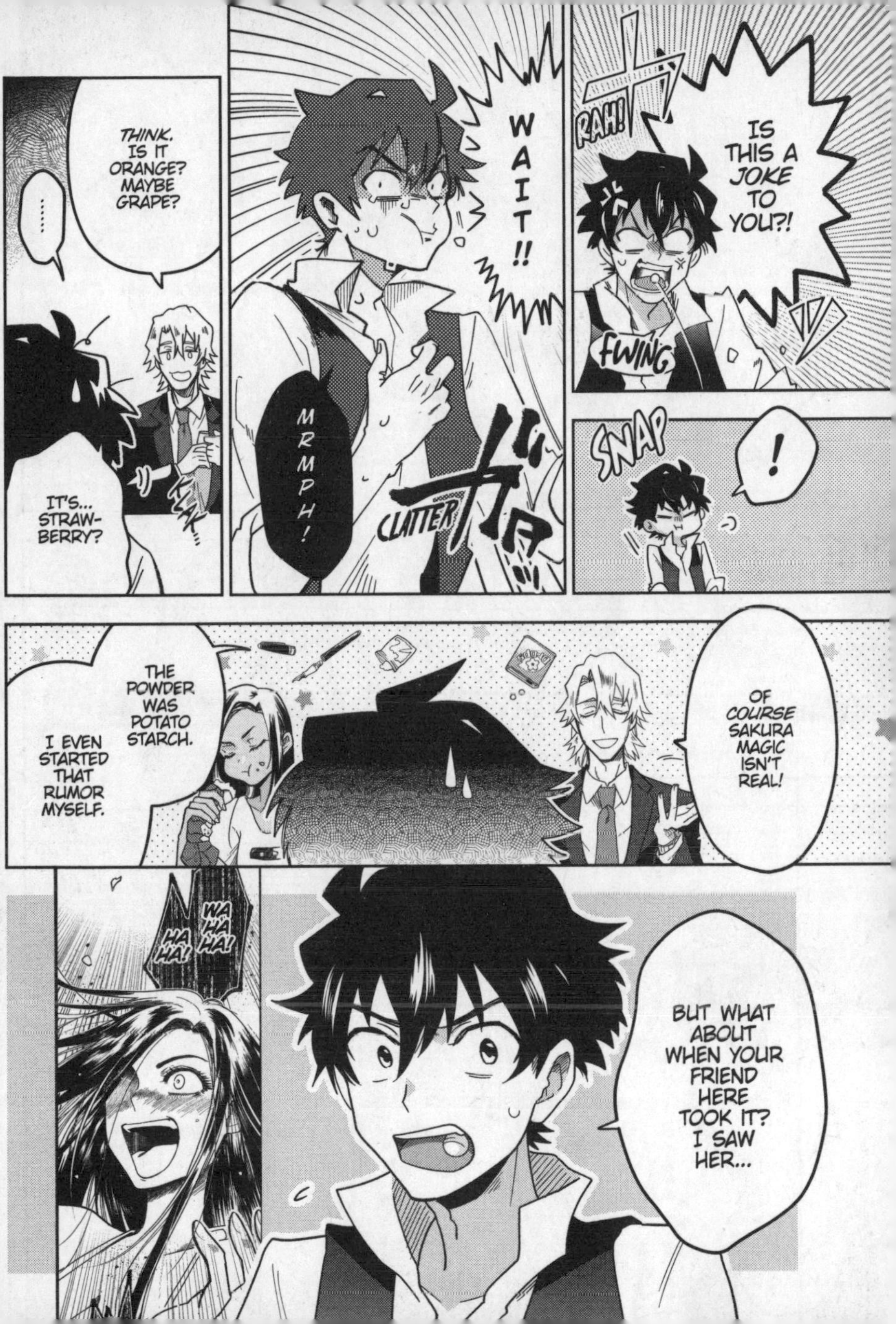

RAH!
IS THIS A JOKE TO YOU?!
FWING
SNAP
!
WAIT!!
MRMPH!
CLATTER
THINK. IS IT ORANGE? MAYBE GRAPE?
......
IT'S... STRAWBERRY?
OF COURSE SAKURA MAGIC ISN'T REAL!
THE POWDER WAS POTATO STARCH.
I EVEN STARTED THAT RUMOR MYSELF.
BUT WHAT ABOUT WHEN YOUR FRIEND HERE TOOK IT? I SAW HER...
WA HA HA!
HA HA!

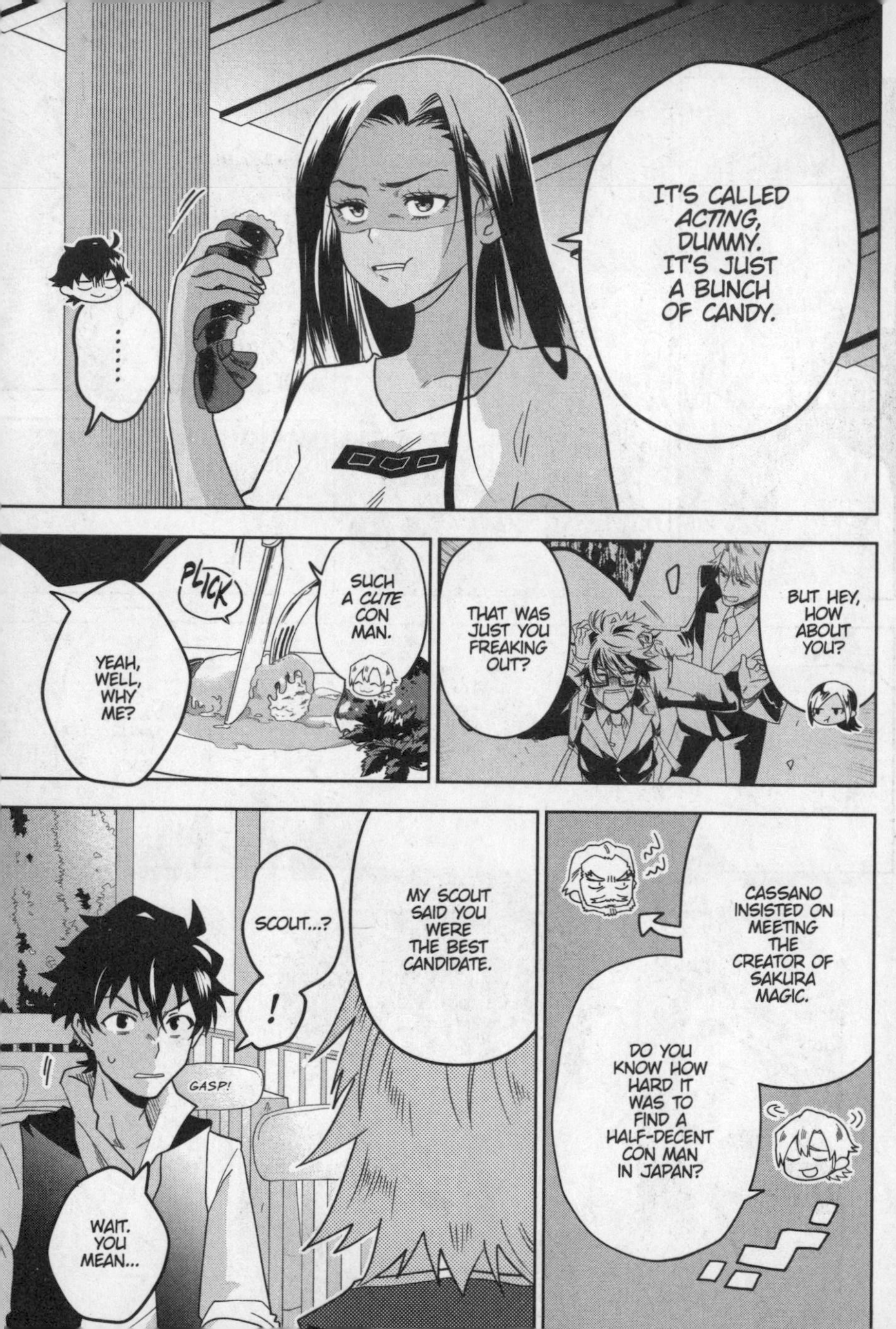
IT'S CALLED ACTING, DUMMY. IT'S JUST A BUNCH OF CANDY.
......
BUT HEY, HOW ABOUT YOU?
THAT WAS JUST YOU FREAKING OUT?
SUCH A CUTE CON MAN.
PLICK
YEAH, WELL, WHY ME?
CASSANO INSISTED ON MEETING THE CREATOR OF SAKURA MAGIC.
DO YOU KNOW HOW HARD IT WAS TO FIND A HALF-DECENT CON MAN IN JAPAN?
MY SCOUT SAID YOU WERE THE BEST CANDIDATE.
SCOUT...?
!
GASP!
WAIT. YOU MEAN...

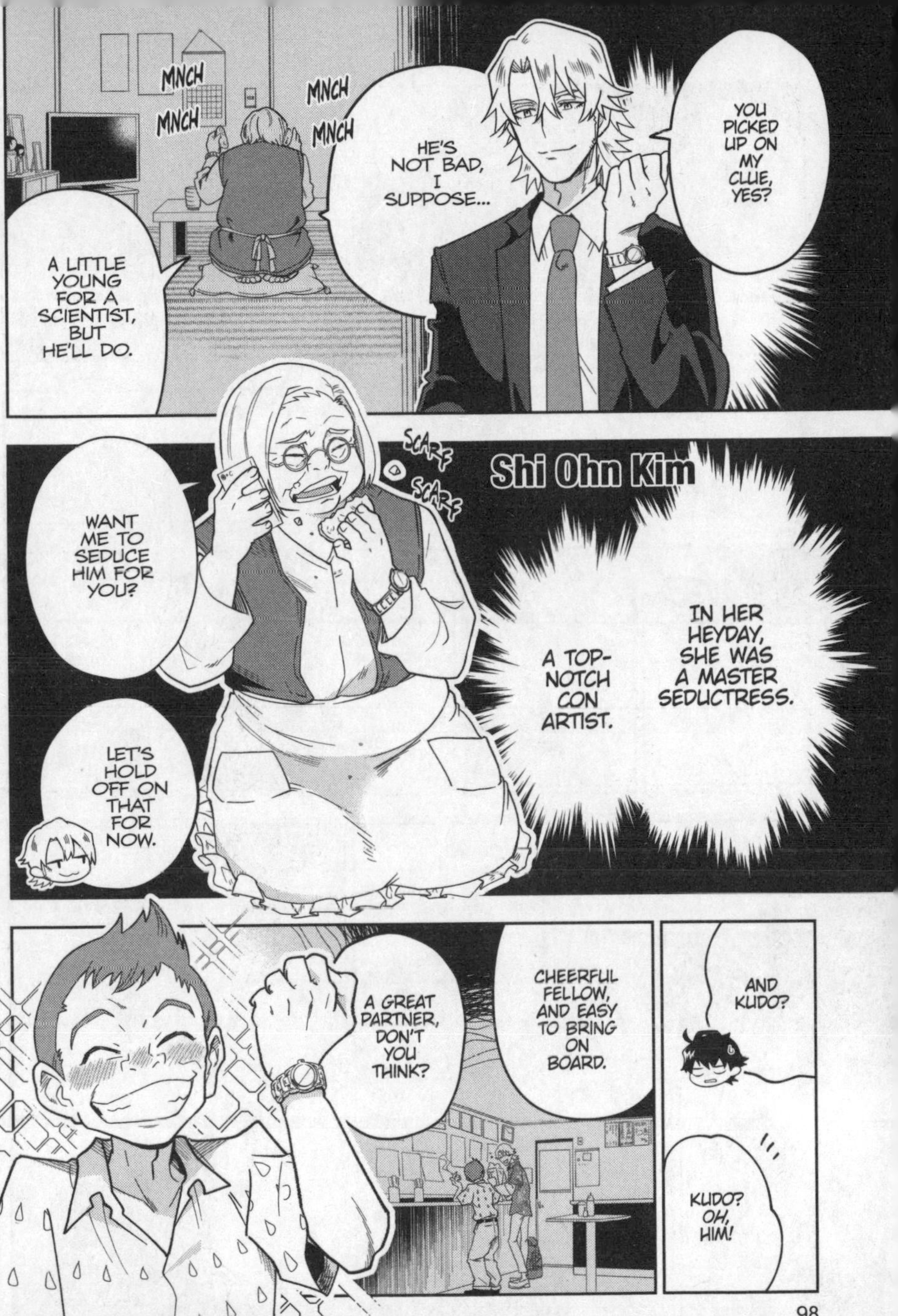
YOU PICKED UP ON MY CLUE, YES?
HE'S NOT BAD, I SUPPOSE...
MNCH MNCH
MNCH MNCH
A LITTLE YOUNG FOR A SCIENTIST, BUT HE'LL DO.
IN HER HEYDAY, SHE WAS A MASTER SEDUCTRESS.
A TOP-NOTCH CON ARTIST.
Shi Ohn Kim
SCARF SCARF
WANT ME TO SEDUCE HIM FOR YOU?
LET'S HOLD OFF ON THAT FOR NOW.
AND KUDO?
KUDO? OH, HIM!
CHEERFUL FELLOW, AND EASY TO BRING ON BOARD.
A GREAT PARTNER, DON'T YOU THINK?

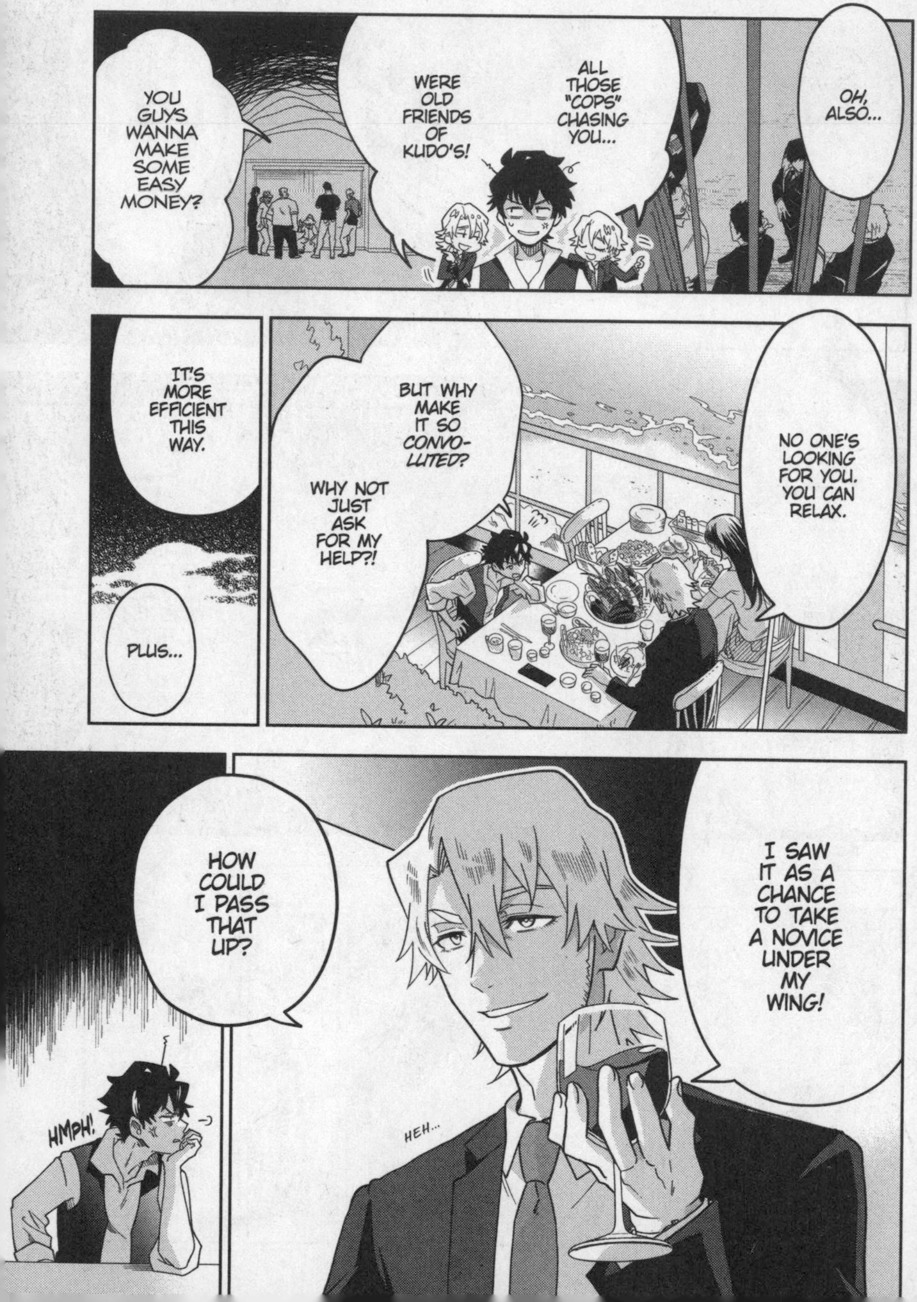
OH, ALSO...
ALL THOSE "COPS" CHASING YOU...
WERE OLD FRIENDS OF KUDO'S!
YOU GUYS WANNA MAKE SOME EASY MONEY?
NO ONE'S LOOKING FOR YOU. YOU CAN RELAX.
BUT WHY MAKE IT SO CONVO-LUTED?
WHY NOT JUST ASK FOR MY HELP?!
IT'S MORE EFFICIENT THIS WAY.
PLUS...
I SAW IT AS A CHANCE TO TAKE A NOVICE UNDER MY WING!
HEH...
HOW COULD I PASS THAT UP?
HMPH!

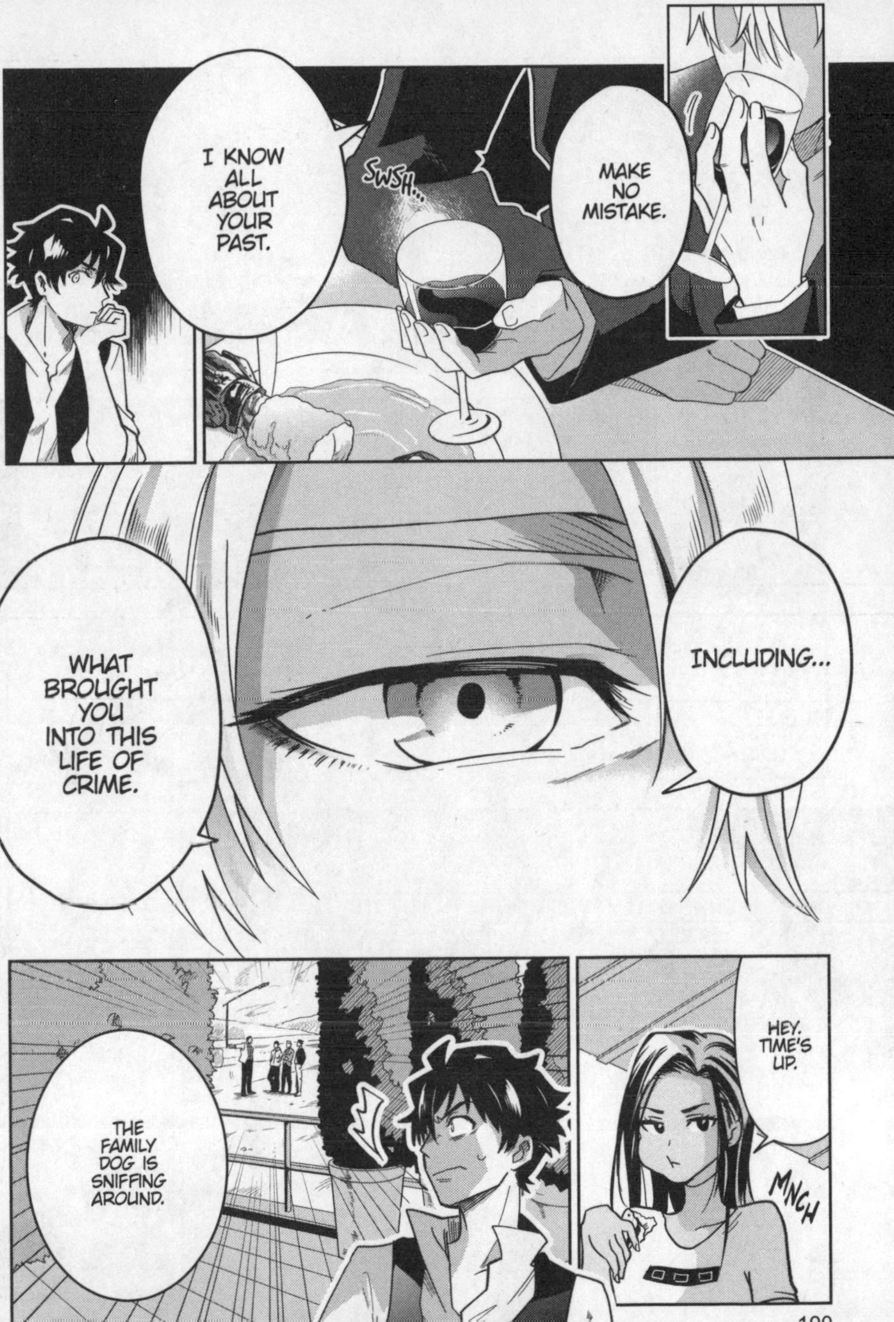
MAKE NO MISTAKE.
SWSH...
I KNOW ALL ABOUT YOUR PAST.
INCLUDING...
WHAT BROUGHT YOU INTO THIS LIFE OF CRIME.
HEY. TIME'S UP.
MNCH
THE FAMILY DOG IS SNIFFING AROUND.

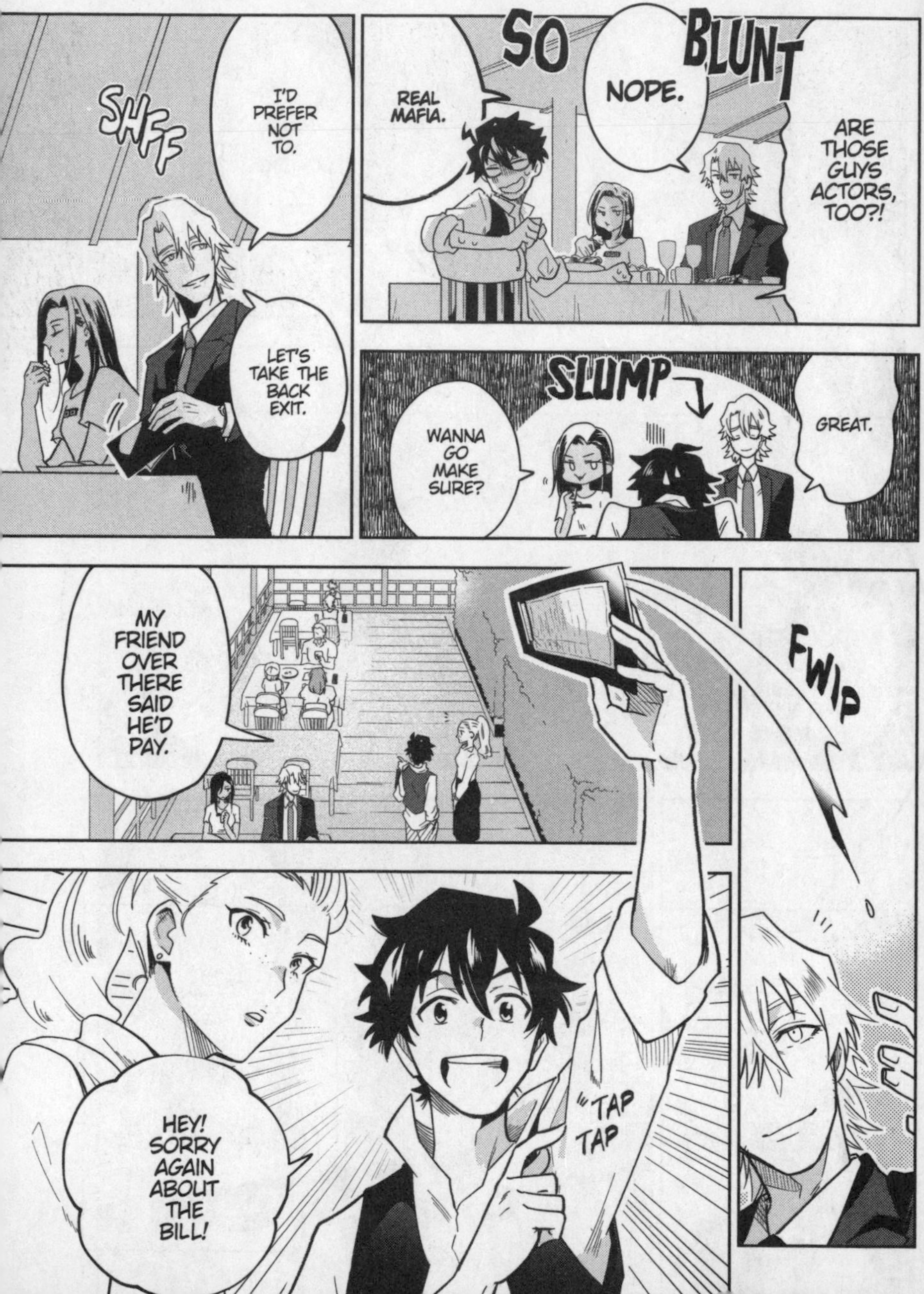
ARE THOSE GUYS ACTORS, TOO?!
NOPE.
SO BLUNT
REAL MAFIA.
GREAT.
SLUMP
WANNA GO MAKE SURE?
I'D PREFER NOT TO.
SHFF
LET'S TAKE THE BACK EXIT.
FWIP
MY FRIEND OVER THERE SAID HE'D PAY.
TAP TAP
HEY! SORRY AGAIN ABOUT THE BILL!

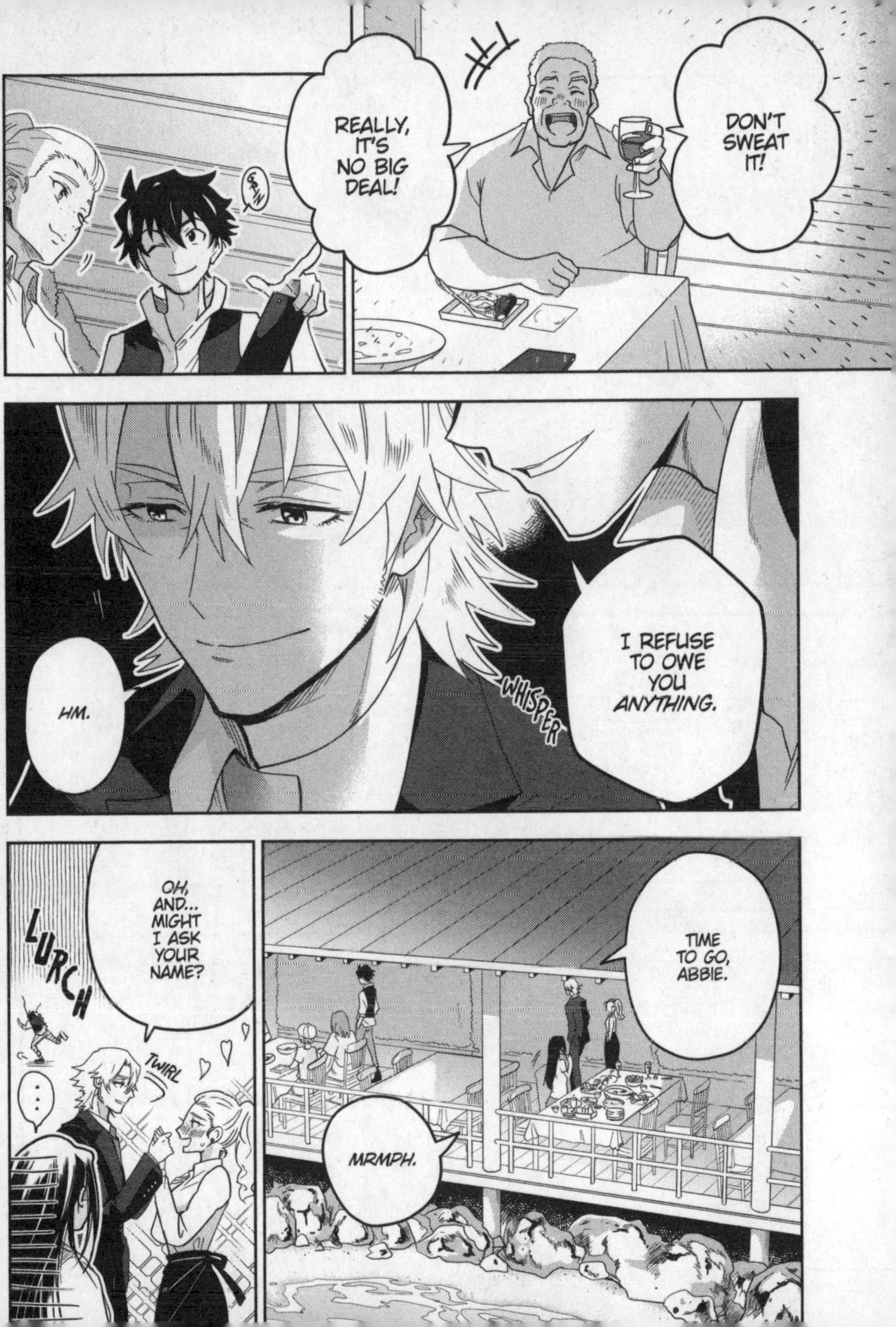
DON'T SWEAT IT!
REALLY, IT'S NO BIG DEAL!
GRIN
I REFUSE TO OWE YOU ANYTHING.
WHISPER
HM.
TIME TO GO, ABBIE.
MRMPH.
OH, AND... MIGHT I ASK YOUR NAME?
LURCH
TWIRL
...

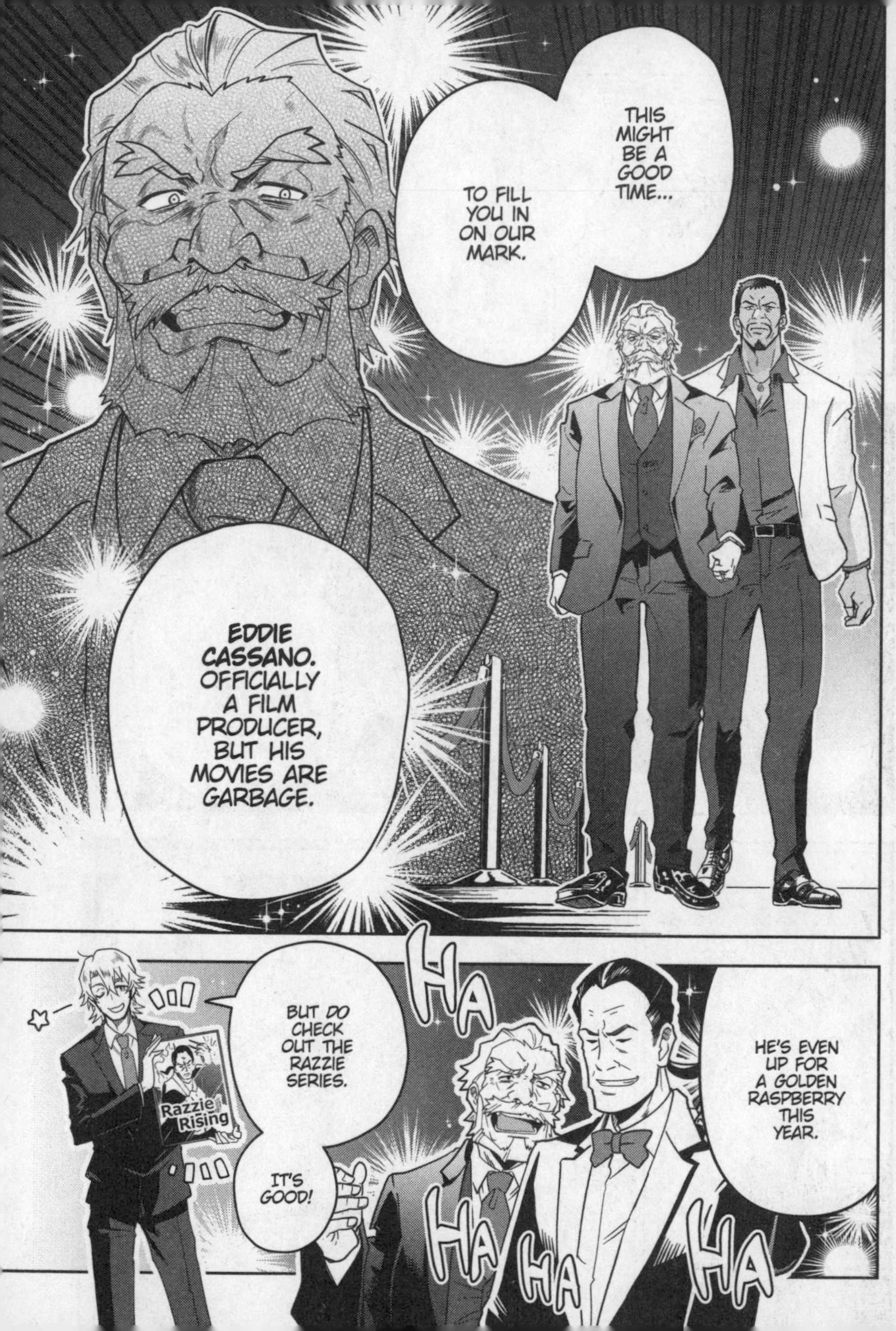
THIS MIGHT BE A GOOD TIME...
TO FILL YOU IN ON OUR MARK.
EDDIE CASSANO. OFFICIALLY A FILM PRODUCER, BUT HIS MOVIES ARE GARBAGE.
HE'S EVEN UP FOR A GOLDEN RASPBERRY THIS YEAR.
HA
HA HA HA HA
BUT DO CHECK OUT THE RAZZIE SERIES.
IT'S GOOD!
Razzie Rising

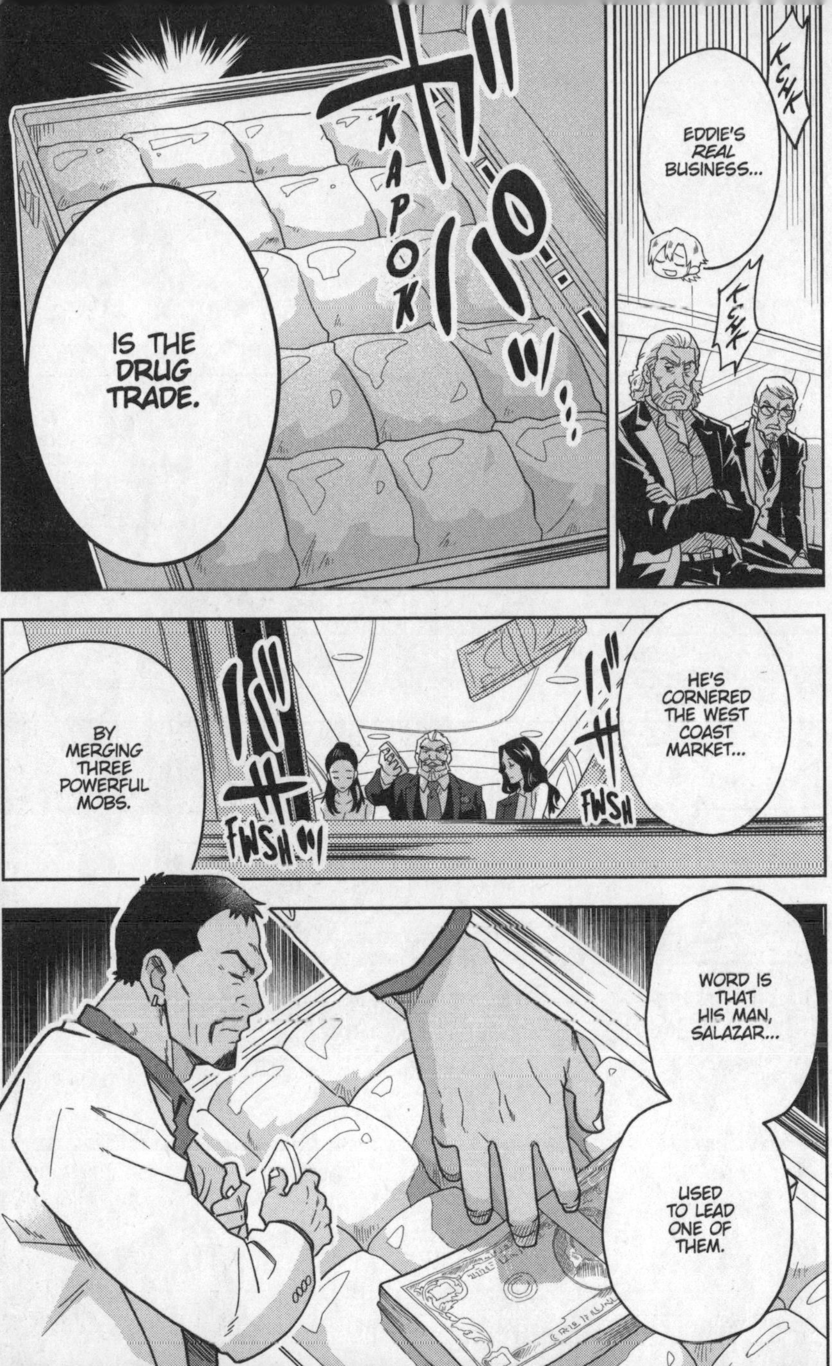
KCHK
EDDIE'S *REAL* BUSINESS...
KCHK
KAPOK
IS THE DRUG TRADE.
HE'S CORNERED THE WEST COAST MARKET...
FWSH
FWSH
BY MERGING THREE POWERFUL MOBS.
WORD IS THAT HIS MAN, SALAZAR...
USED TO LEAD ONE OF THEM.

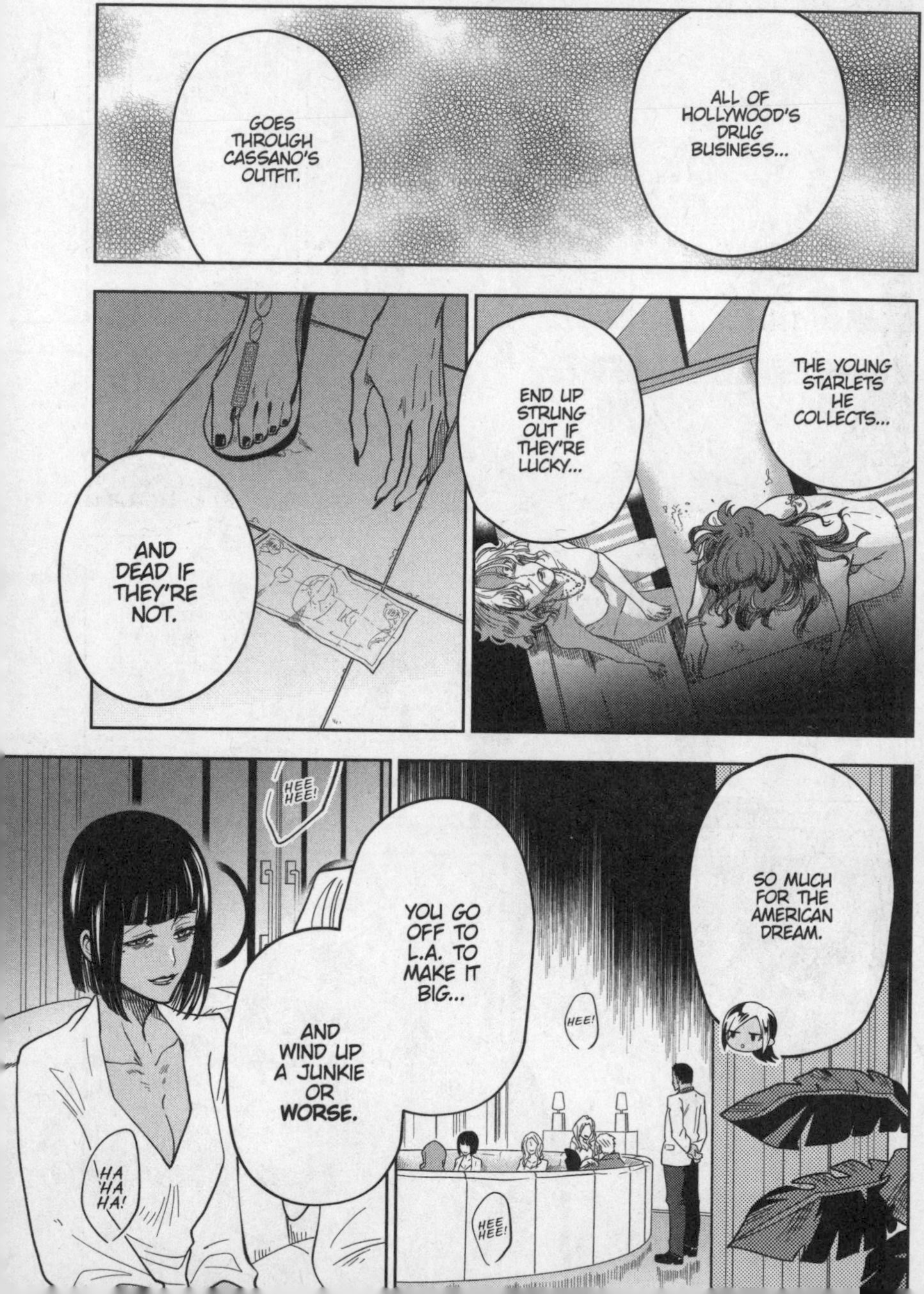
ALL OF HOLLYWOOD'S DRUG BUSINESS...
GOES THROUGH CASSANO'S OUTFIT.
THE YOUNG STARLETS HE COLLECTS...
END UP STRUNG OUT IF THEY'RE LUCKY...
AND DEAD IF THEY'RE NOT.
SO MUCH FOR THE AMERICAN DREAM.
HEE!
HEE HEE!
HEE HEE!
YOU GO OFF TO L.A. TO MAKE IT BIG...
AND WIND UP A JUNKIE OR WORSE.
HA HA HA!

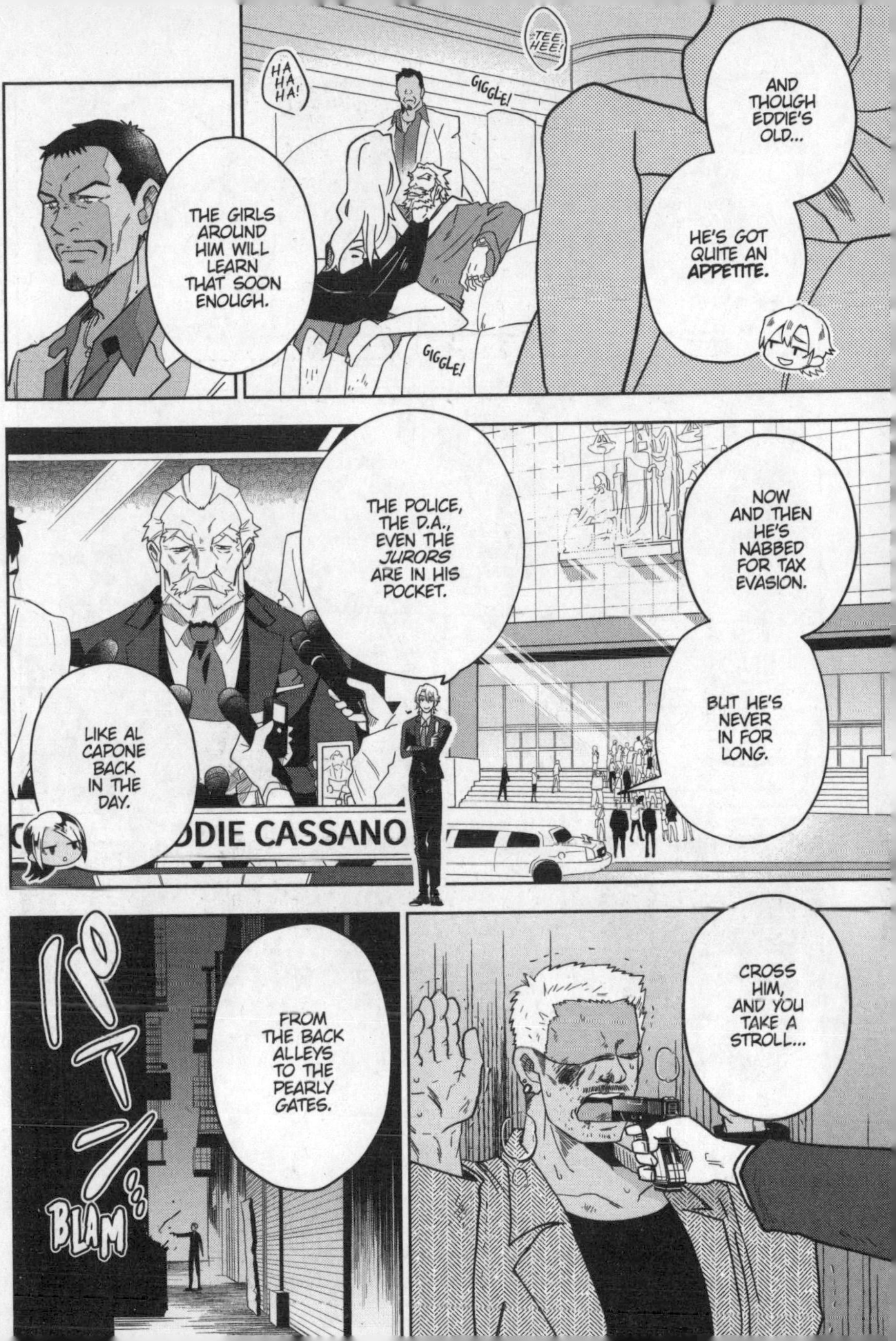
TEE HEE!
HA HA HA!
GIGGLE!
AND THOUGH EDDIE'S OLD...
HE'S GOT QUITE AN APPETITE.
GIGGLE!
THE GIRLS AROUND HIM WILL LEARN THAT SOON ENOUGH.
NOW AND THEN HE'S NABBED FOR TAX EVASION.
BUT HE'S NEVER IN FOR LONG.
THE POLICE, THE D.A., EVEN THE JURORS ARE IN HIS POCKET.
LIKE AL CAPONE BACK IN THE DAY.
DDIE CASSANO
CROSS HIM, AND YOU TAKE A STROLL...
FROM THE BACK ALLEYS TO THE PEARLY GATES.
BLAM

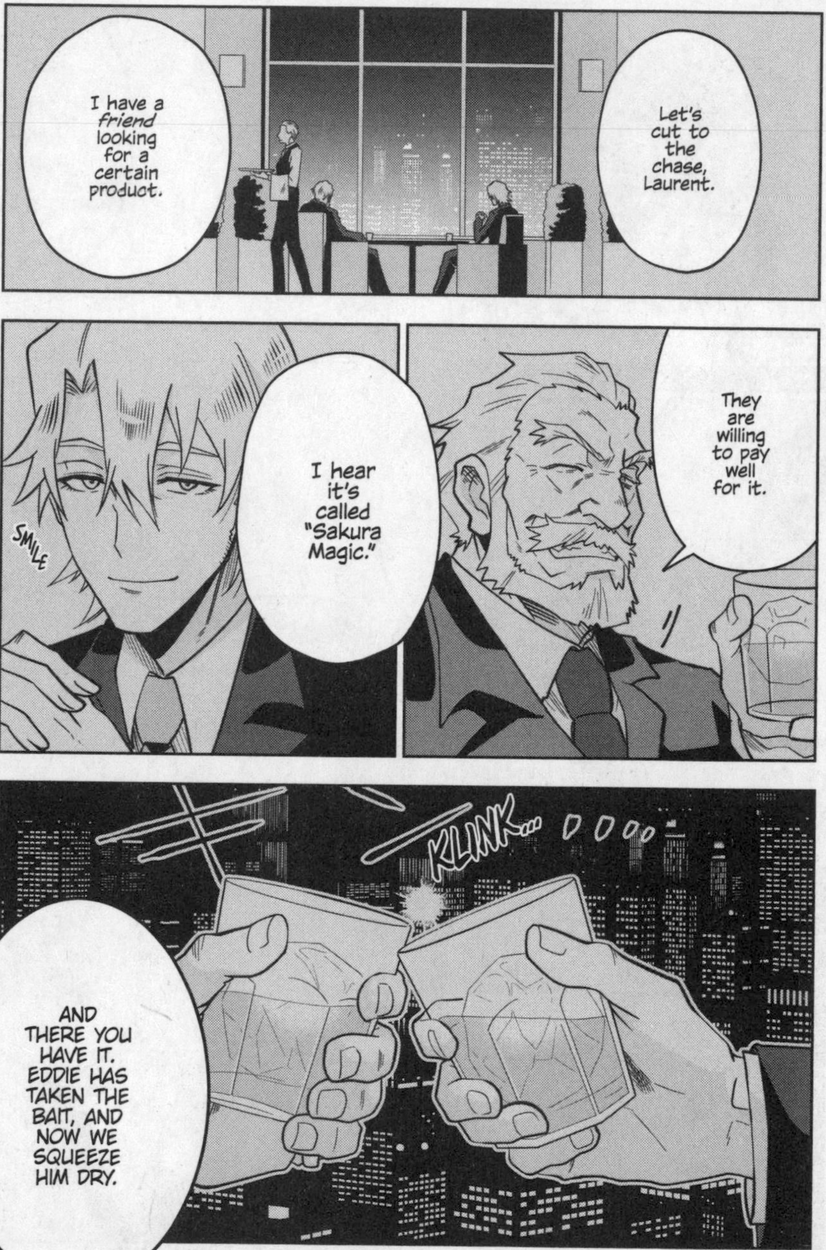
Let's cut to the chase, Laurent.
I have a *friend* looking for a certain product.
They are willing to pay well for it.
I hear it's called "Sakura Magic."
SMILE
KLINK...
AND THERE YOU HAVE IT. EDDIE HAS TAKEN THE BAIT, AND NOW WE SQUEEZE HIM DRY.

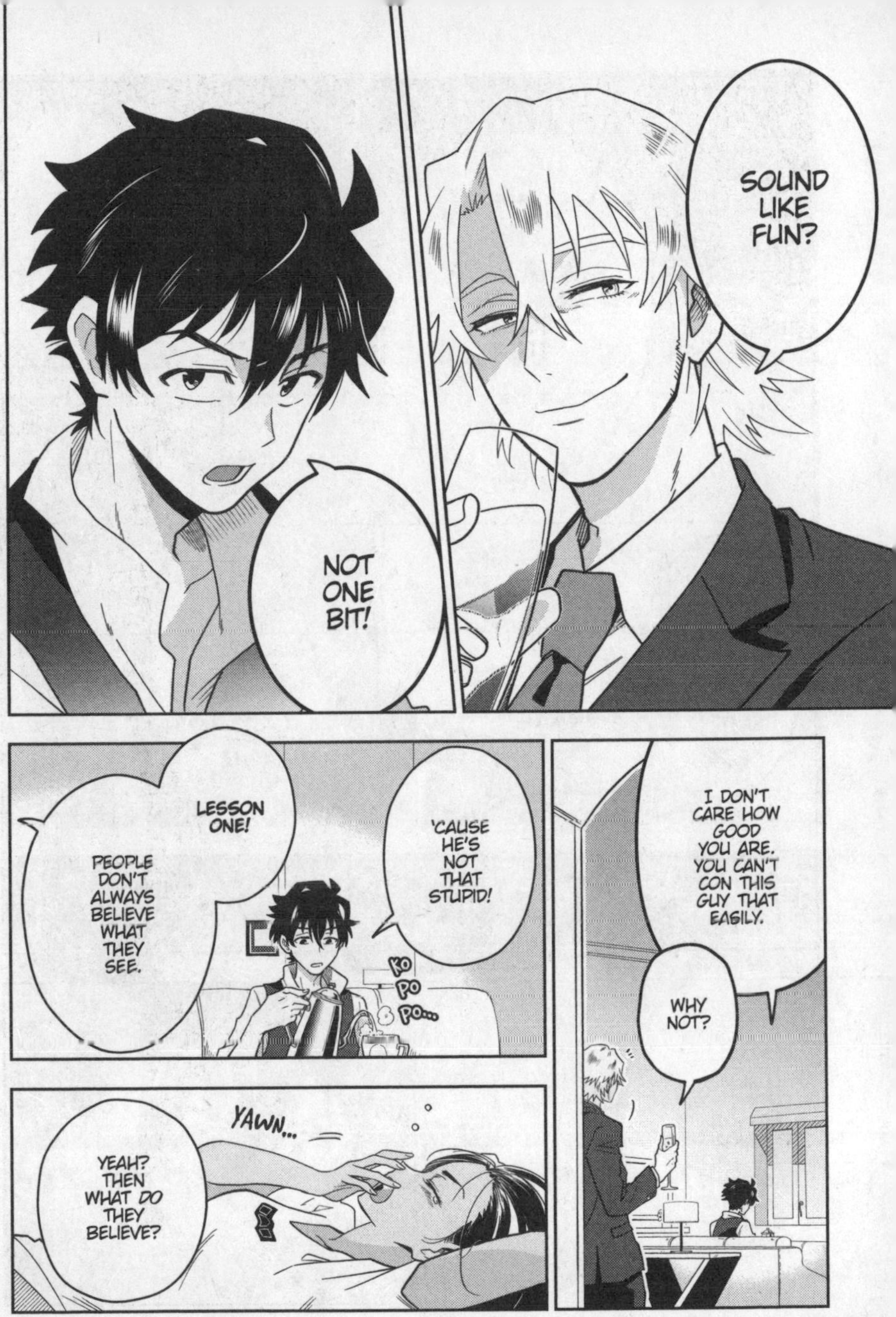
SOUND LIKE FUN?
NOT ONE BIT!
I DON'T CARE HOW GOOD YOU ARE. YOU CAN'T CON THIS GUY THAT EASILY.
WHY NOT?
'CAUSE HE'S NOT THAT STUPID!
KO PO PO...
LESSON ONE!
PEOPLE DON'T ALWAYS BELIEVE WHAT THEY SEE.
YAWN...
YEAH? THEN WHAT DO THEY BELIEVE?

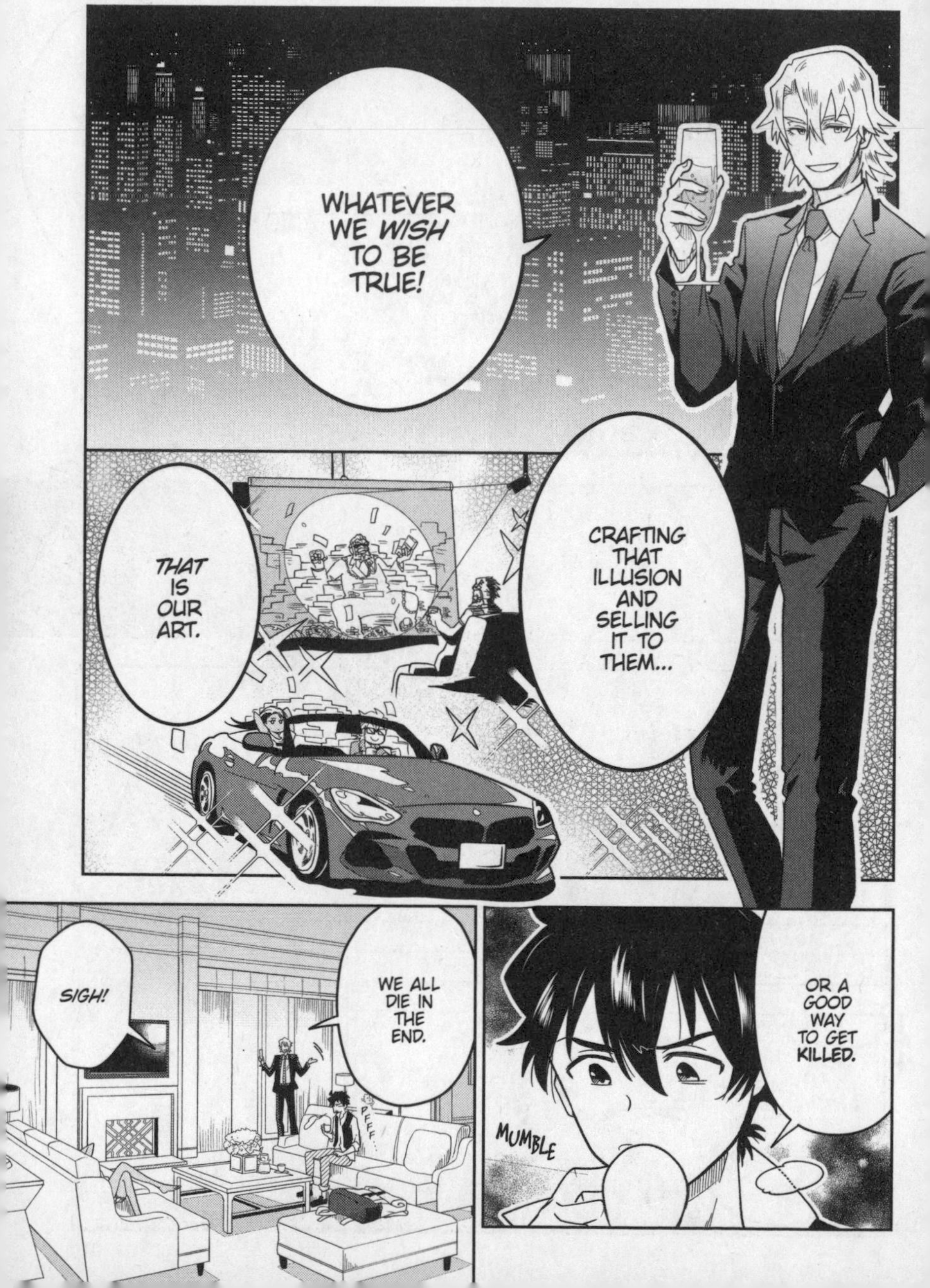
WHATEVER WE *WISH* TO BE TRUE!
CRAFTING THAT ILLUSION AND SELLING IT TO THEM...
THAT IS OUR ART.
OR A GOOD WAY TO GET KILLED.
MUMBLE
WE ALL DIE IN THE END.
PFFF...
SIGH!

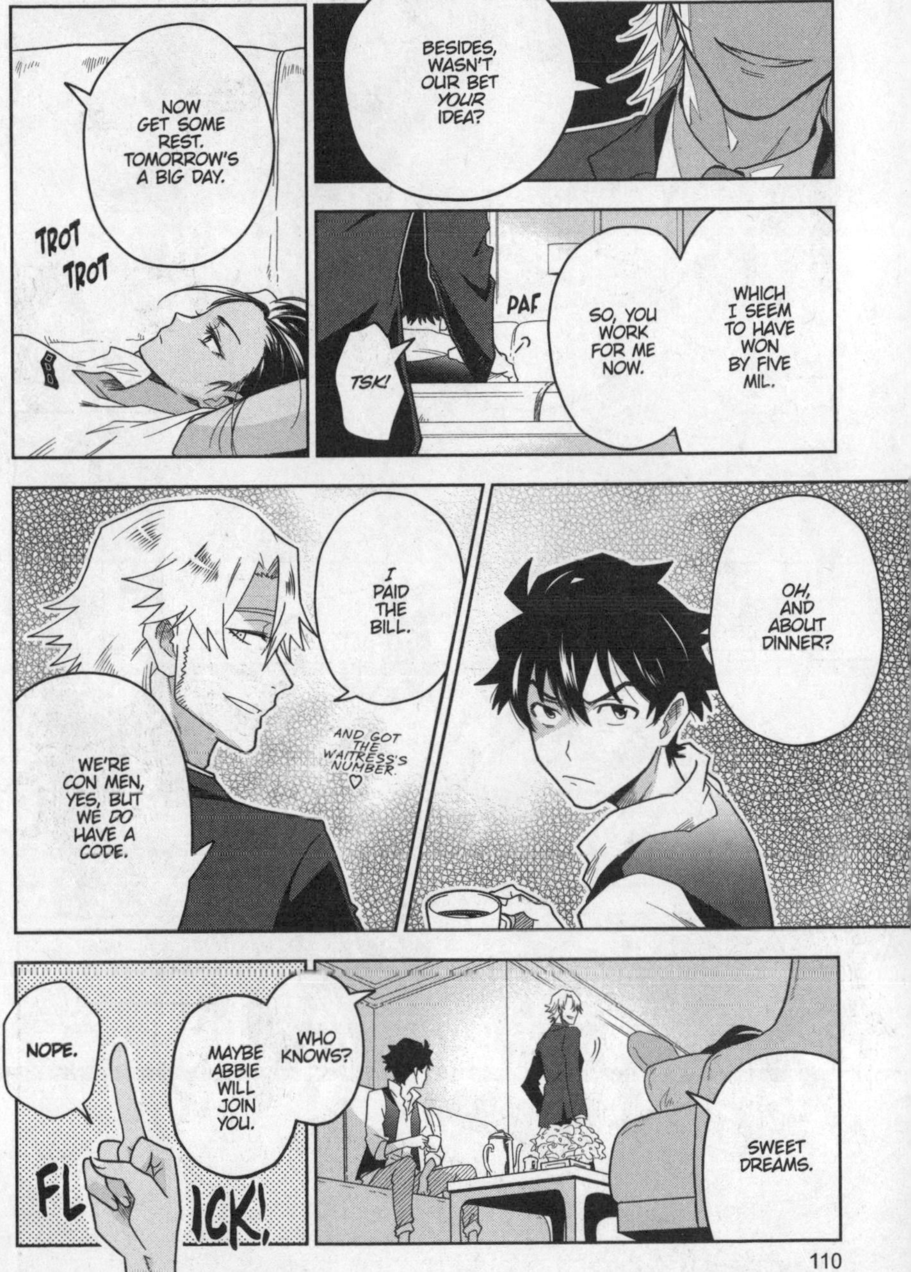
BESIDES, WASN'T OUR BET *YOUR* IDEA?
WHICH I SEEM TO HAVE WON BY FIVE MIL.
SO, YOU WORK FOR ME NOW.
PAF
TSK!
NOW GET SOME REST. TOMORROW'S A BIG DAY.
TROT TROT
OH, AND ABOUT DINNER?
I PAID THE BILL.
AND GOT THE WAITRESS'S NUMBER. ♡
WE'RE CON MEN, YES, BUT WE *DO* HAVE A CODE.
SWEET DREAMS.
WHO KNOWS?
MAYBE ABBIE WILL JOIN YOU.
NOPE.
FLICK!

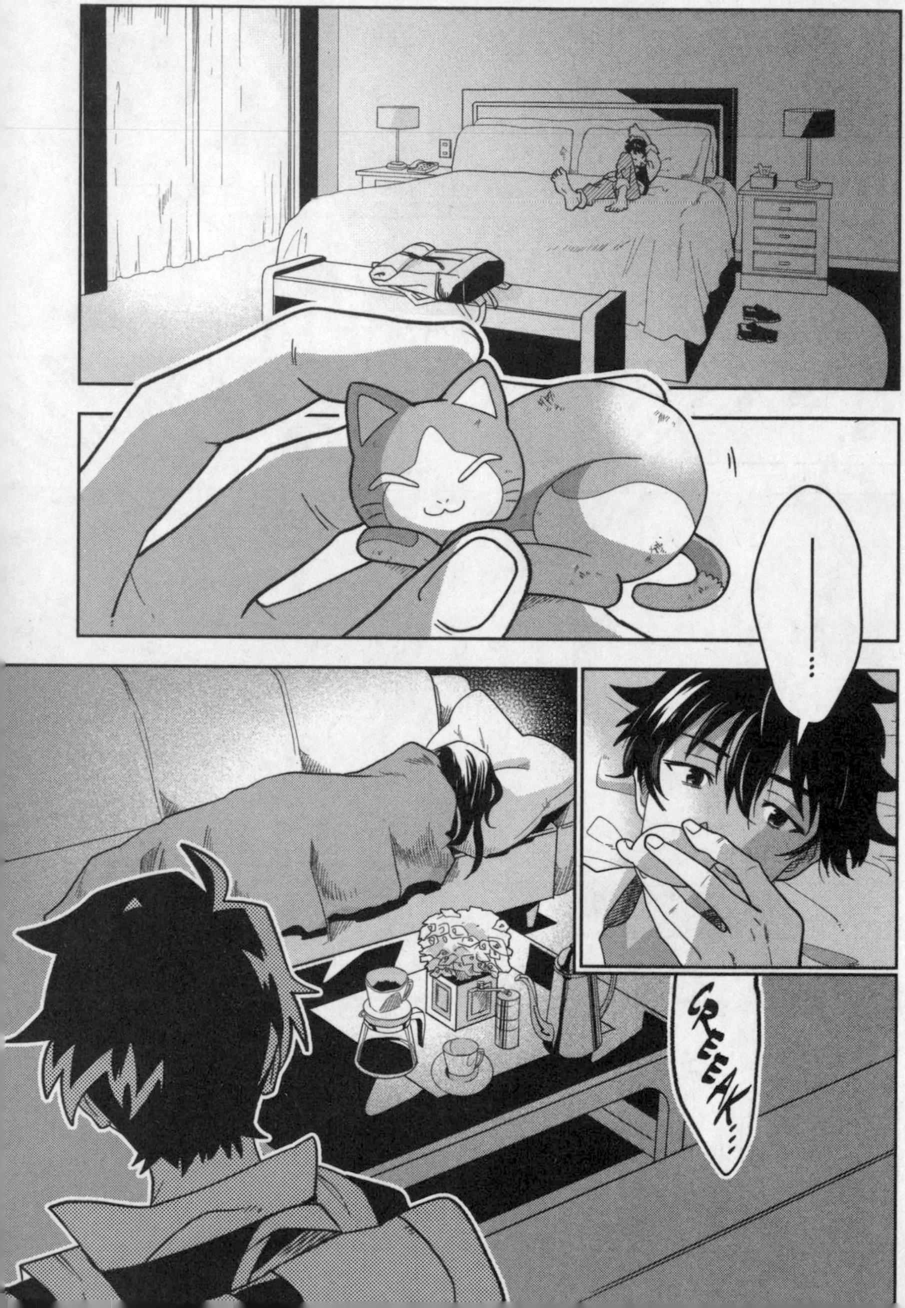
—...
CREEAK...

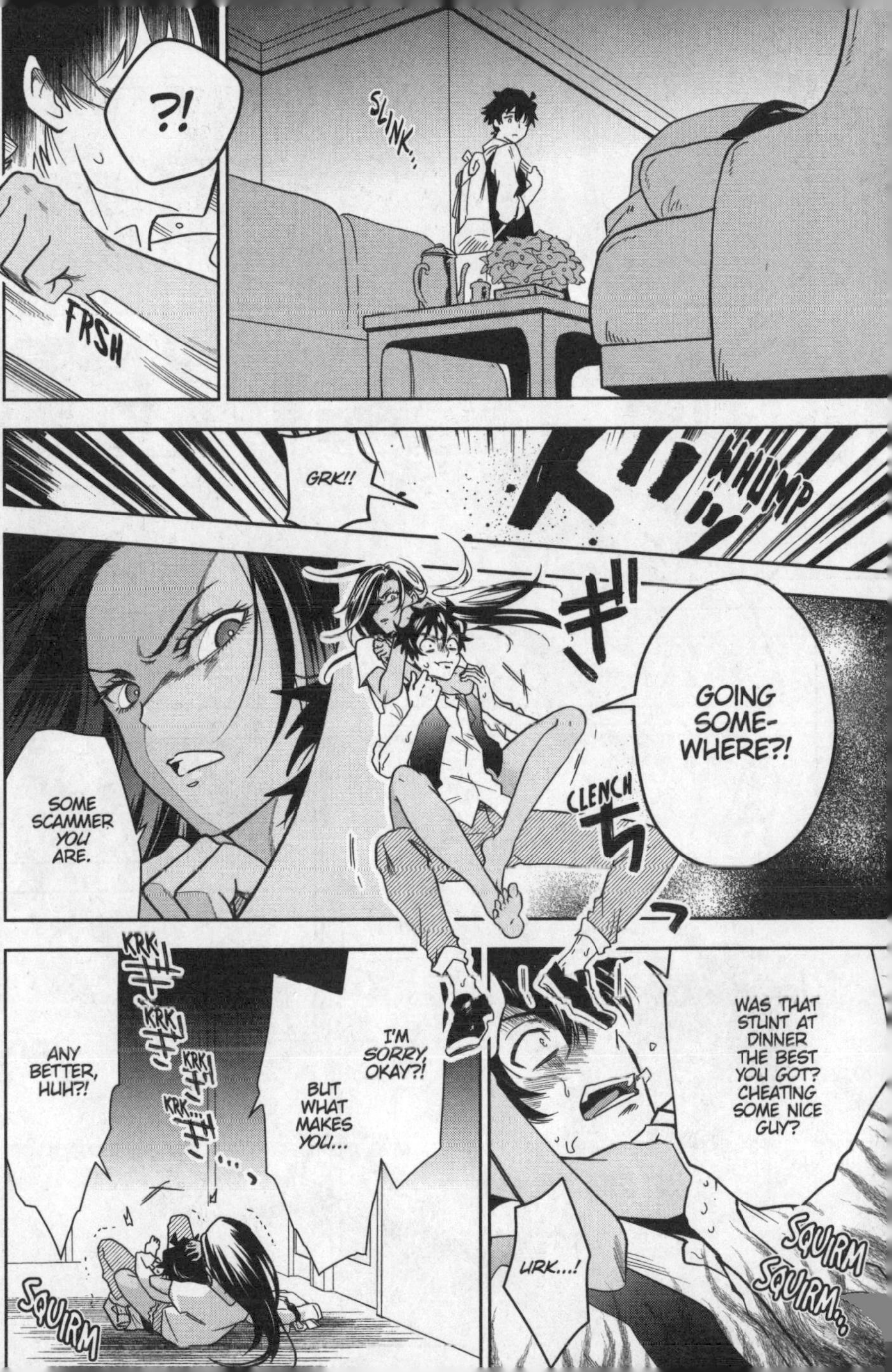
SLINK...
?!
FRSH
WHUMP
GRK!!
GOING SOME-WHERE?!
CLENCH
SOME SCAMMER YOU ARE.
WAS THAT STUNT AT DINNER THE BEST YOU GOT? CHEATING SOME NICE GUY?
SQUIRM SQUIRM...
URK...!
I'M SORRY, OKAY?!
BUT WHAT MAKES YOU...
ANY BETTER, HUH?!
KRK
KRK
KRK
KRK...
SQUIRM

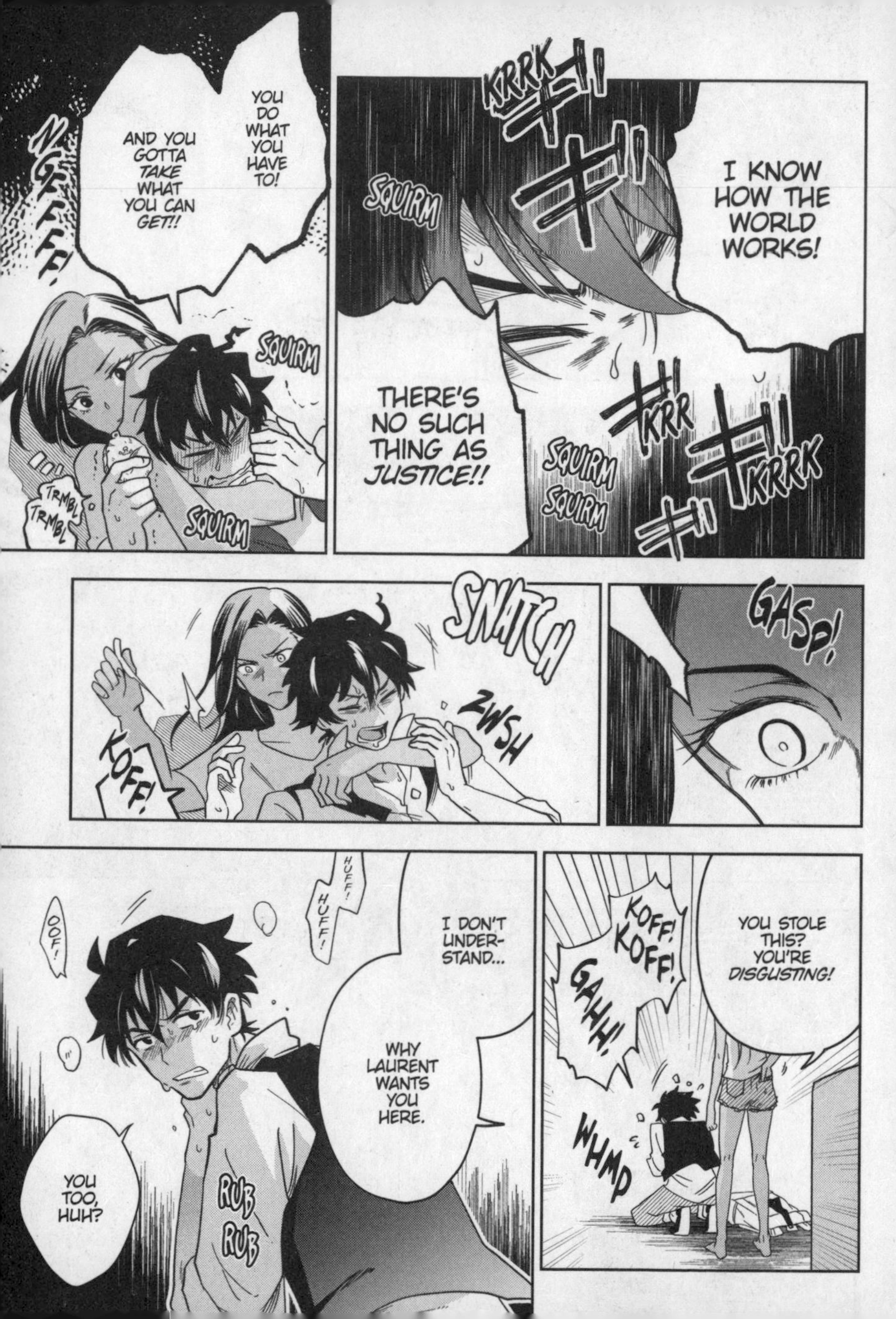
KRRK
SQUIRM
I KNOW HOW THE WORLD WORKS!
THERE'S NO SUCH THING AS JUSTICE!!
KRR
KRRK
SQUIRM SQUIRM
YOU DO WHAT YOU HAVE TO!
AND YOU GOTTA TAKE WHAT YOU CAN GET!!
NGFFFF!
SQUIRM
TRMBL TRMBL
SQUIRM
GASP!
SNATCH
ZWSH
KOFF!
YOU STOLE THIS? YOU'RE DISGUSTING!
KOFF! KOFF!
GAHH!
WHMP
HUFF! HUFF!
I DON'T UNDER-STAND...
WHY LAURENT WANTS YOU HERE.
OOF!
YOU TOO, HUH?
RUB RUB

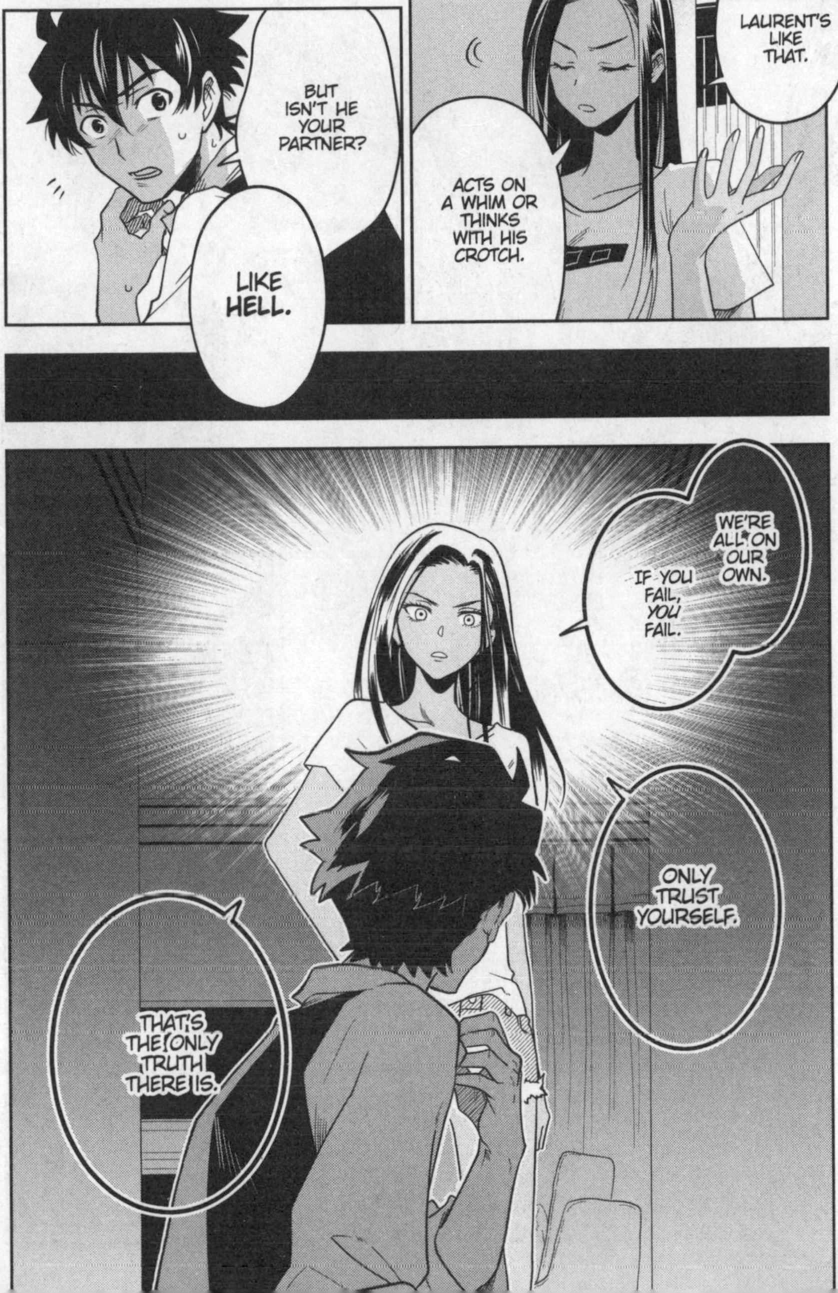
LAURENT'S LIKE THAT.
ACTS ON A WHIM OR THINKS WITH HIS CROTCH.
BUT ISN'T HE YOUR PARTNER?
LIKE HELL.
WE'RE ALL ON OUR OWN.
IF YOU FAIL, YOU FAIL.
ONLY TRUST YOURSELF.
THAT'S THE ONLY TRUTH THERE IS.

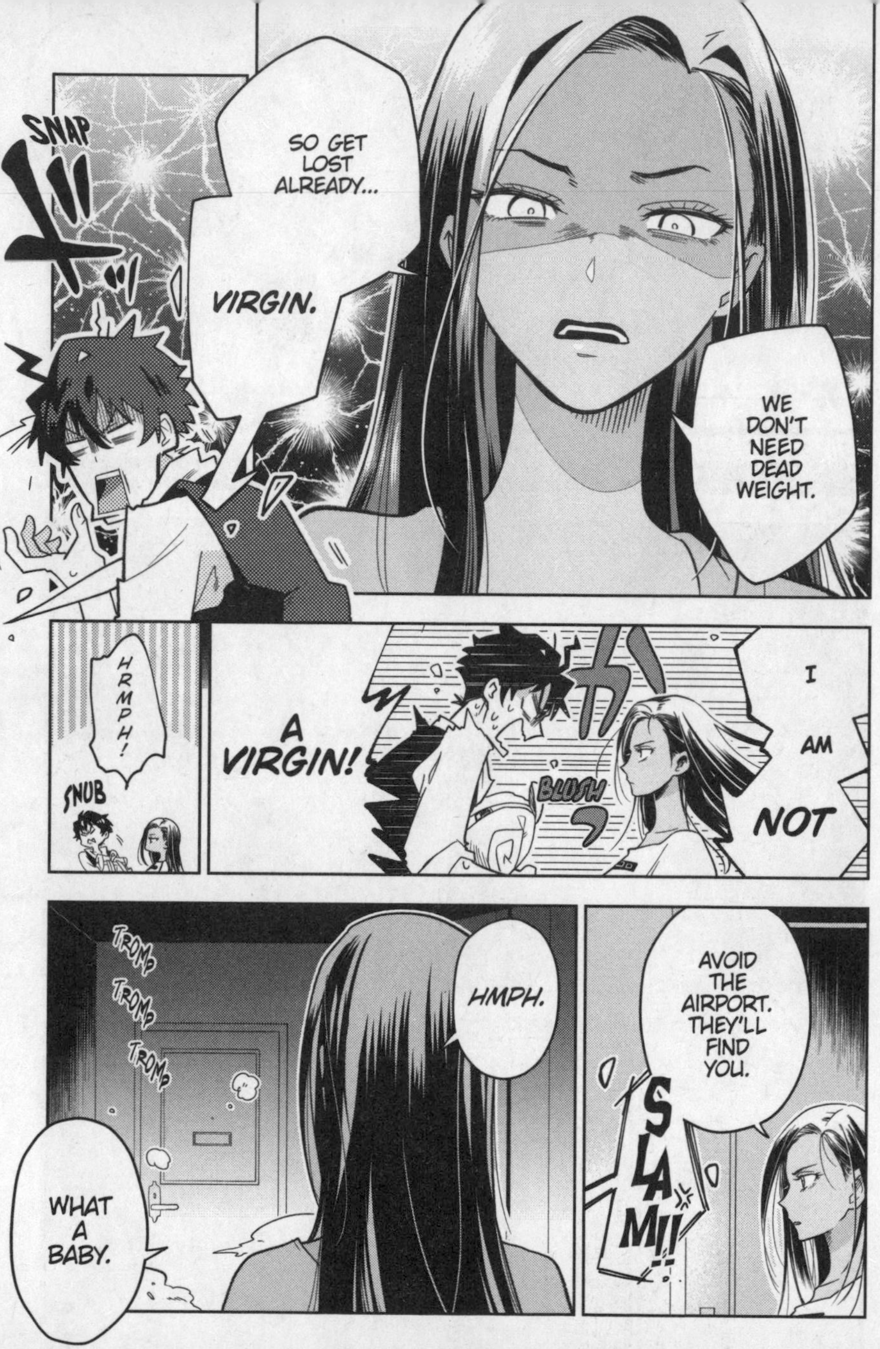
WE DON'T NEED DEAD WEIGHT.
SO GET LOST ALREADY... VIRGIN.
SNAP
I AM NOT A VIRGIN!
BLUSH
HRMPH!
SNUB
AVOID THE AIRPORT. THEY'LL FIND YOU.
SLAM!!
HMPH.
TROMP
TROMP
TROMP
WHAT A BABY.

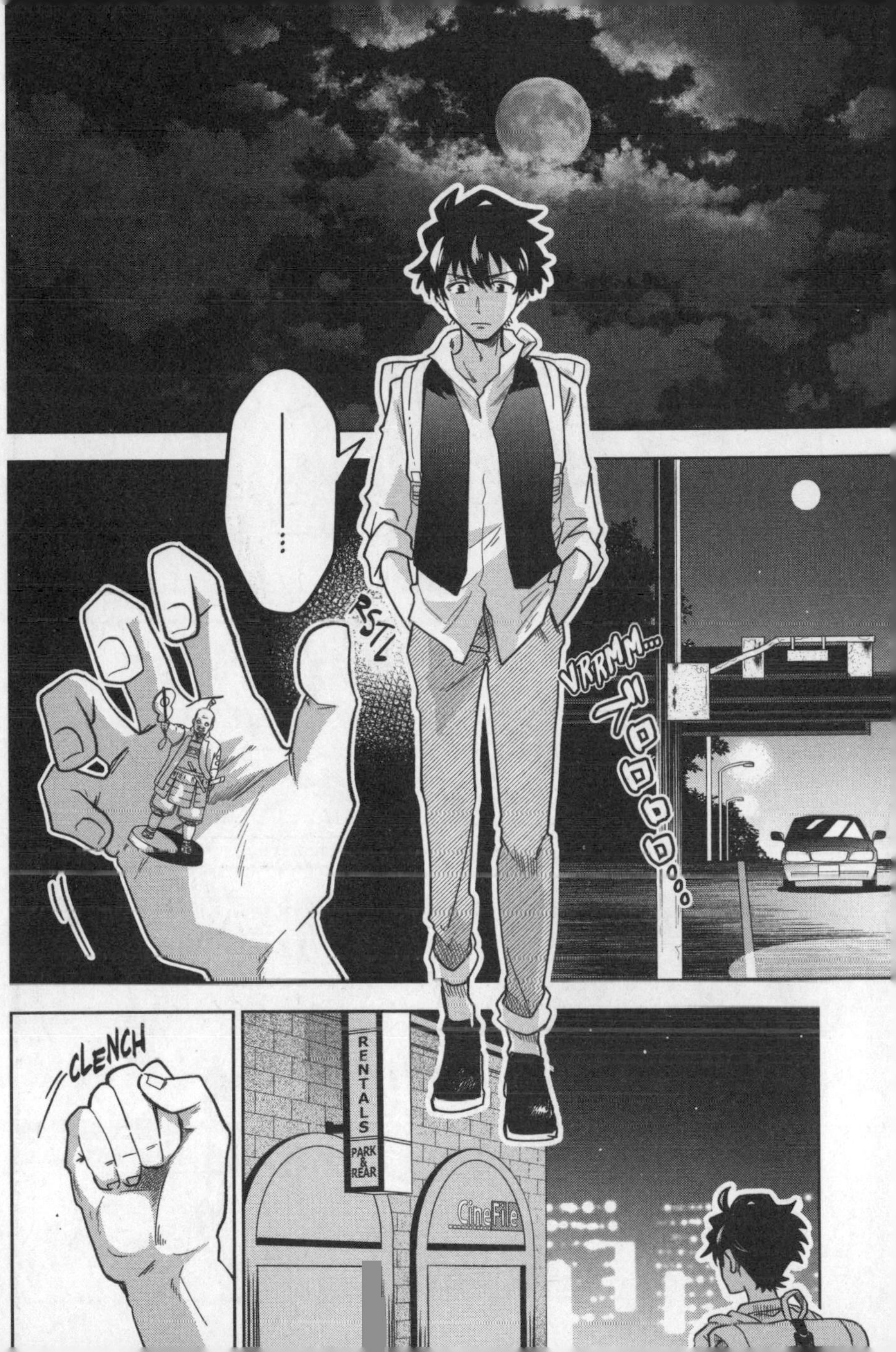

VRRMM...
ブロロロ...
RSTL
—...
RENTALS
PARK & REAR
CineFile
CLENCH

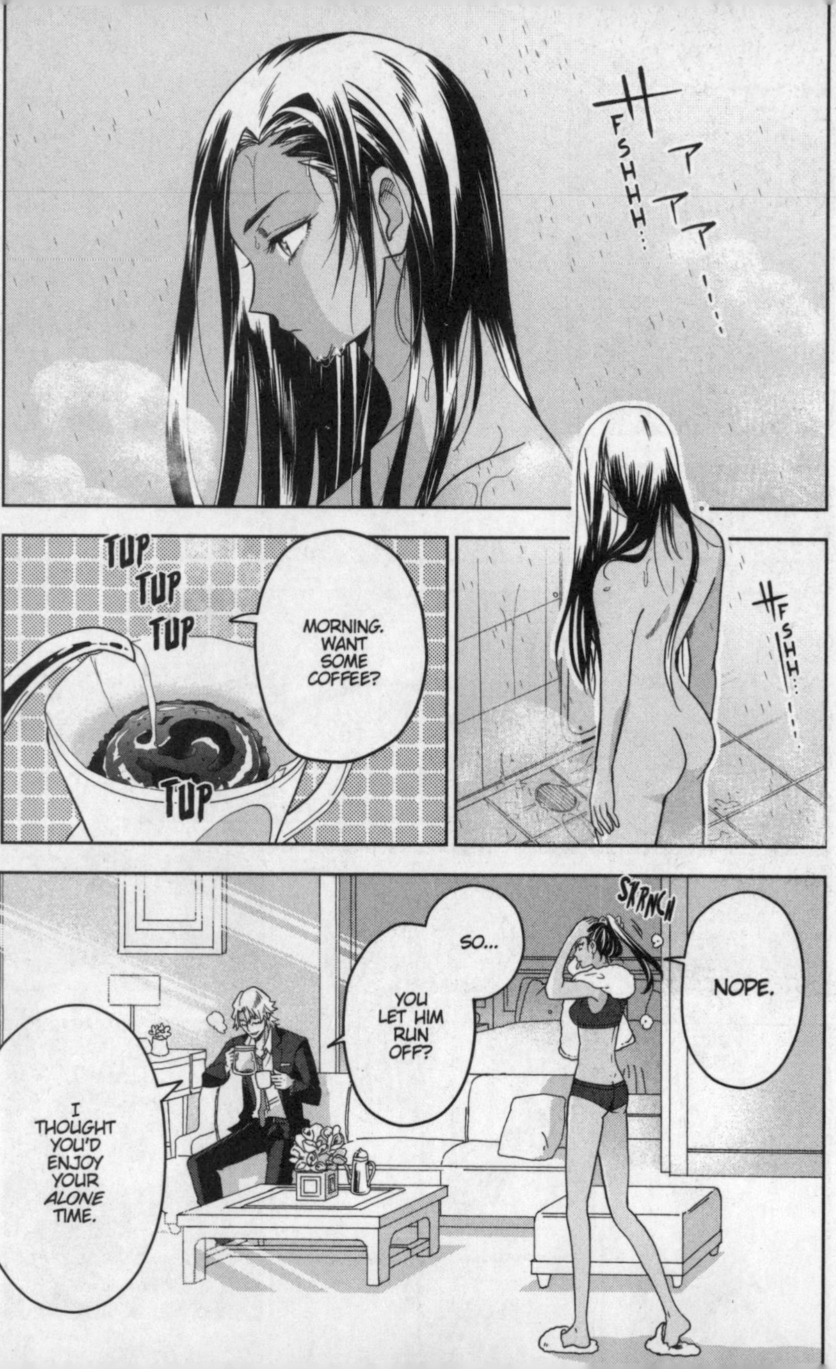
FSHHH...
FSHH...
TUP
TUP
TUP
TUP
MORNING. WANT SOME COFFEE?
SKRNCH
NOPE.
SO...
YOU LET HIM RUN OFF?
I THOUGHT YOU'D ENJOY YOUR *ALONE* TIME.

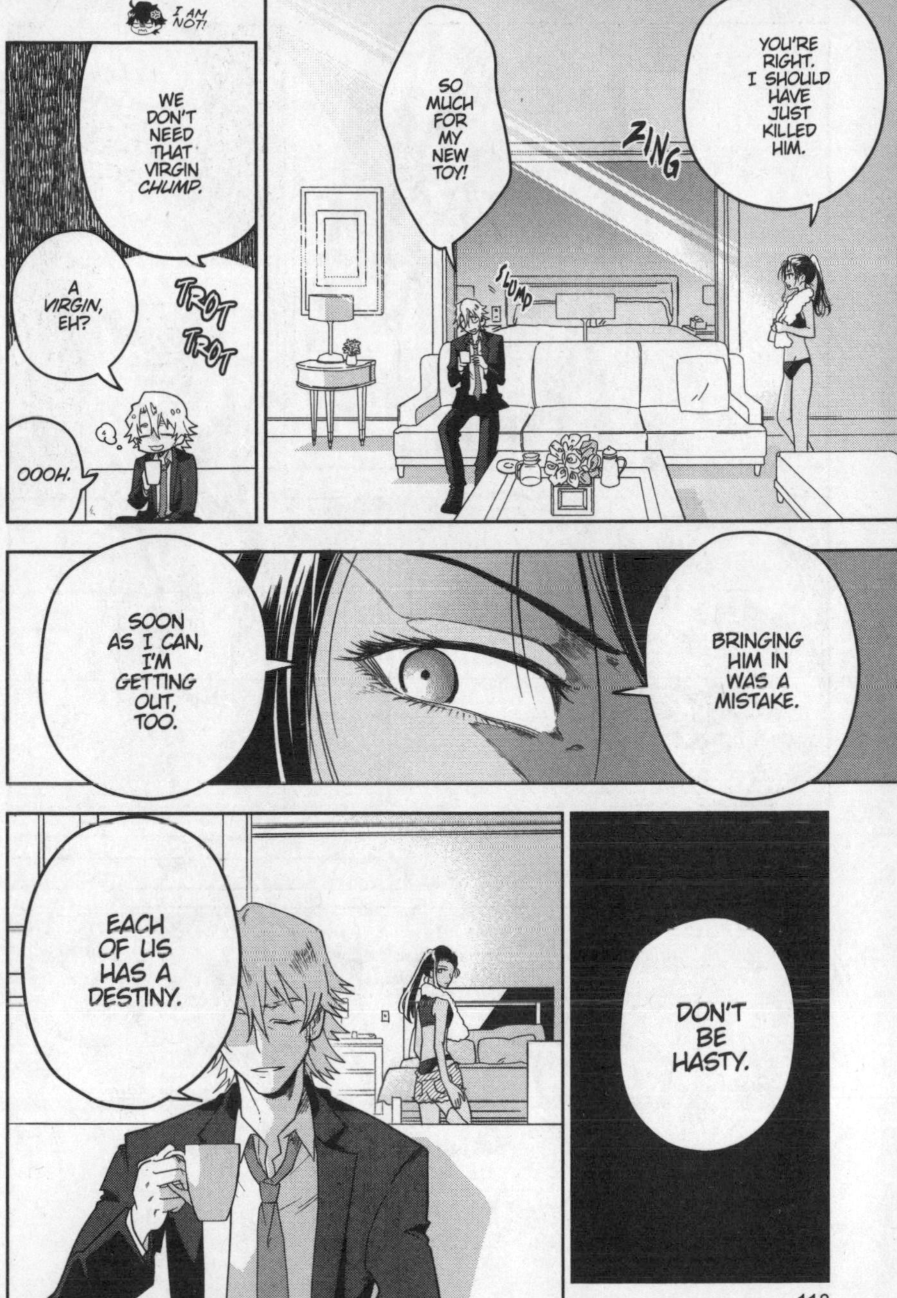
YOU'RE RIGHT. I SHOULD HAVE JUST KILLED HIM.
ZING
SO MUCH FOR MY NEW TOY!
SLUMP
I AM NOT!
WE DON'T NEED THAT VIRGIN CHUMP.
A VIRGIN, EH?
TROT TROT
OOOH.
BRINGING HIM IN WAS A MISTAKE.
SOON AS I CAN, I'M GETTING OUT, TOO.
DON'T BE HASTY.
EACH OF US HAS A DESTINY.

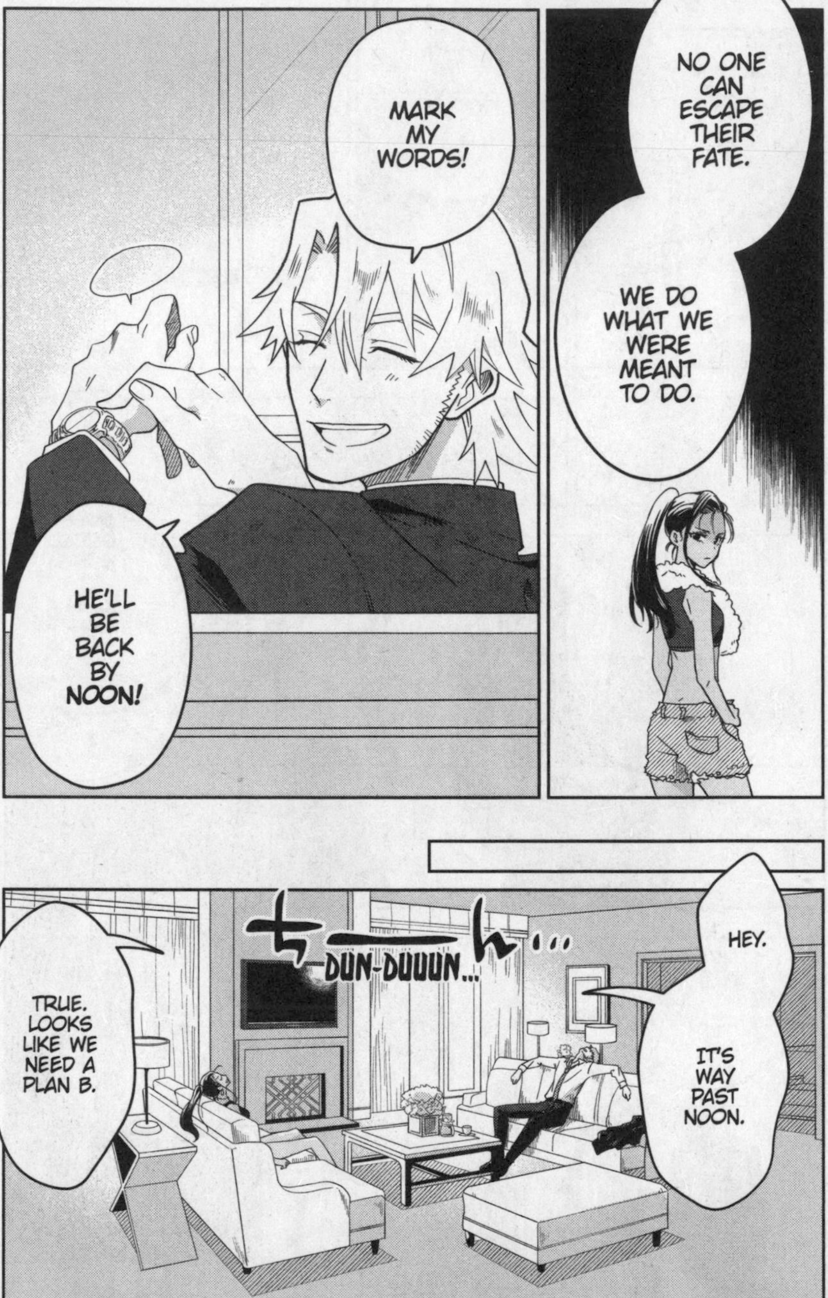
NO ONE CAN ESCAPE THEIR FATE.
WE DO WHAT WE WERE MEANT TO DO.
MARK MY WORDS!
HE'LL BE BACK BY NOON!
HEY.
IT'S WAY PAST NOON.
ち——ん...
DUN-DUUUN...
TRUE. LOOKS LIKE WE NEED A PLAN B.

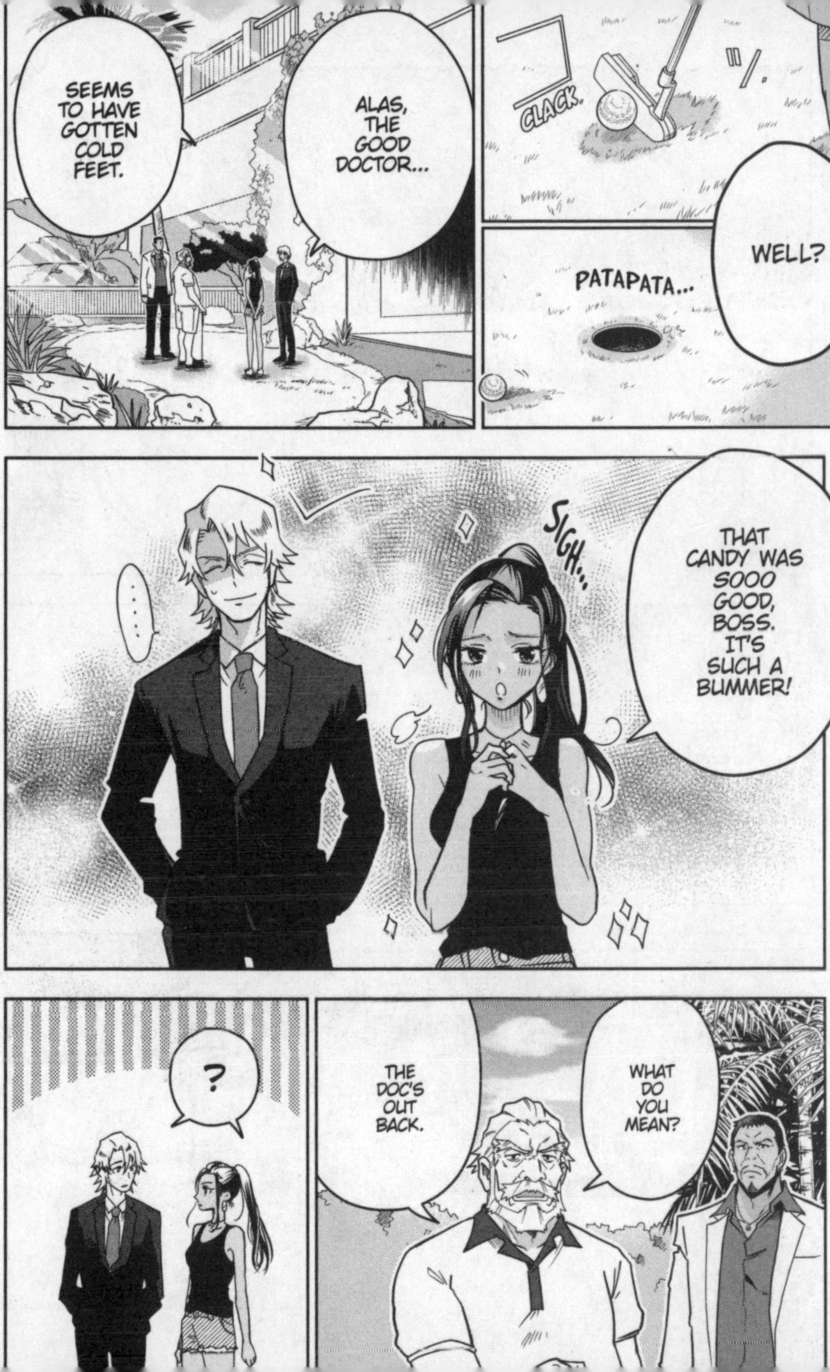
CLACK.
WELL?
PATAPATA...
ALAS, THE GOOD DOCTOR...
SEEMS TO HAVE GOTTEN COLD FEET.
THAT CANDY WAS SOOO GOOD, BOSS. IT'S SUCH A BUMMER!
SIGH...
......
WHAT DO YOU MEAN?
THE DOC'S OUT BACK.
?

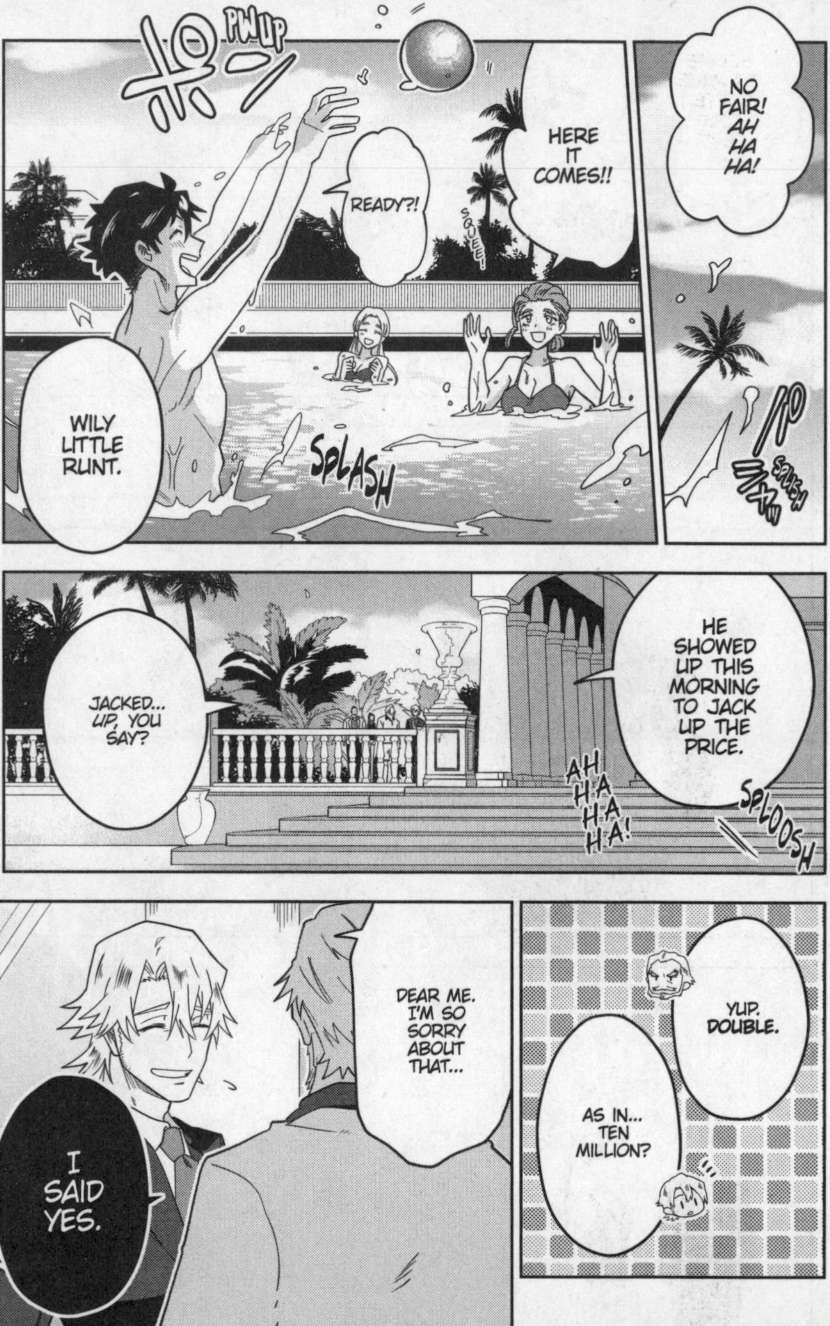
NO FAIR! AH HA HA!
SPLISH
HERE IT COMES!!
READY?!
PWUP
SQUEE!
WILY LITTLE RUNT.
SPLASH
HE SHOWED UP THIS MORNING TO JACK UP THE PRICE.
SPLOOSH
AHAHAHAHA!
JACKED... UP, YOU SAY?
YUP. DOUBLE.
AS IN... TEN MILLION?
DEAR ME. I'M SO SORRY ABOUT THAT...
I SAID YES.

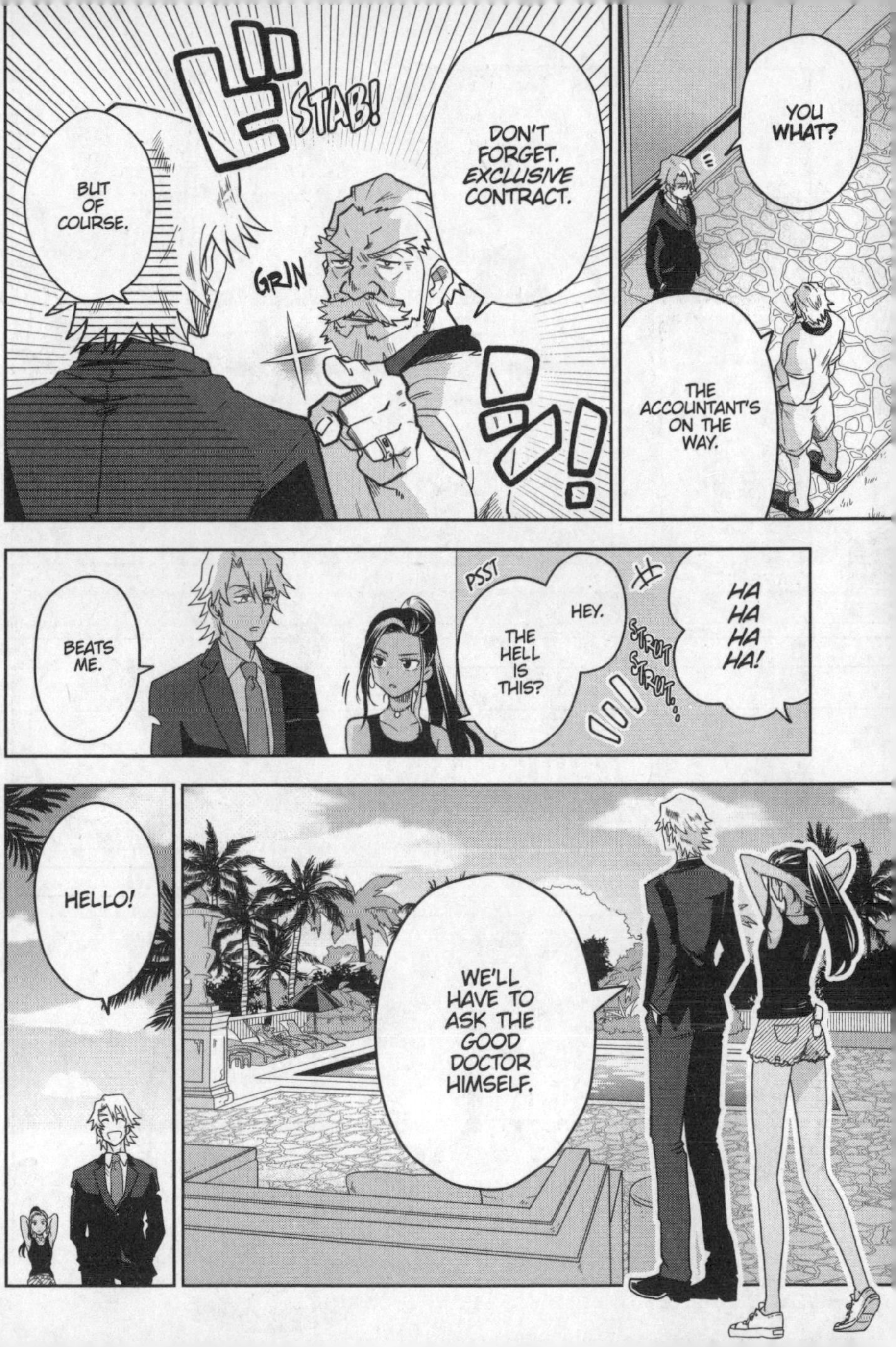
YOU WHAT?
THE ACCOUNTANT'S ON THE WAY.
DON'T FORGET. *EXCLUSIVE* CONTRACT.
STAB!
GRIN
BUT OF COURSE.
HA HA HA HA!
STRUT STRUT
HEY.
THE HELL IS THIS?
PSST
BEATS ME.
WE'LL HAVE TO ASK THE GOOD DOCTOR HIMSELF.
HELLO!

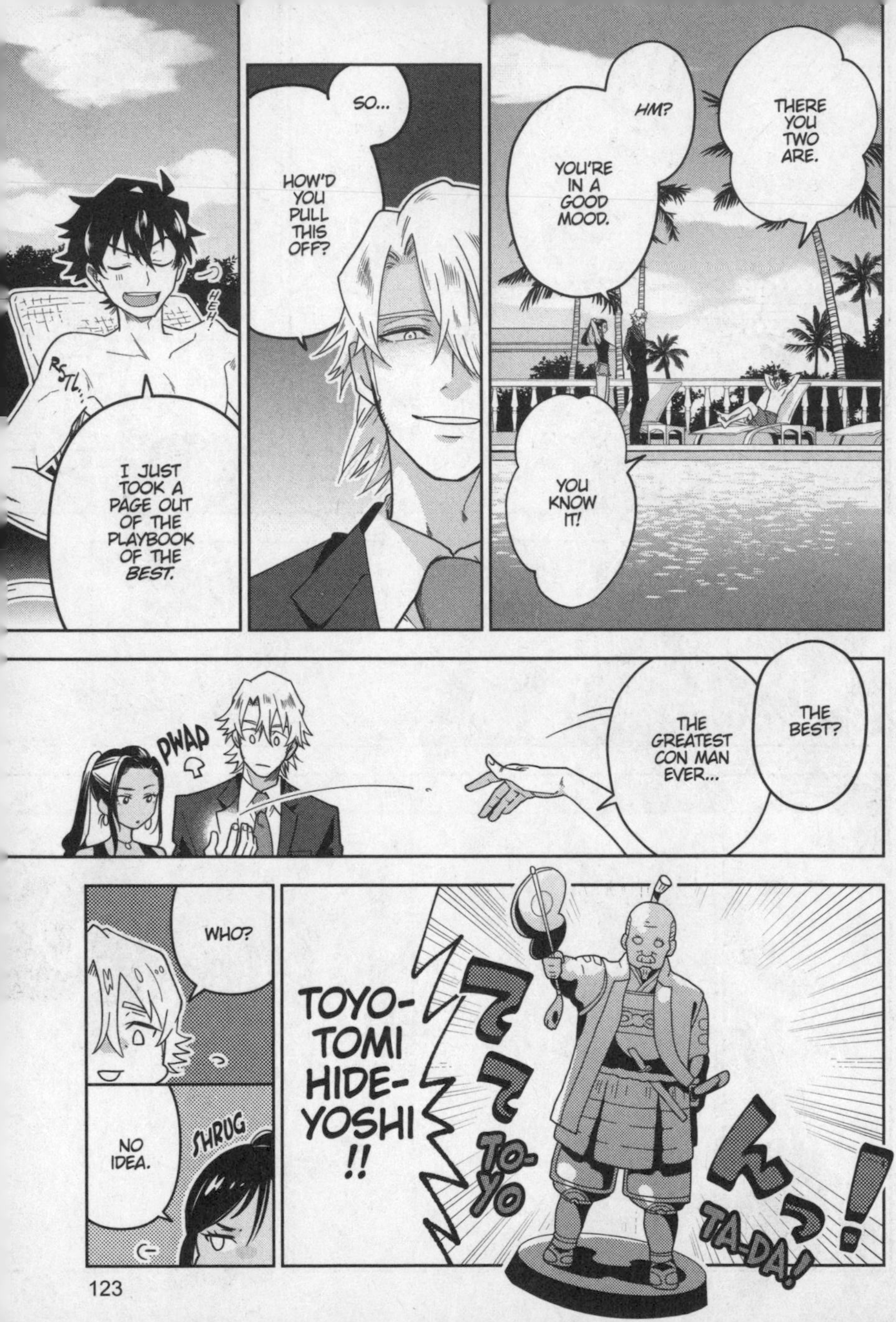
THERE YOU TWO ARE.
HM?
YOU'RE IN A GOOD MOOD.
YOU KNOW IT!
SO...
HOW'D YOU PULL THIS OFF?
HEH!
RSTL...
I JUST TOOK A PAGE OUT OF THE PLAYBOOK OF THE BEST.
THE BEST?
THE GREATEST CON MAN EVER...
PWAP
TOYO-TOMI HIDE-YOSHI!!
TO-YO
TA-DA!
WHO?
SHRUG
NO IDEA.

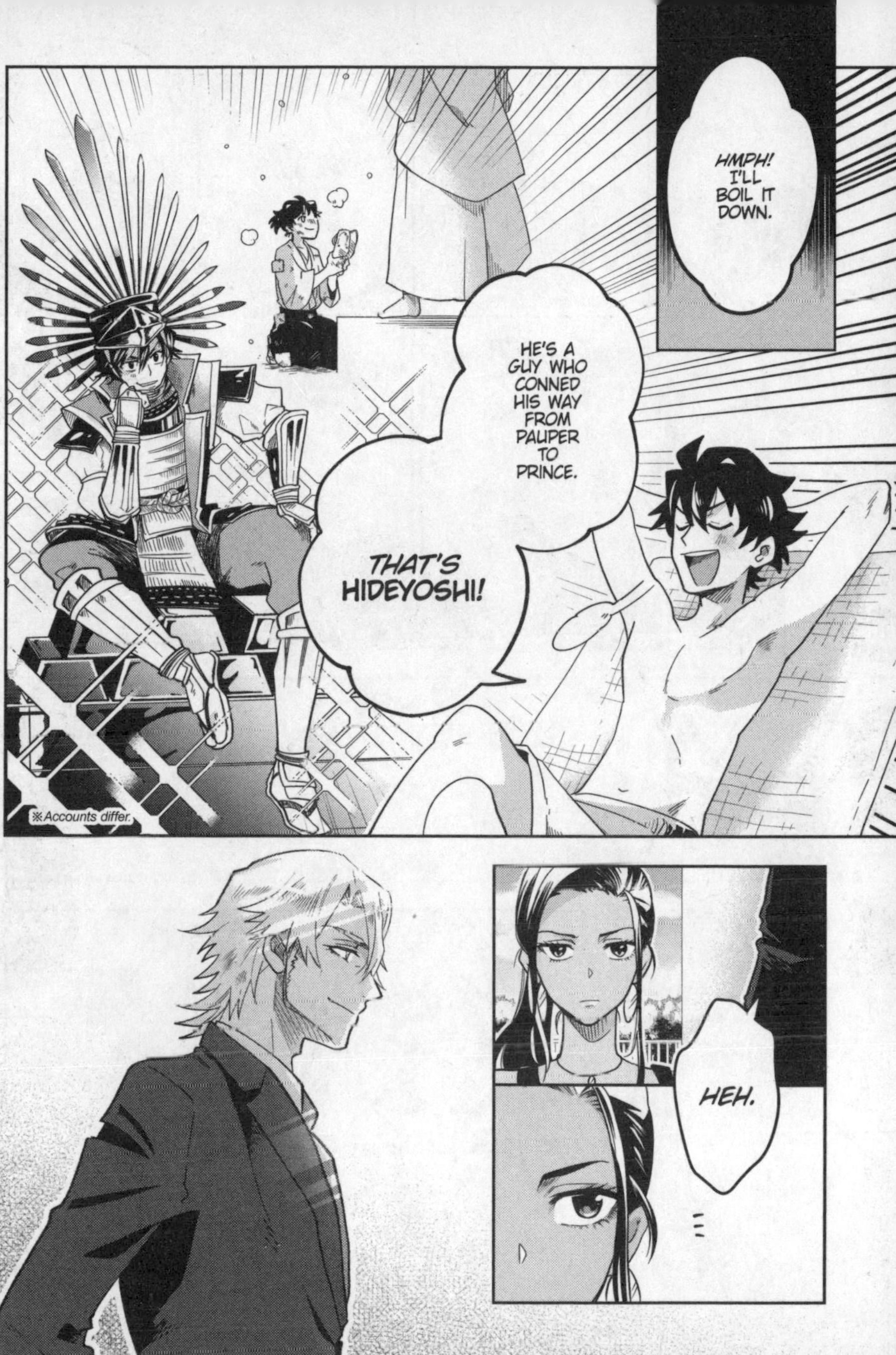
HMPH! I'LL BOIL IT DOWN.
HE'S A GUY WHO CONNED HIS WAY FROM PAUPER TO PRINCE.
THAT'S HIDEYOSHI!
※Accounts differ.
HEH.

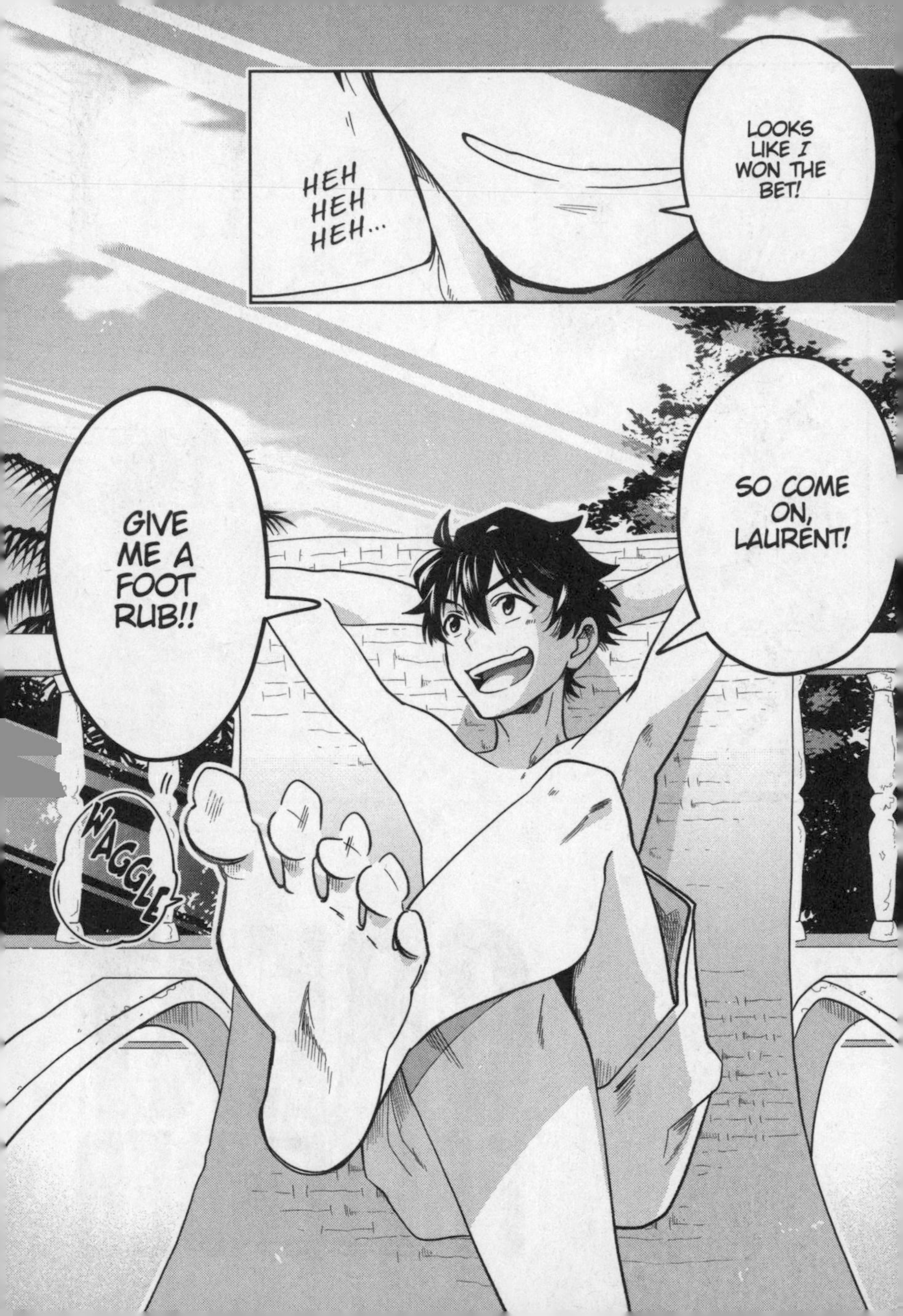
LOOKS LIKE I WON THE BET!
HEH HEH HEH...
SO COME ON, LAURENT!
GIVE ME A FOOT RUB!!
WAGGLE

GREAT

グレートプリテンダー

PRETENDER

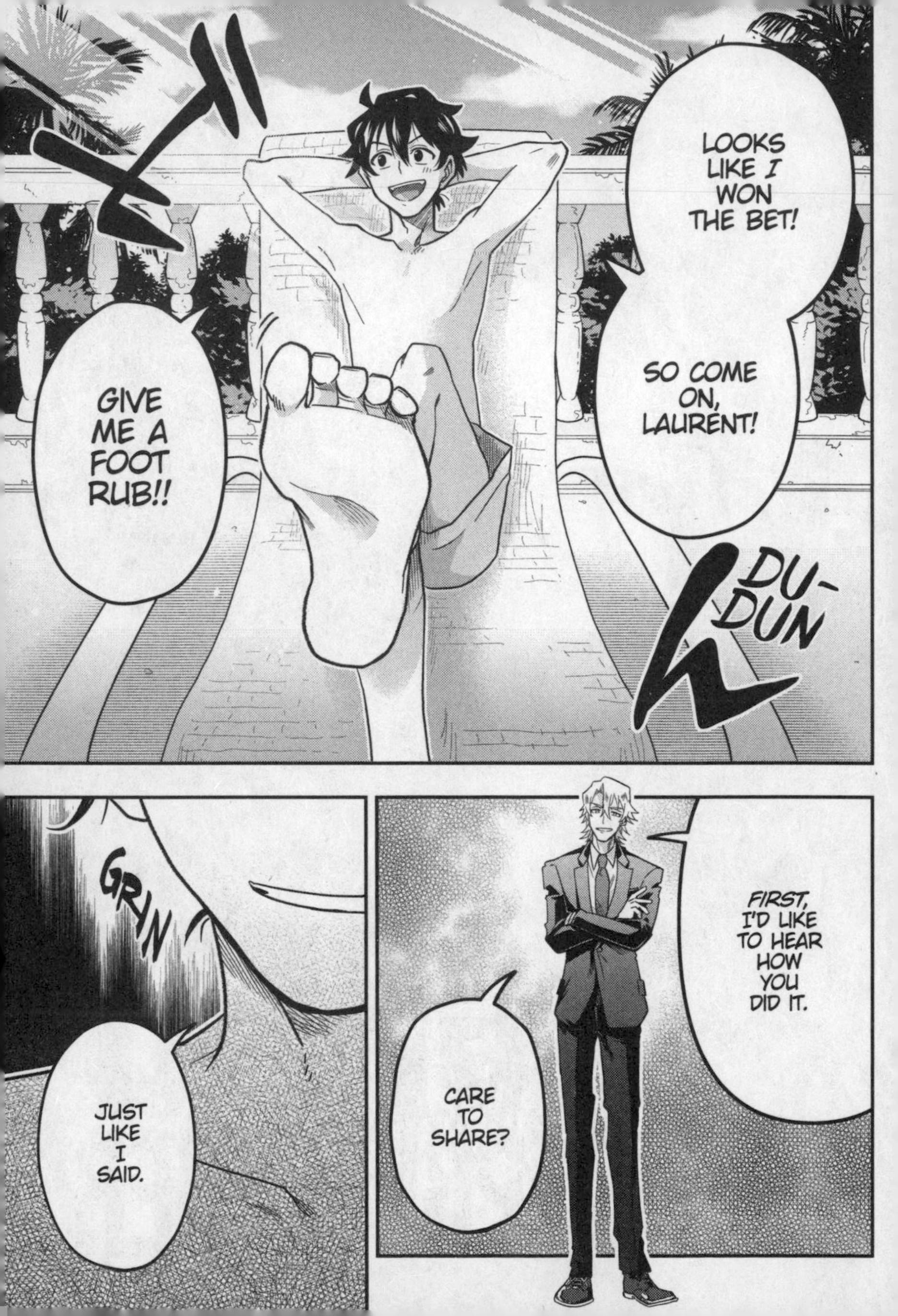
LOOKS LIKE I WON THE BET!
SO COME ON, LAURENT!
DU-DUN
GIVE ME A FOOT RUB!!
FIRST, I'D LIKE TO HEAR HOW YOU DID IT.
CARE TO SHARE?
GRIN
JUST LIKE I SAID.

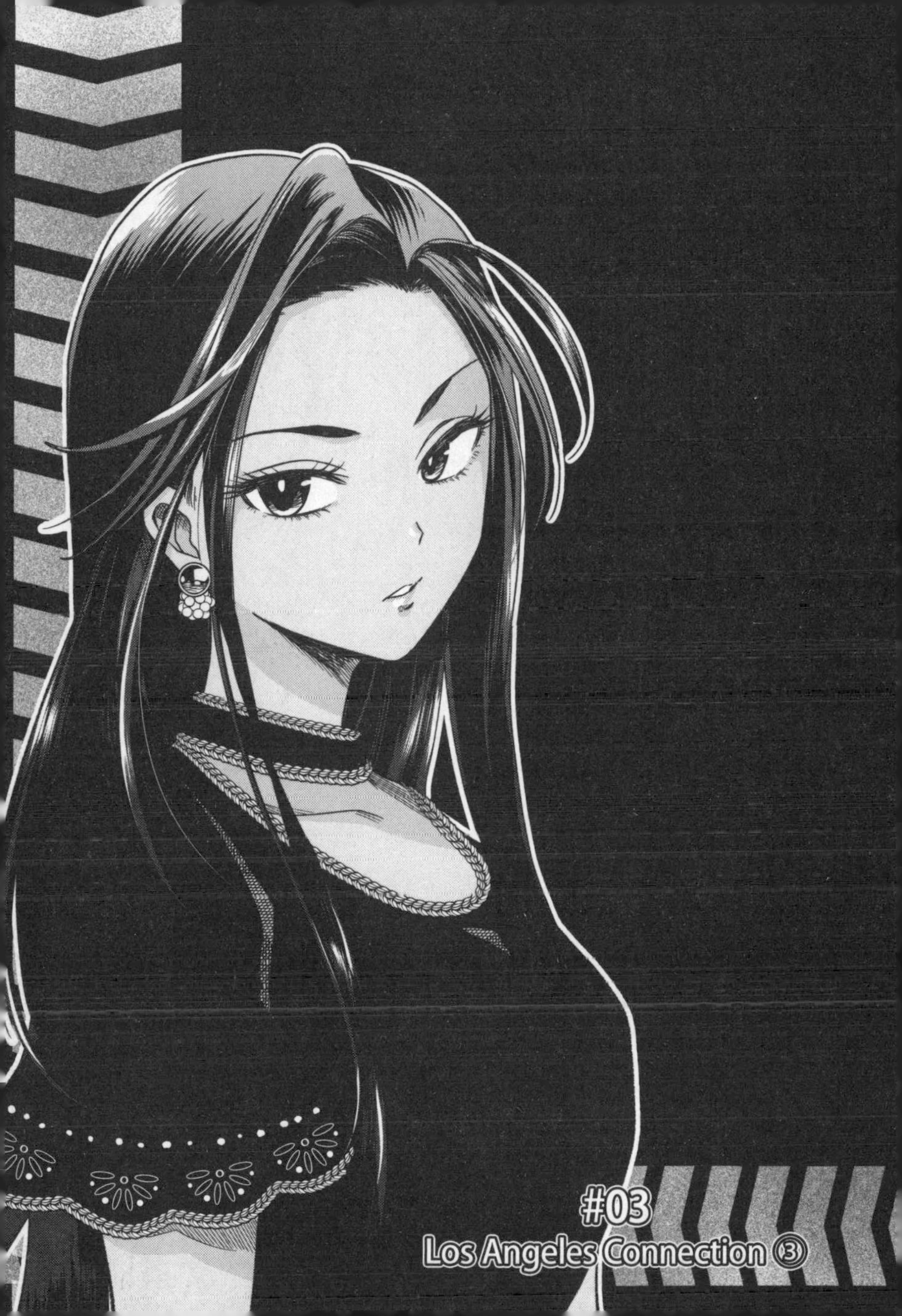
#03
Los Angeles Connection ③

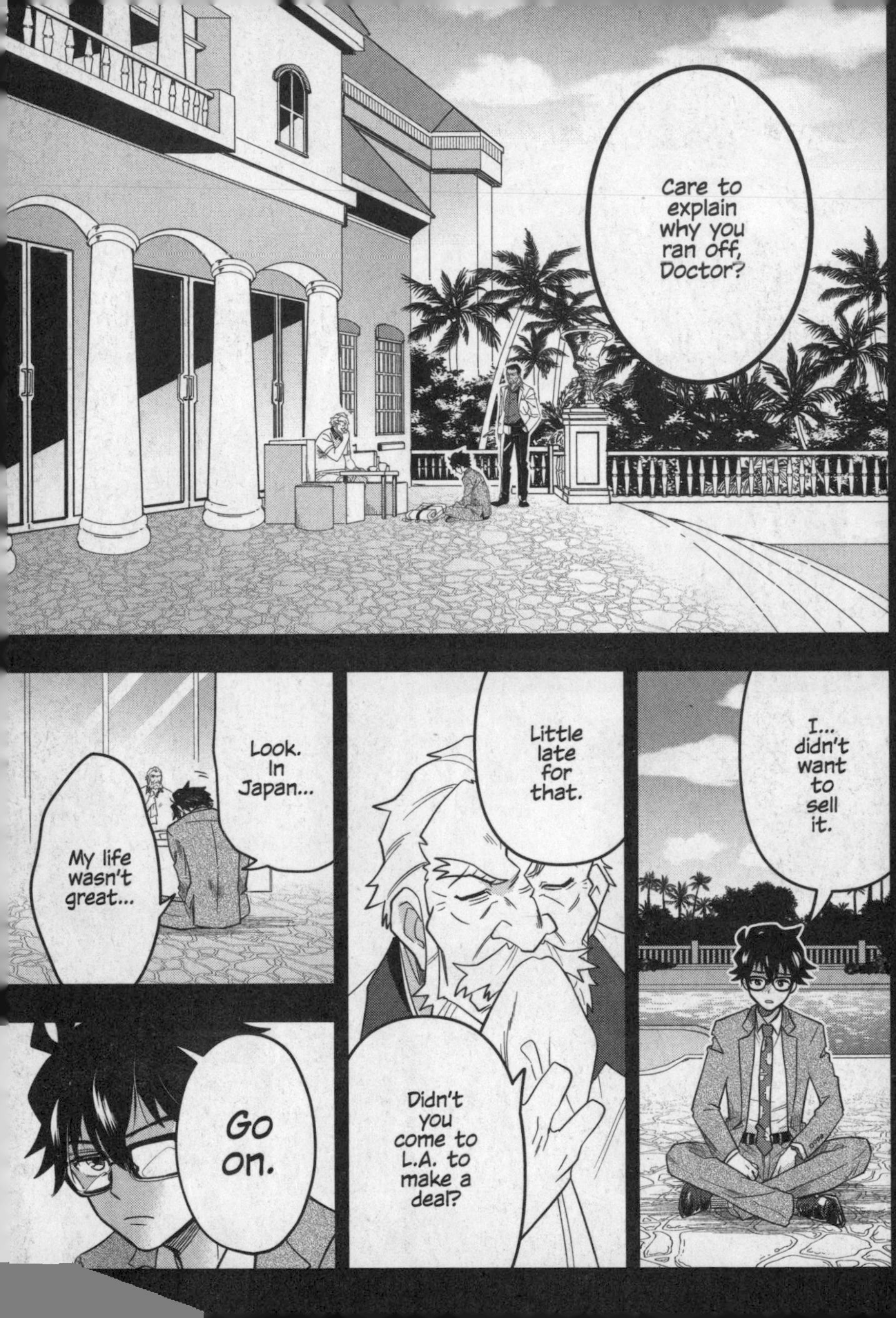
Care to explain why you ran off, Doctor?
I... didn't want to sell it.
Little late for that.
Didn't you come to L.A. to make a deal?
Look. In Japan...
My life wasn't great...
Go on.

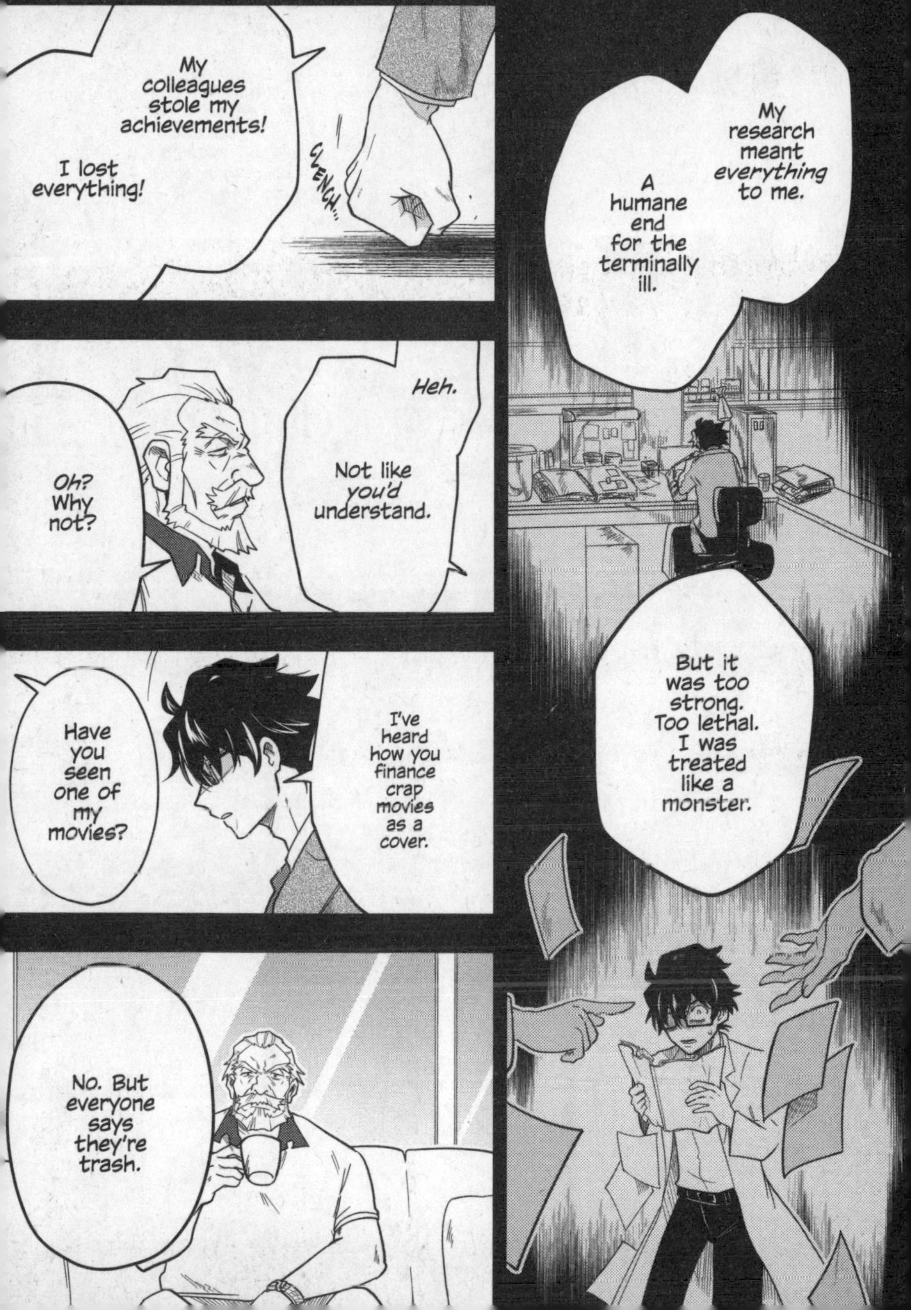
My research meant everything to me.
A humane end for the terminally ill.
But it was too strong. Too lethal. I was treated like a monster.
My colleagues stole my achievements!
I lost everything!
CLENCH...
Heh.
Not like you'd understand.
Oh? Why not?
I've heard how you finance crap movies as a cover.
Have you seen one of my movies?
No. But everyone says they're trash.

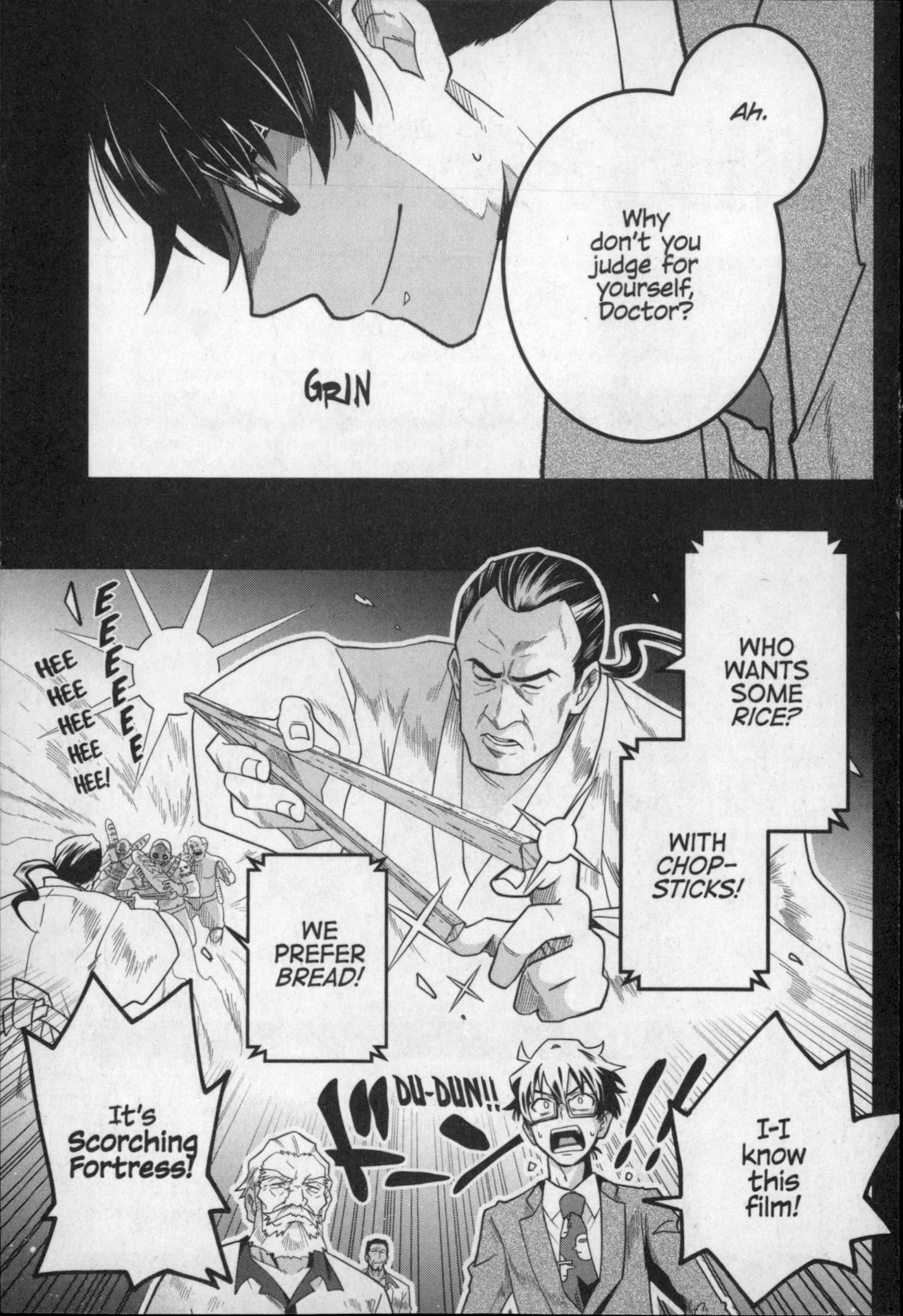
Ah.
Why don't you judge for yourself, Doctor?
GRIN
WHO WANTS SOME RICE?
WITH CHOP-STICKS!
WE PREFER BREAD!
EEEEEEE
HEE HEE HEE HEE HEE!
I-I know this film!
DU-DUN!!
It's Scorching Fortress!

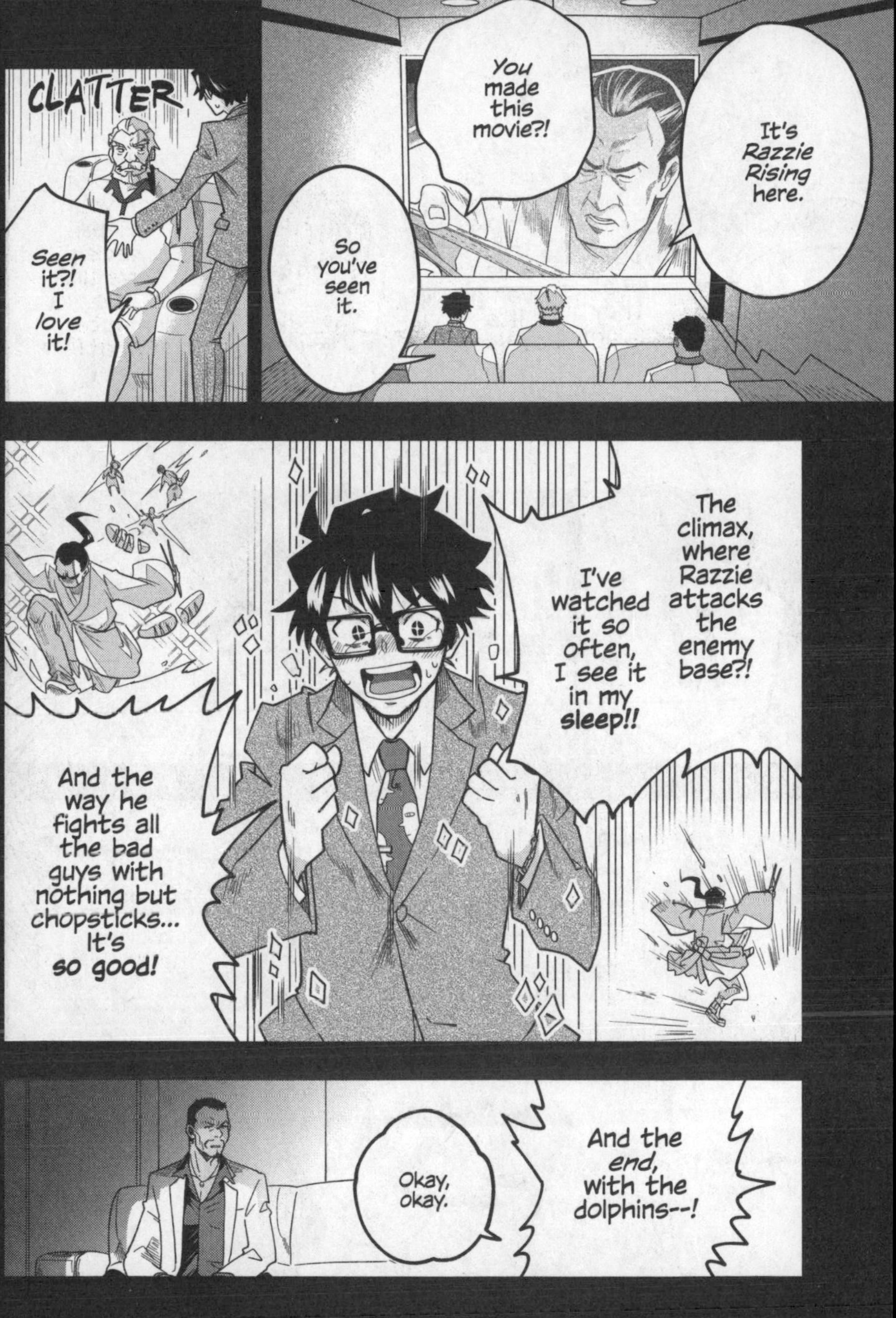
It's Razzie Rising here.
You made this movie?!
So you've seen it.
CLATTER
Seen it?! I love it!
The climax, where Razzie attacks the enemy base?!
I've watched it so often, I see it in my sleep!!
And the way he fights all the bad guys with nothing but chopsticks... It's so good!
And the *end*, with the dolphins--!
Okay, okay.

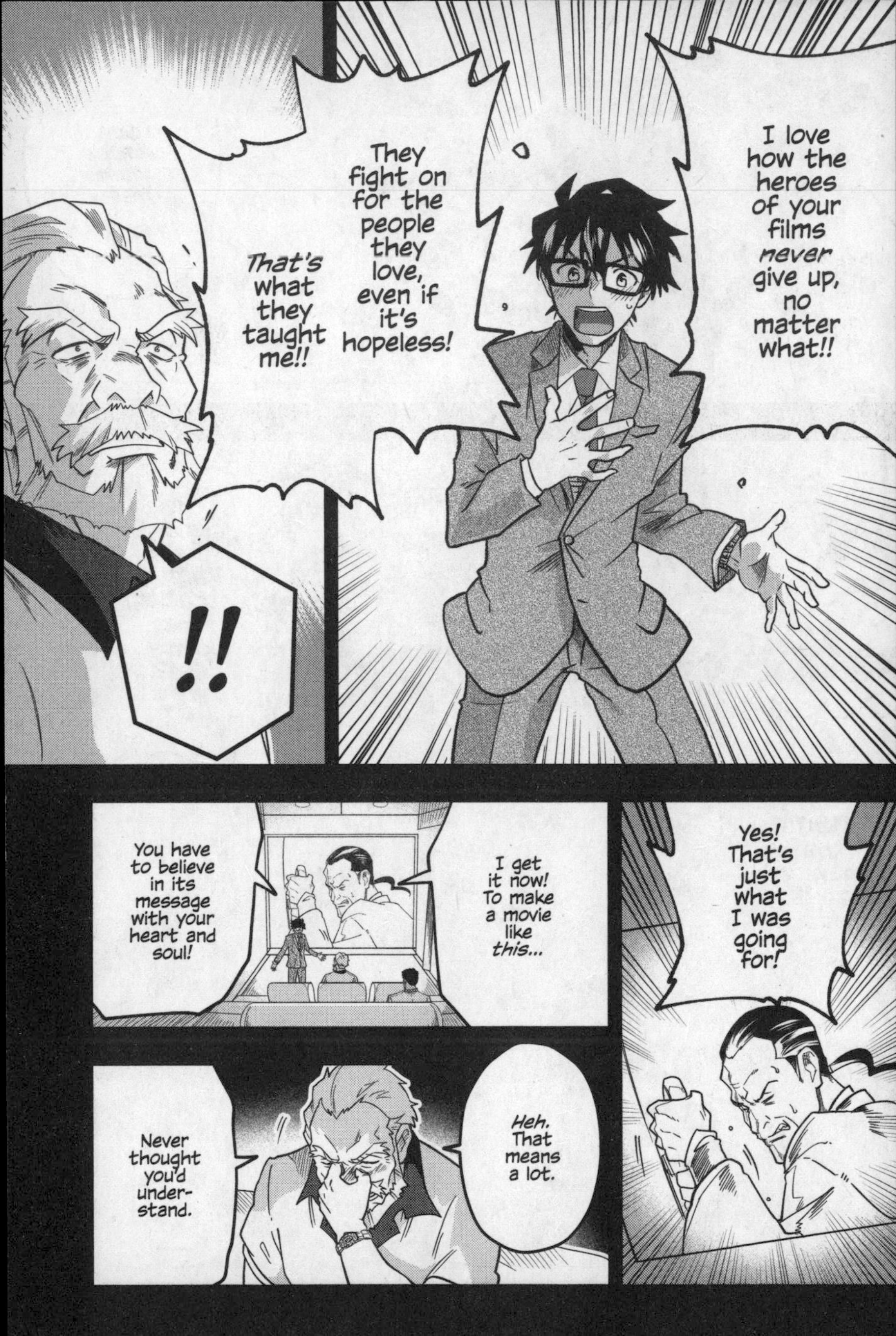
I love how the heroes of your films *never* give up, no matter what!!
They fight on for the people they love, even if it's hopeless!
That's what they taught me!!
!!
Yes! That's just what I was going for!
I get it now! To make a movie like *this*...
You have to believe in its message with your heart and soul!
Heh. That means a lot.
Never thought you'd under-stand.

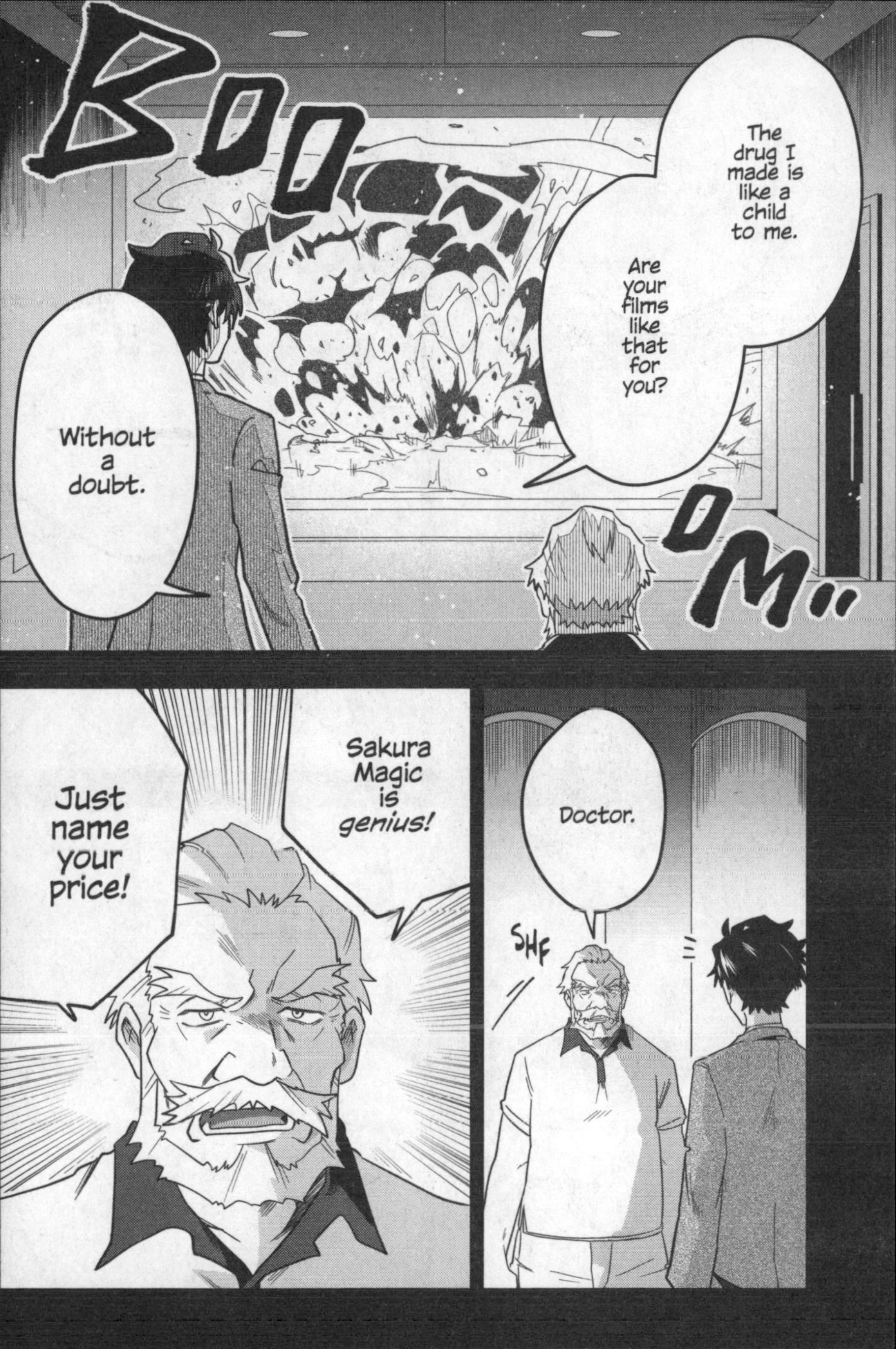
BOOOM!!
The drug I made is like a child to me.
Are your films like that for you?
Without a doubt.
Doctor.
SHF
Sakura Magic is genius!
Just name your price!

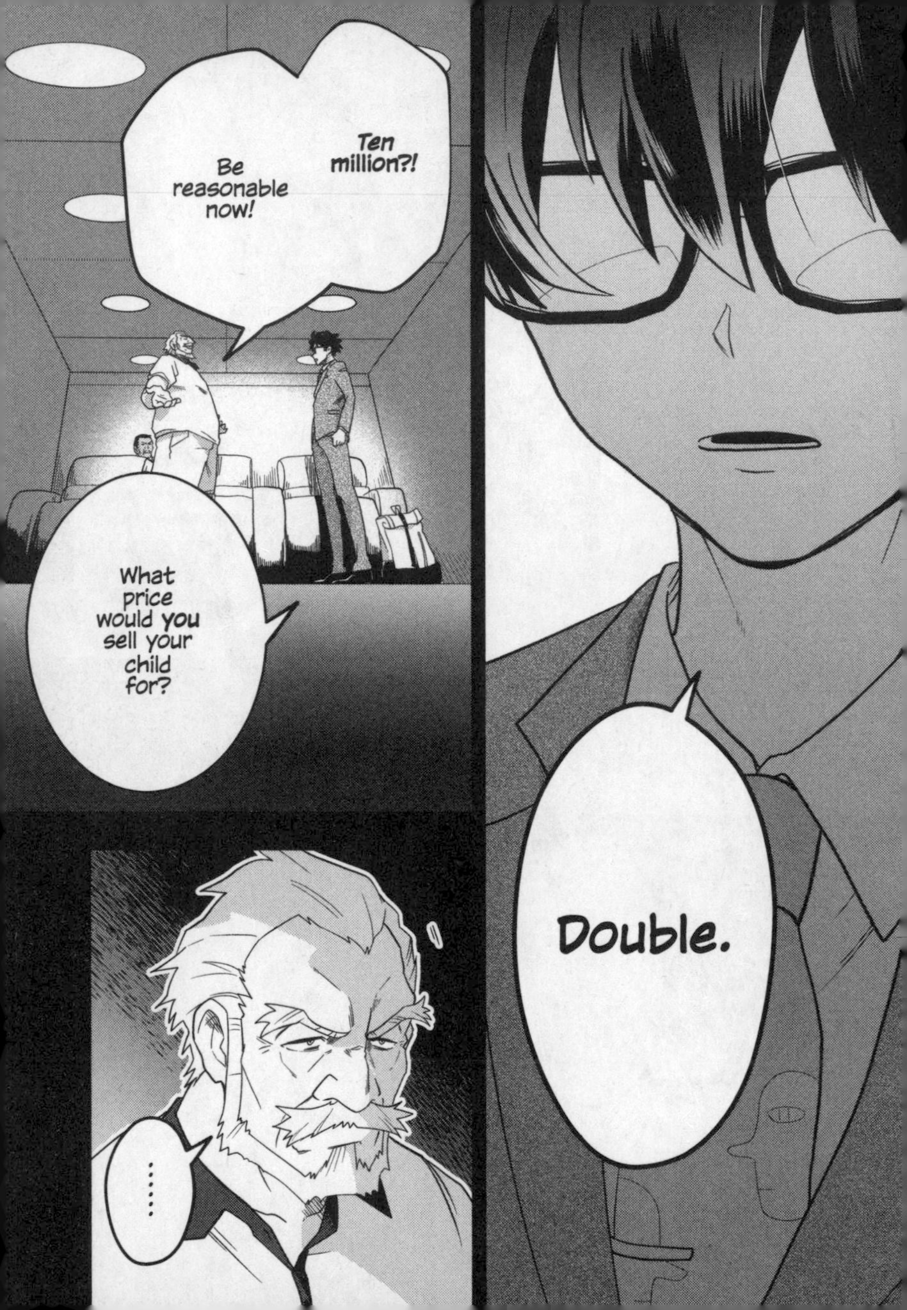
Ten million?!
Be reasonable now!
What price would you sell your child for?
Double.
......

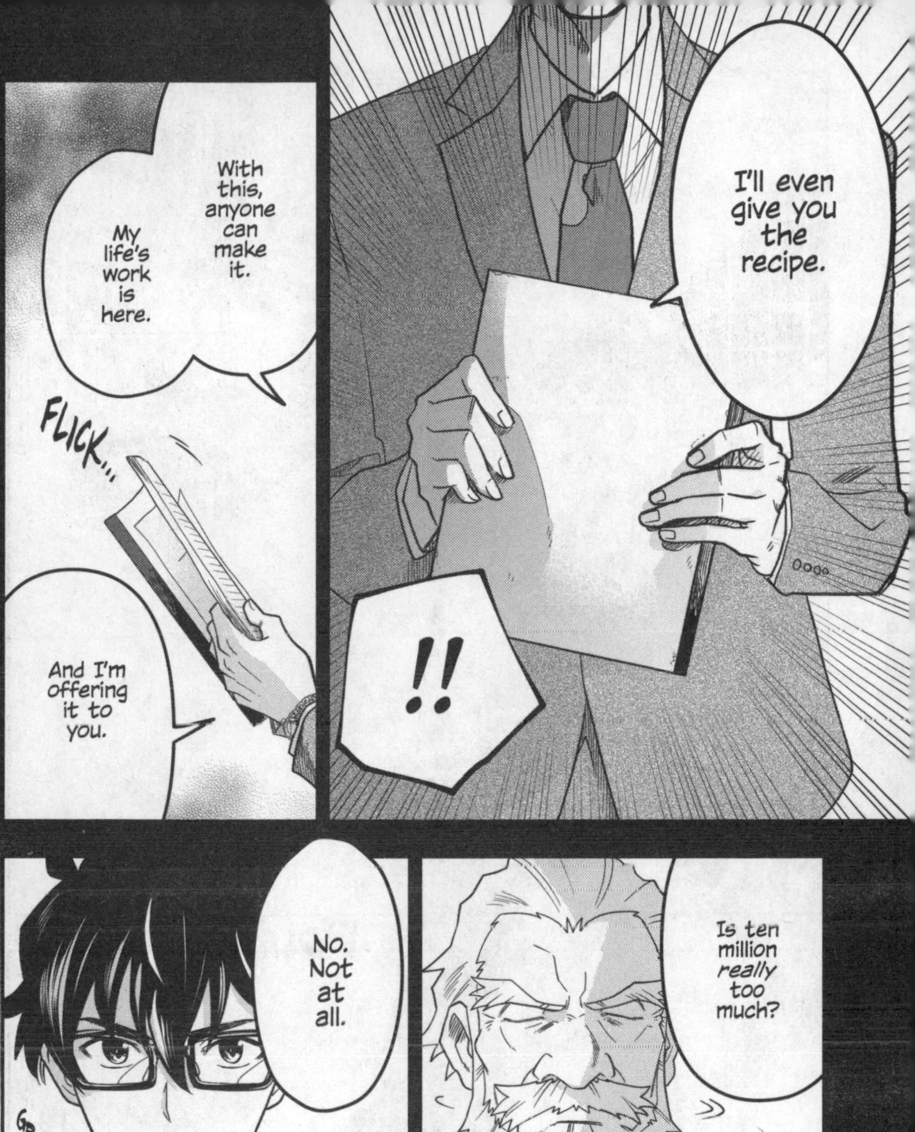

I'll even give you the recipe.
!!
With this, anyone can make it.
My life's work is here.
FLICK...
And I'm offering it to you.
Is ten million *really* too much?
No. Not at all.
GRIN

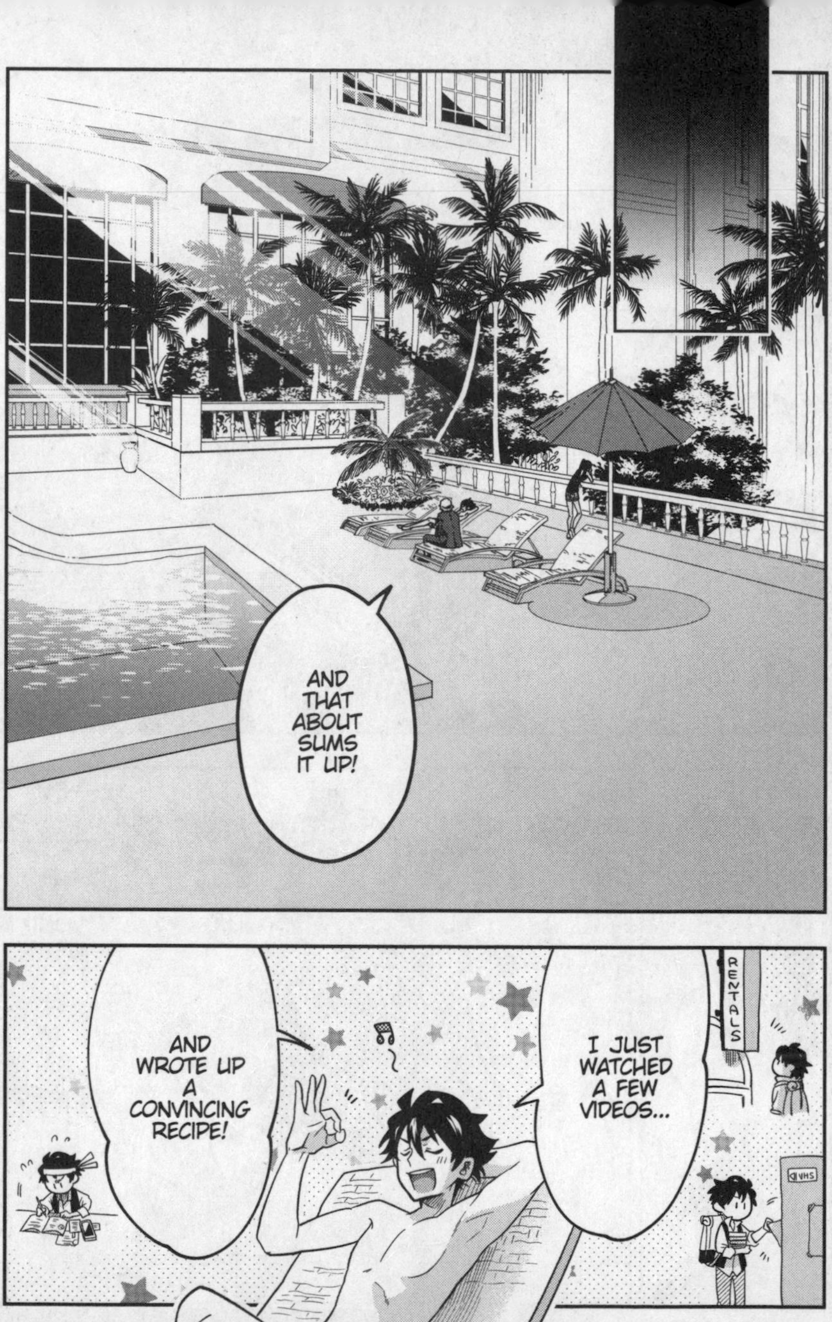
AND THAT ABOUT SUMS IT UP!
RENTALS
I JUST WATCHED A FEW VIDEOS...
VHS
AND WROTE UP A CONVINCING RECIPE!

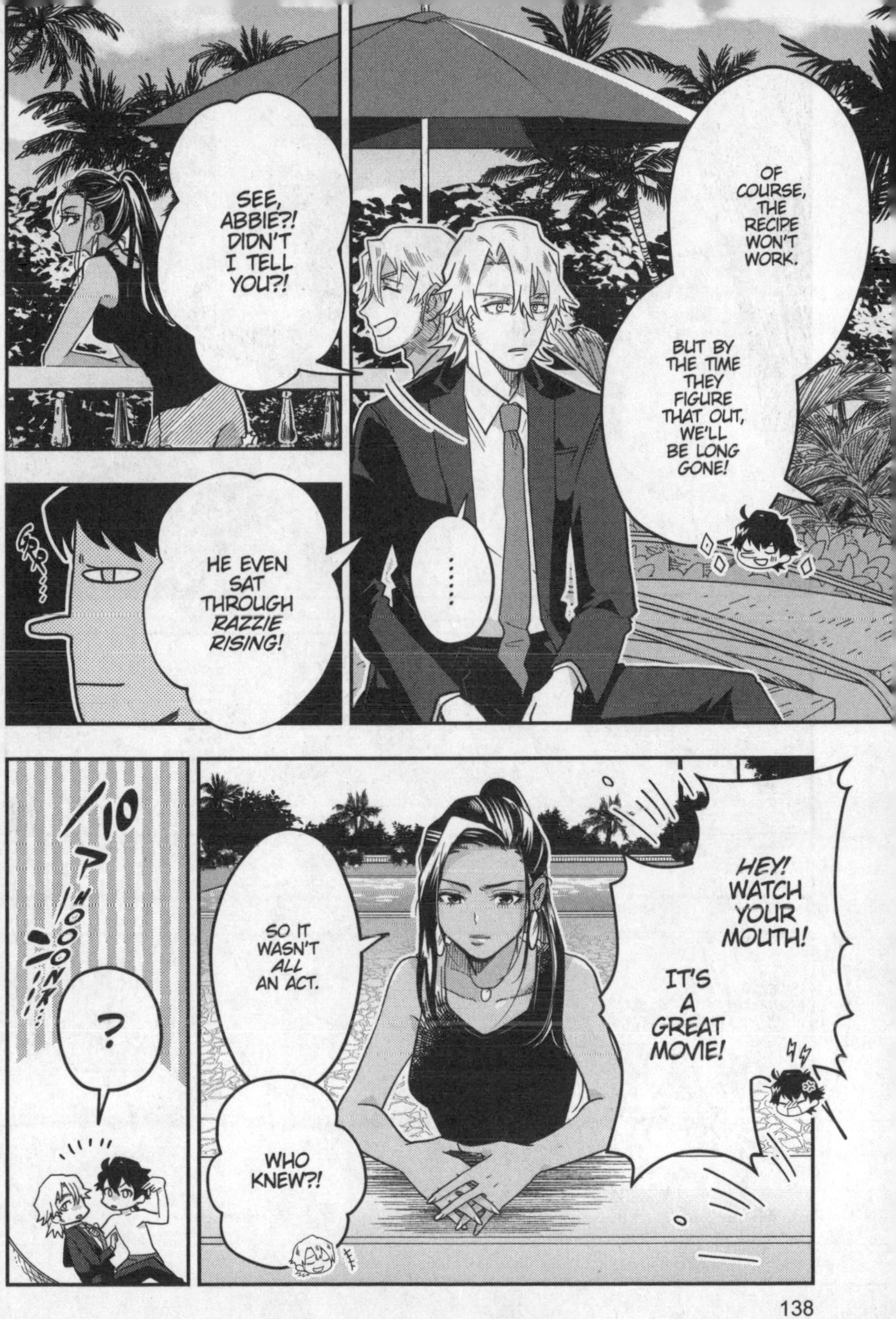
OF COURSE, THE RECIPE WON'T WORK.
BUT BY THE TIME THEY FIGURE THAT OUT, WE'LL BE LONG GONE!
......
SEE, ABBIE?! DIDN'T I TELL YOU?!
GRR...
HE EVEN SAT THROUGH *RAZZIE RISING!*
SO IT WASN'T *ALL* AN ACT.
WHO KNEW?!
HEY! WATCH YOUR MOUTH!
IT'S A GREAT MOVIE!
?

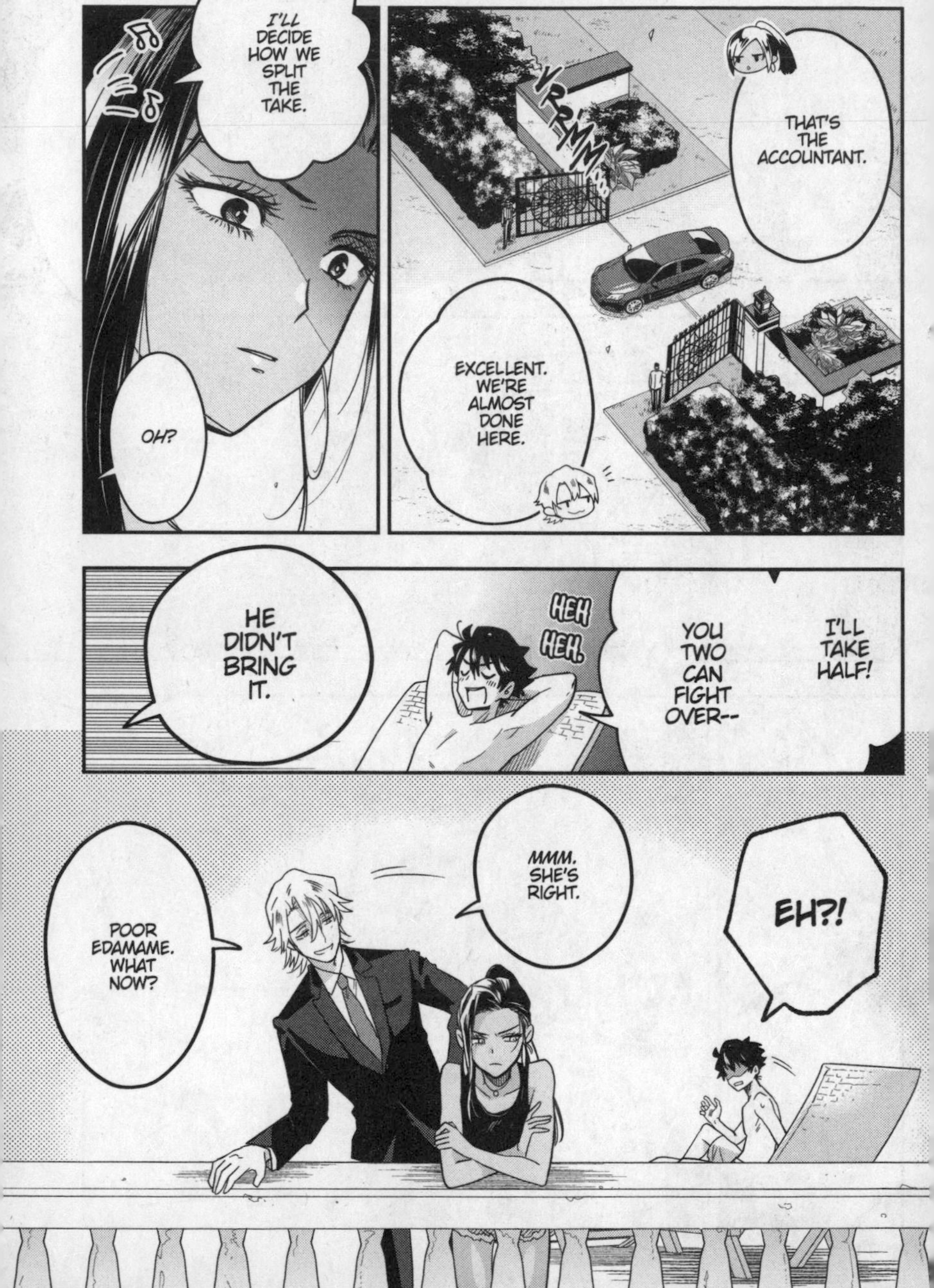
THAT'S THE ACCOUNTANT.
VRMMM
EXCELLENT. WE'RE ALMOST DONE HERE.
I'LL DECIDE HOW WE SPLIT THE TAKE.
OH?
I'LL TAKE HALF!
YOU TWO CAN FIGHT OVER--
HEH HEH.
HE DIDN'T BRING IT.
EH?!
MMM. SHE'S RIGHT.
POOR EDAMAME. WHAT NOW?

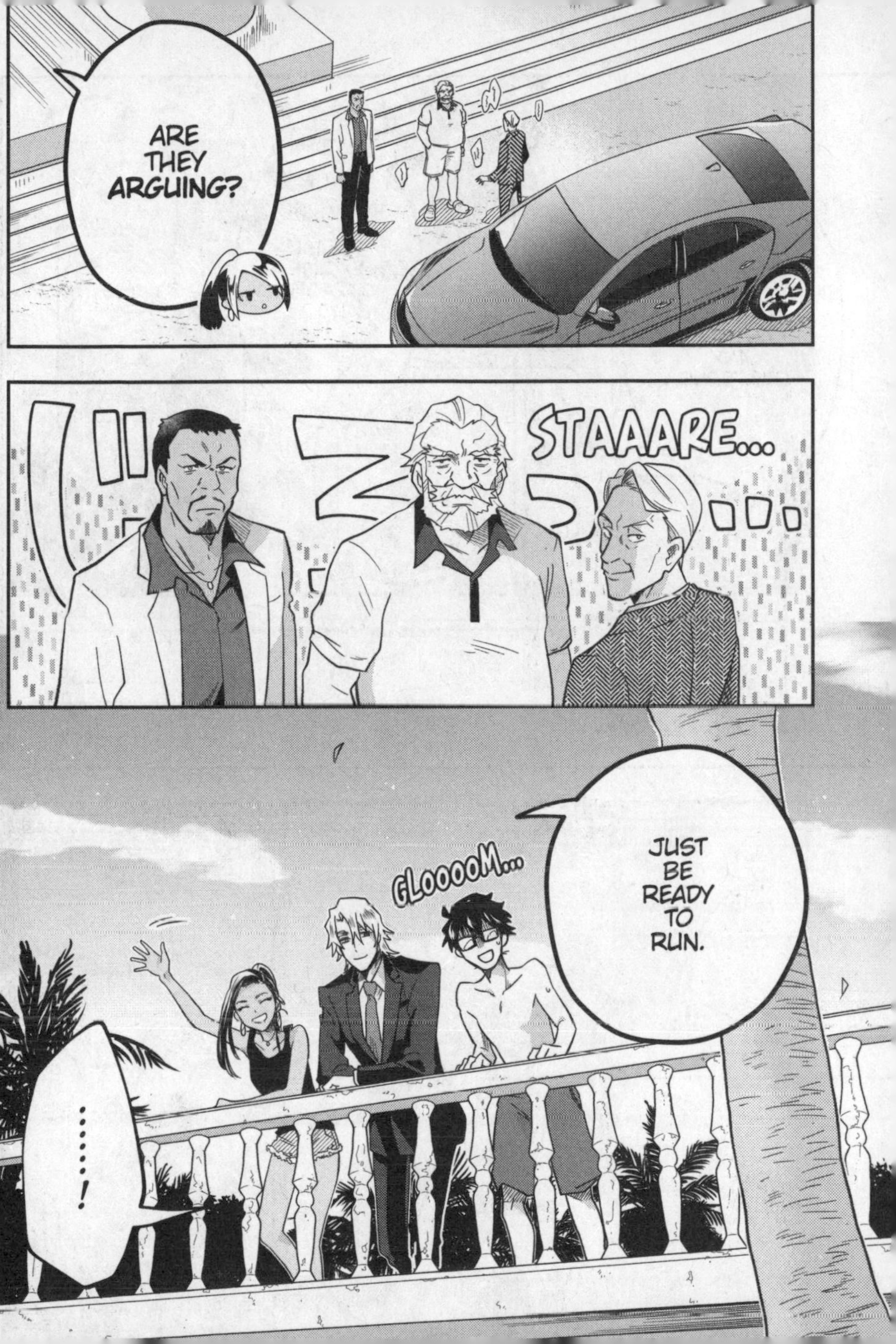
ARE THEY ARGUING?
STAAARE...
JUST BE READY TO RUN.
GLOOOOM...
......!

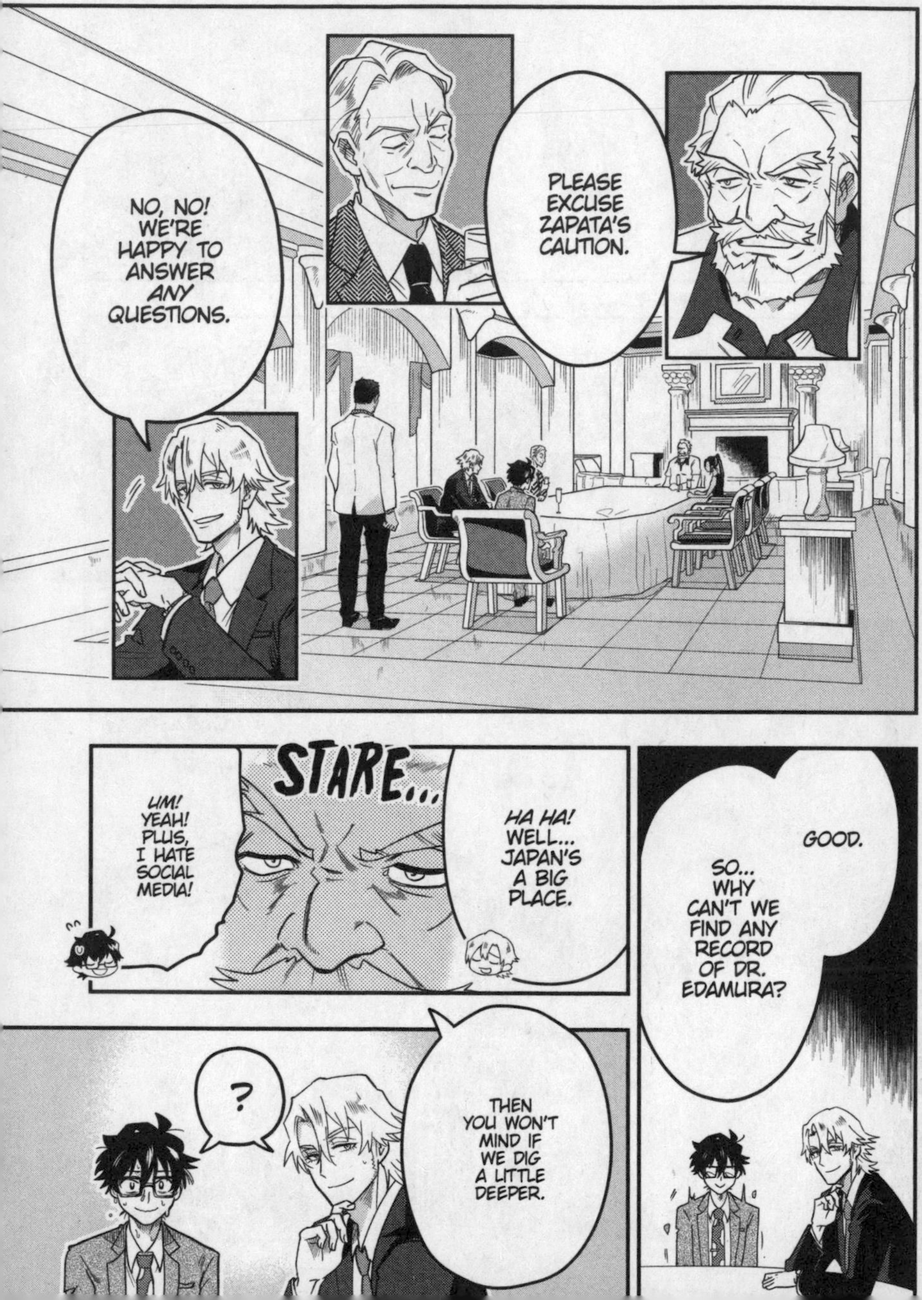
PLEASE EXCUSE ZAPATA'S CAUTION.
NO, NO! WE'RE HAPPY TO ANSWER ANY QUESTIONS.
GOOD.
SO... WHY CAN'T WE FIND ANY RECORD OF DR. EDAMURA?
HA HA! WELL... JAPAN'S A BIG PLACE.
STARE...
UM! YEAH! PLUS, I HATE SOCIAL MEDIA!
THEN YOU WON'T MIND IF WE DIG A LITTLE DEEPER.
?

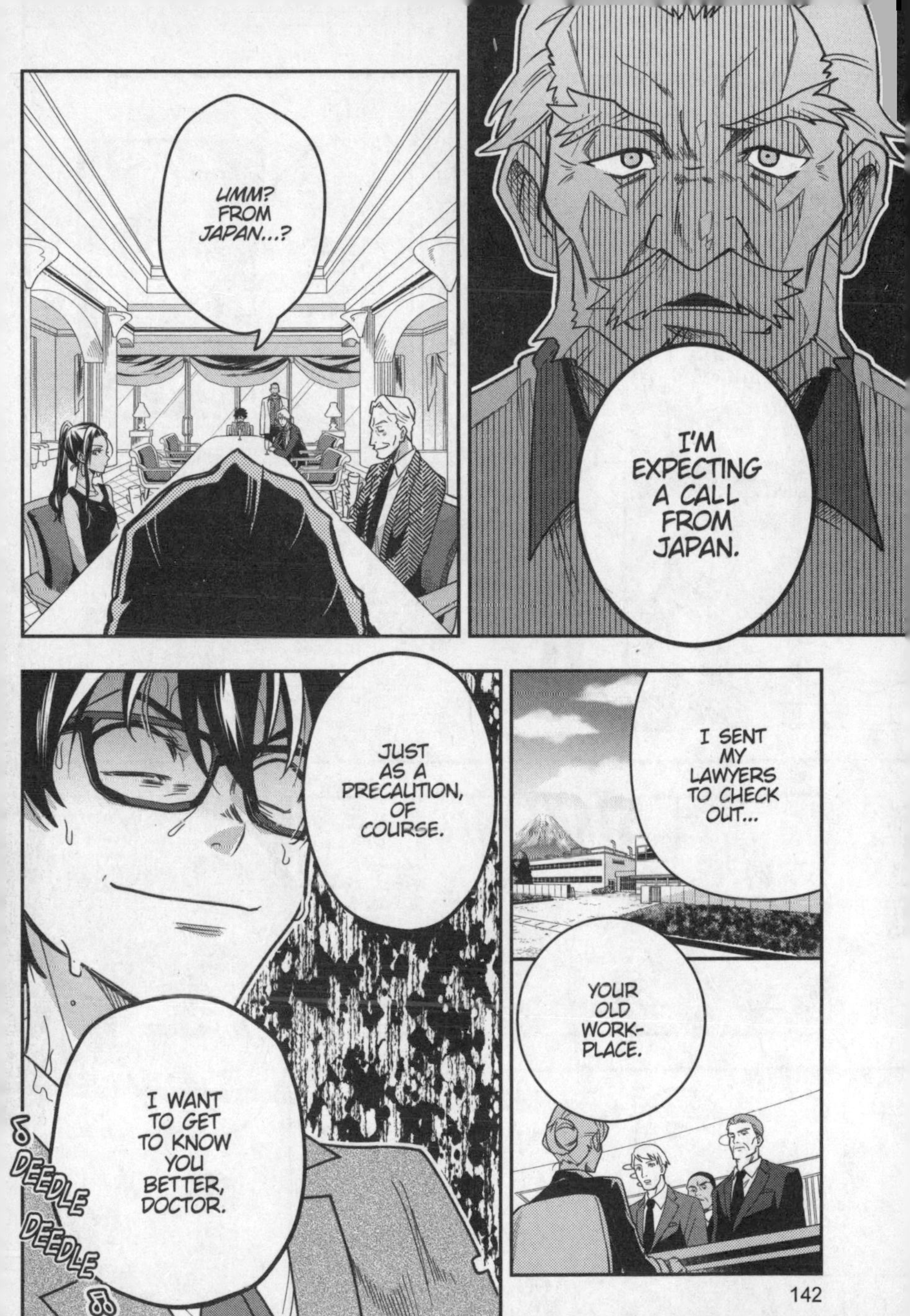
I'M EXPECTING A CALL FROM JAPAN.
UMM? FROM JAPAN...?
I SENT MY LAWYERS TO CHECK OUT...
YOUR OLD WORK-PLACE.
JUST AS A PRECAUTION, OF COURSE.
I WANT TO GET TO KNOW YOU BETTER, DOCTOR.
DEEDLE DEEDLE

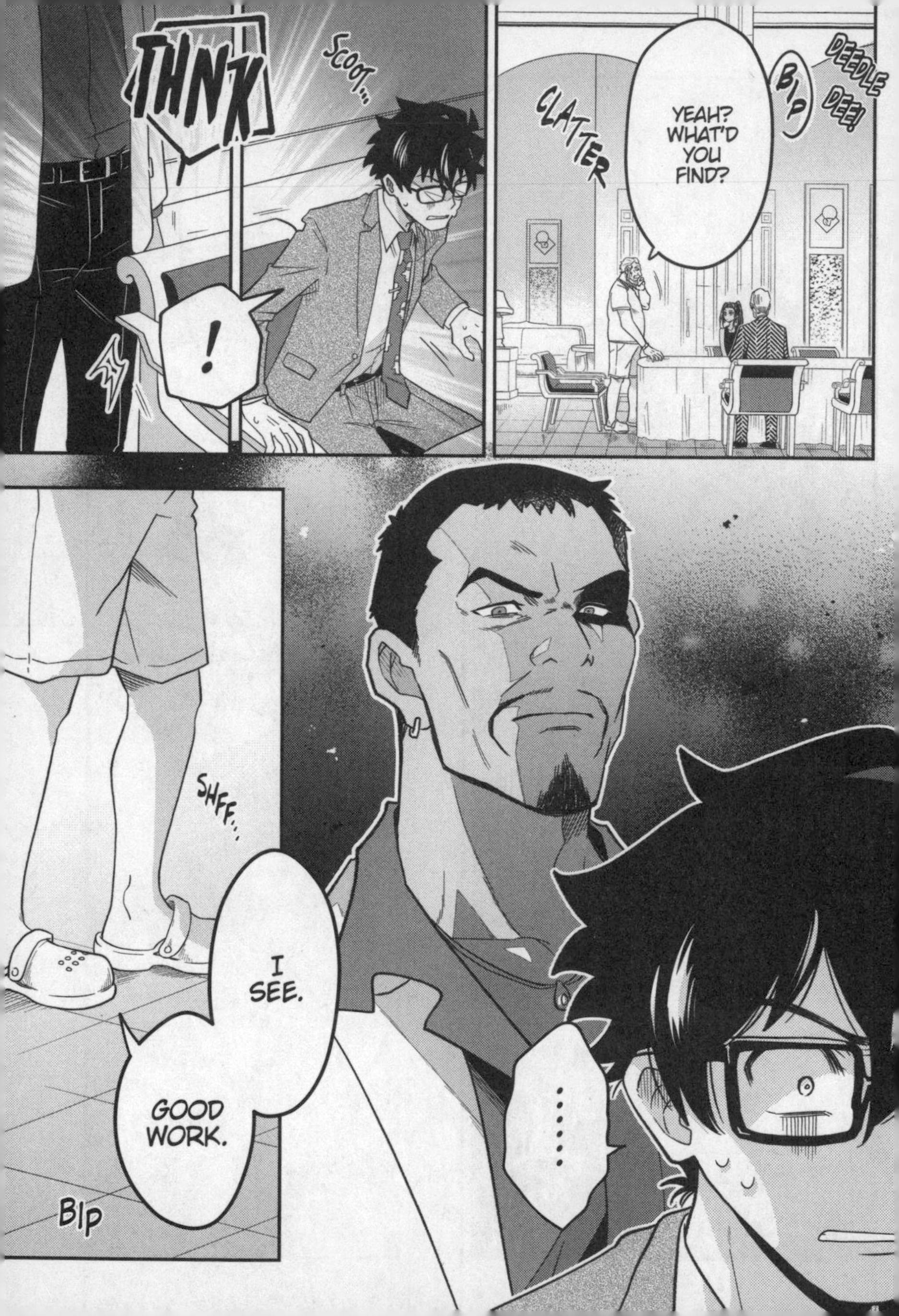
DEEDLE DEE!
BIP
YEAH? WHAT'D YOU FIND?
CLATTER
THNK
SCOOT...
!
......
SHFF...
I SEE.
GOOD WORK.
BIP

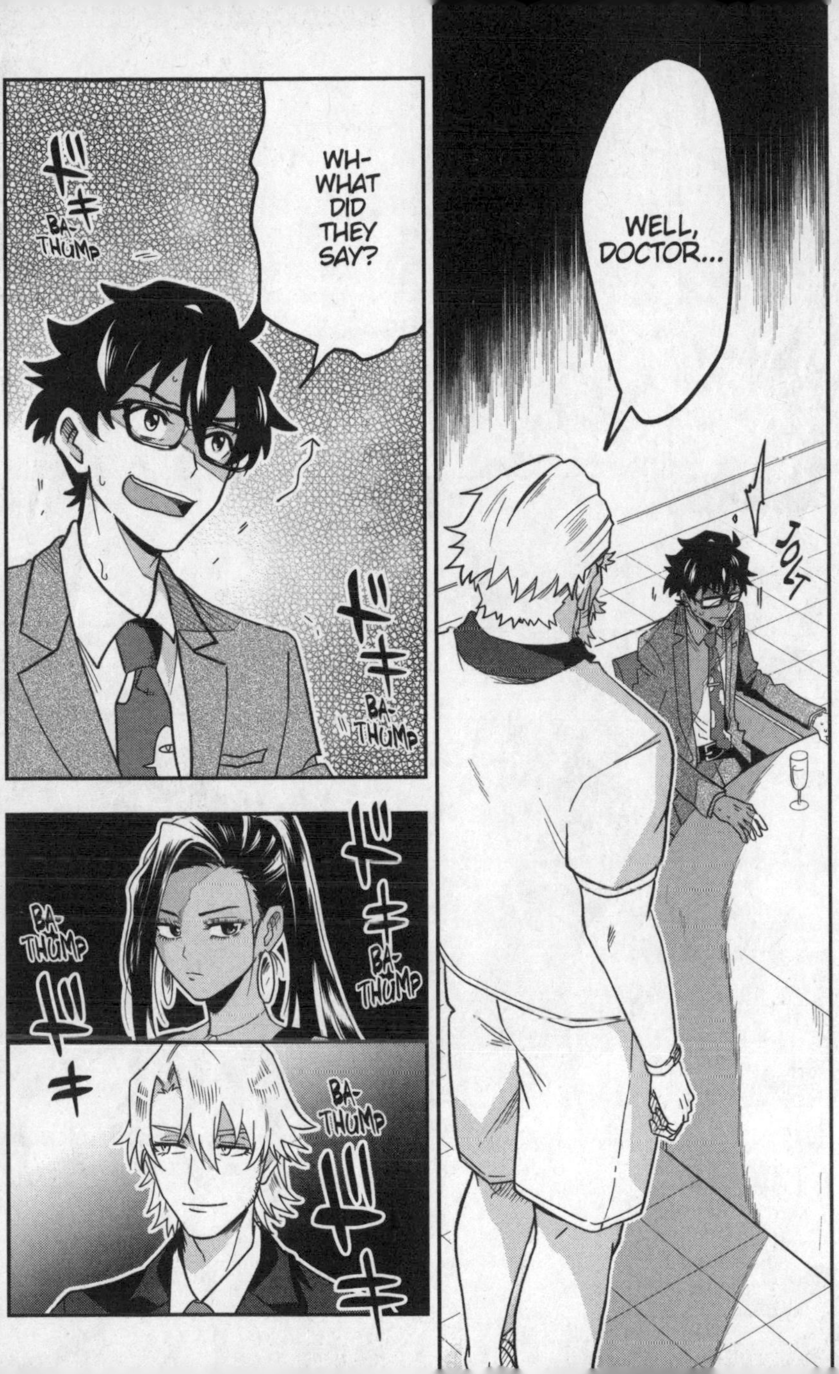
WELL, DOCTOR...
JOLT
WH-WHAT DID THEY SAY?
BA-THUMP
BA-THUMP
BA-THUMP
BA-THUMP
BA-THUMP

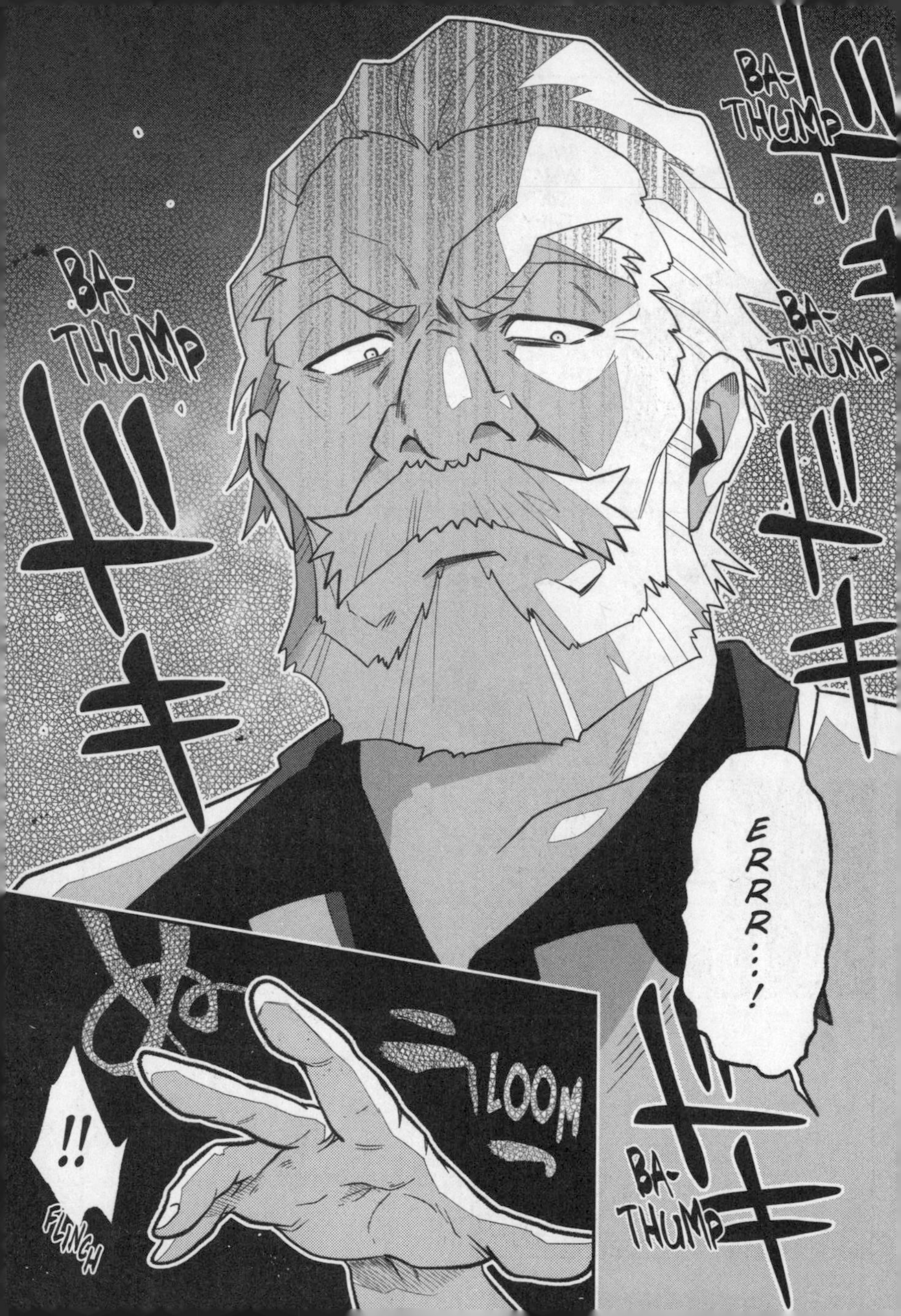
BA-THUMP
BA-THUMP
BA-THUMP
ERRR...!
BA-THUMP
LOOM
!!
FLINCH

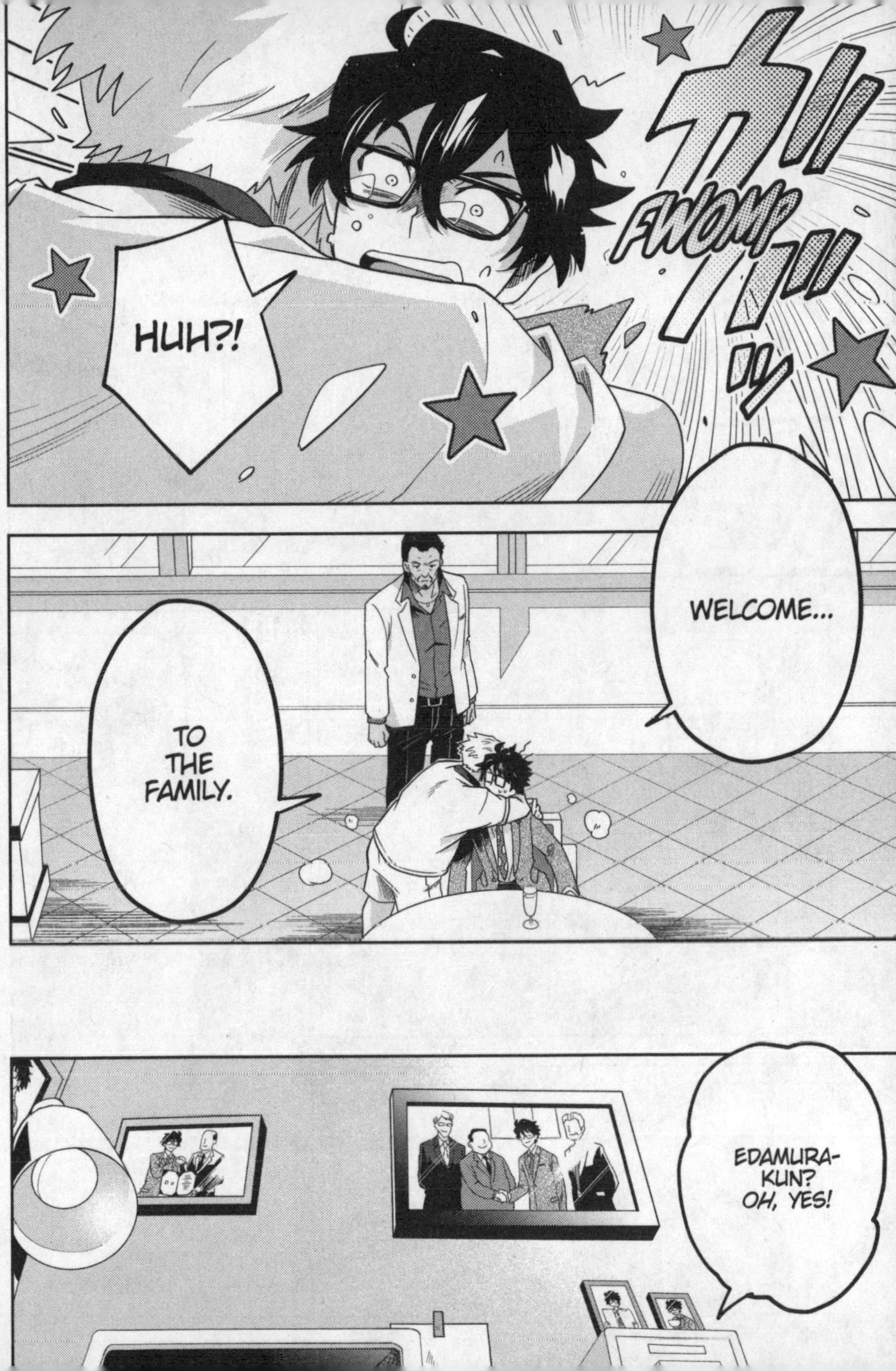
FWOMP
HUH?!
WELCOME...
TO THE FAMILY.
EDAMURA-KUN? OH, YES!

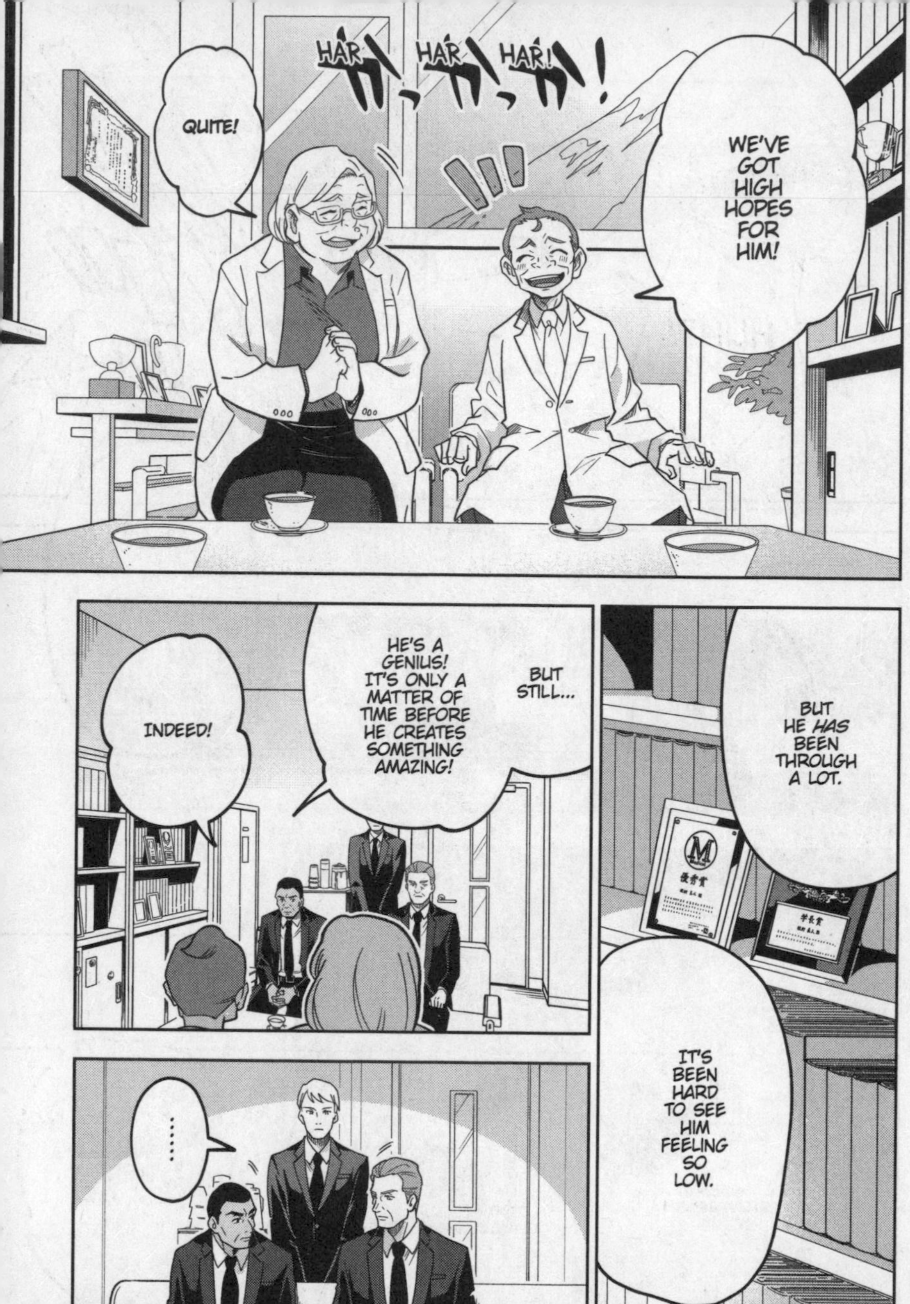
WE'VE GOT HIGH HOPES FOR HIM!
HAR HAR HAR!
カ、カ、カ！
QUITE!
BUT HE *HAS* BEEN THROUGH A LOT.
IT'S BEEN HARD TO SEE HIM FEELING SO LOW.
BUT STILL...
HE'S A GENIUS! IT'S ONLY A MATTER OF TIME BEFORE HE CREATES SOMETHING AMAZING!
INDEED!
......

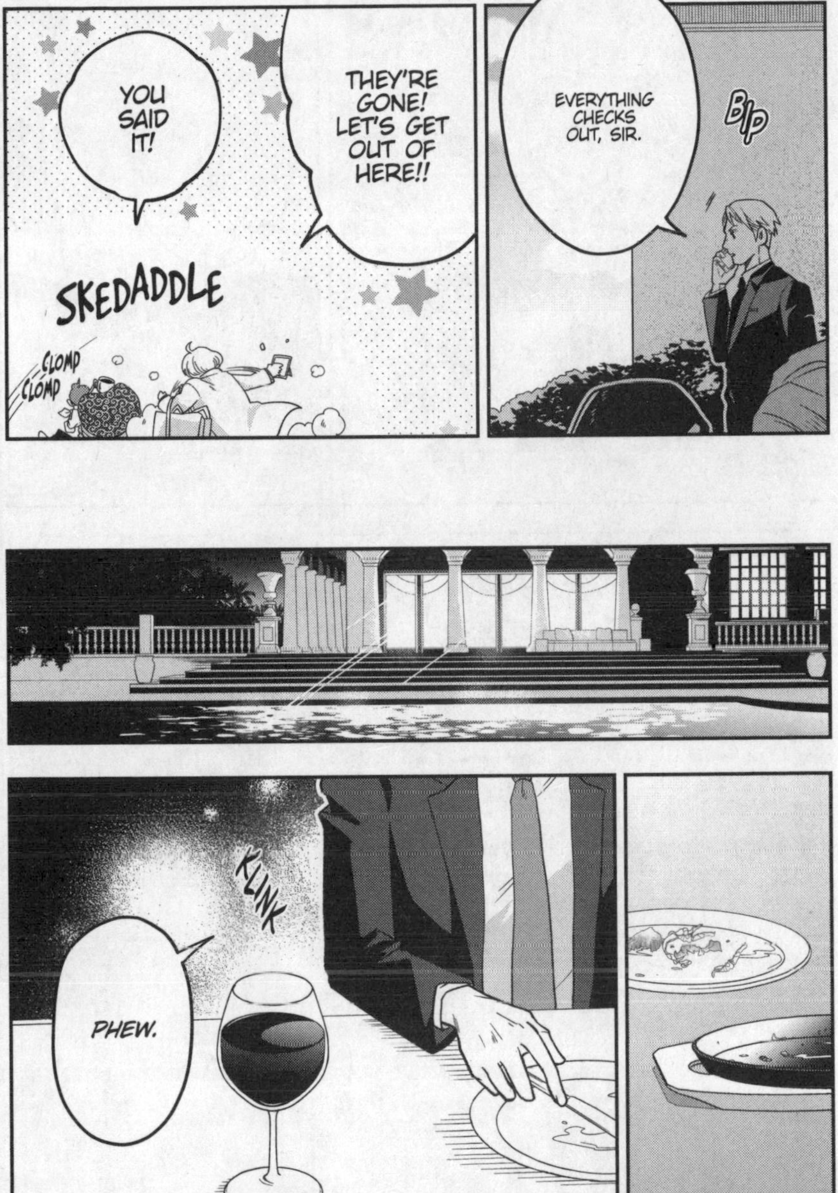
EVERYTHING CHECKS OUT, SIR.
BIP
THEY'RE GONE! LET'S GET OUT OF HERE!!
YOU SAID IT!
SKEDADDLE
CLOMP CLOMP
KLINK
PHEW.

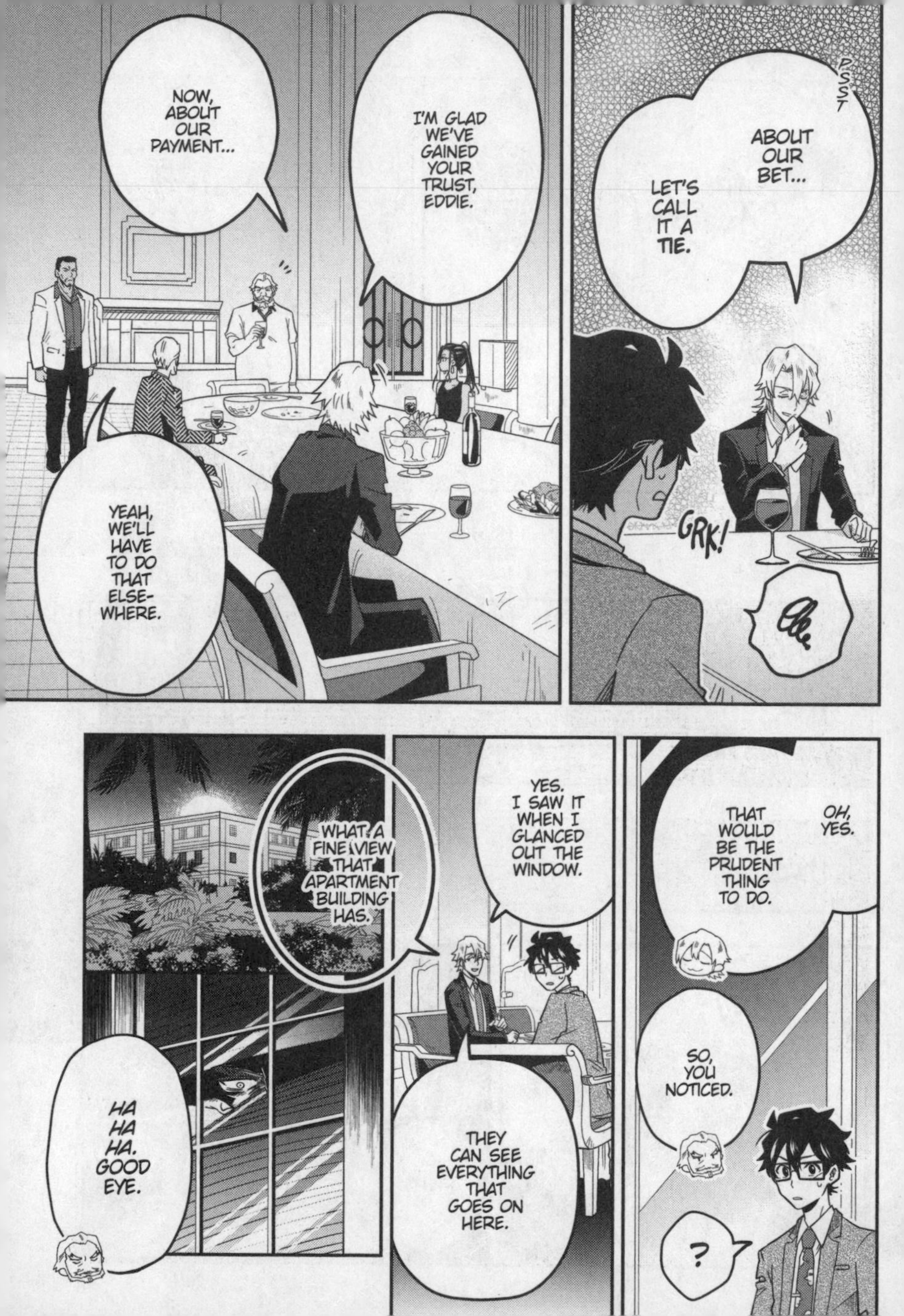
PSST
ABOUT OUR BET...
LET'S CALL IT A TIE.
GRK!
I'M GLAD WE'VE GAINED YOUR TRUST, EDDIE.
NOW, ABOUT OUR PAYMENT...
YEAH, WE'LL HAVE TO DO THAT ELSE-WHERE.
OH, YES.
THAT WOULD BE THE PRUDENT THING TO DO.
SO, YOU NOTICED.
?
YES. I SAW IT WHEN I GLANCED OUT THE WINDOW.
THEY CAN SEE EVERYTHING THAT GOES ON HERE.
WHAT A FINE VIEW THAT APARTMENT BUILDING HAS.
HA HA HA. GOOD EYE.

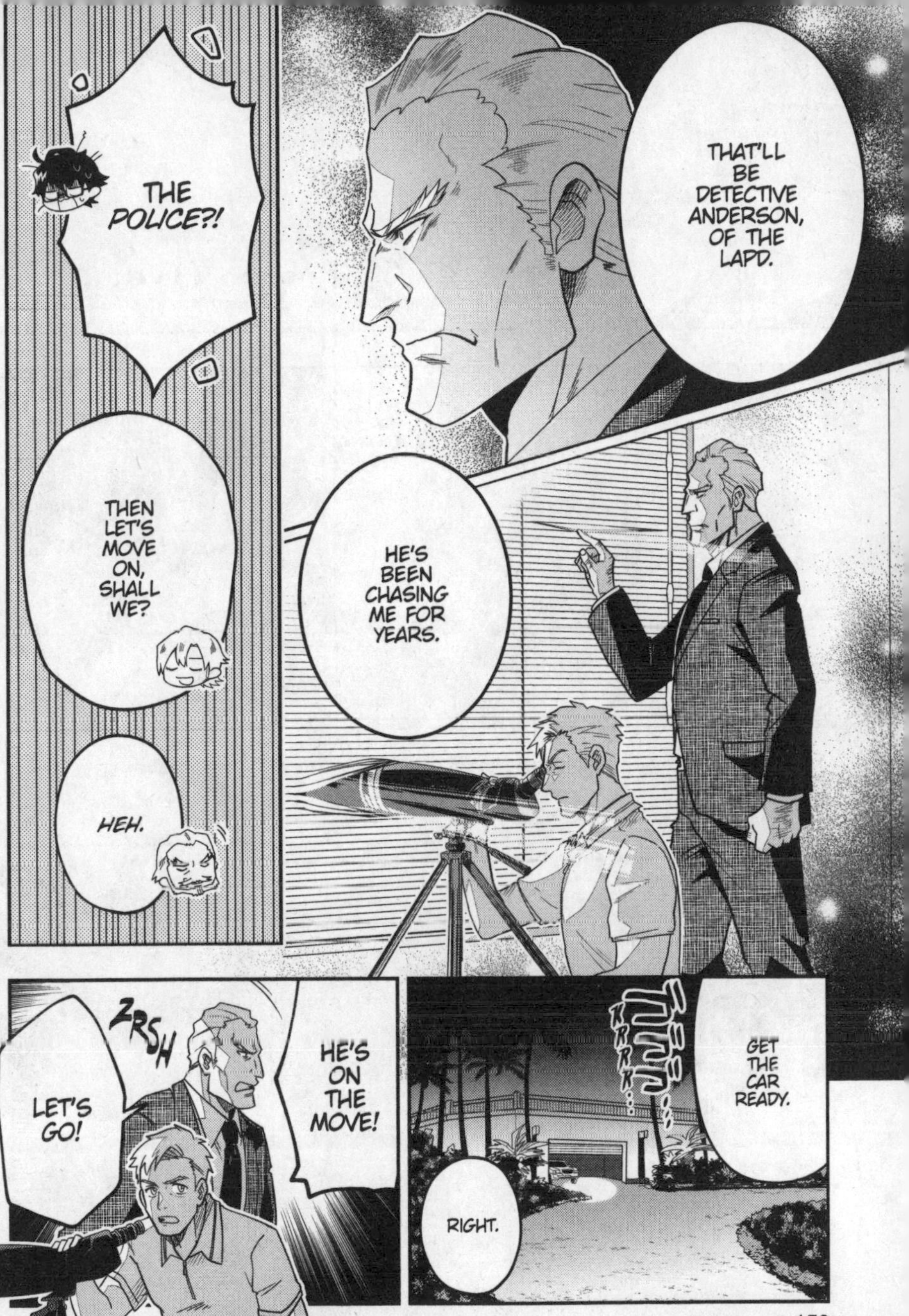
THAT'LL BE DETECTIVE ANDERSON, OF THE LAPD.
HE'S BEEN CHASING ME FOR YEARS.
THE POLICE?!
THEN LET'S MOVE ON, SHALL WE?
HEH.
KRRR...
GET THE CAR READY.
RIGHT.
HE'S ON THE MOVE!
ZRSH
LET'S GO!

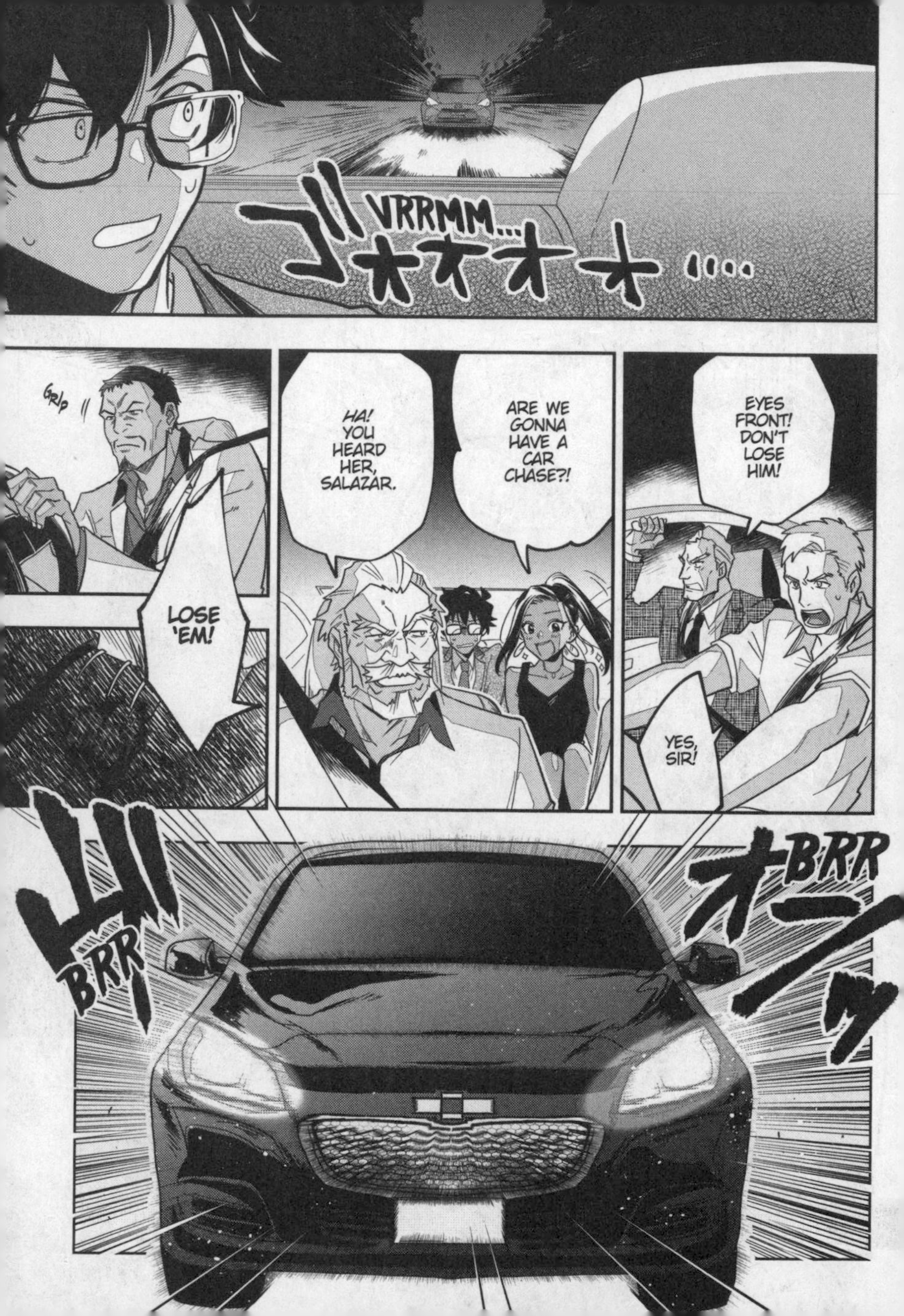
VRRMM...
EYES FRONT! DON'T LOSE HIM!
YES, SIR!
ARE WE GONNA HAVE A CAR CHASE?!
HA! YOU HEARD HER, SALAZAR.
GRIP
LOSE 'EM!
BRR
BRR

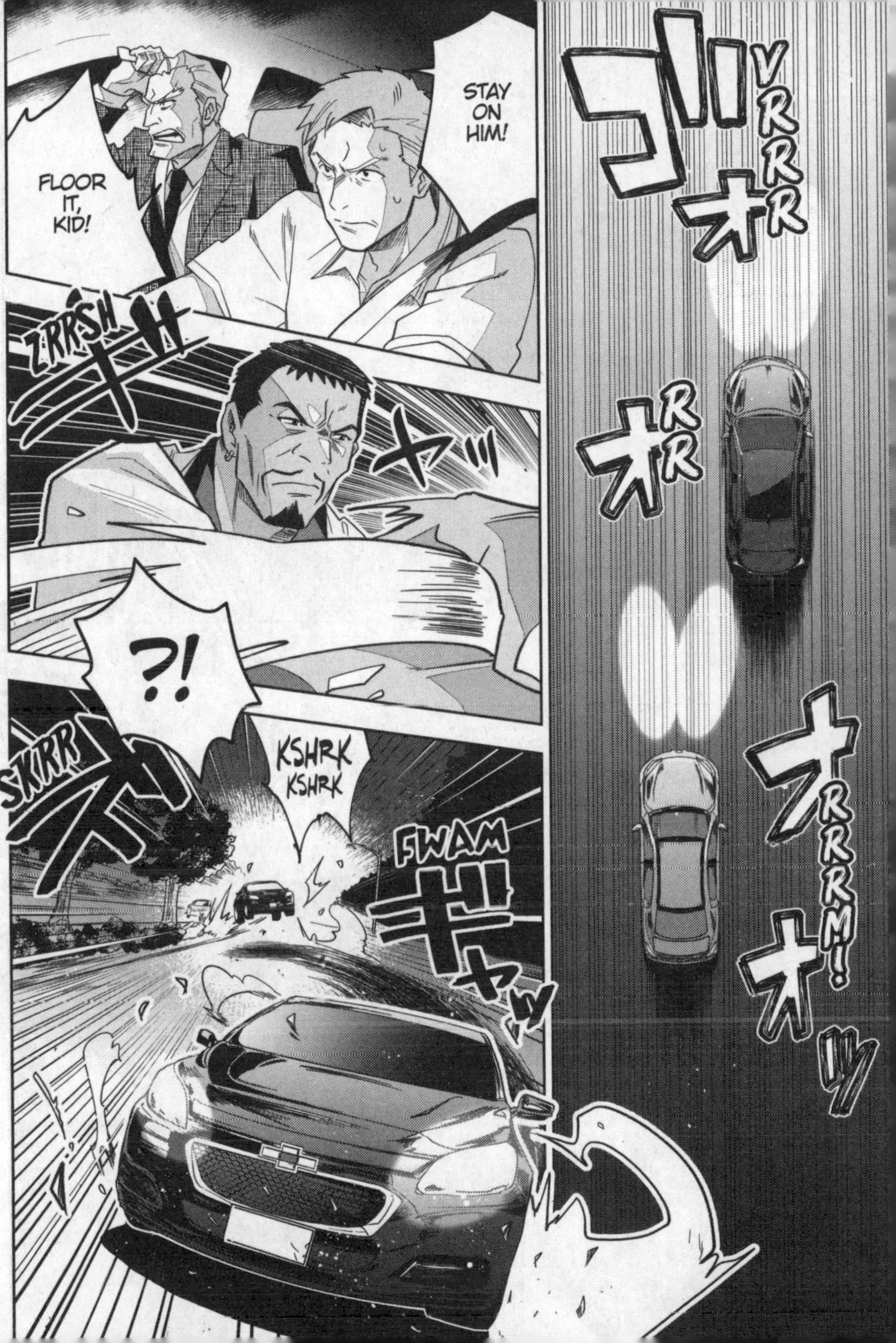
VRRR
RR
RRRRM!
STAY ON HIM!
FLOOR IT, KID!
ZRRSH
?!
KSHRK KSHRK
FWAM
SKRR

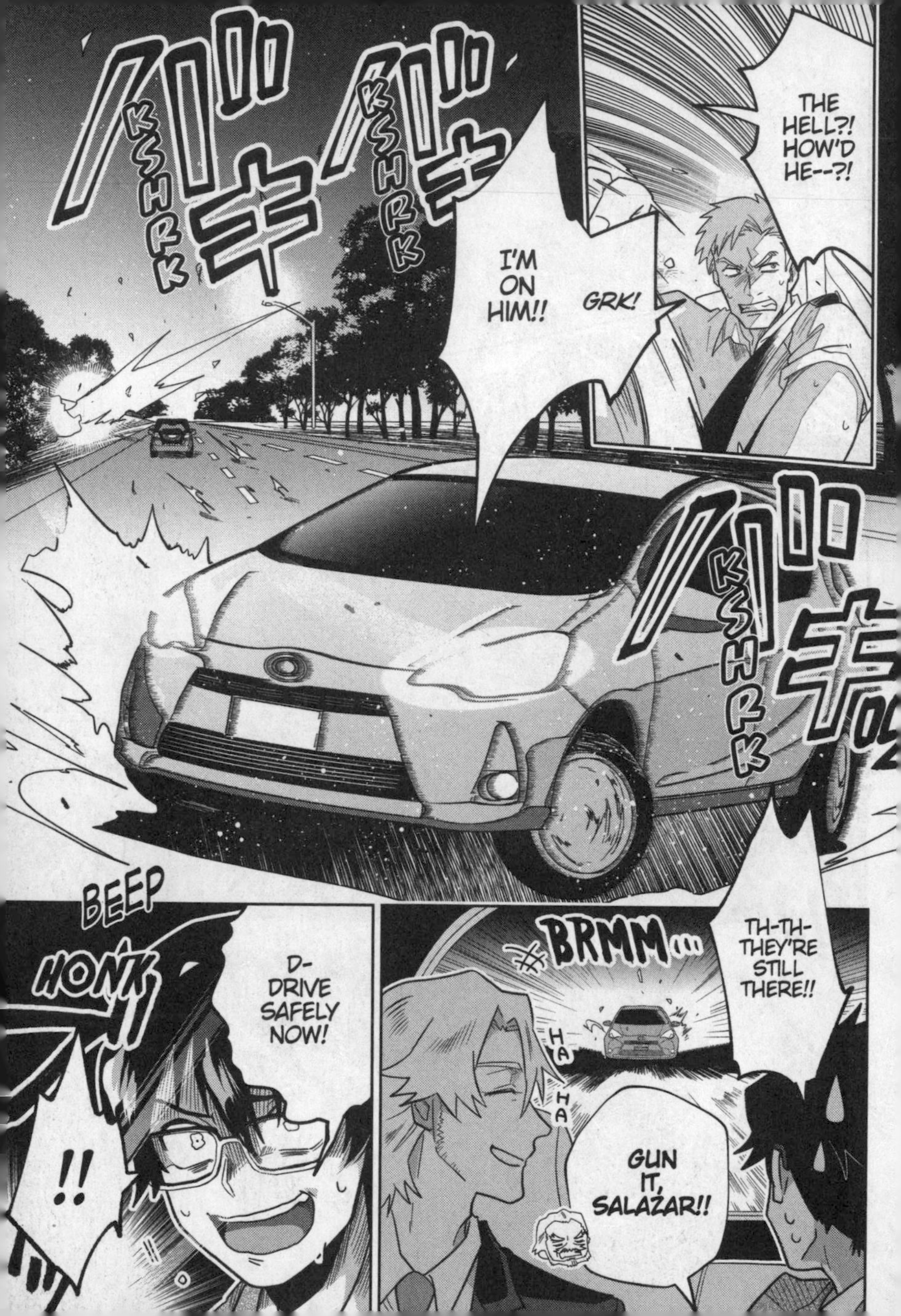
THE HELL?! HOW'D HE--?!
GRK!
I'M ON HIM!!
KSHRK
KSHRK
KSHRK
TH-TH- THEY'RE STILL THERE!!
BRMM...
HA HA
GUN IT, SALAZAR!!
BEEP
HONK
D- DRIVE SAFELY NOW!
!!

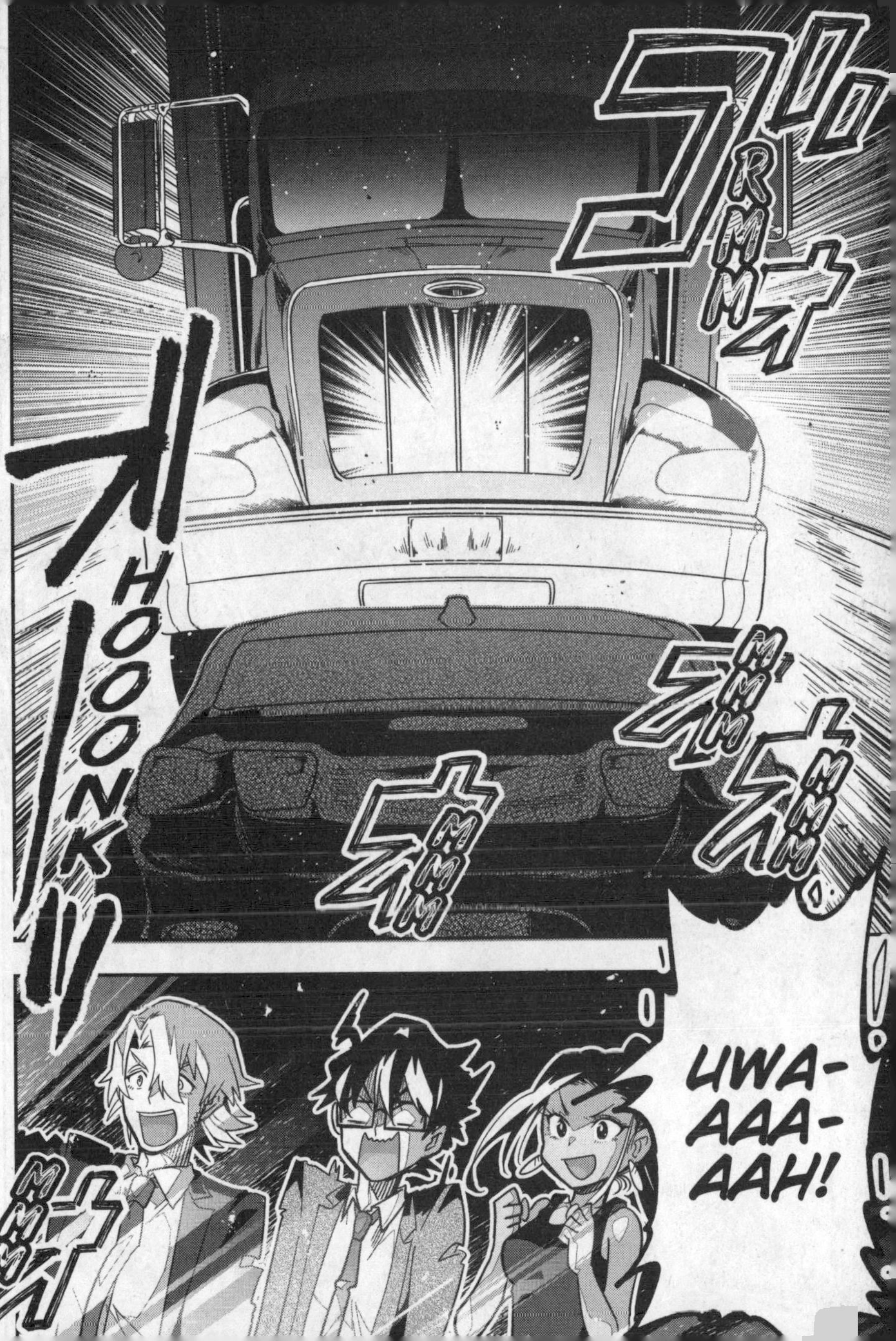
RMMM
MMMM
MMMM
MMMM
HOOOONK
UWA-
AAA-
AAH!
MMM

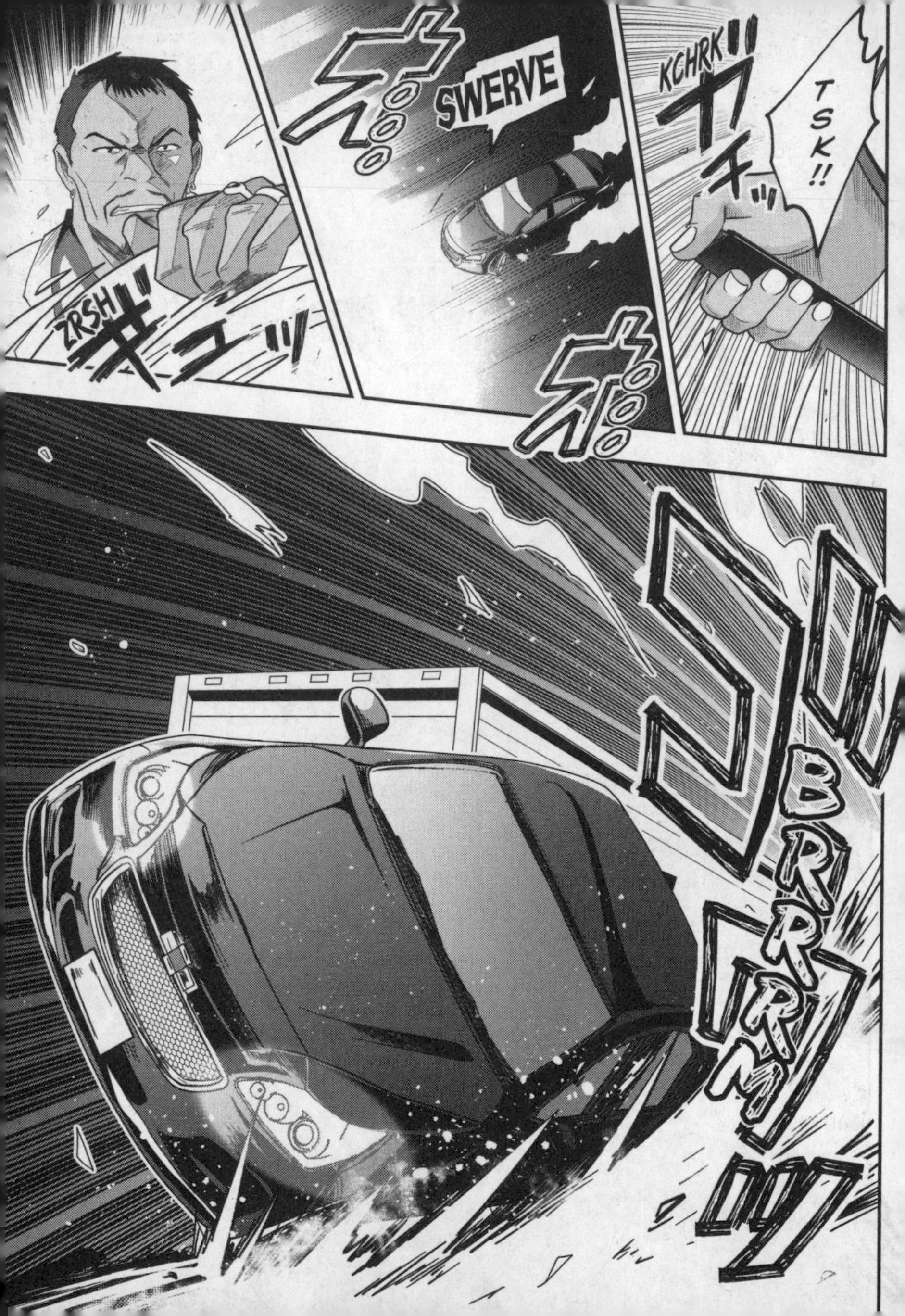
TSK!!
KCHRK
SWERVE
ZRSH
BRRRM

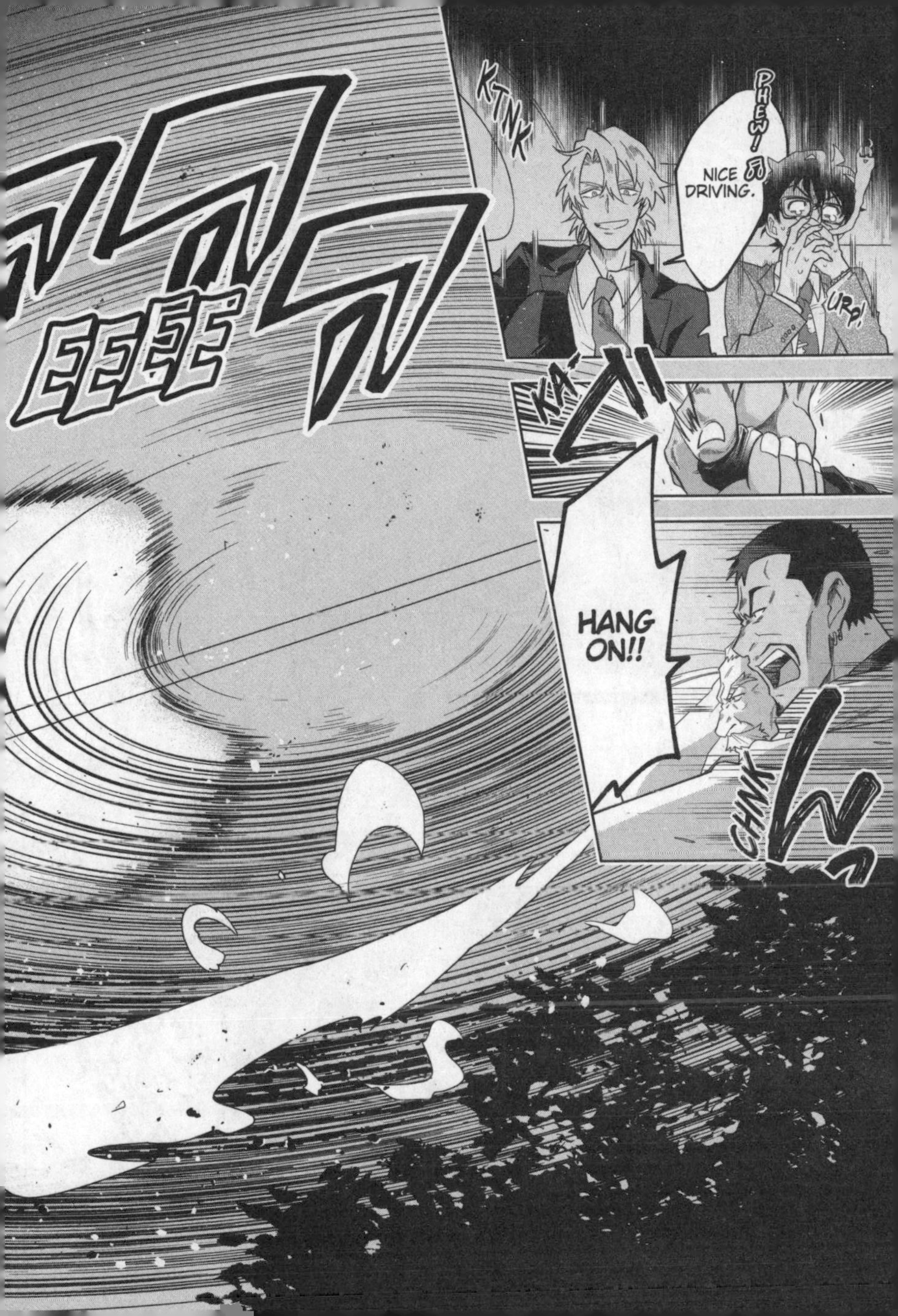
KTNK
PHEW!
NICE DRIVING.
URP!
KA'
HANG ON!!
CHINK
EEEE

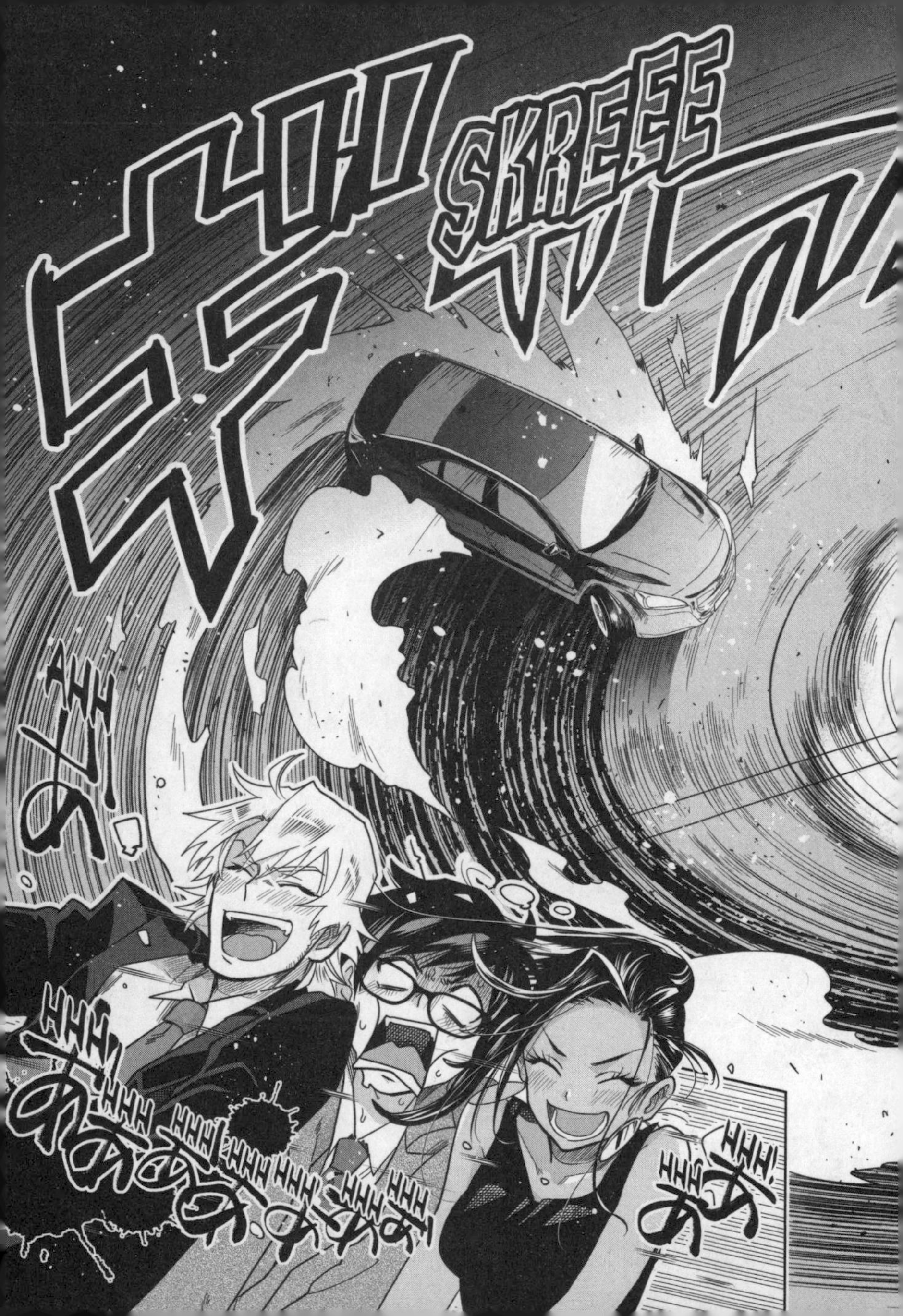
SKREEEE
AHH
HHHH
HHHH
HHH
HHH
HHH
HHH
HHH
HHH!

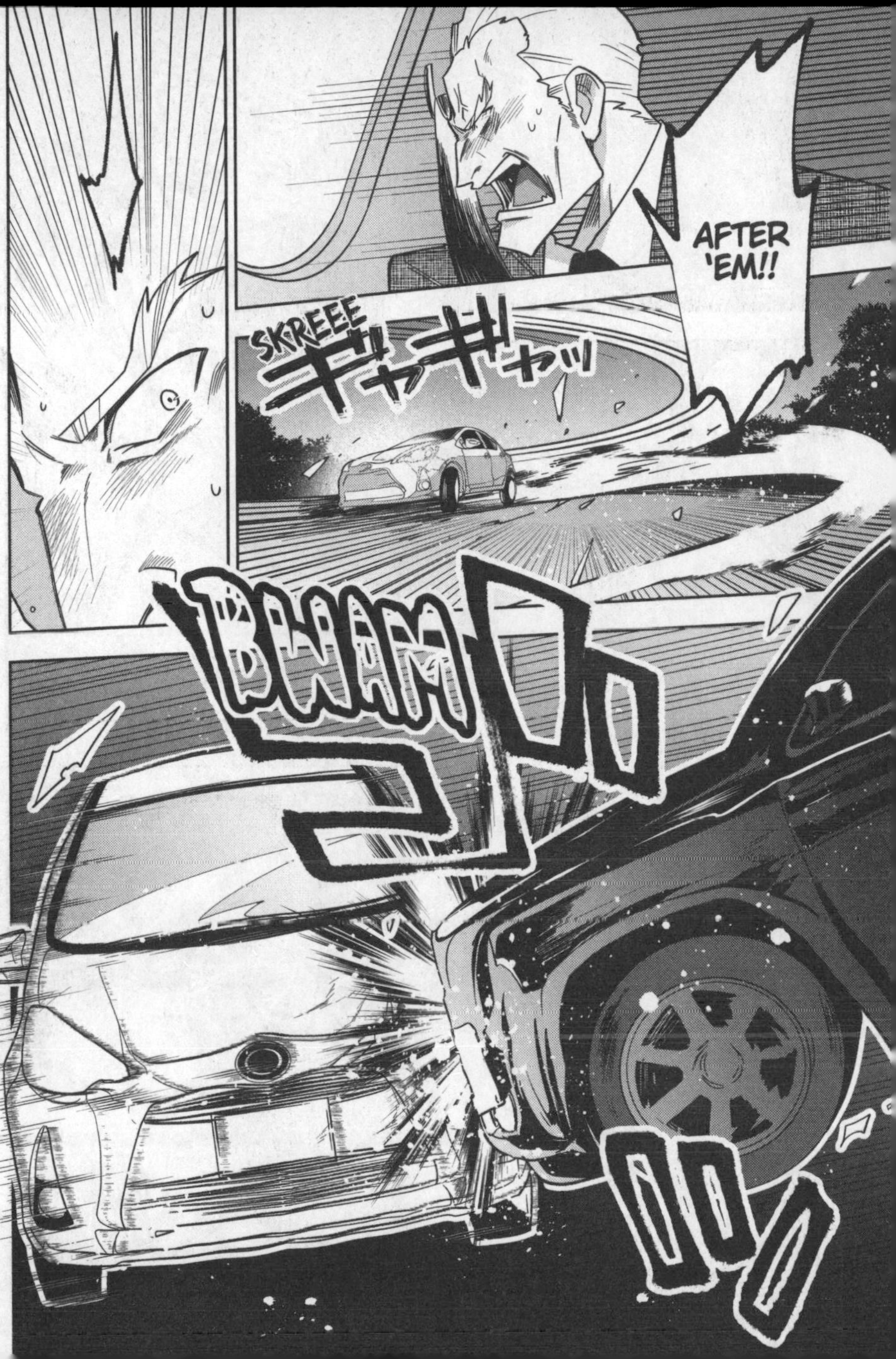
AFTER 'EM!!
SKREEE
BWAM

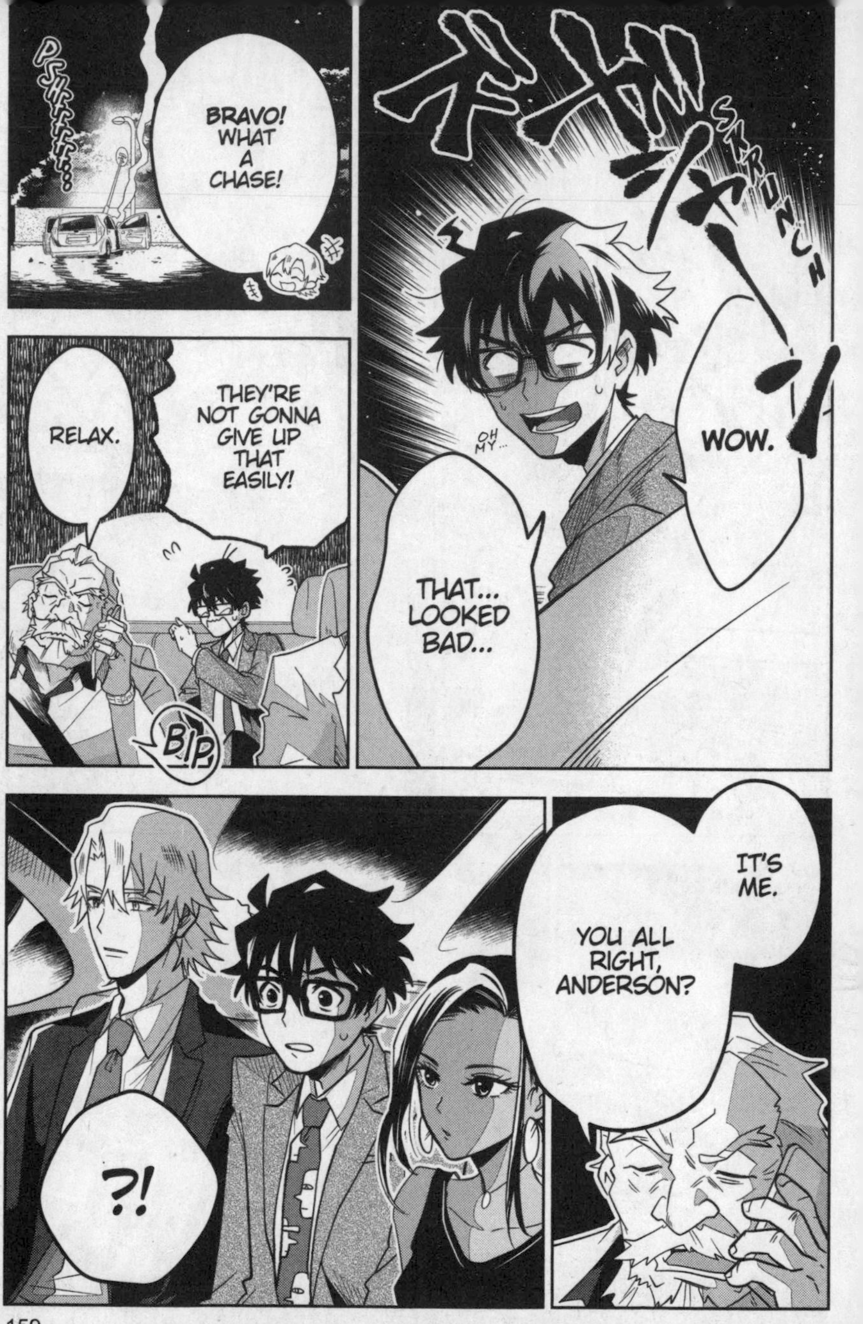
SKRUNCH
WOW.
OH MY...
THAT... LOOKED BAD...
BRAVO! WHAT A CHASE!
THEY'RE NOT GONNA GIVE UP THAT EASILY!
RELAX.
BIP
IT'S ME.
YOU ALL RIGHT, ANDERSON?
?!

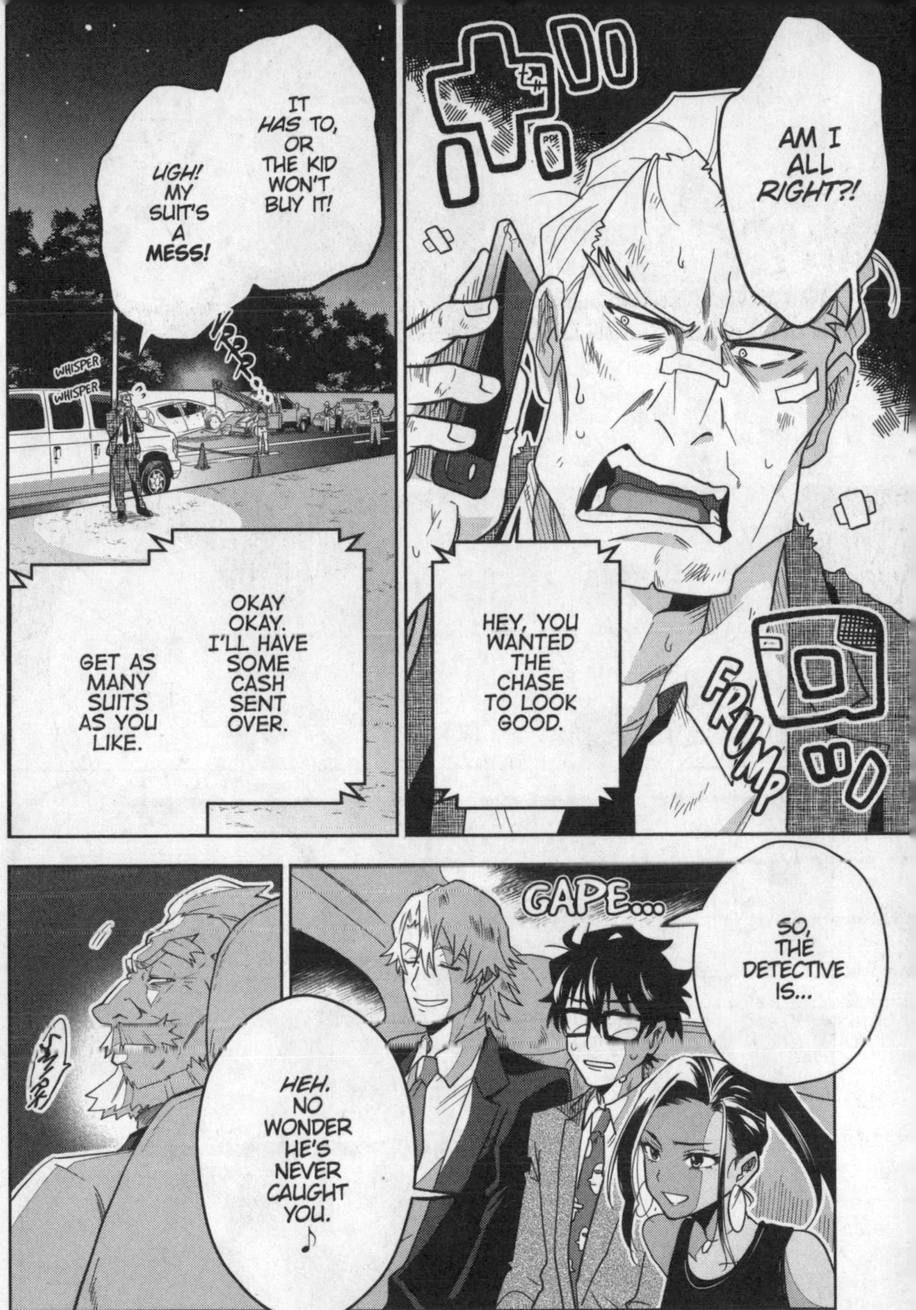
AM I ALL RIGHT?!
HEY, YOU WANTED THE CHASE TO LOOK GOOD.
FRUMP
IT HAS TO, OR THE KID WON'T BUY IT!
UGH! MY SUIT'S A MESS!
WHISPER
WHISPER
OKAY OKAY. I'LL HAVE SOME CASH SENT OVER.
GET AS MANY SUITS AS YOU LIKE.
SO, THE DETECTIVE IS...
GAPE...
HEH. NO WONDER HE'S NEVER CAUGHT YOU. ♪
SMIRK

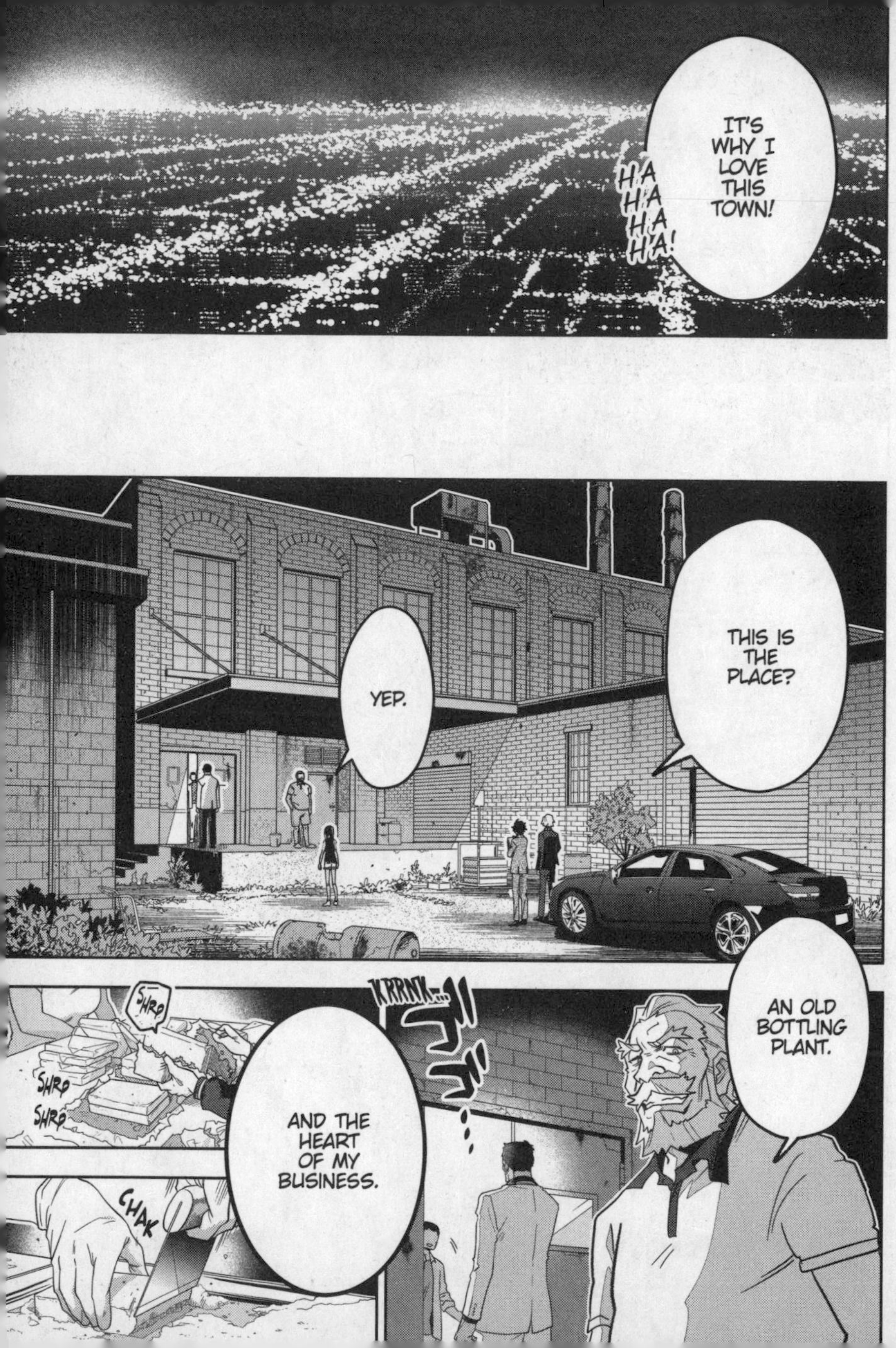
IT'S WHY I LOVE THIS TOWN!
HA HA HA HA!
THIS IS THE PLACE?
YEP.
AN OLD BOTTLING PLANT.
KRRNK...!!
AND THE HEART OF MY BUSINESS.
SHRP
SHRP SHRP
CHAK

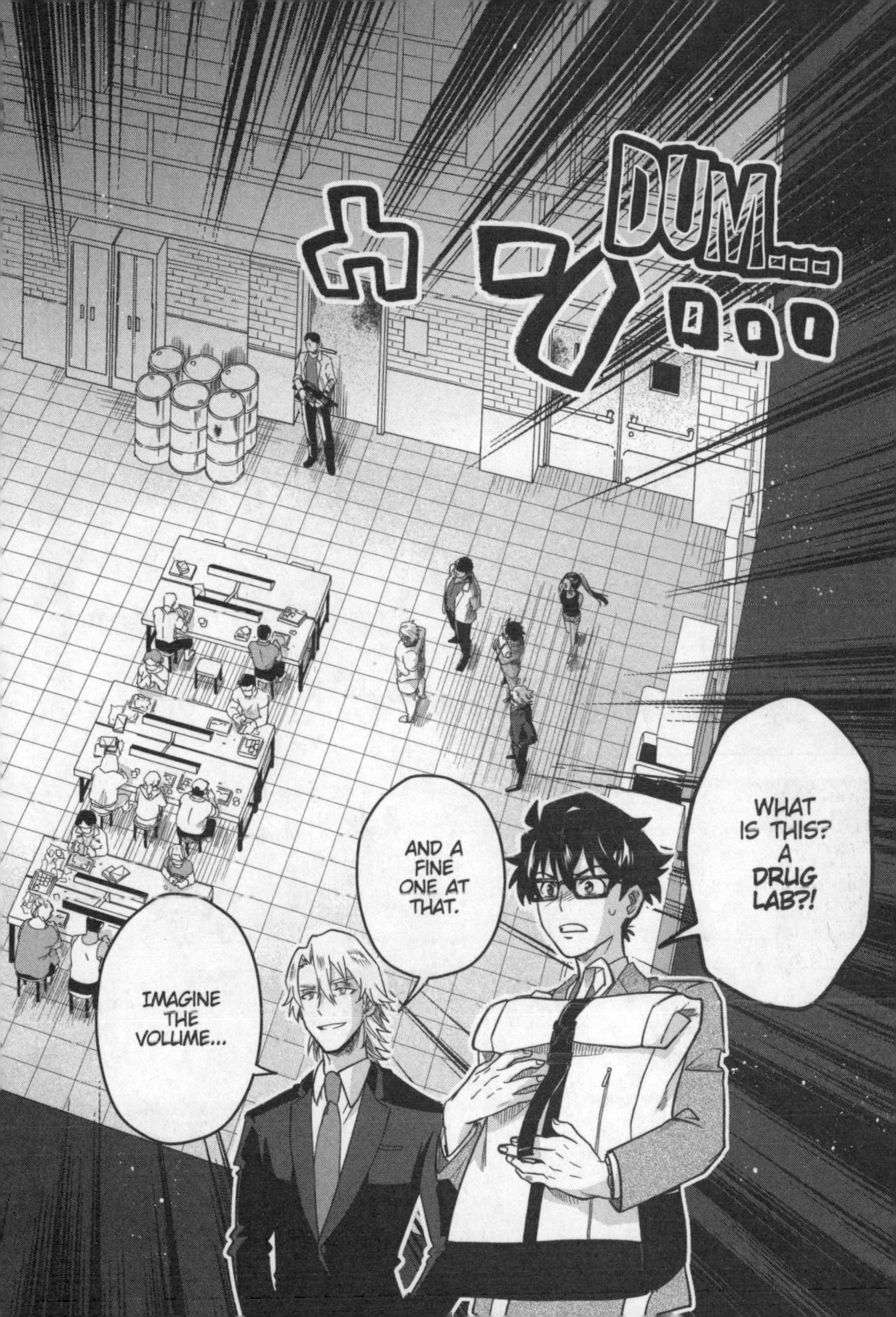
DUM...
WHAT IS THIS? A DRUG LAB?!
AND A FINE ONE AT THAT.
IMAGINE THE VOLUME...

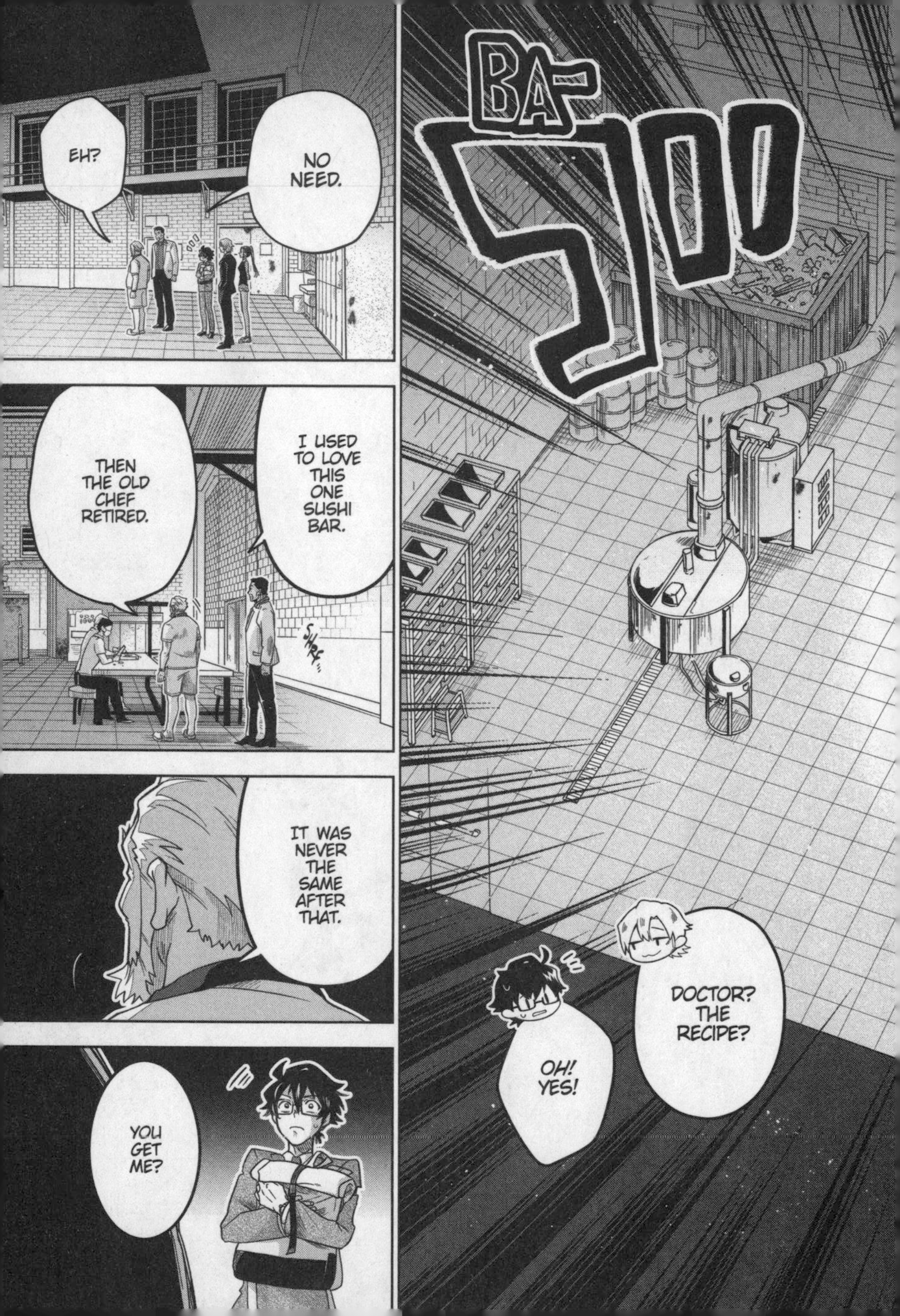
BA-
DOCTOR? THE RECIPE?
OH! YES!
NO NEED.
EH?
I USED TO LOVE THIS ONE SUSHI BAR.
THEN THE OLD CHEF RETIRED.
IT WAS NEVER THE SAME AFTER THAT.
YOU GET ME?

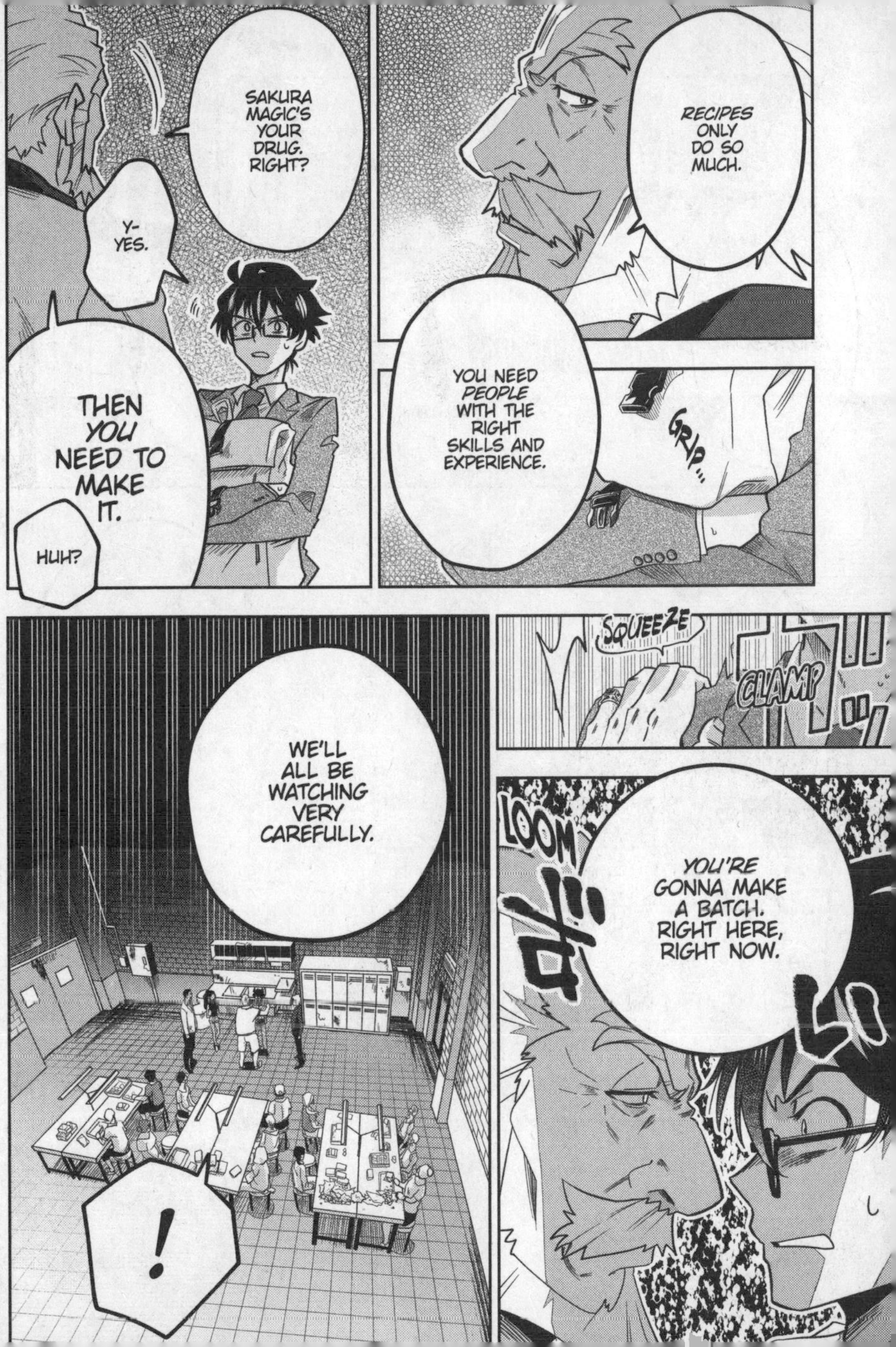
RECIPES ONLY DO SO MUCH.
YOU NEED PEOPLE WITH THE RIGHT SKILLS AND EXPERIENCE.
GRIP...
SAKURA MAGIC'S YOUR DRUG. RIGHT?
Y-YES.
THEN YOU NEED TO MAKE IT.
HUH?
SQUEEZE
CLAMP
LOOM
YOU'RE GONNA MAKE A BATCH. RIGHT HERE, RIGHT NOW.
WE'LL ALL BE WATCHING VERY CAREFULLY.
!

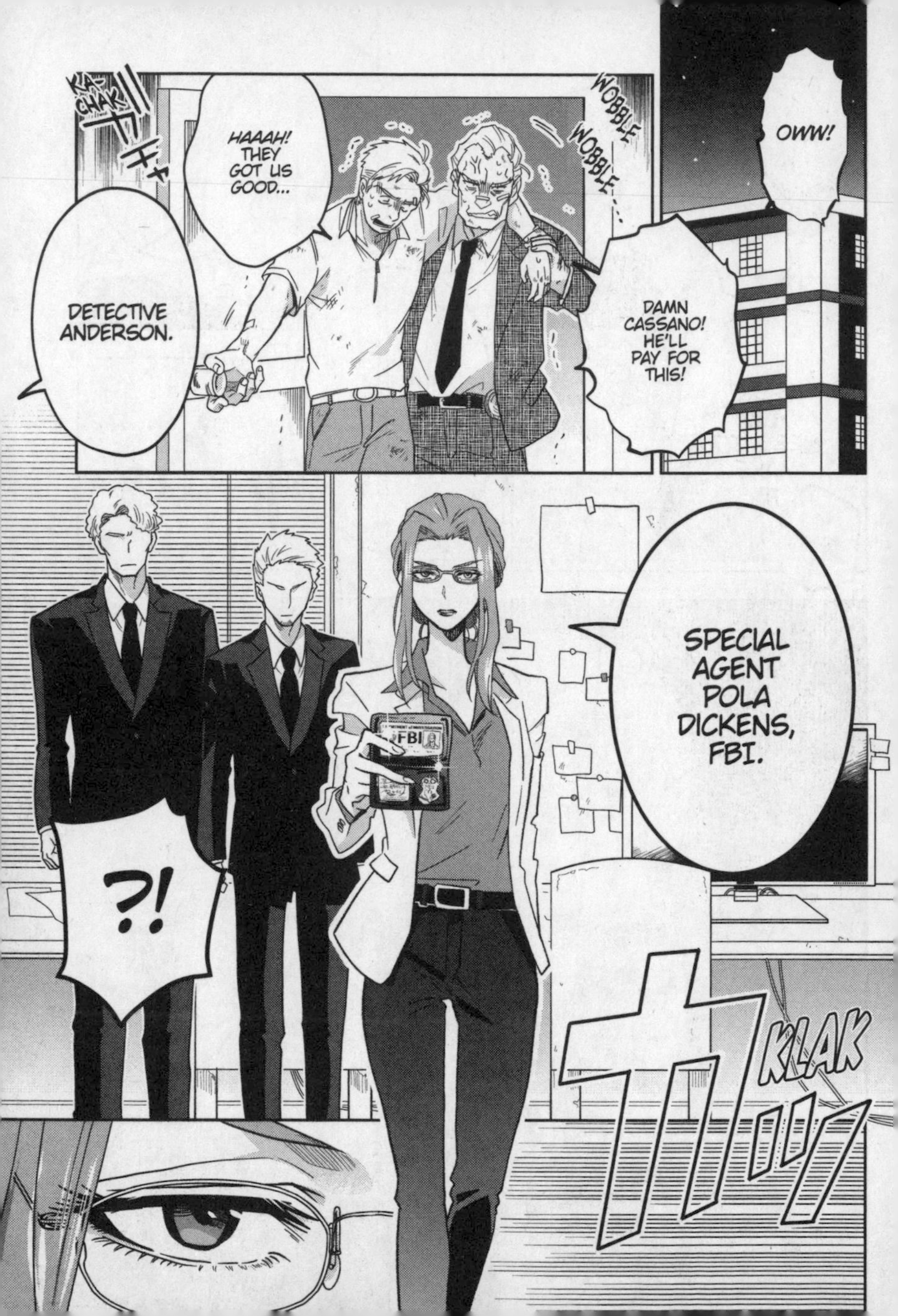
OWW!
WOBBLE WOBBLE...
DAMN CASSANO! HE'LL PAY FOR THIS!
HAAAH! THEY GOT US GOOD...
KA-CHAK
DETECTIVE ANDERSON.
SPECIAL AGENT POLA DICKENS, FBI.
FBI
?!
KLAK

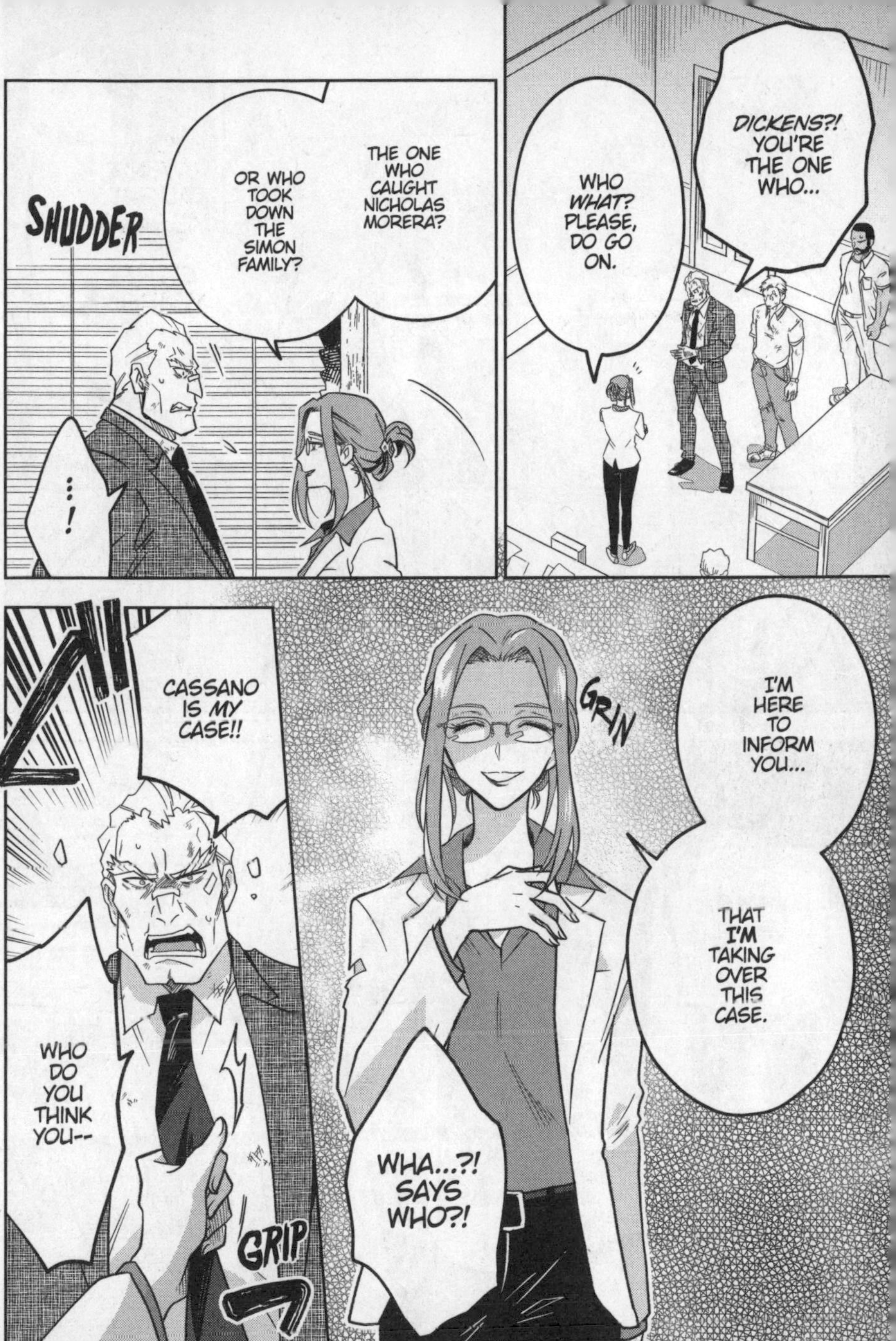
DICKENS?! YOU'RE THE ONE WHO...
WHO WHAT? PLEASE, DO GO ON.
THE ONE WHO CAUGHT NICHOLAS MORERA?
OR WHO TOOK DOWN THE SIMON FAMILY?
SHUDDER
...!
I'M HERE TO INFORM YOU...
THAT I'M TAKING OVER THIS CASE.
GRIN
WHA...?! SAYS WHO?!
CASSANO IS MY CASE!!
WHO DO YOU THINK YOU--
GRIP

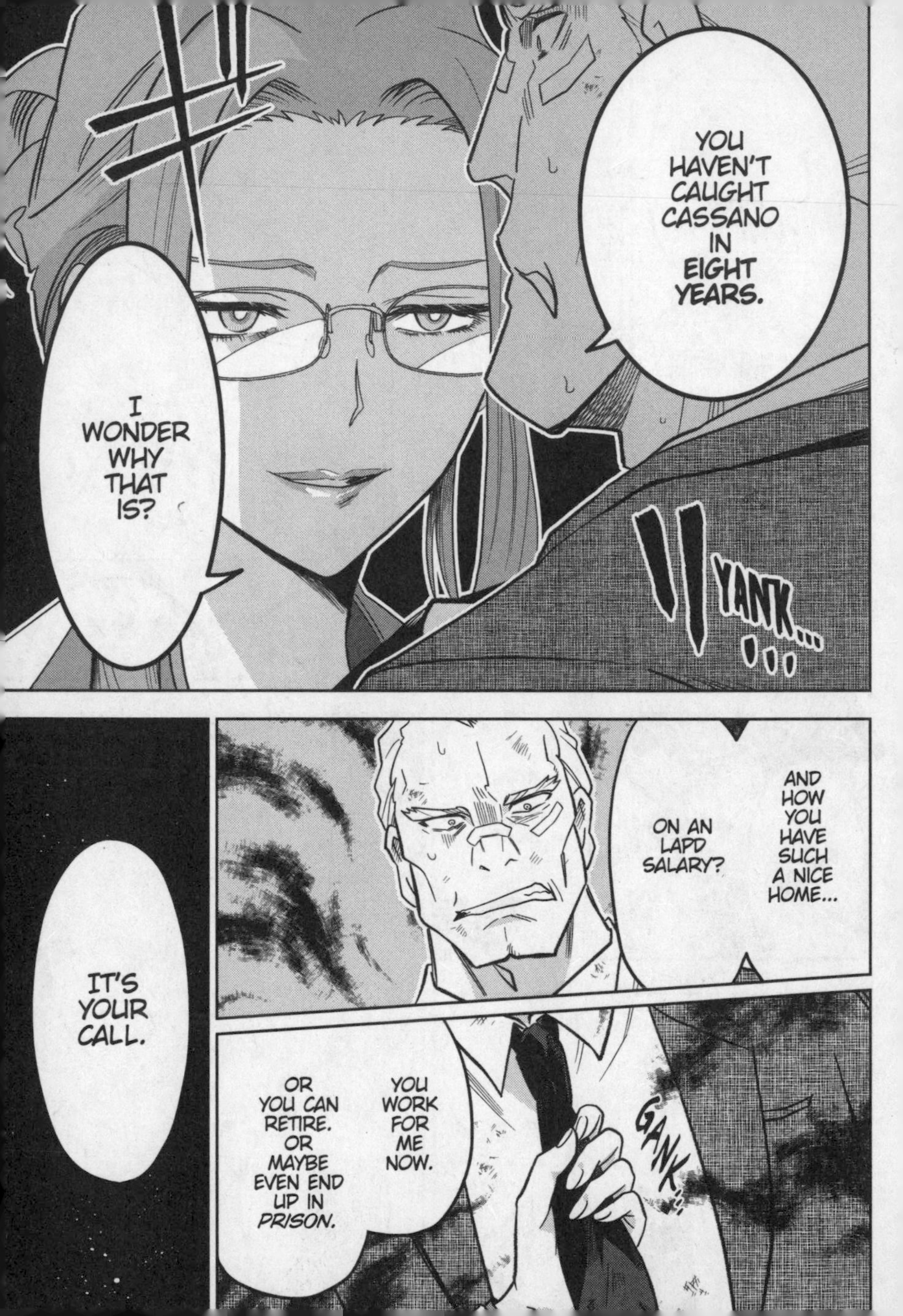
YOU HAVEN'T CAUGHT CASSANO IN EIGHT YEARS.
I WONDER WHY THAT IS?
YANK...
AND HOW YOU HAVE SUCH A NICE HOME...
ON AN LAPD SALARY?
YOU WORK FOR ME NOW.
OR YOU CAN RETIRE. OR MAYBE EVEN END UP IN *PRISON*.
GANK!!
IT'S YOUR CALL.

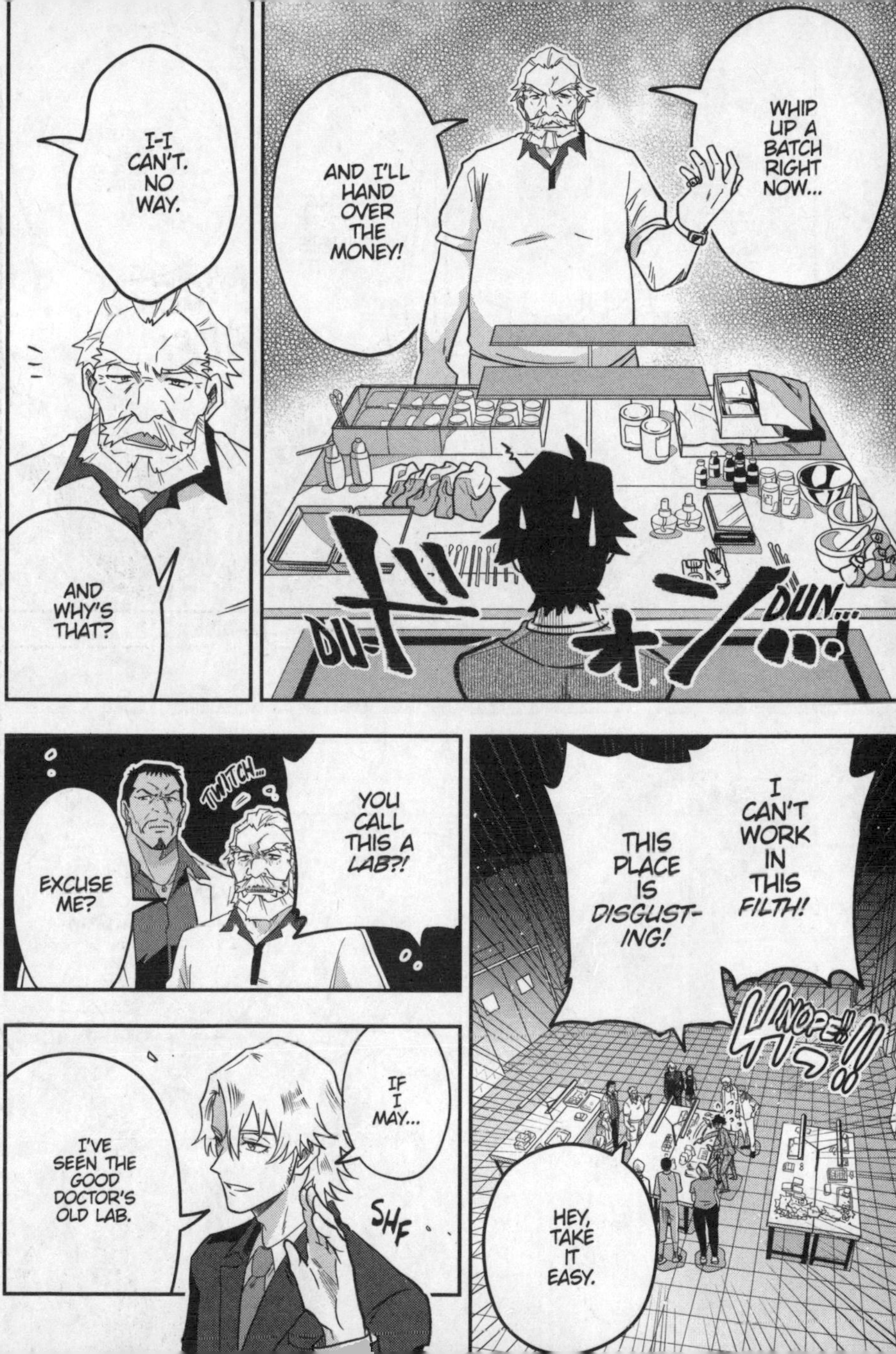
WHIP UP A BATCH RIGHT NOW...
AND I'LL HAND OVER THE MONEY!
DUN...
DU-
I-I CAN'T. NO WAY.
AND WHY'S THAT?
I CAN'T WORK IN THIS FILTH!
THIS PLACE IS DISGUSTING!
NOPE!!
HEY, TAKE IT EASY.
YOU CALL THIS A LAB?!
TWITCH...
EXCUSE ME?
IF I MAY...
SHF
I'VE SEEN THE GOOD DOCTOR'S OLD LAB.

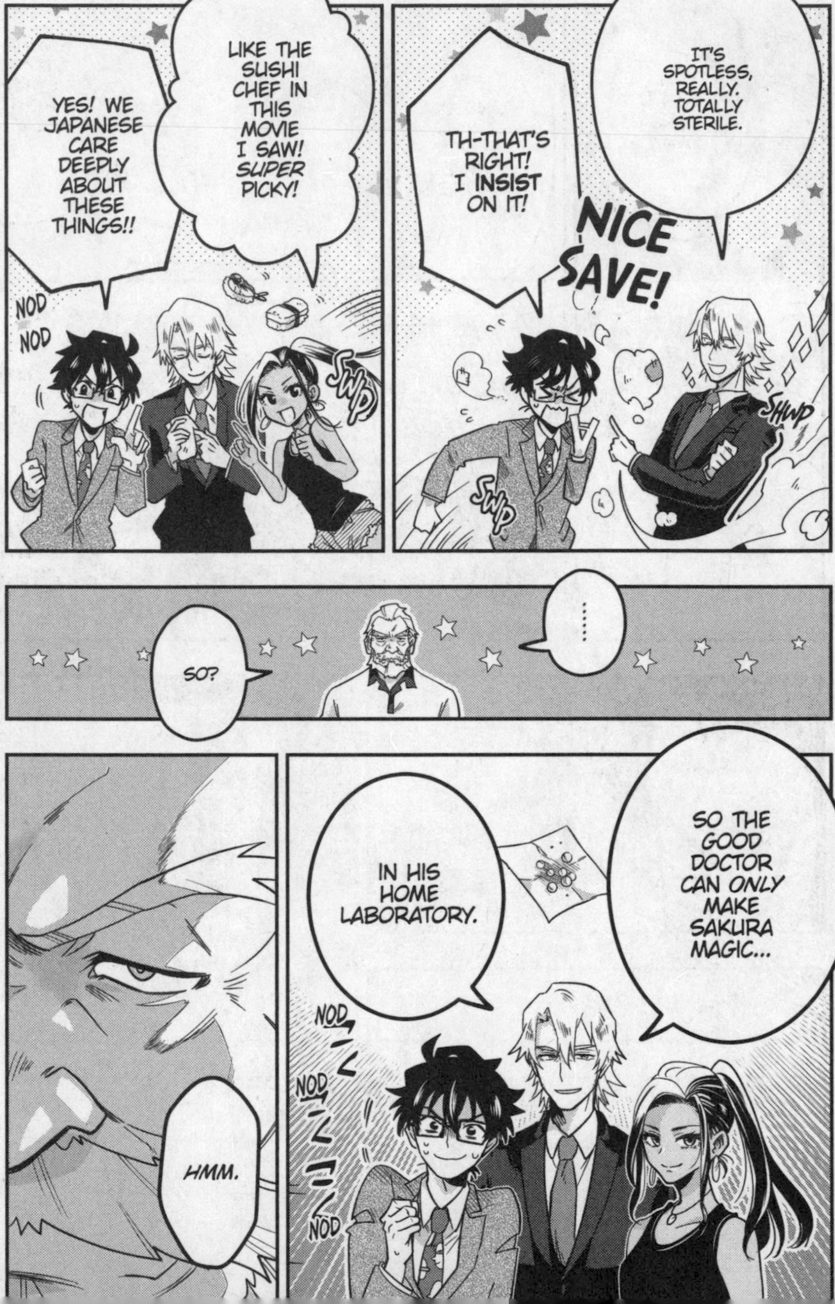
IT'S SPOTLESS, REALLY. TOTALLY STERILE.
TH-THAT'S RIGHT! I INSIST ON IT!
NICE SAVE!
SHWP
SWP
LIKE THE SUSHI CHEF IN THIS MOVIE I SAW! SUPER PICKY!
YES! WE JAPANESE CARE DEEPLY ABOUT THESE THINGS!!
NOD NOD
SWP
......
SO?
SO THE GOOD DOCTOR CAN ONLY MAKE SAKURA MAGIC...
IN HIS HOME LABORATORY.
NOD
NOD
NOD
HMM.

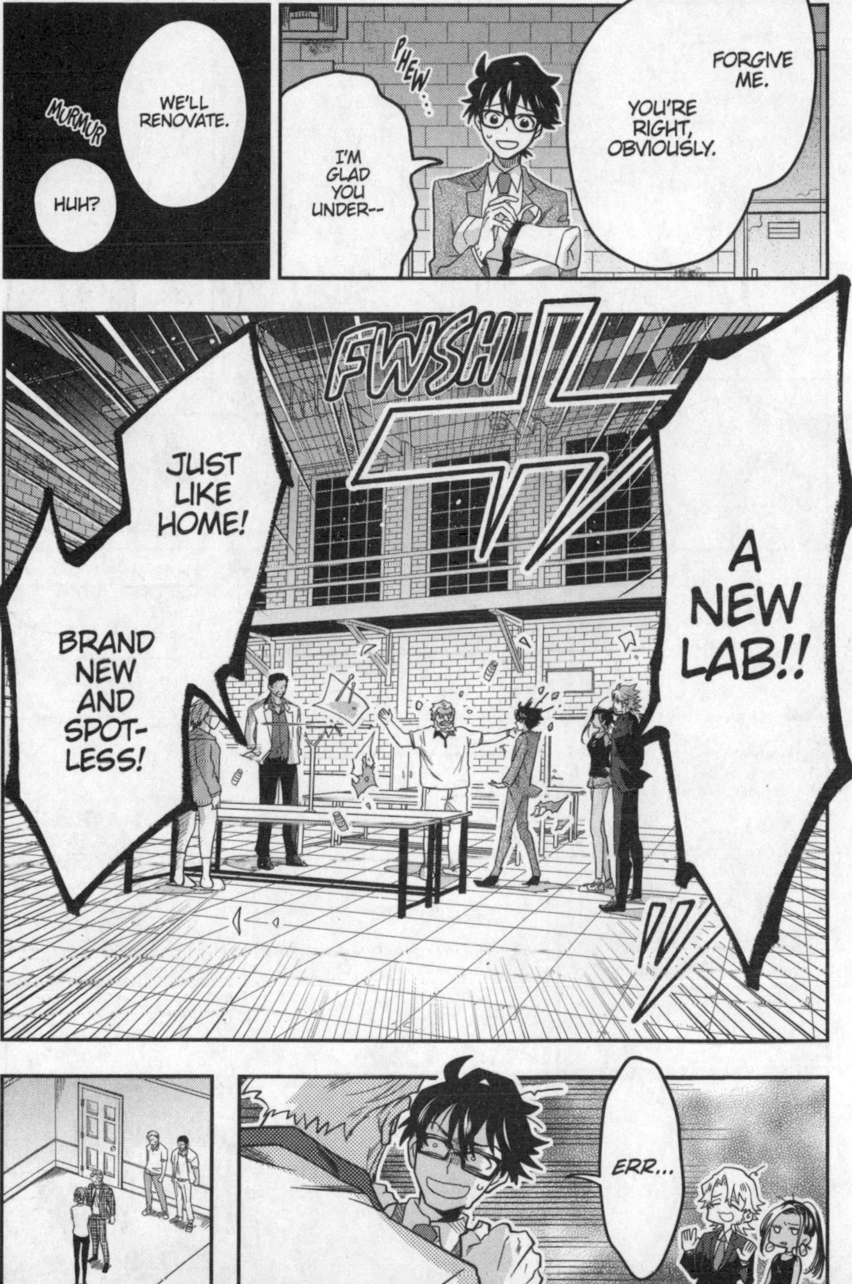
FORGIVE ME.
YOU'RE RIGHT, OBVIOUSLY.
PHEW...
I'M GLAD YOU UNDER--
WE'LL RENOVATE.
MURMUR
HUH?
FWSH
A NEW LAB!!
JUST LIKE HOME!
BRAND NEW AND SPOT-LESS!
ERR...

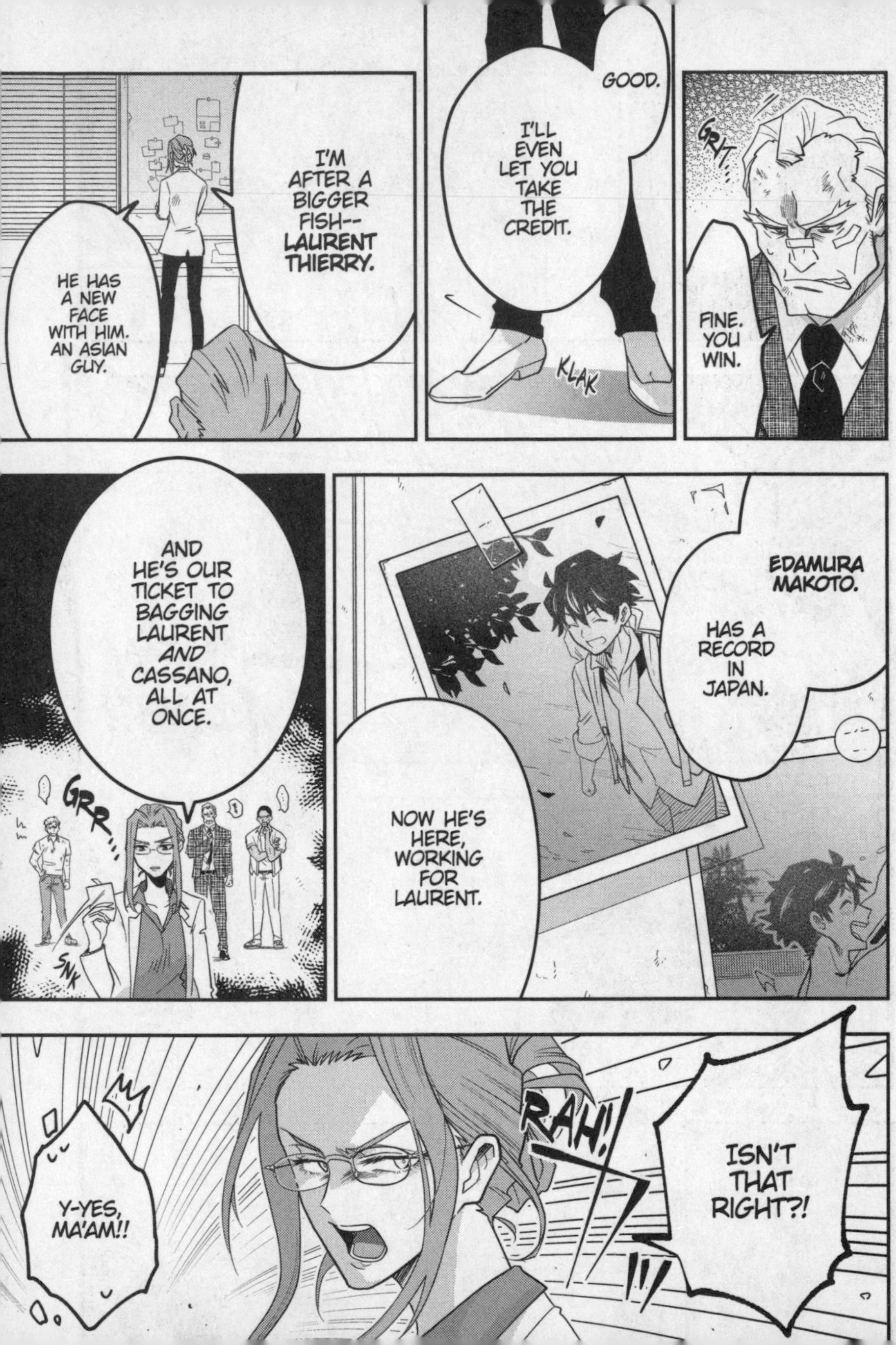
GRIT...
FINE. YOU WIN.
GOOD.
I'LL EVEN LET YOU TAKE THE CREDIT.
KLAK
I'M AFTER A BIGGER FISH--LAURENT THIERRY.
HE HAS A NEW FACE WITH HIM. AN ASIAN GUY.
EDAMURA MAKOTO.
HAS A RECORD IN JAPAN.
NOW HE'S HERE, WORKING FOR LAURENT.
AND HE'S OUR TICKET TO BAGGING LAURENT *AND* CASSANO, ALL AT ONCE.
GRR...
SNK
ISN'T THAT RIGHT?!
RAH!
Y-YES, MA'AM!!

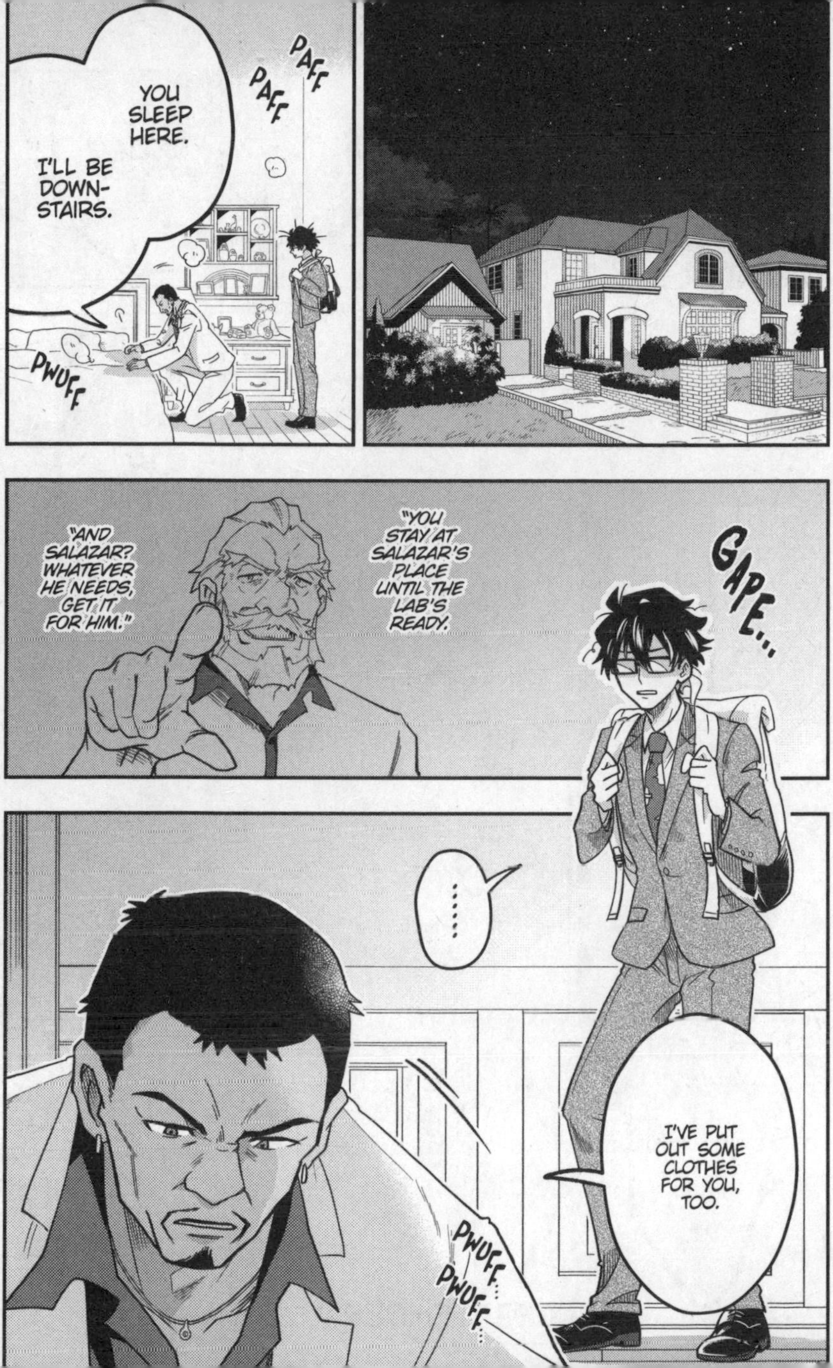
PAFF
PAFF
YOU SLEEP HERE.
I'LL BE DOWN-STAIRS.
PWUFF
GAPE...
"YOU STAY AT SALAZAR'S PLACE UNTIL THE LAB'S READY.
"AND SALAZAR? WHATEVER HE NEEDS, GET IT FOR HIM."
......
I'VE PUT OUT SOME CLOTHES FOR YOU, TOO.
PWUFF...
PWUFF...

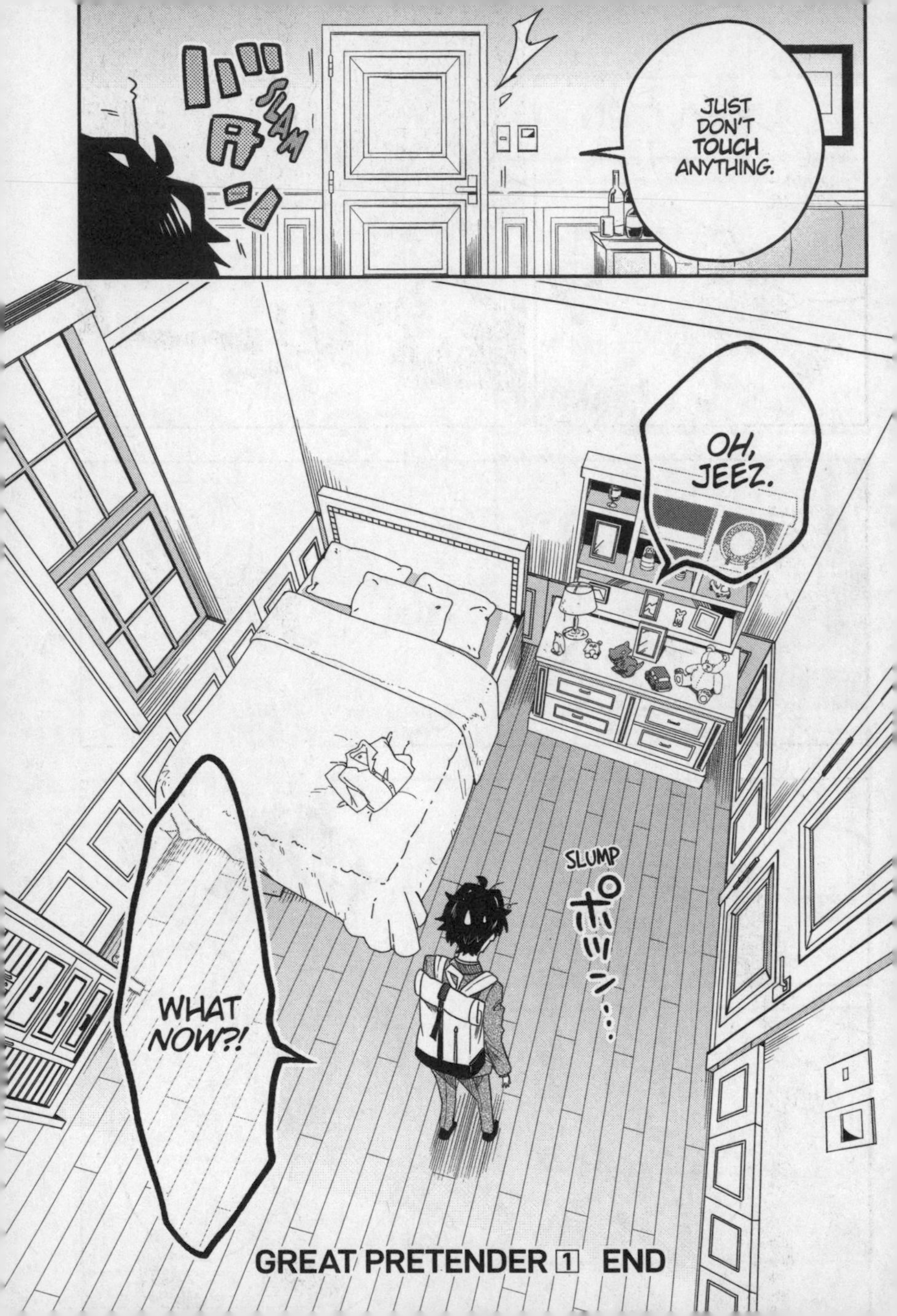
JUST DON'T TOUCH ANYTHING.
SLAM
OH, JEEZ.
SLUMP
ポツン…
WHAT NOW?!
GREAT PRETENDER 1 END

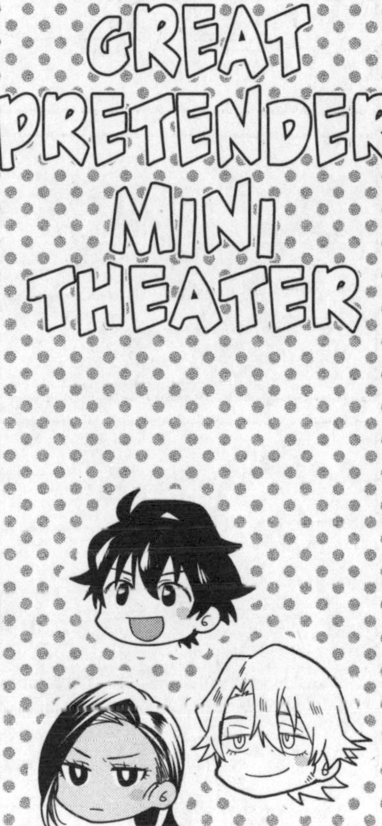
GREAT PRETENDER MINI THEATER

UNINVITED

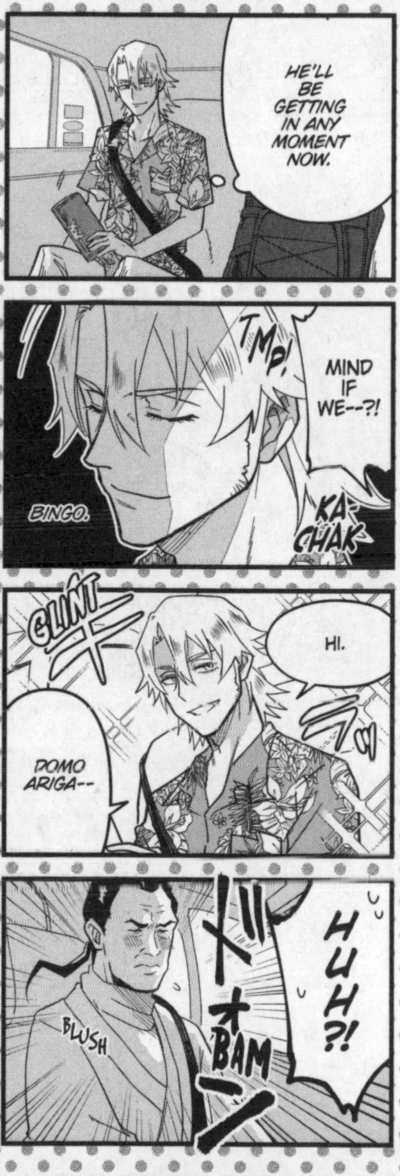
HE'LL BE GETTING IN ANY MOMENT NOW.
TMP!
MIND IF WE--?!
KA-CHAK
BINGO.
HI.
GLINT
DOMO ARIGA--
HUH?!
BAM
BLUSH

A MOLE'S FIRST DAY

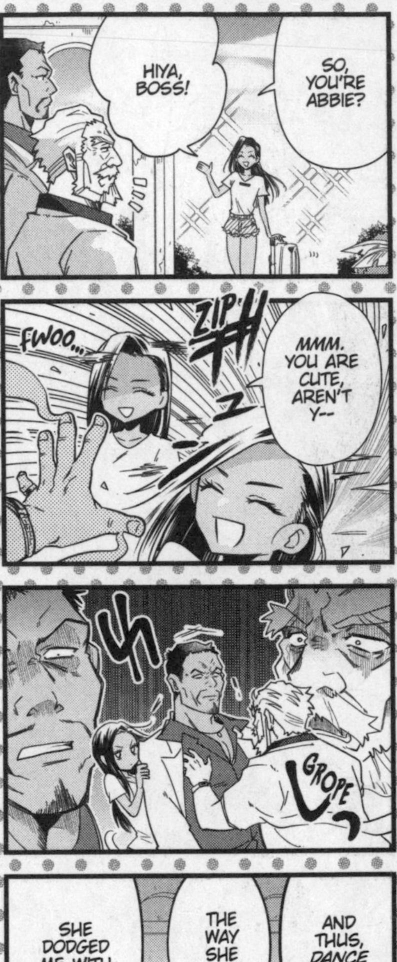
SO, YOU'RE ABBIE?
HIYA, BOSS!
MMM. YOU ARE CUTE, AREN'T Y--
ZIP
FWOO...
GROPE
AND THUS, DANCE LESSONS?
THE WAY SHE MOVED...
SHE DODGED ME WITH SUCH GRACE.

CONVERTING THE MASSES

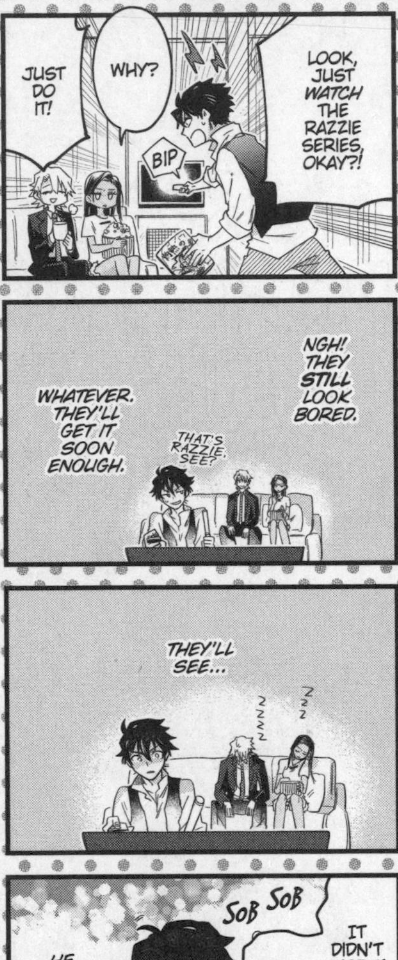
LOOK, JUST *WATCH* THE RAZZIE SERIES, OKAY?!
WHY?
JUST DO IT!
BIP
NGH! THEY **STILL** LOOK BORED.
THAT'S RAZZIE. SEE?
WHATEVER. THEY'LL GET IT SOON ENOUGH.
THEY'LL SEE...
SOB SOB
IT DIDN'T WORK!
I'M SO SORRY, RAZZIE! I FAILED YOU!
HE NEVER TRIED AGAIN.
SNIFF

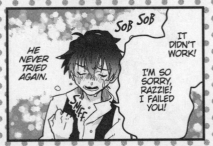

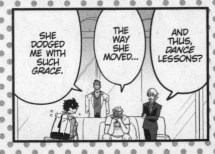

BELLY OF THE BEAST

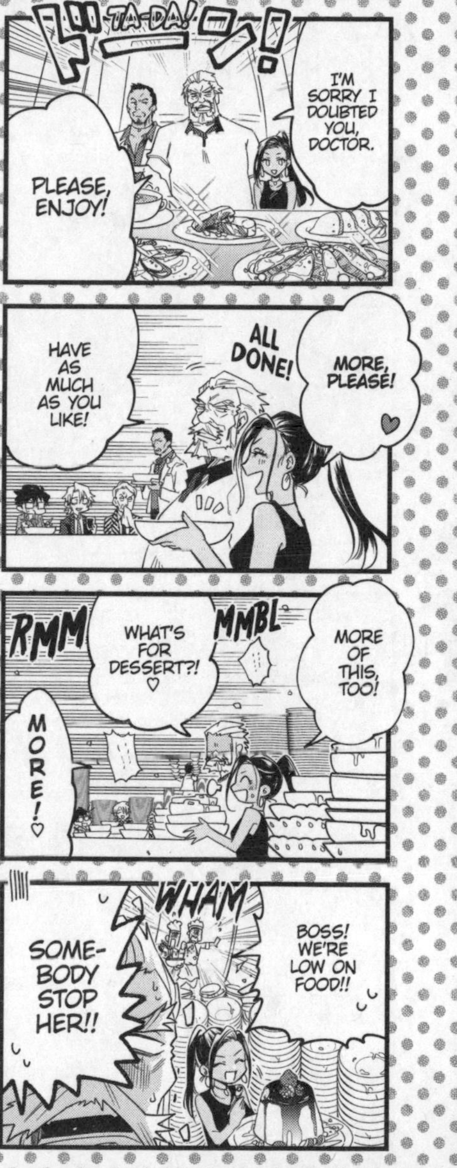
TA-DA!
I'M SORRY I DOUBTED YOU, DOCTOR.
PLEASE, ENJOY!
MORE, PLEASE! ♡
ALL DONE!
HAVE AS MUCH AS YOU LIKE!
MORE OF THIS, TOO!
MMBL
WHAT'S FOR DESSERT?! ♡
RMM
MORE!♡
BOSS! WE'RE LOW ON FOOD!!
WHAM
SOME-BODY STOP HER!!

FINISH YOUR DINNER

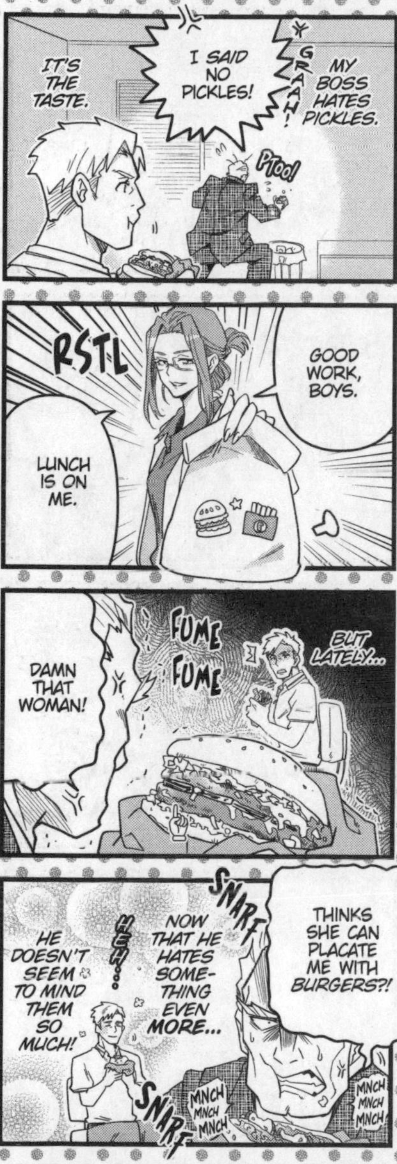
MY BOSS HATES PICKLES.
GRAAH!
I SAID NO PICKLES!
IT'S THE TASTE.
PTOO!
GOOD WORK, BOYS.
RSTL
LUNCH IS ON ME.
BUT LATELY...
FUME FUME
DAMN THAT WOMAN!
THINKS SHE CAN PLACATE ME WITH BURGERS?!
SNARF
NOW THAT HE HATES SOME-THING EVEN MORE...
HEH...
HE DOESN'T SEEM TO MIND THEM SO MUCH!
MNCH MNCH MNCH
MNCH MNCH MNCH
SNARF

KUDO BLUES

I HOPE THE KID'S OKAY
SIGH...
YOU WOR-RIED?
OF COURSE I AM!
I CARE ABOUT HIM, Y'KNOW?
I WANT THIS NEW THING OF HIS TO WORK OUT.
'CAUSE IF IT *DOESN'T*, HE'LL COME BACK AND KILL ME!
I JUST WANTED A NICE WATCH!!
SO IT DAMN WELL BETT WO
MNCH MNCH
AH. THE TRUTH COMES OUT.
MNCH

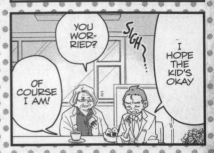

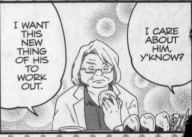

AFTERWORD

Hello, hello! It's me, Daichi Marui! Thanks for reading this first volume of the manga adaptation of *Great Pretender*!

This is my first serialized manga, so things are hectic, but I'm excited to be involved in such a wonderful project!

It's been a blast so far, and I'm looking forward to more! See you next volume!!

Special Thanks

To my editor, K-sama, to Sabatoban-sama and Tsubota Izumi-sama for their help, and to all you readers for your support.

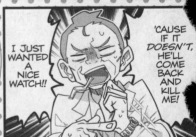

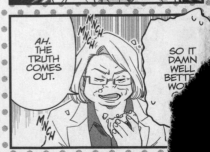

SEVEN SEAS ENTERTAINMENT PRESENTS

GREAT PRETENDER
Vol. 1

TRANSLATION
Stephen Kohler

ADAPTATION
Brett Hallahan

LETTERING
Bambi Eloriaga-Amago
Roland Amago

COVER DESIGN
Hanase Qi

PROOFREADER
B. Lana Guggenheim

COPY EDITOR
Dawn Davis

EDITOR
Shannon Fay

PREPRESS TECHNICIAN
Jon Rasmussen-Silverstein

PRODUCTION ASSOCIATE
Christa Miesner

PRODUCTION MANAGER
Lissa Pattillo

MANAGING EDITOR
Julie Davis

ASSOCIATE PUBLISHER
Adam Arnold

PUBLISHER
Jason DeAngelis

GREAT PRETENDER vol.1
©WIT STUDIO/Great Pretenders
©Daichi Marui 2020
Originally published in Japan in 2020 by MAG Garden Corporation, TOKYO.
English translation rights arranged through TOHAN CORPORATION, Tokyo.

Seven Seas press and purchase enquiries can be sent to Marketing Manager Lianne
Sentar at press@gomanga.com. Information regarding the distribution and purchase of
digital editions is available from Digital Manager CK Russell at digital@gomanga.com.

ISBN: 978-1-64827-583-8
Printed in Canada
First Printing: July 2021
10 9 8 7 6 5 4 3 2 1

READING DIRECTIONS

This book reads from *right to left*,
Japanese style. If this is your first time
reading manga, you start reading from
the top right panel on each page and
take it from there. If you get lost, just
follow the numbered diagram here.
It may seem backwards at first,
but you'll get the hang of it! Have fun!!

Follow us online: www.SevenSeasEntertainment.com

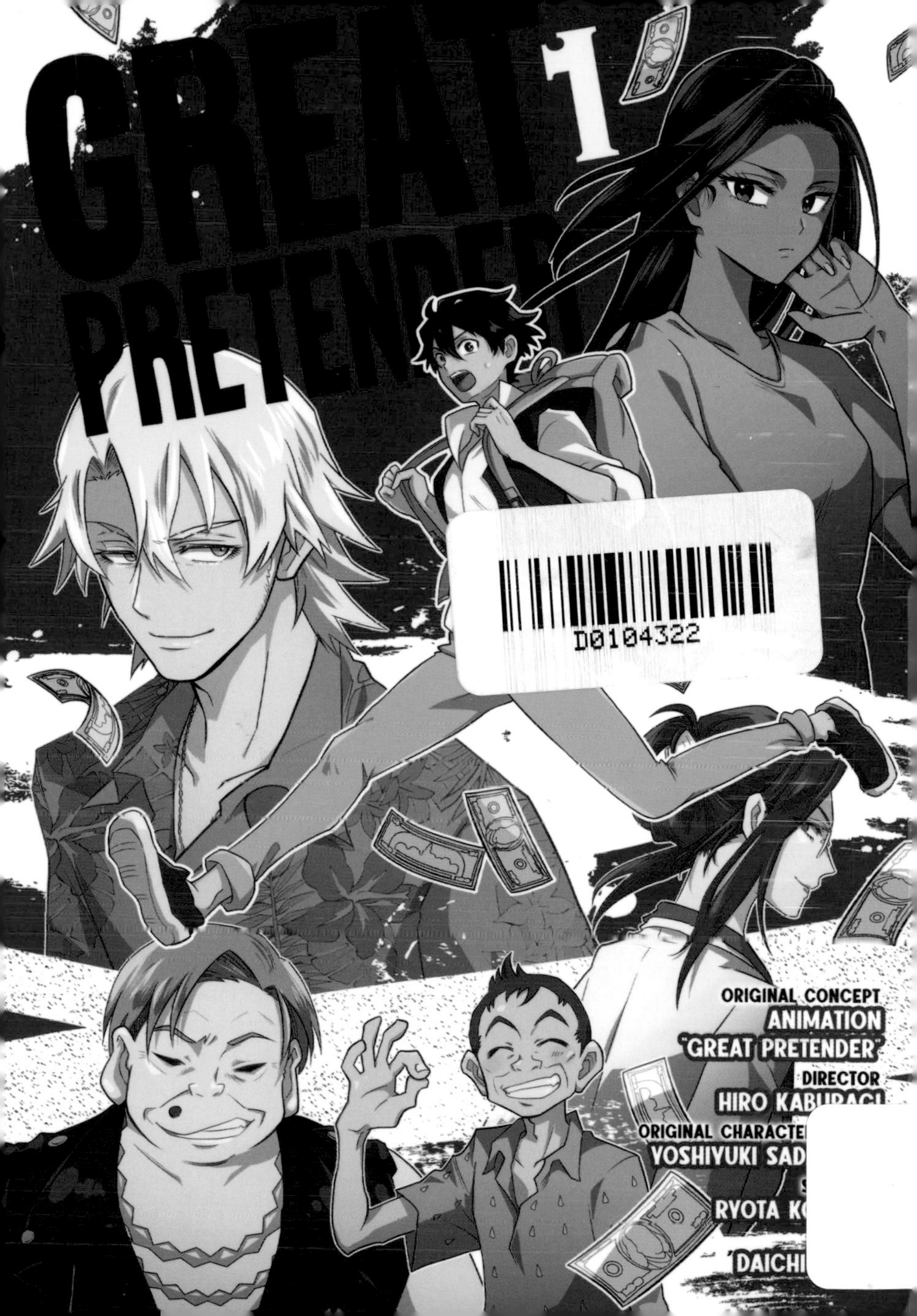
GREAT PRETENDER
1
ORIGINAL CONCEPT
ANIMATION
"GREAT PRETENDER"
DIRECTOR
HIRO KABURAGI
ORIGINAL CHARACTE
YOSHIYUKI SAD
RYOTA KO
DAICHI